X-TREME X-MEN

prisoner of fire

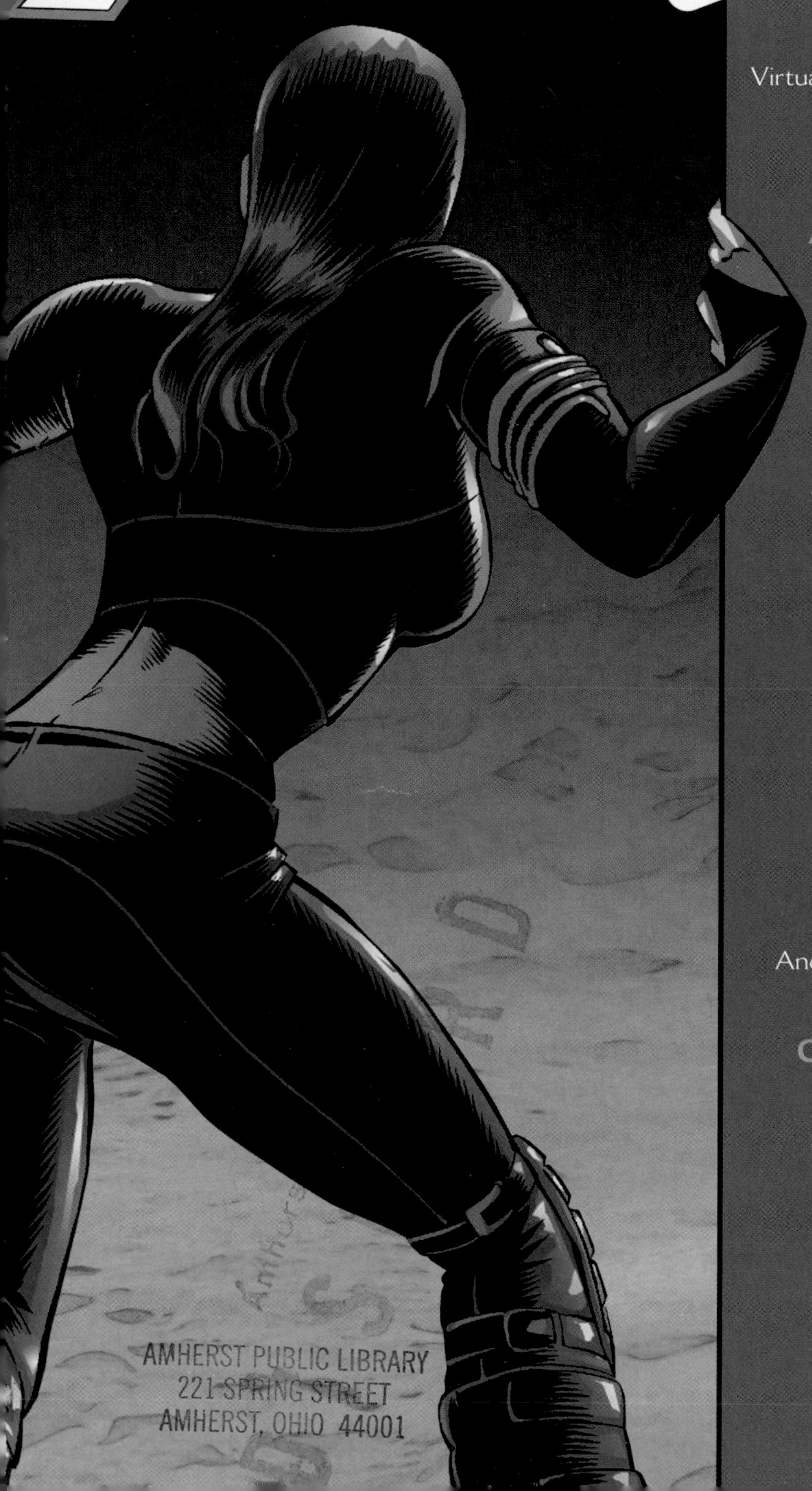

Writer
Chris Claremont

...er
...ey

...y Pepoy,
...und &
...ndu Florea

Colorists
Liquid! Graphics

Letterer
Virtual Calligraphy's Rus Wooton
with Cory Petit

Cover Art
Salvador Larroca

Assistant Editors
Stephanie Moore &
Cory Sedlmeier

Editor
Mike Marts

Annual 2001

Writer
Chris Claremont

Penciler
Salvador Larroca

Inker
Sandu Florea

Colorist
Liquid! Graphics

Letters
Tom Orzechowski

Editors
Andrew Lis & Mark Powers

Collections Editor
Jeff Youngquist

Assistant Editor
Jennifer Grünwald

Book Designer
Carrie Beadle

Editor in Chief
Joe Quesada

Publisher
Dan Buckley

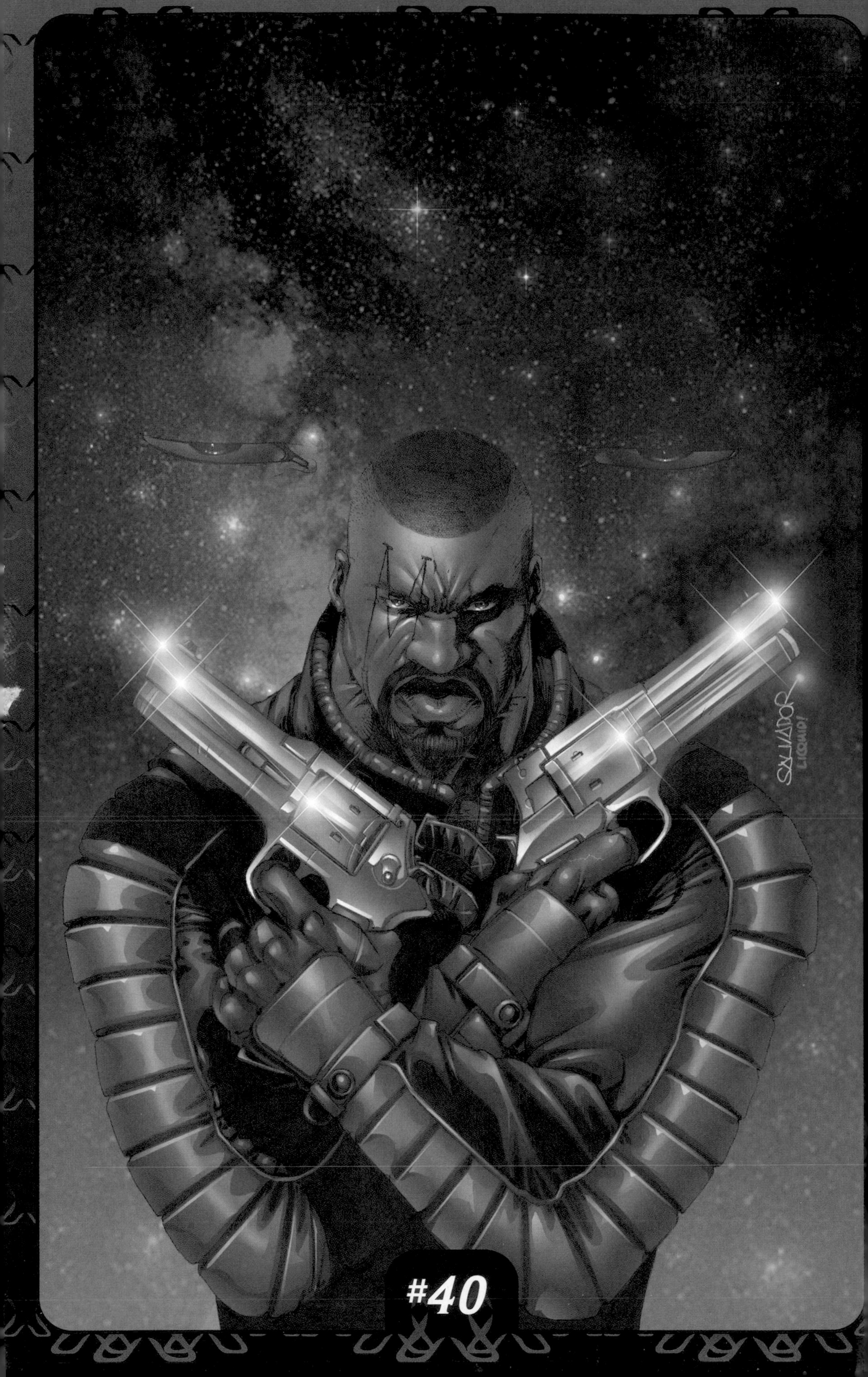
#40

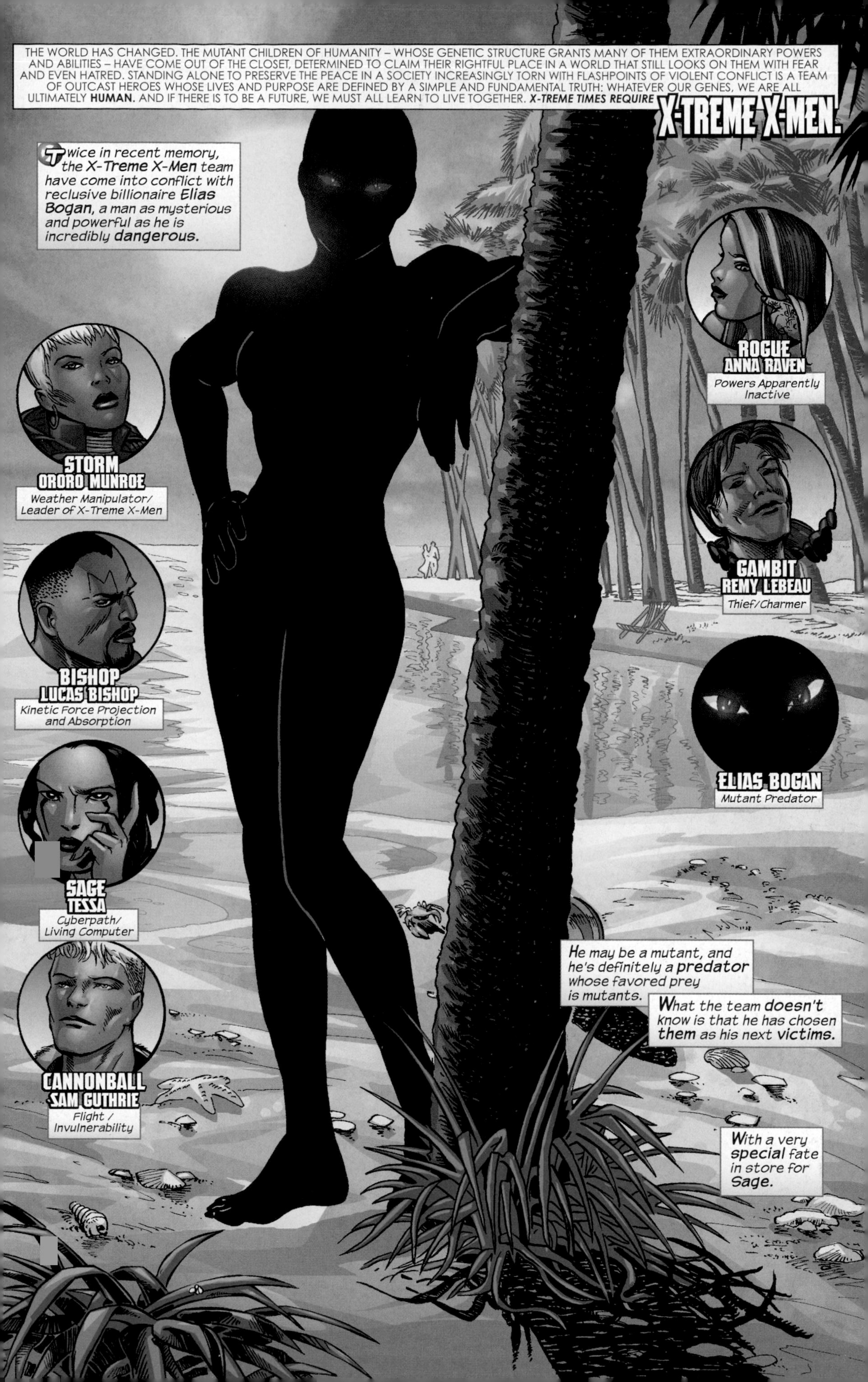
THE WORLD HAS CHANGED. THE MUTANT CHILDREN OF HUMANITY – WHOSE GENETIC STRUCTURE GRANTS MANY OF THEM EXTRAORDINARY POWERS AND ABILITIES – HAVE COME OUT OF THE CLOSET, DETERMINED TO CLAIM THEIR RIGHTFUL PLACE IN A WORLD THAT STILL LOOKS ON THEM WITH FEAR AND EVEN HATRED. STANDING ALONE TO PRESERVE THE PEACE IN A SOCIETY INCREASINGLY TORN WITH FLASHPOINTS OF VIOLENT CONFLICT IS A TEAM OF OUTCAST HEROES WHOSE LIVES AND PURPOSE ARE DEFINED BY A SIMPLE AND FUNDAMENTAL TRUTH: WHATEVER OUR GENES, WE ARE ALL ULTIMATELY HUMAN. AND IF THERE IS TO BE A FUTURE, WE MUST ALL LEARN TO LIVE TOGETHER. X-TREME TIMES REQUIRE
X-TREME X-MEN.
Twice in recent memory, the X-Treme X-Men team have come into conflict with reclusive billionaire Elias Bogan, a man as mysterious and powerful as he is incredibly dangerous.
STORM ORORO MUNROE
Weather Manipulator/ Leader of X-Treme X-Men
BISHOP LUCAS BISHOP
Kinetic Force Projection and Absorption
SAGE TESSA
Cyberpath/ Living Computer
CANNONBALL SAM GUTHRIE
Flight / Invulnerability
ROGUE ANNA RAVEN
Powers Apparently Inactive
GAMBIT REMY LEBEAU
Thief/Charmer
ELIAS BOGAN
Mutant Predator
He may be a mutant, and he's definitely a predator whose favored prey is mutants.
What the team doesn't know is that he has chosen them as his next victims.
With a very special fate in store for Sage.

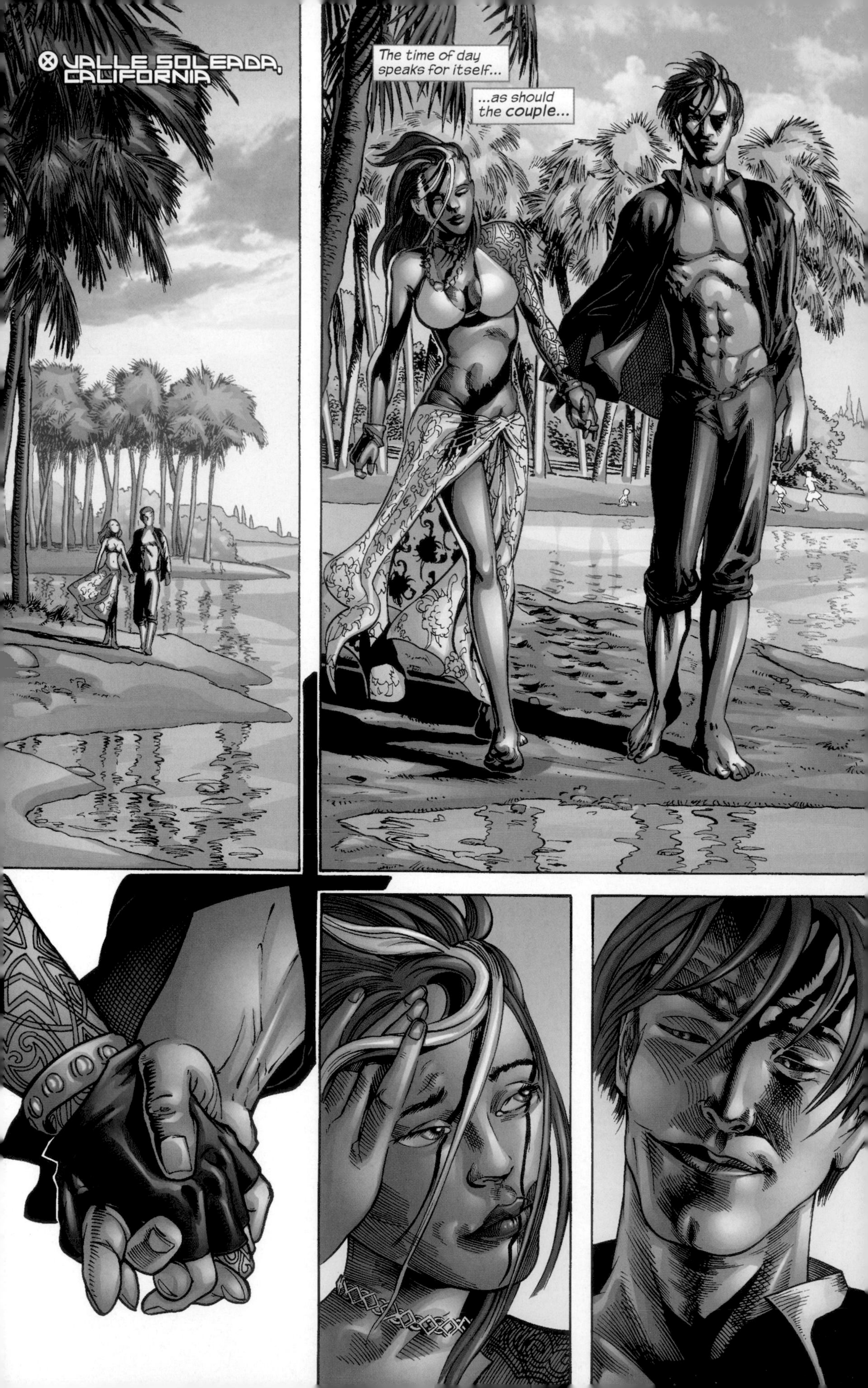
VALLE SOLEADA, CALIFORNIA
The time of day speaks for itself...
...as should the couple...

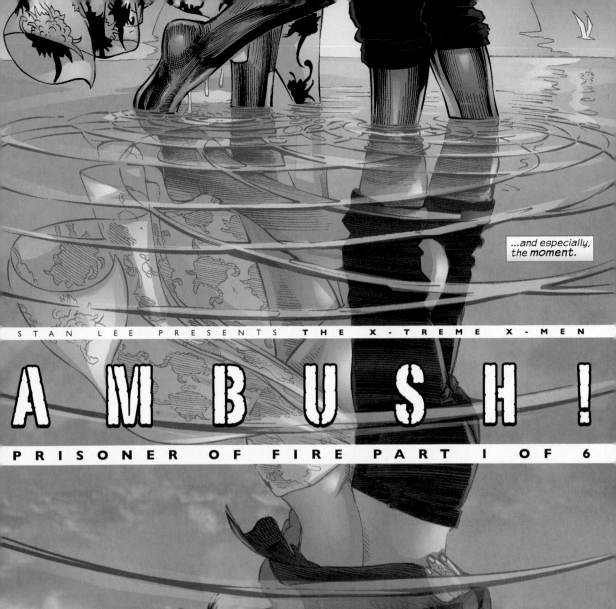

...and especially, the moment.

STAN LEE PRESENTS THE X-TREME X-MEN

AMBUSH!

PRISONER OF FIRE PART 1 OF 6

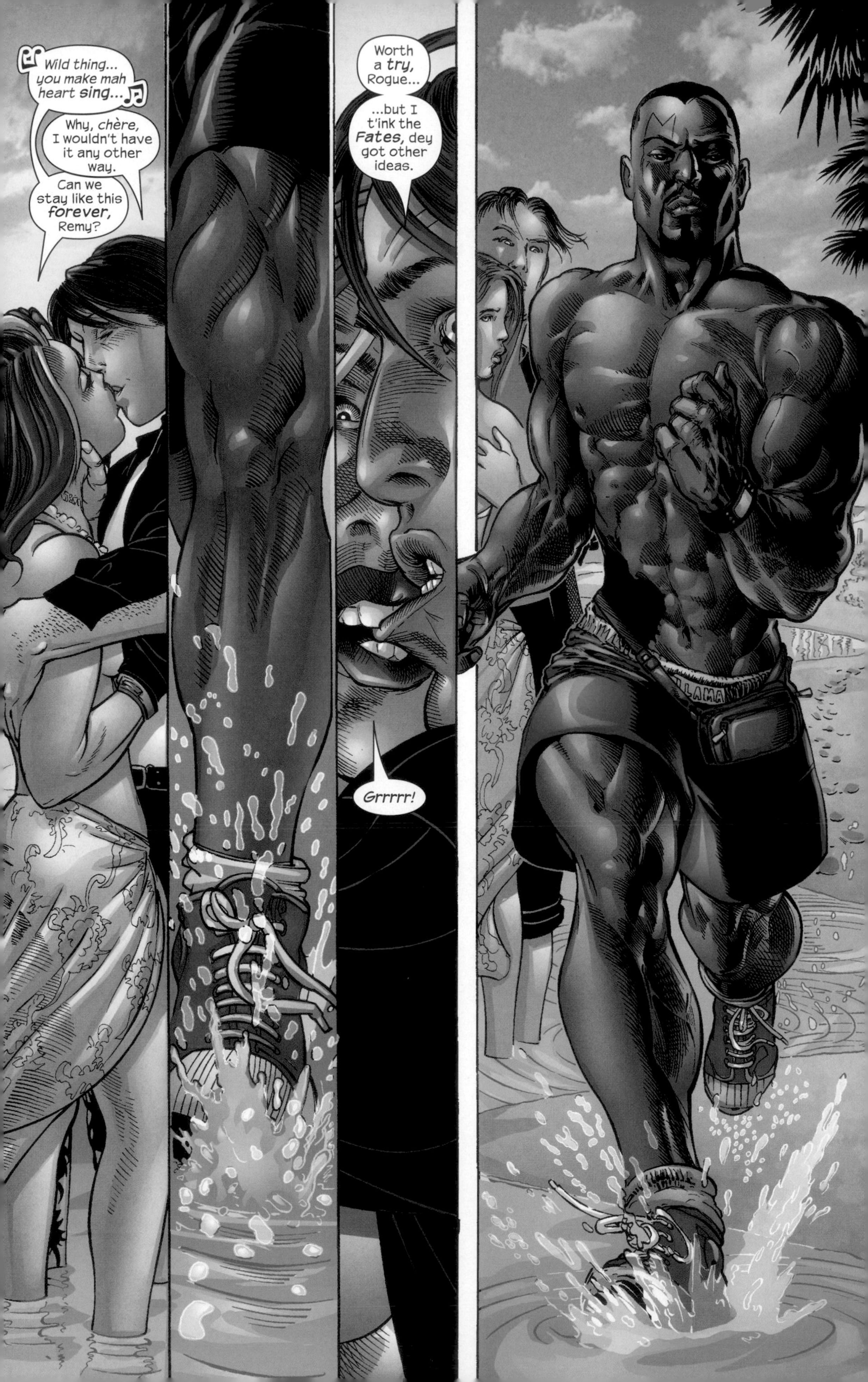
Wild thing... you make mah heart sing...
Why, chère, I wouldn't have it any other way.
Can we stay like this forever, Remy?
Worth a try, Rogue...
...but I t'ink the Fates, dey got other ideas.
Grrrrr!

Of *all* the beaches in all the *world*... ...why does *Bishop* have to go running on *this* one?

Man's on a *mission*, Rogue. Prob'ly din't even *see* us.

Don't you b'lieve it, sugah.

Bishop's just like *Sage*. He sees *everything*.

He lives *his* life.

We live *ours*.

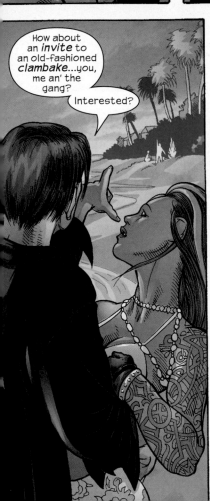

How about an *invite* to an old-fashioned *clambake*...you, me an' the gang?

Interested?

Oh, Remy, that sounds *wonderful!*

But--Ah've never been to one before! Who'll handle the *cookin'*?

Ha. You gon' *insult* me, naughty girl... ...you ain't *never* gon' have your *wicked way* wit' me.

Wanna *bet*?

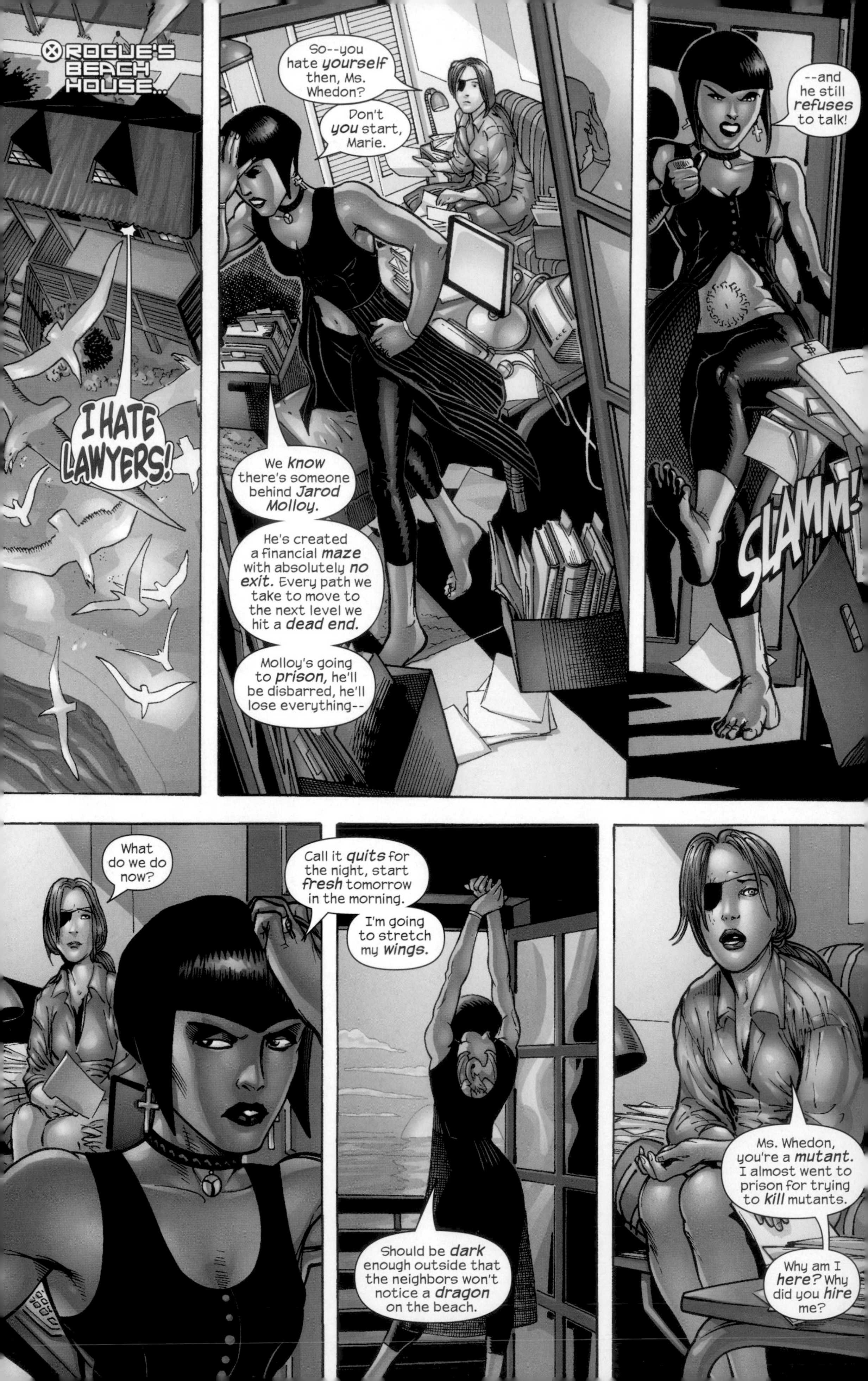
ROGUE'S BEACH HOUSE...
I HATE LAWYERS!
So--you hate yourself then, Ms. Whedon?
Don't you start, Marie.
We know there's someone behind Jarod Molloy.
He's created a financial maze with absolutely no exit. Every path we take to move to the next level we hit a dead end.
Molloy's going to prison, he'll be disbarred, he'll lose everything--
--and he still refuses to talk!
SLAMM!
What do we do now?
Call it quits for the night, start fresh tomorrow in the morning.
I'm going to stretch my wings.
Should be dark enough outside that the neighbors won't notice a dragon on the beach.
Ms. Whedon, you're a mutant. I almost went to prison for trying to kill mutants.
Why am I here? Why did you hire me?

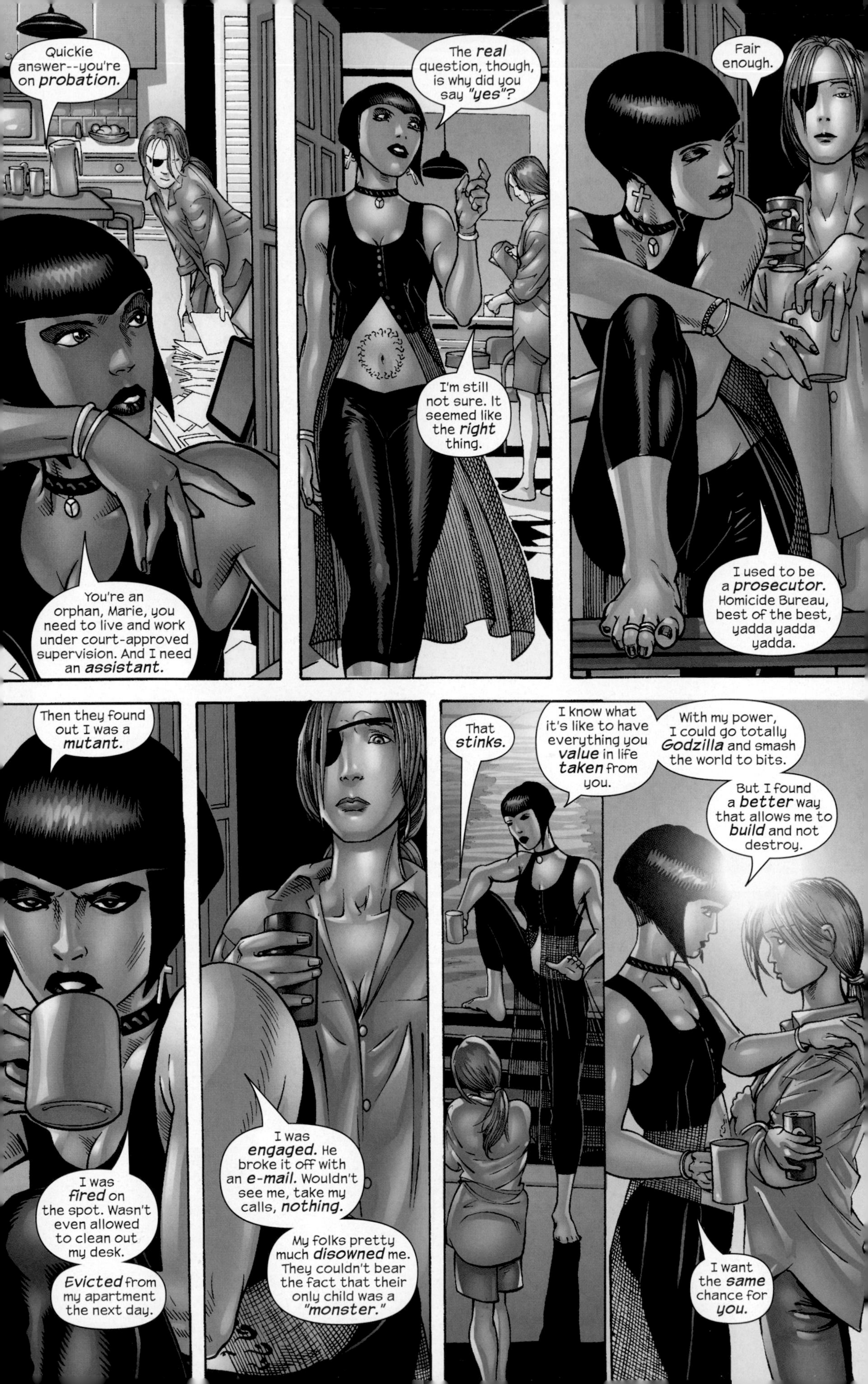
Quickie answer--you're on *probation.*
You're an orphan, Marie, you need to live and work under court-approved supervision. And I need an *assistant.*
The *real* question, though, is why did you say *"yes"*?
I'm still not sure. It seemed like the *right* thing.
Fair enough.
I used to be a *prosecutor.* Homicide Bureau, best of the best, yadda yadda yadda.
Then they found out I was a *mutant.*
I was *fired* on the spot. Wasn't even allowed to clean out my desk.
Evicted from my apartment the next day.
I was *engaged.* He broke it off with an *e-mail.* Wouldn't see me, take my calls, *nothing.*
My folks pretty much *disowned* me. They couldn't bear the fact that their only child was a *"monster."*
That *stinks.*
I know what it's like to have everything you *value* in life *taken* from you.
With my power, I could go totally *Godzilla* and smash the world to bits.
But I found a *better* way that allows me to *build* and not destroy.
I want the *same* chance for *you.*

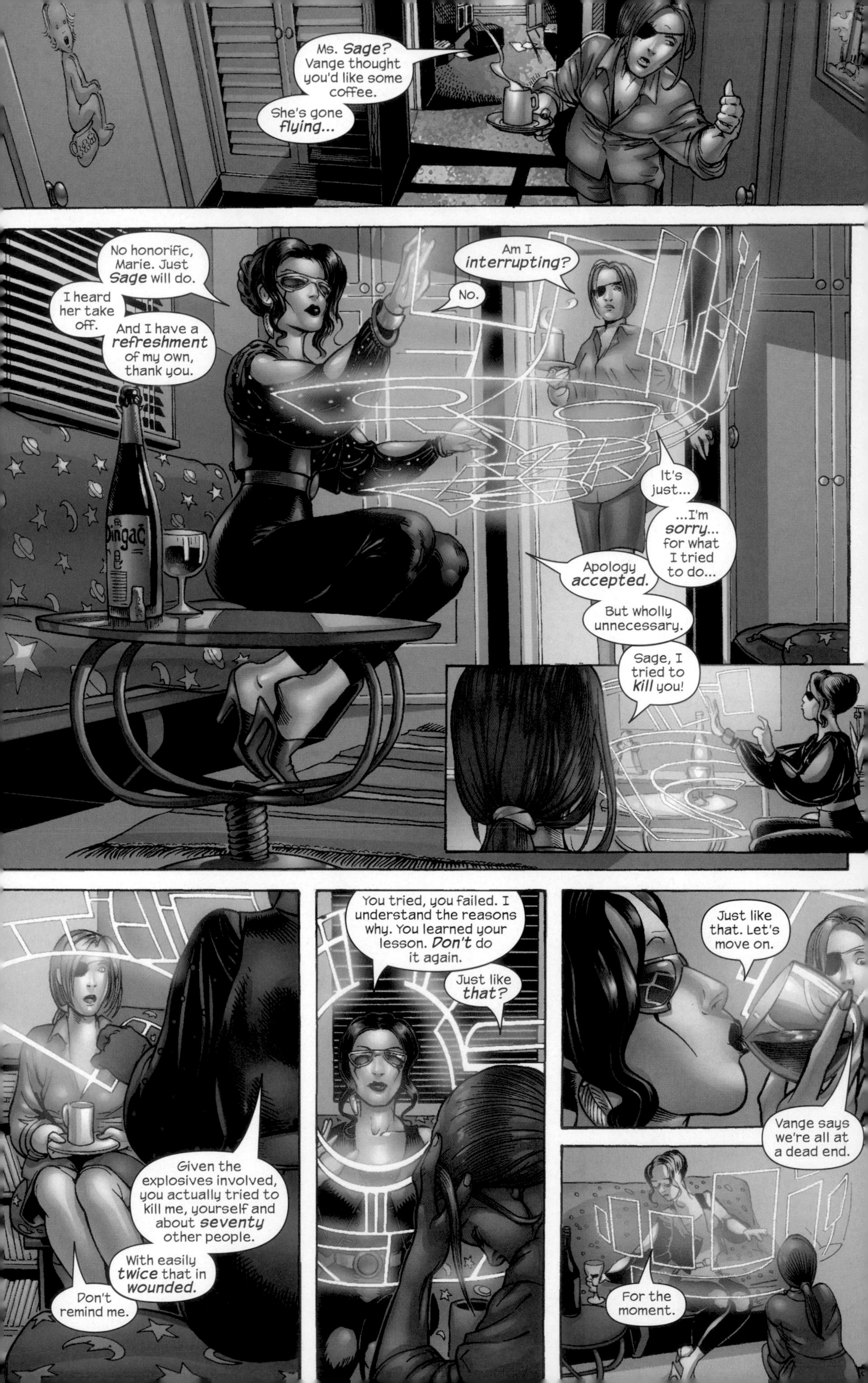
Ms. Sage? Vange thought you'd like some coffee.
She's gone flying...
No honorific, Marie. Just Sage will do.
I heard her take off.
And I have a refreshment of my own, thank you.
Am I interrupting?
No.
It's just...
...I'm sorry... for what I tried to do...
Apology accepted.
But wholly unnecessary.
Sage, I tried to kill you!
Given the explosives involved, you actually tried to kill me, yourself and about seventy other people.
With easily twice that in wounded.
Don't remind me.
You tried, you failed. I understand the reasons why. You learned your lesson. Don't do it again.
Just like that?
Just like that. Let's move on.
Vange says we're all at a dead end.
For the moment.

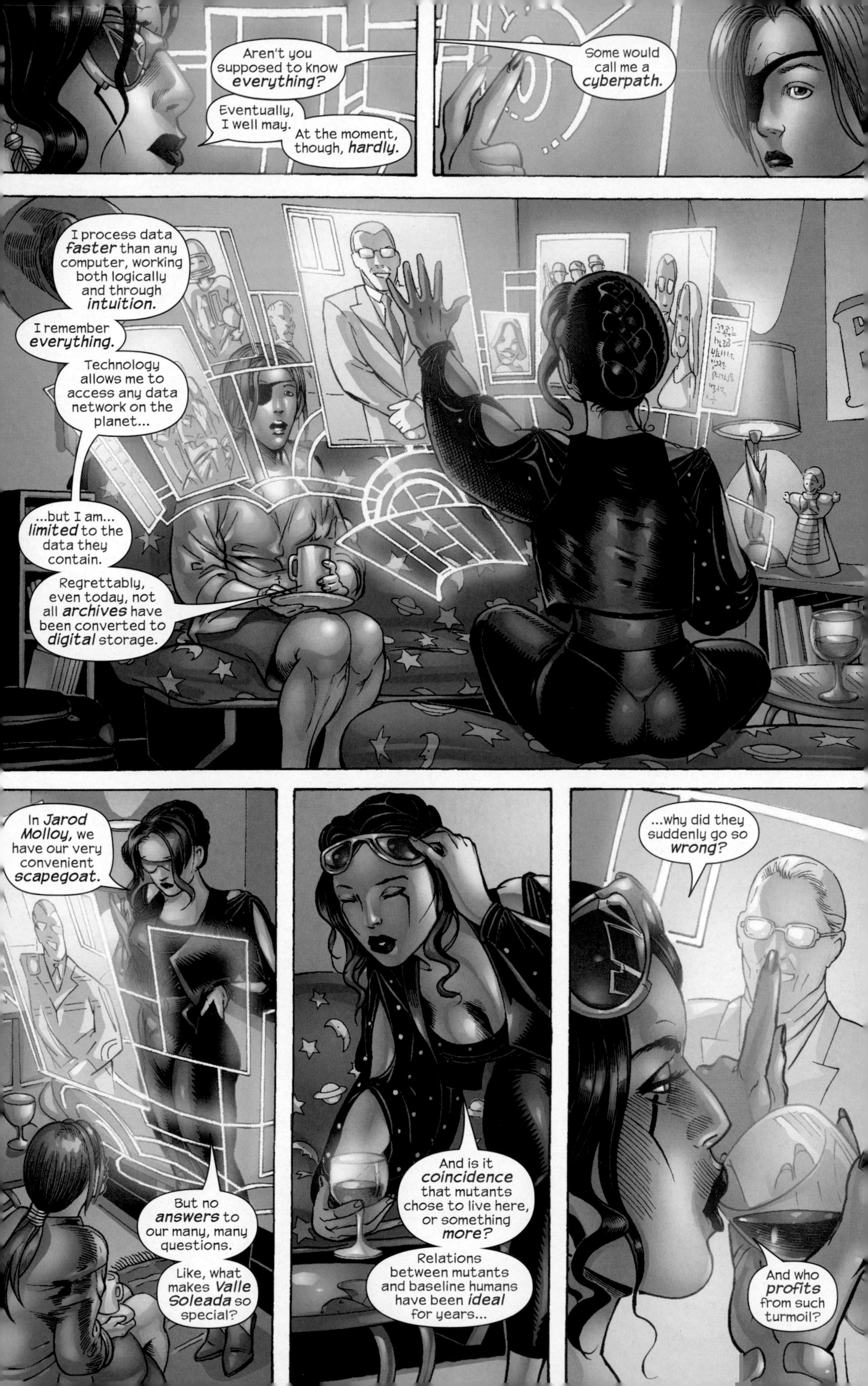

Aren't you supposed to know everything?
Eventually, I well may.
At the moment, though, hardly.
Some would call me a cyberpath.
I process data faster than any computer, working both logically and through intuition.
I remember everything.
Technology allows me to access any data network on the planet...
...but I am... limited to the data they contain.
Regrettably, even today, not all archives have been converted to digital storage.
In Jarod Molloy, we have our very convenient scapegoat.
But no answers to our many, many questions.
Like, what makes Valle Soleada so special?
And is it coincidence that mutants chose to live here, or something more?
Relations between mutants and baseline humans have been ideal for years...
...why did they suddenly go so wrong?
And who profits from such turmoil?

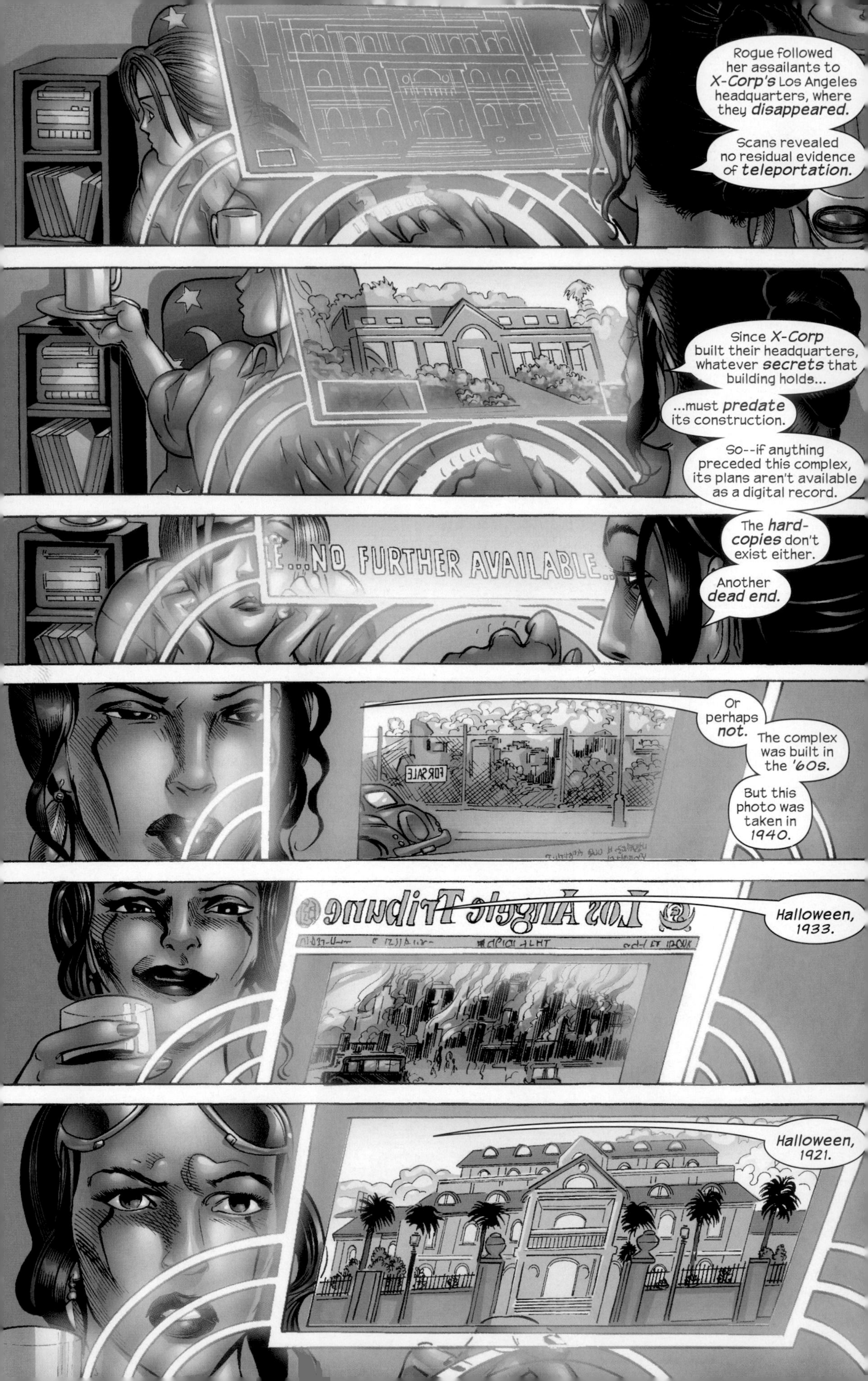
Rogue followed her assailants to X-Corp's Los Angeles headquarters, where they disappeared.
Scans revealed no residual evidence of teleportation.
Since X-Corp built their headquarters, whatever secrets that building holds...
...must predate its construction.
So--if anything preceded this complex, its plans aren't available as a digital record.
...NO FURTHER AVAILABLE...
The hard-copies don't exist either.
Another dead end.
Or perhaps not.
The complex was built in the '60s.
But this photo was taken in 1940.
Halloween, 1933.
Halloween, 1921.

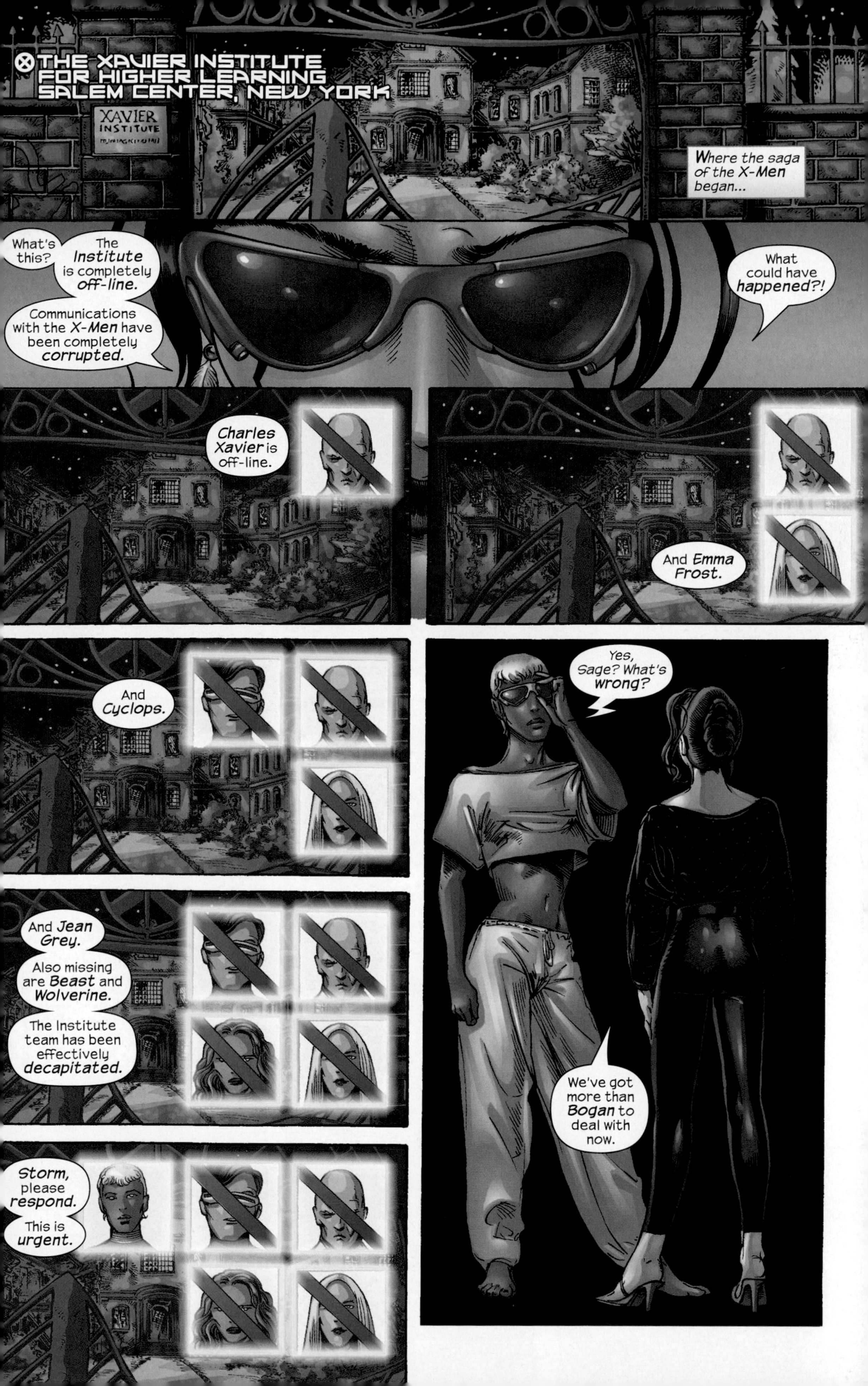
THE XAVIER INSTITUTE FOR HIGHER LEARNING SALEM CENTER, NEW YORK
XAVIER INSTITUTE
Where the saga of the X-Men began...
What's this?
The Institute is completely off-line.
Communications with the X-Men have been completely corrupted.
What could have happened?!
Charles Xavier is off-line.
And Emma Frost.
And Cyclops.
And Jean Grey.
Also missing are Beast and Wolverine.
The Institute team has been effectively decapitated.
Storm, please respond.
This is urgent.
Yes, Sage? What's wrong?
We've got more than Bogan to deal with now.

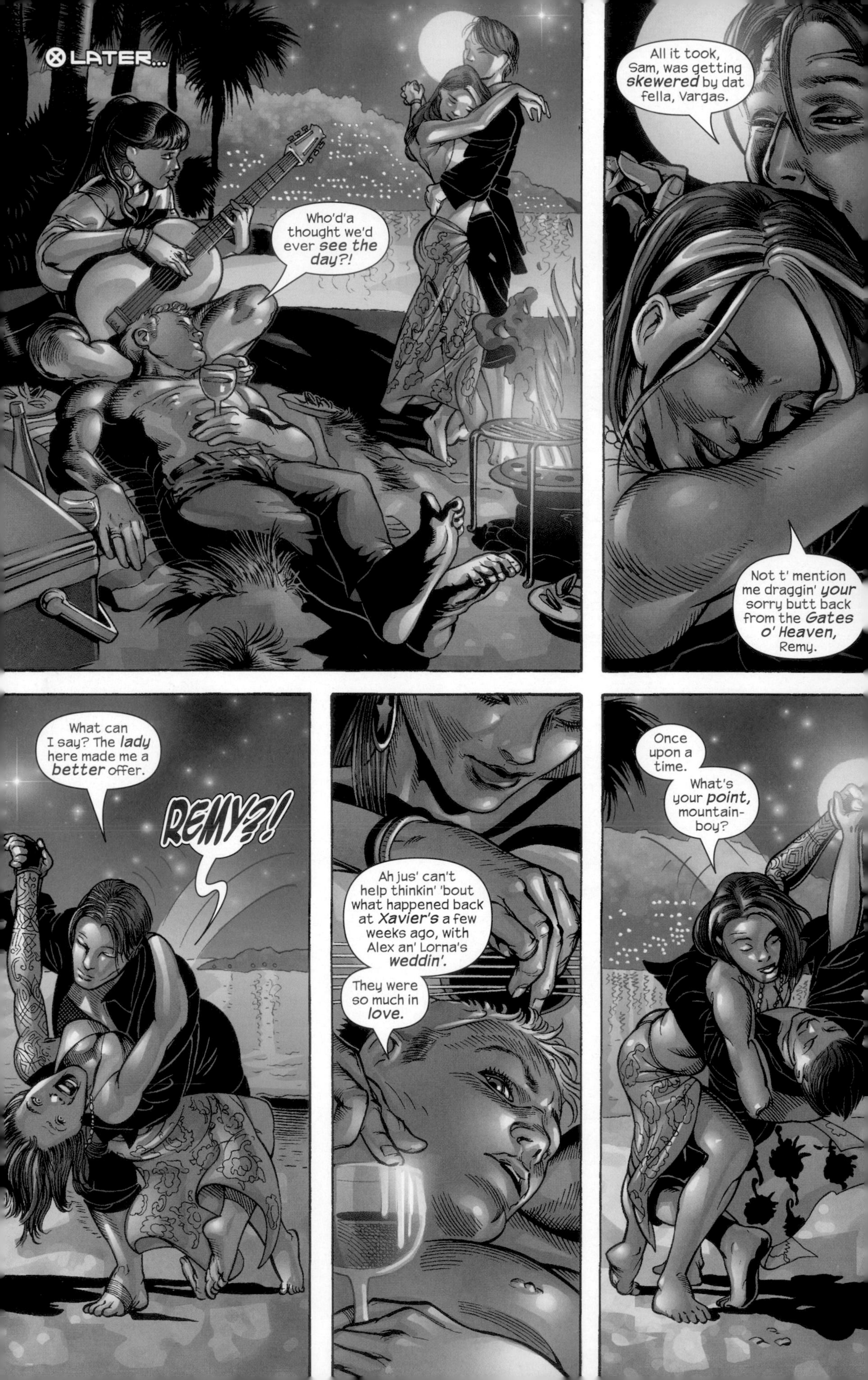
LATER...
Who'd'a thought we'd ever see the day?!
All it took, Sam, was getting skewered by dat fella, Vargas.
Not t' mention me draggin' your sorry butt back from the Gates o' Heaven, Remy.
What can I say? The lady here made me a better offer.
REMY?!
Ah jus' can't help thinkin' 'bout what happened back at Xavier's a few weeks ago, with Alex an' Lorna's weddin'.
They were so much in love.
Once upon a time.
What's your point, mountain-boy?

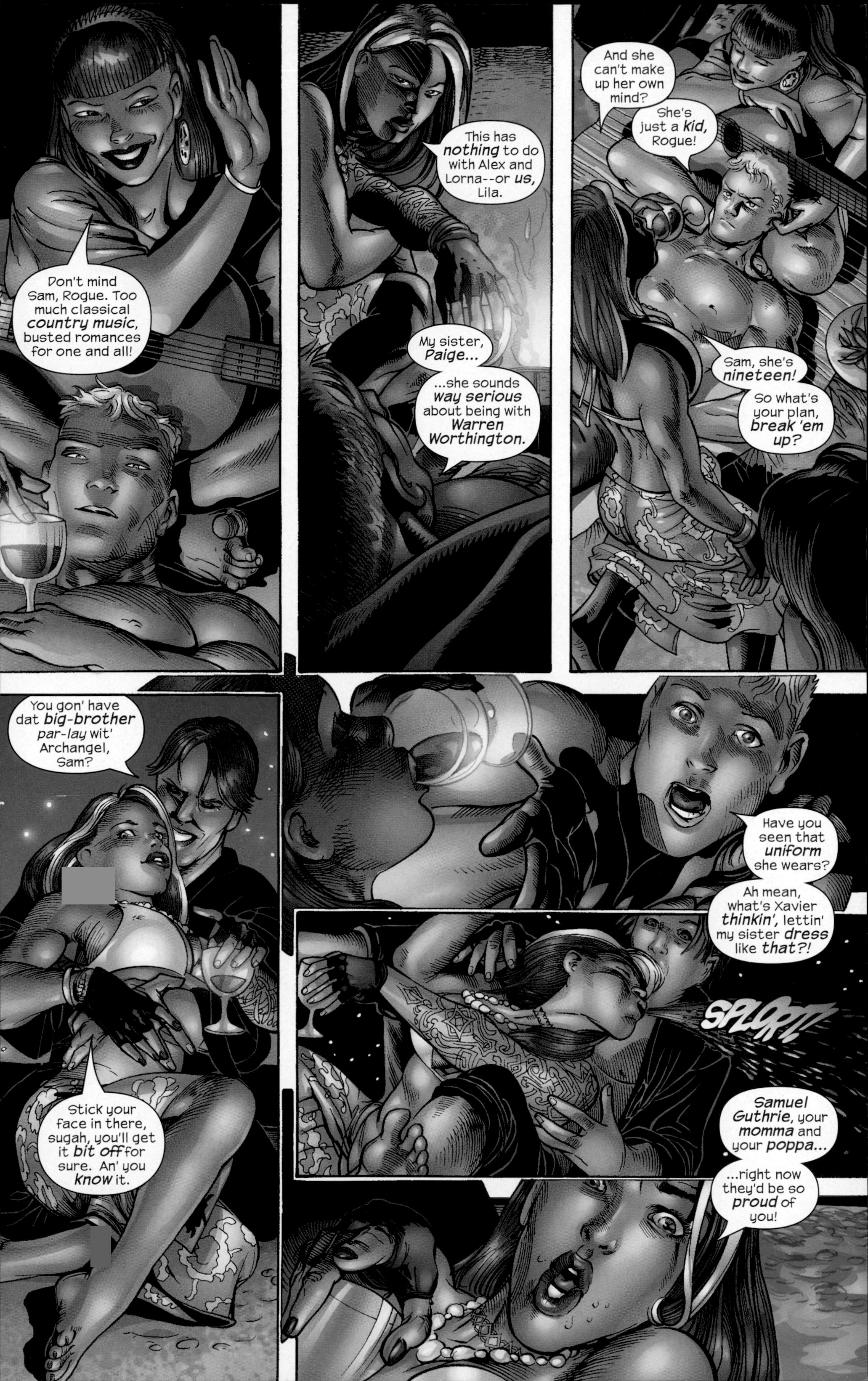
Don't mind Sam, Rogue. Too much classical country music, busted romances for one and all!
This has nothing to do with Alex and Lorna--or us, Lila.
My sister, Paige...
...she sounds way serious about being with Warren Worthington.
And she can't make up her own mind?
She's just a kid, Rogue!
Sam, she's nineteen!
So what's your plan, break 'em up?
You gon' have dat big-brother par-lay wit' Archangel, Sam?
Stick your face in there, sugah, you'll get it bit off for sure. An' you know it.
Have you seen that uniform she wears?
Ah mean, what's Xavier thinkin', lettin' my sister dress like that?!
SPLORT!
Samuel Guthrie, your momma and your poppa...
...right now they'd be so proud of you!

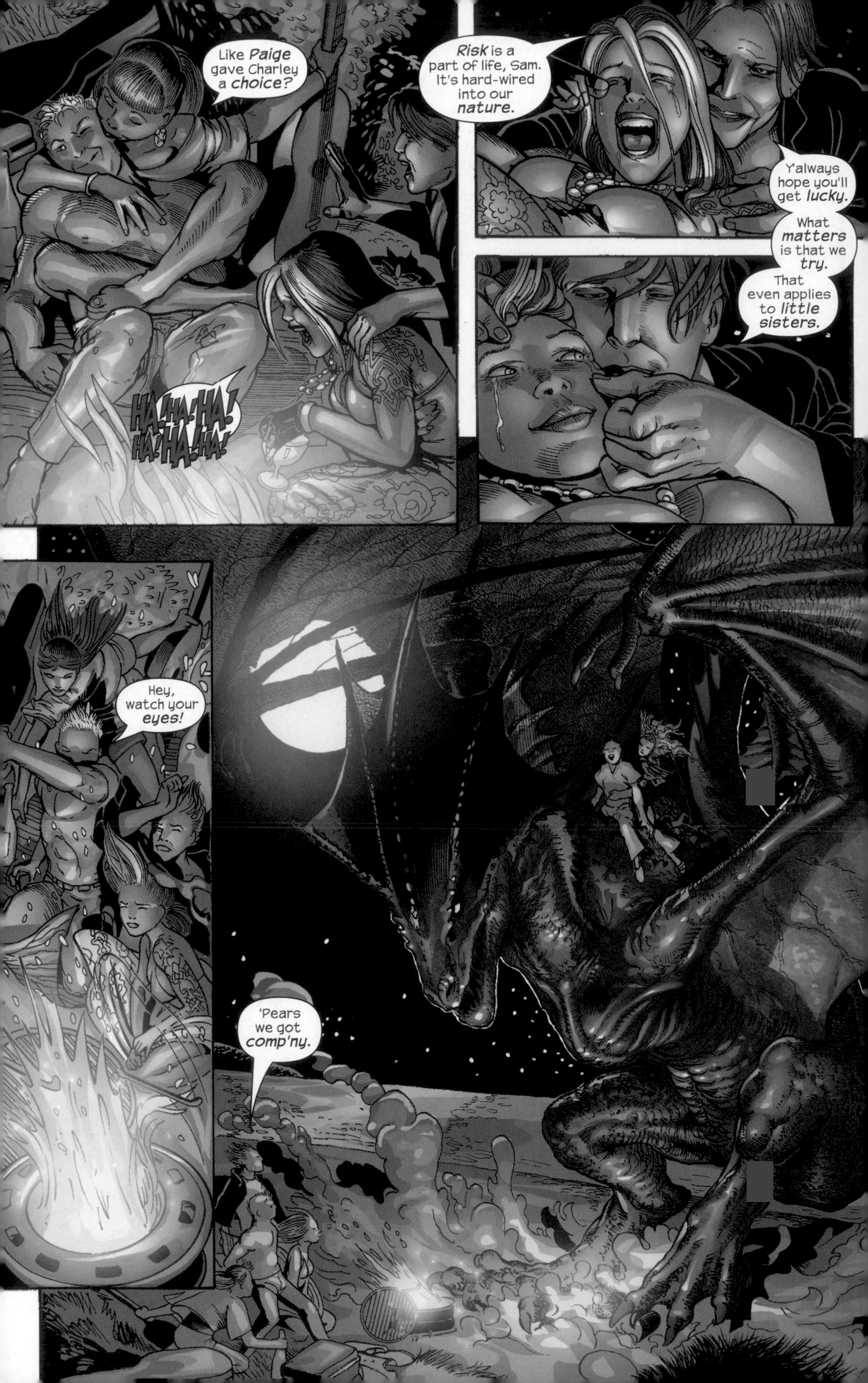

Like Paige gave Charley a choice?
HA!HA!HA! HA!HA!HA!
Risk is a part of life, Sam. It's hard-wired into our nature.
Y'always hope you'll get lucky.
What matters is that we try.
That even applies to little sisters.
Hey, watch your eyes!
'Pears we got comp'ny.

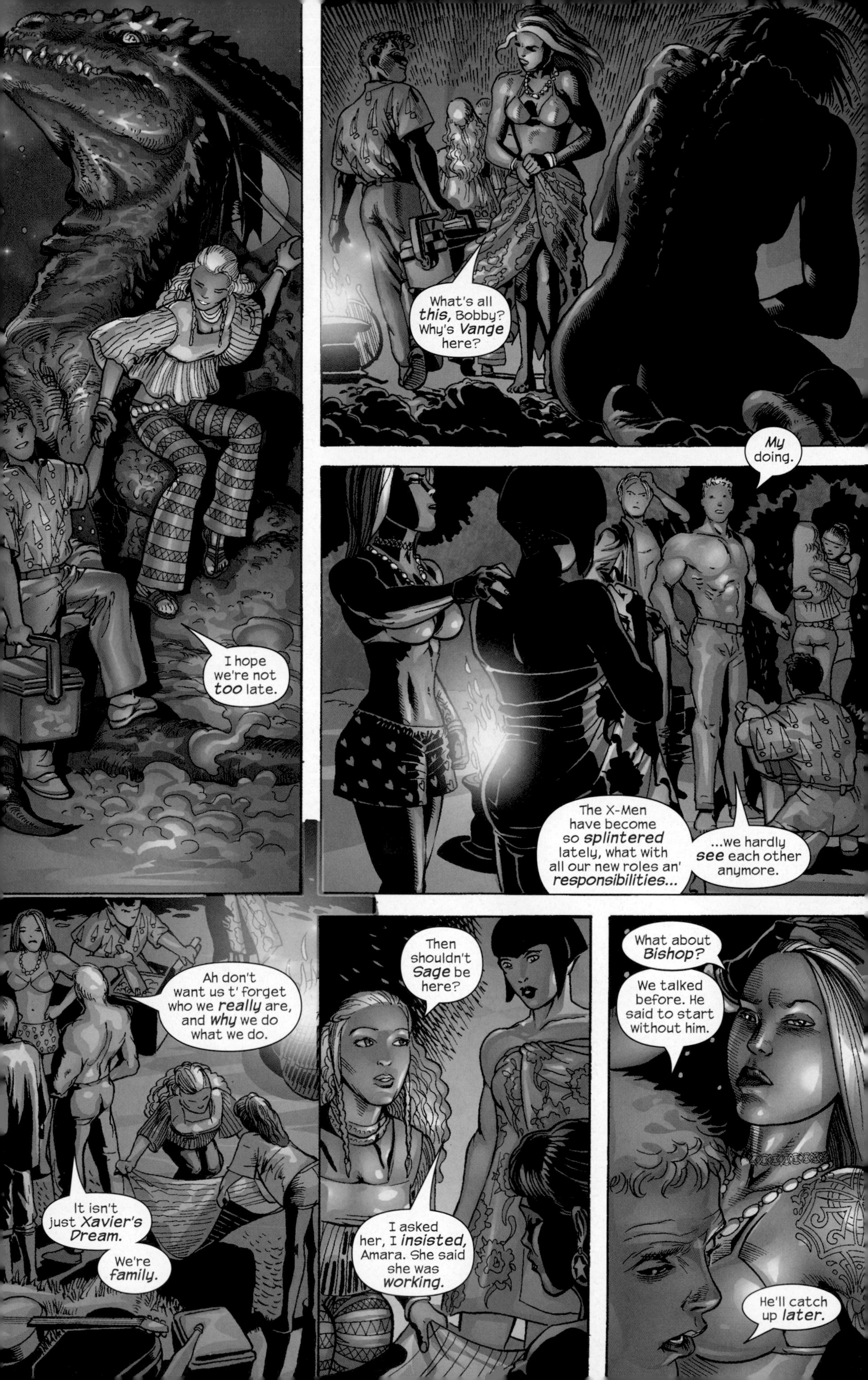

I hope we're not *too* late.
What's all *this,* Bobby? Why's *Vange* here?
My doing.
The X-Men have become so *splintered* lately, what with all our new roles an' *responsibilities...*
...we hardly *see* each other anymore.
Ah don't want us t' forget who we *really* are, and *why* we do what we do.
It isn't just *Xavier's Dream.*
We're *family.*
Then shouldn't *Sage* be here?
I asked her, I *insisted,* Amara. She said she was *working.*
What about *Bishop?*
We talked before. He said to start without him.
He'll catch up *later.*

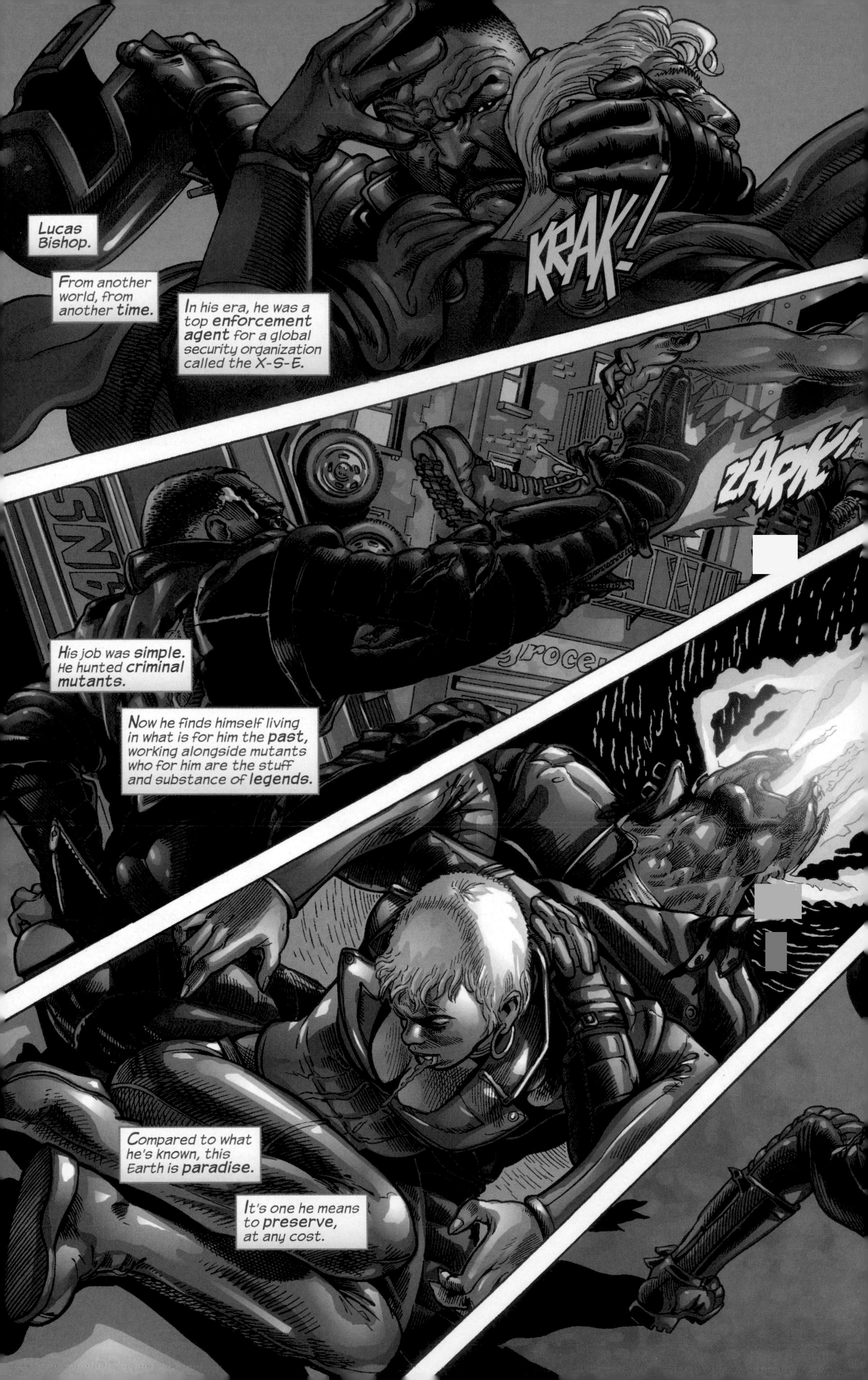
Lucas Bishop.
KRAK!
From another world, from another time.
In his era, he was a top enforcement agent for a global security organization called the X-S-E.
ZARK!
His job was simple. He hunted criminal mutants.
Now he finds himself living in what is for him the past, working alongside mutants who for him are the stuff and substance of legends.
Compared to what he's known, this Earth is paradise.
It's one he means to preserve, at any cost.

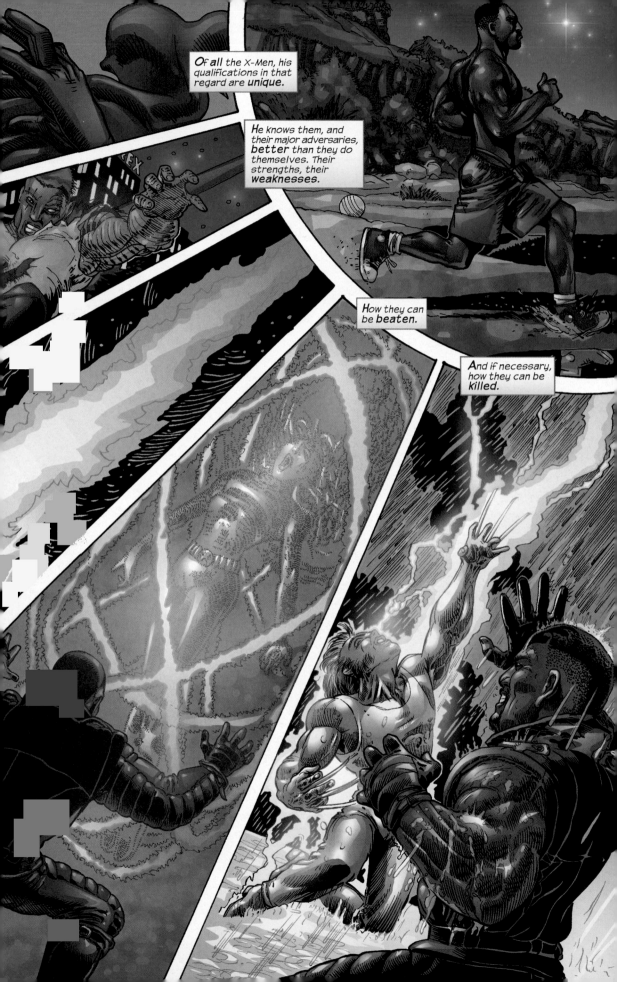

Of all the X-Men, his qualifications in that regard are *unique*.

He knows them, and their major adversaries, *better* than they do themselves. Their strengths, their *weaknesses*.

How they can be *beaten*.

And if necessary, how they can be *killed*.

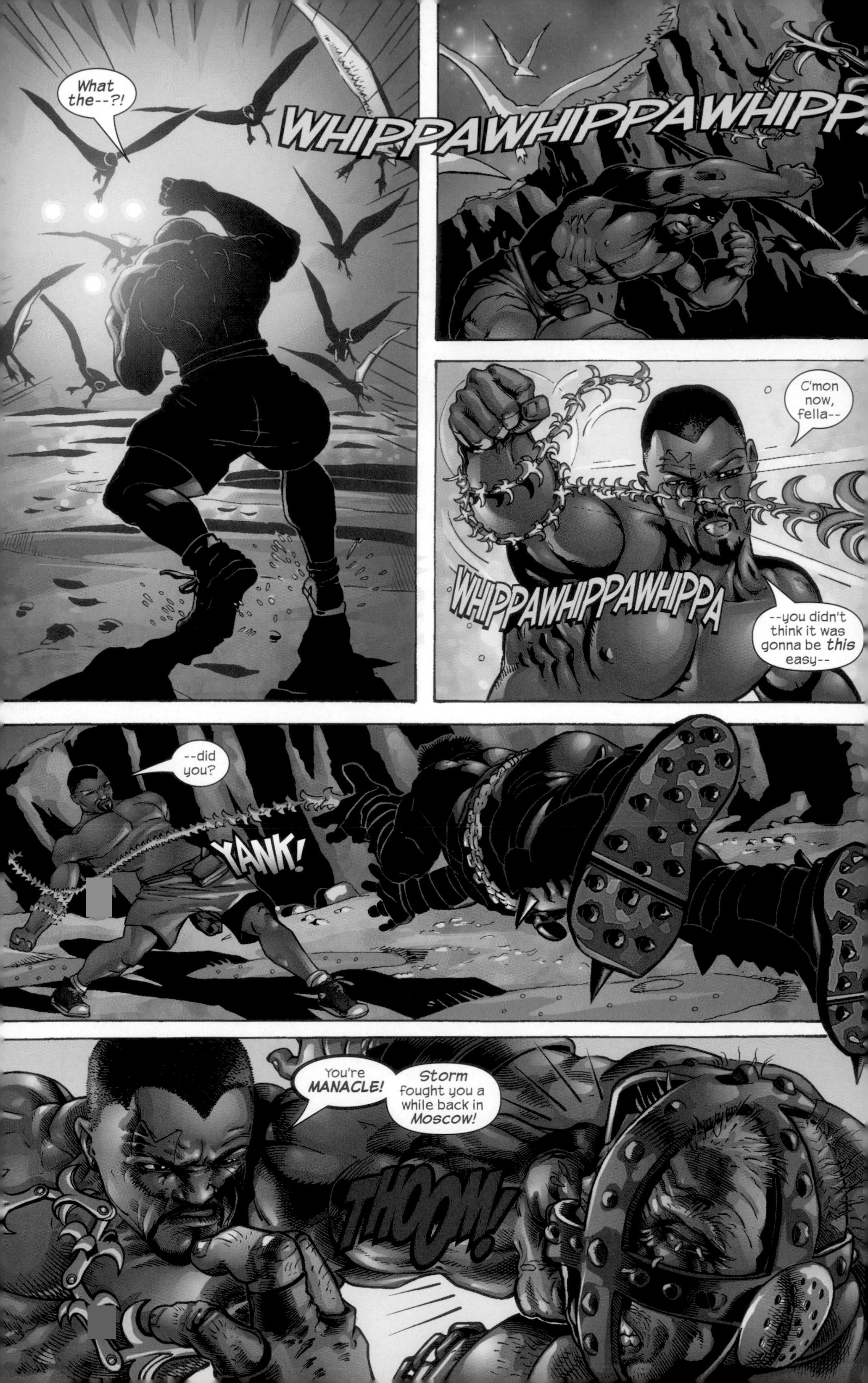
What the--?!
WHIPPAWHIPPAWHIPP
C'mon now, fella--
WHIPPAWHIPPAWHIPPA
--you didn't think it was gonna be this easy--
--did you?
YANK!
You're MANACLE!
Storm fought you a while back in Moscow!
THOOM!

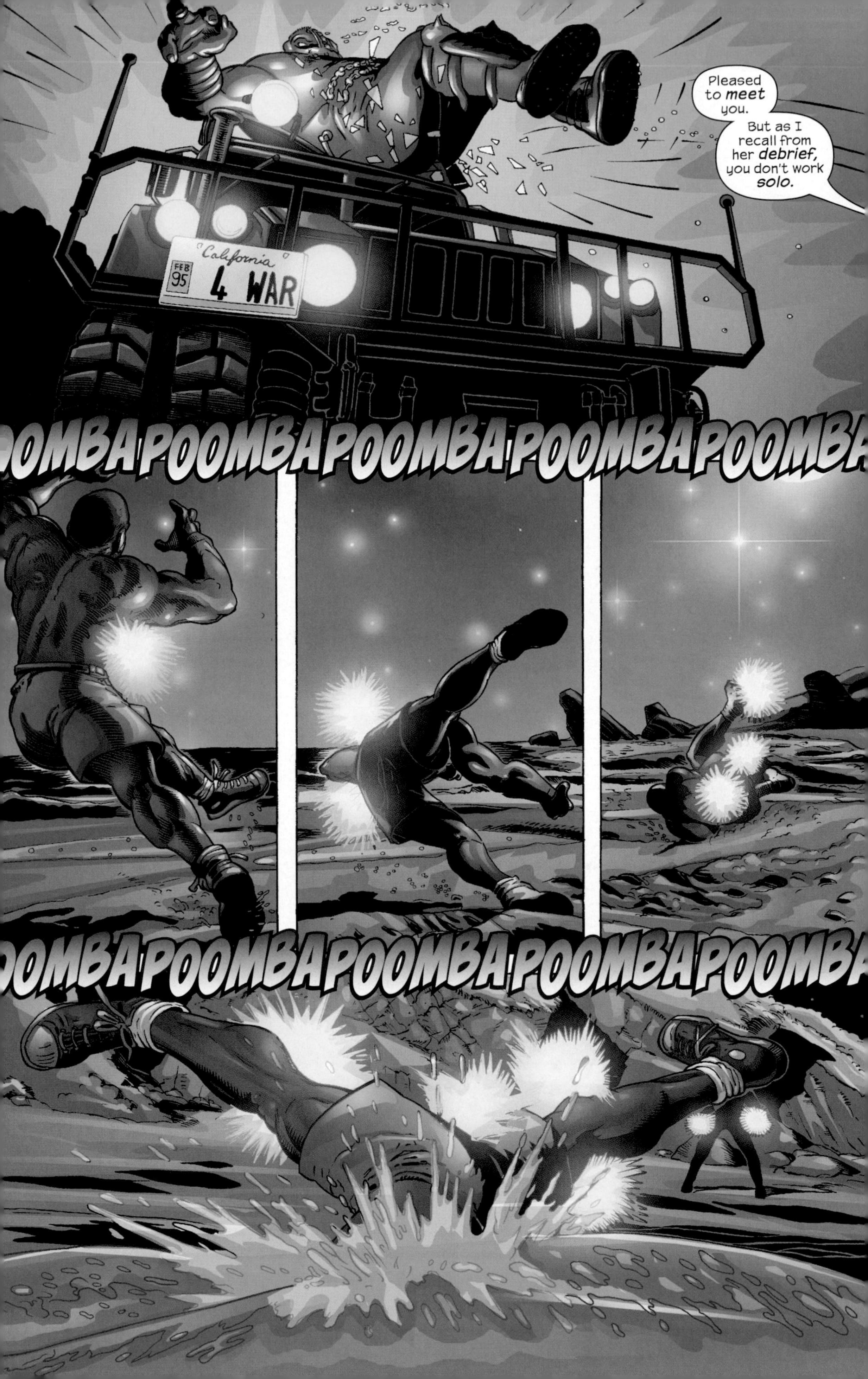
Pleased to *meet* you.
But as I recall from her *debrief,* you don't work *solo.*
California
FEB 95
4 WAR
POOMBAPOOMBAPOOMBAPOOMBAPOOMBA
POOMBAPOOMBAPOOMBAPOOMBAPOOMBA

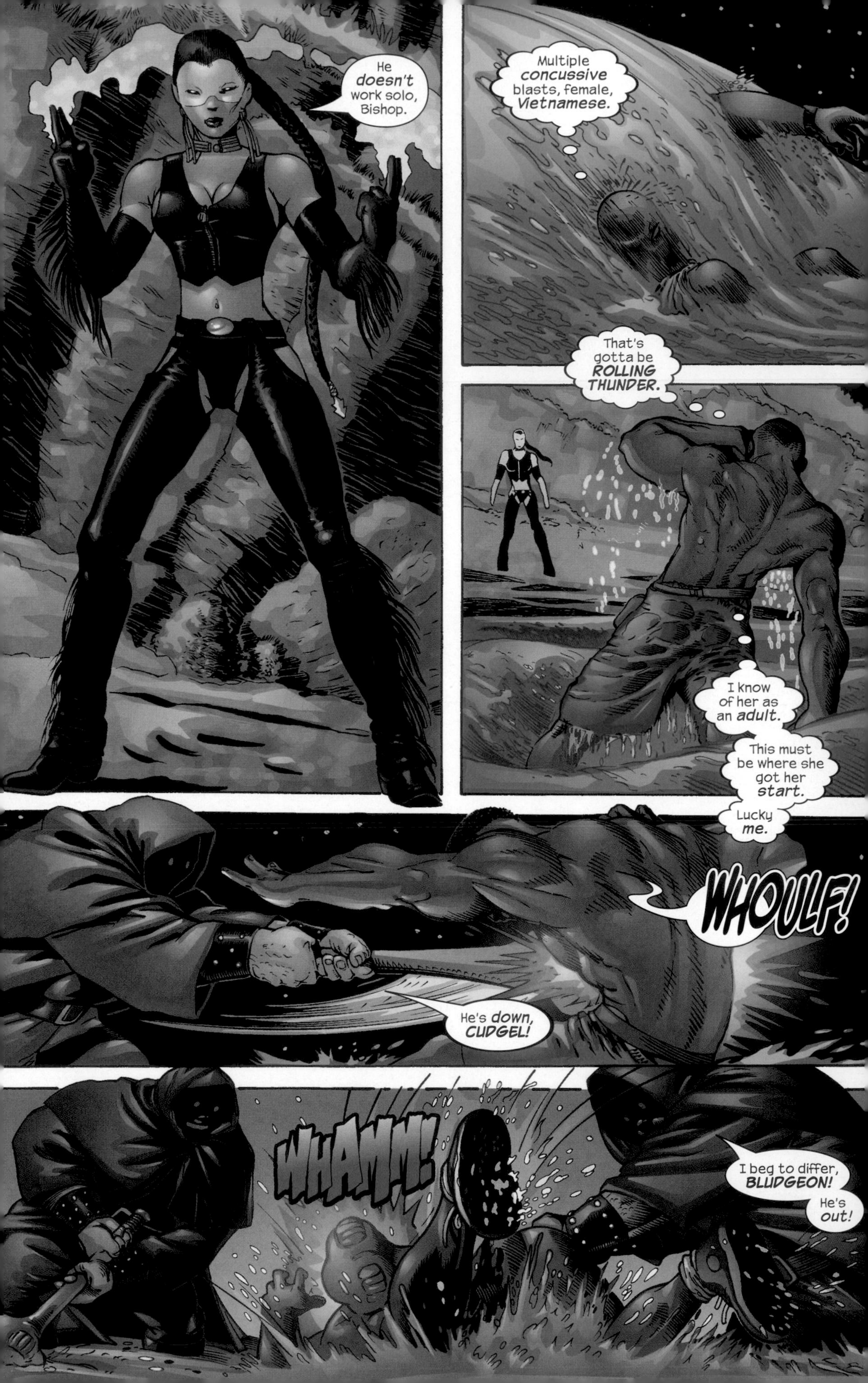
He doesn't work solo, Bishop.
Multiple concussive blasts, female, Vietnamese.
That's gotta be ROLLING THUNDER.
I know of her as an adult.
This must be where she got her start.
Lucky me.
WHOULF!
He's down, CUDGEL!
WHAMM!
I beg to differ, BLUDGEON!
He's out!

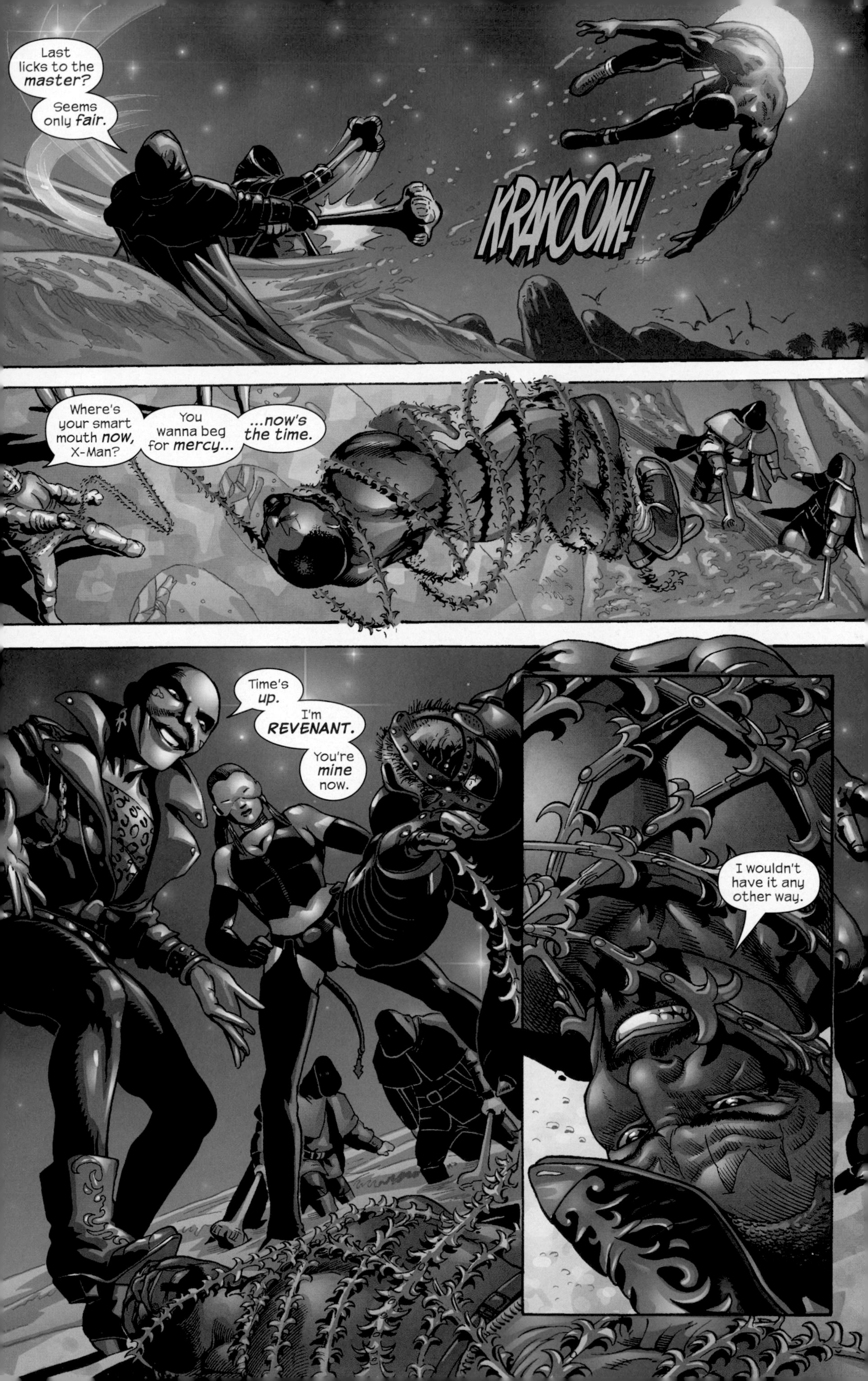
Last licks to the master?
Seems only fair.
KRAKOOM!
Where's your smart mouth now, X-Man?
You wanna beg for mercy...
...now's the time.
Time's up.
I'm REVENANT.
You're mine now.
I wouldn't have it any other way.

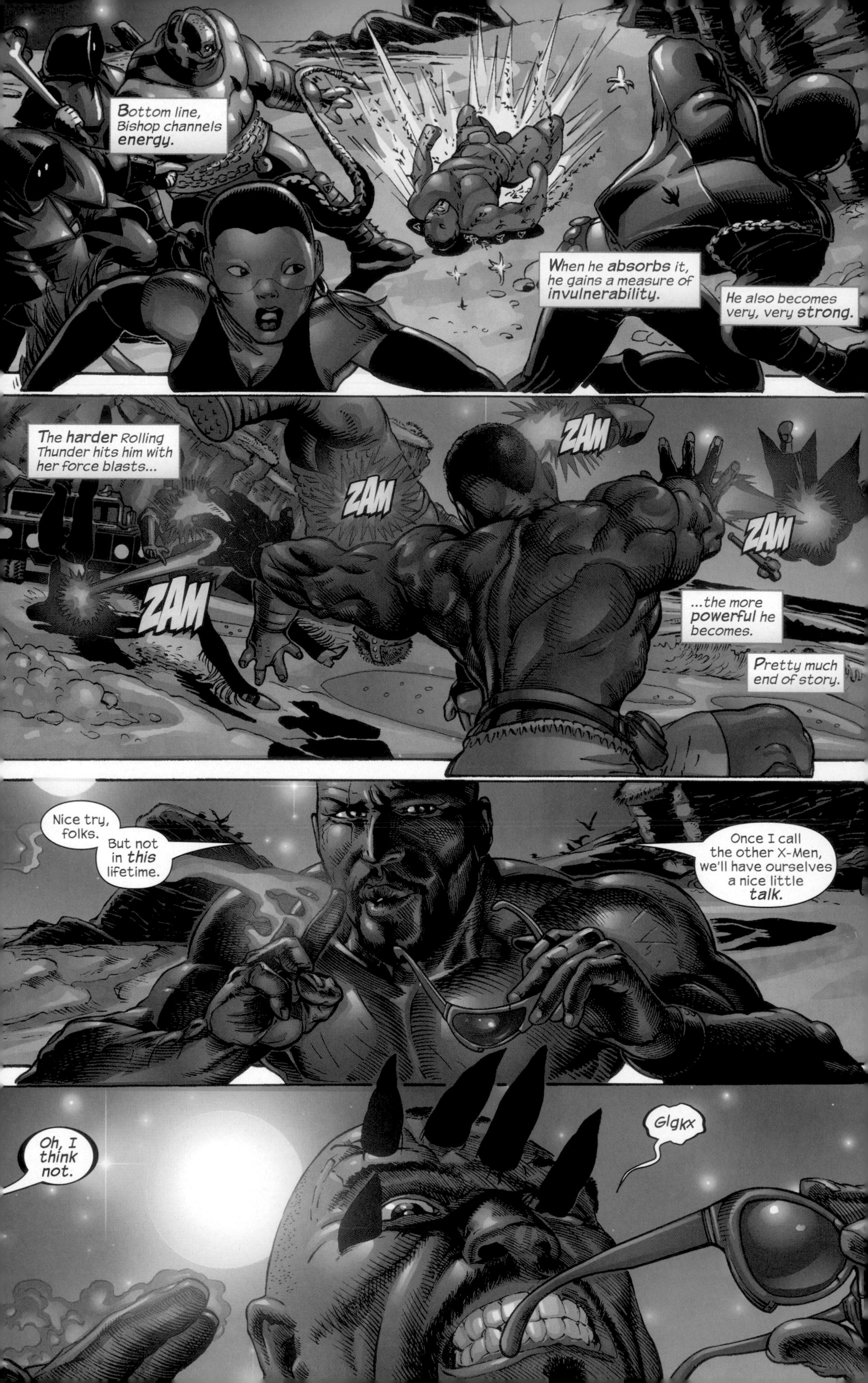
Bottom line, Bishop channels energy.
When he absorbs it, he gains a measure of invulnerability.
He also becomes very, very strong.
The harder Rolling Thunder hits him with her force blasts...
ZAM
ZAM
ZAM
ZAM
...the more powerful he becomes.
Pretty much end of story.
Nice try, folks.
But not in this lifetime.
Once I call the other X-Men, we'll have ourselves a nice little talk.
Oh, I think not.
Glgkx

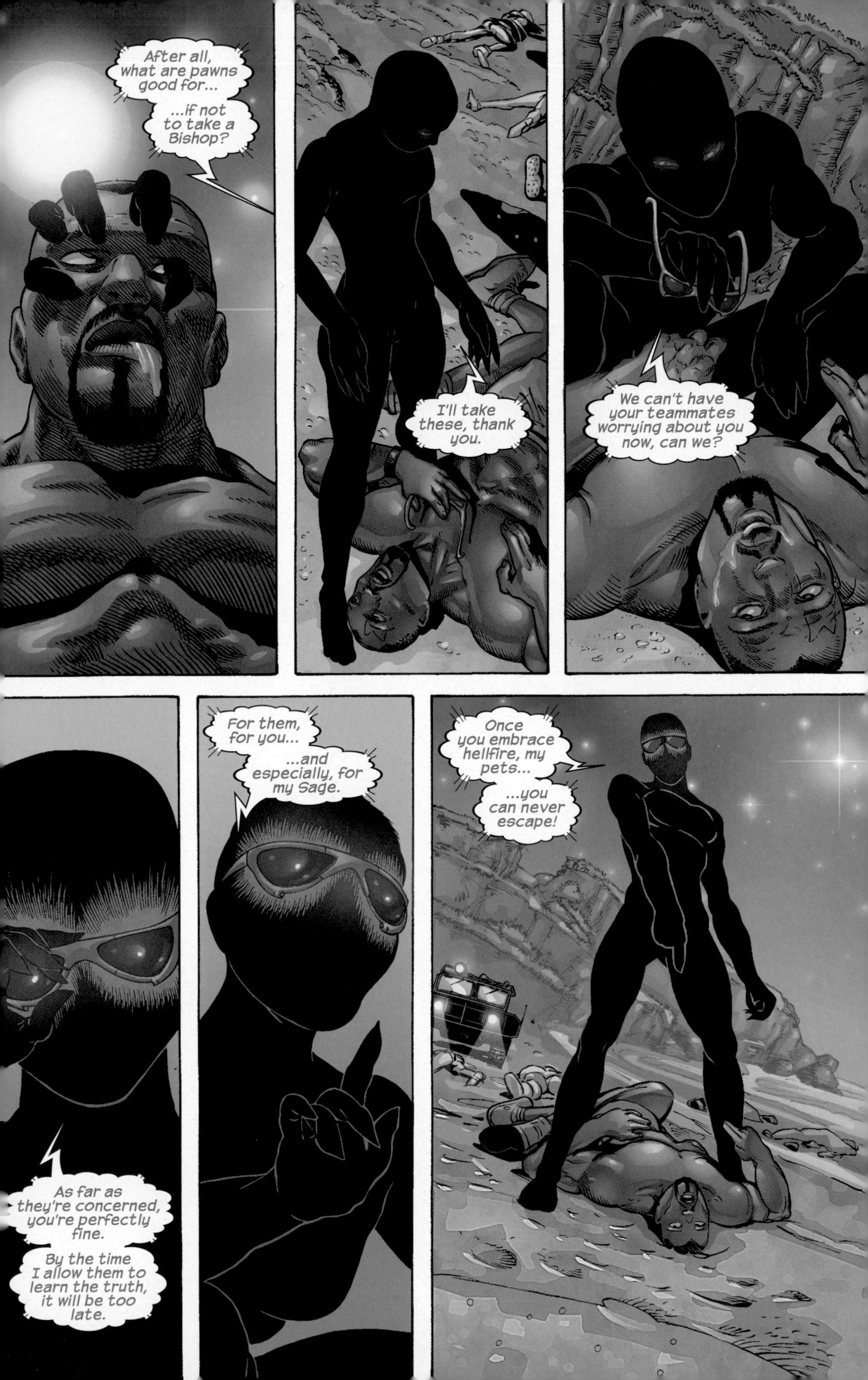
After all, what are pawns good for...
...if not to take a Bishop?
I'll take these, thank you.
We can't have your teammates worrying about you now, can we?
As far as they're concerned, you're perfectly fine.
By the time I allow them to learn the truth, it will be too late.
For them, for you...
...and especially, for my Sage.
Once you embrace hellfire, my pets...
...you can never escape!

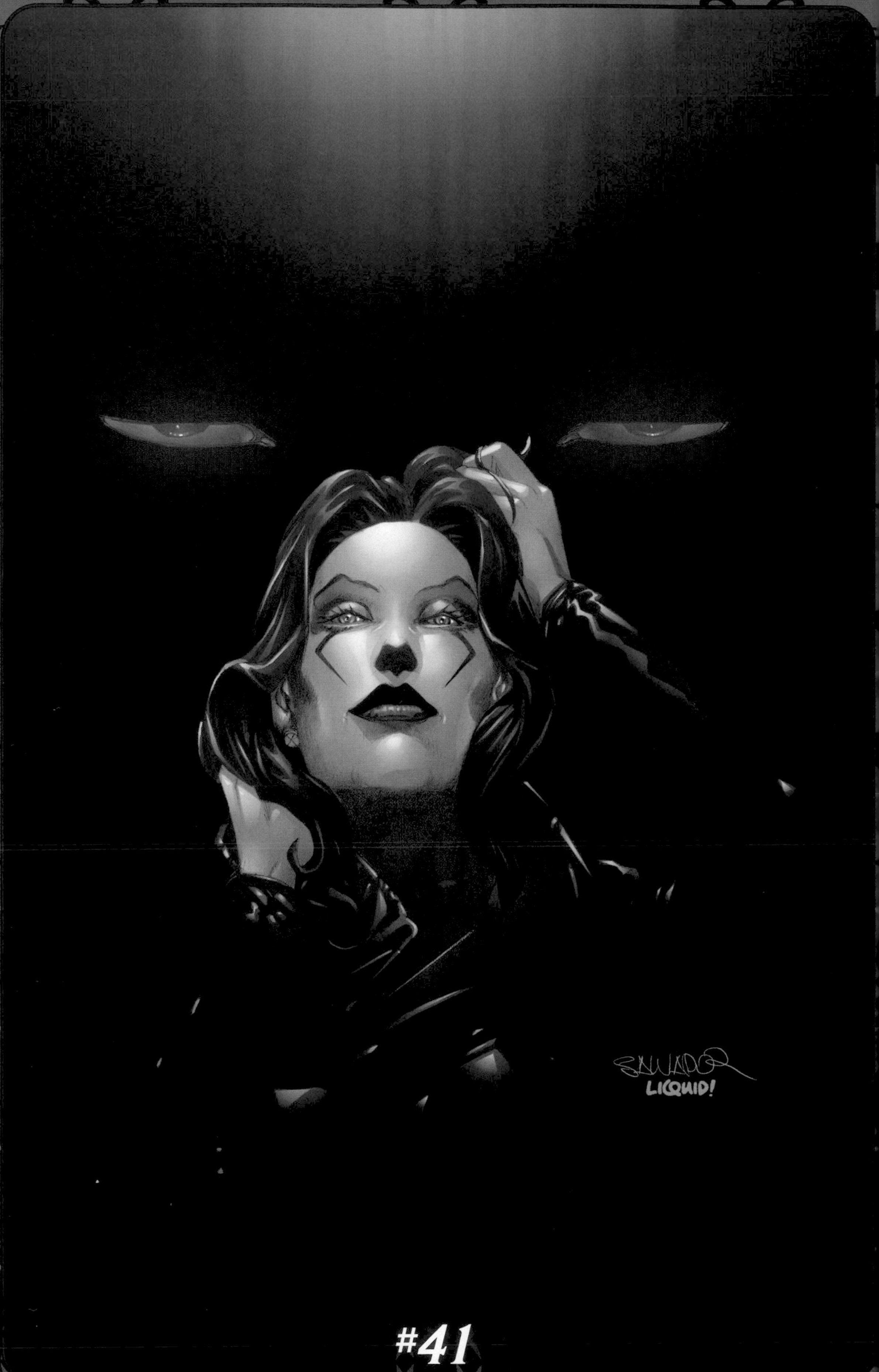
SALVADOR
LICQUID!

#41

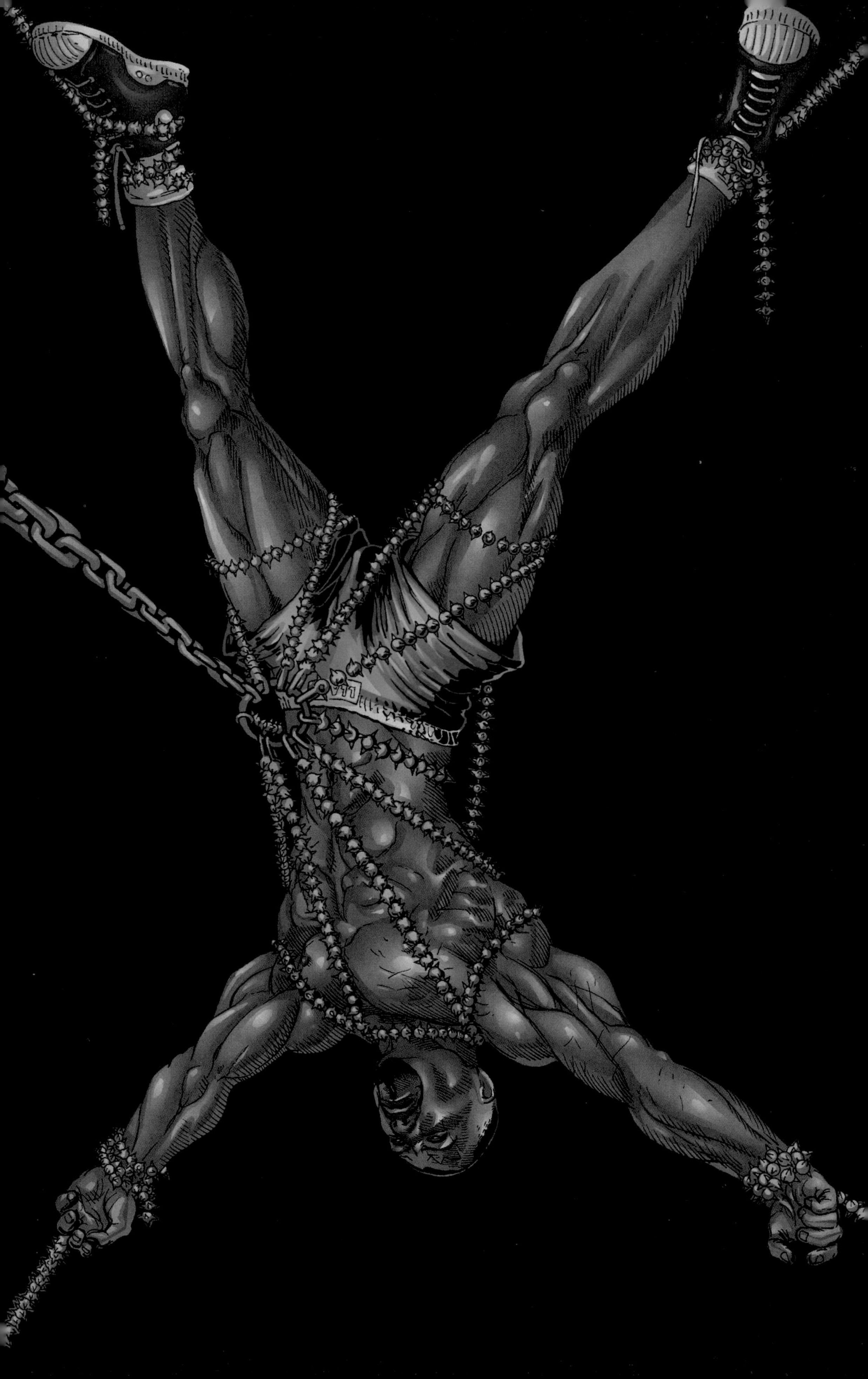

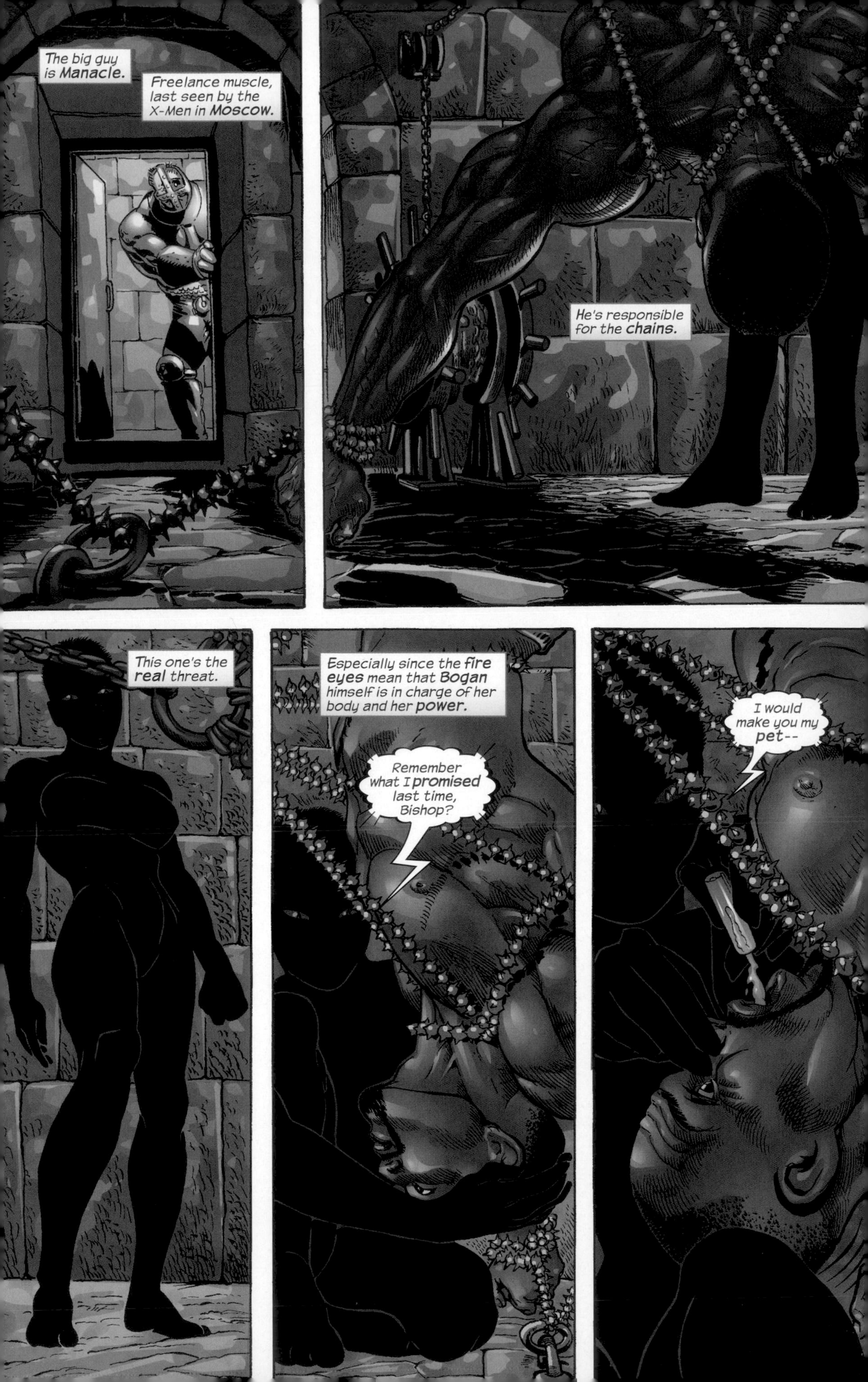
The big guy is Manacle.
Freelance muscle, last seen by the X-Men in Moscow.
He's responsible for the chains.
This one's the real threat.
Especially since the fire eyes mean that Bogan himself is in charge of her body and her power.
Remember what I promised last time, Bishop?
I would make you my pet--

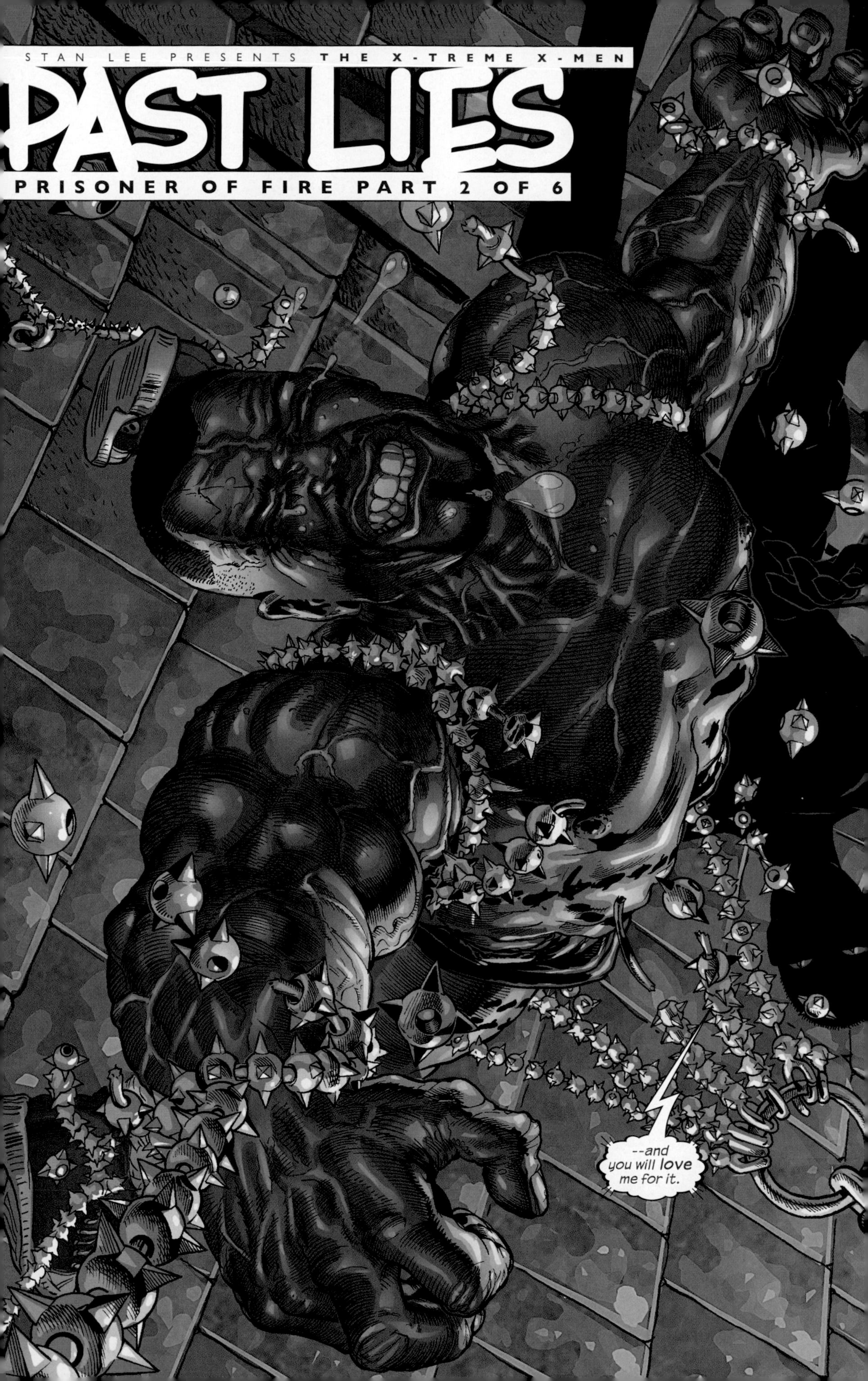
STAN LEE PRESENTS THE X-TREME X-MEN
PAST LIES
PRISONER OF FIRE PART 2 OF 6
--and you will love me for it.

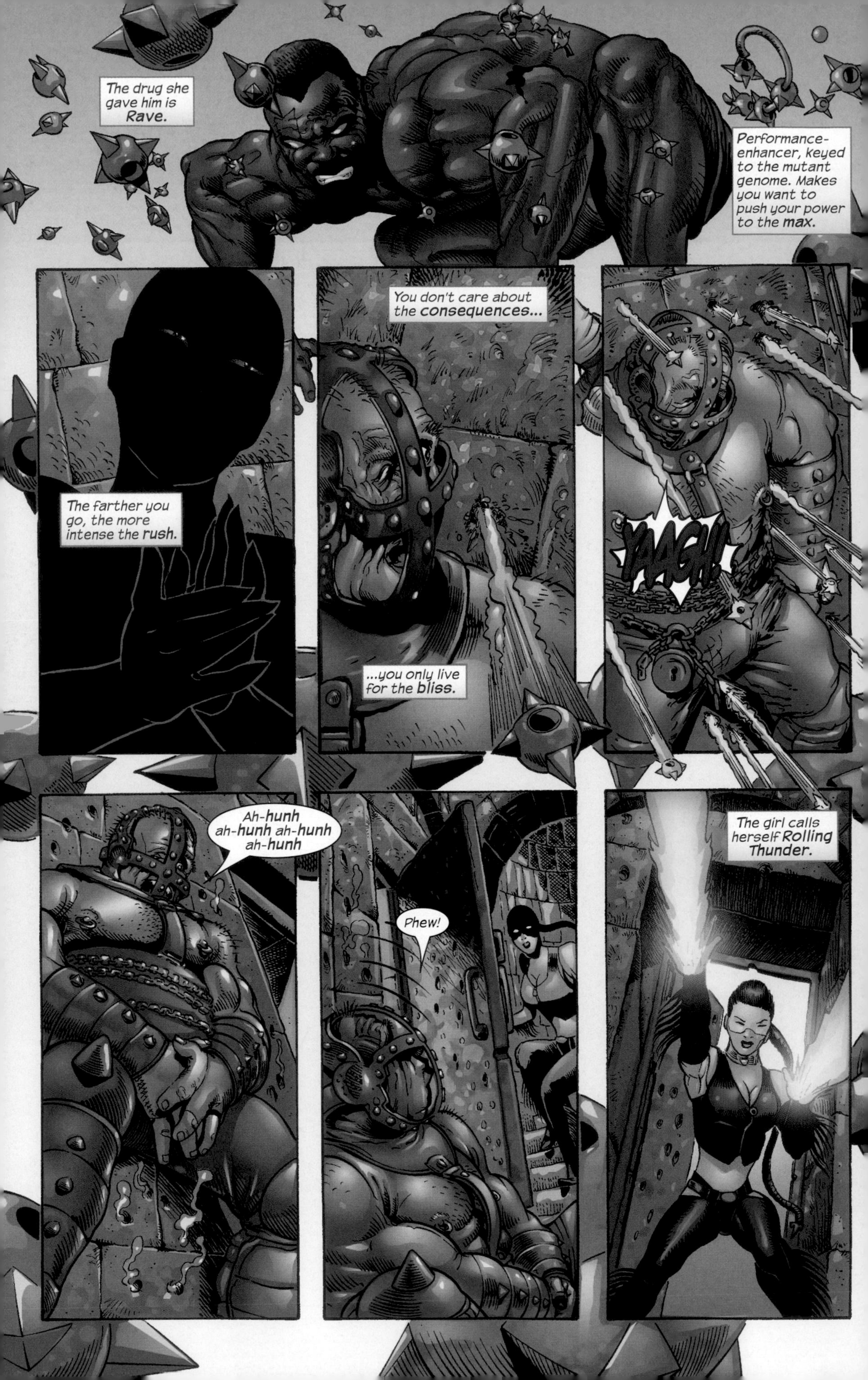
The drug she gave him is Rave.
Performance-enhancer, keyed to the mutant genome. Makes you want to push your power to the max.
The farther you go, the more intense the rush.
You don't care about the consequences...
...you only live for the bliss.
YAAGH!
Ah-hunh ah-hunh ah-hunh ah-hunh
Phew!
The girl calls herself Rolling Thunder.

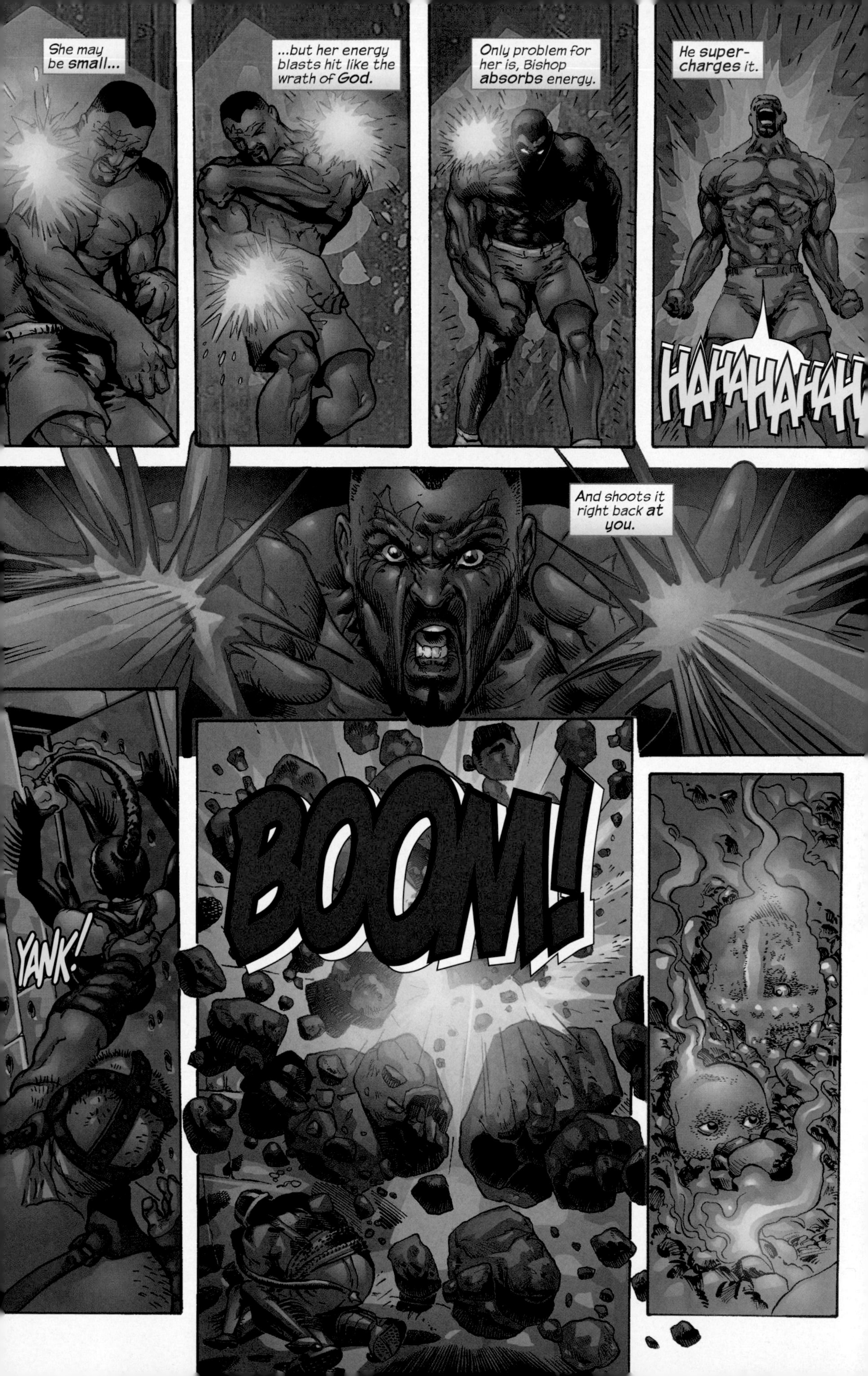
She may be small...
...but her energy blasts hit like the wrath of God.
Only problem for her is, Bishop absorbs energy.
He super-charges it.
HAHAHAHAH
And shoots it right back at you.
YANK!
BOOM!

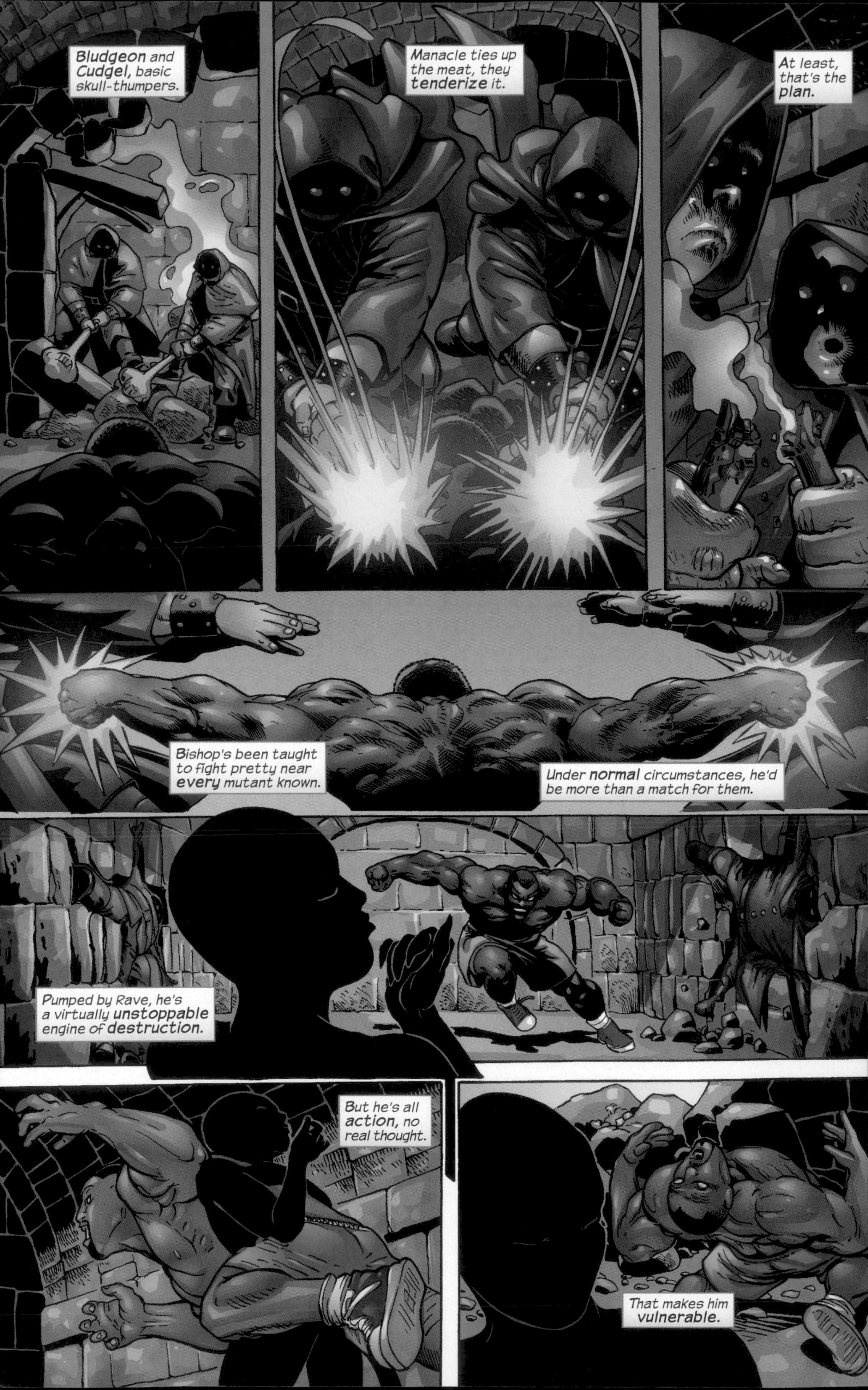
Bludgeon and Cudgel, basic skull-thumpers.
Manacle ties up the meat, they tenderize it.
At least, that's the plan.
Bishop's been taught to fight pretty near every mutant known.
Under normal circumstances, he'd be more than a match for them.
Pumped by Rave, he's a virtually unstoppable engine of destruction.
But he's all action, no real thought.
That makes him vulnerable.

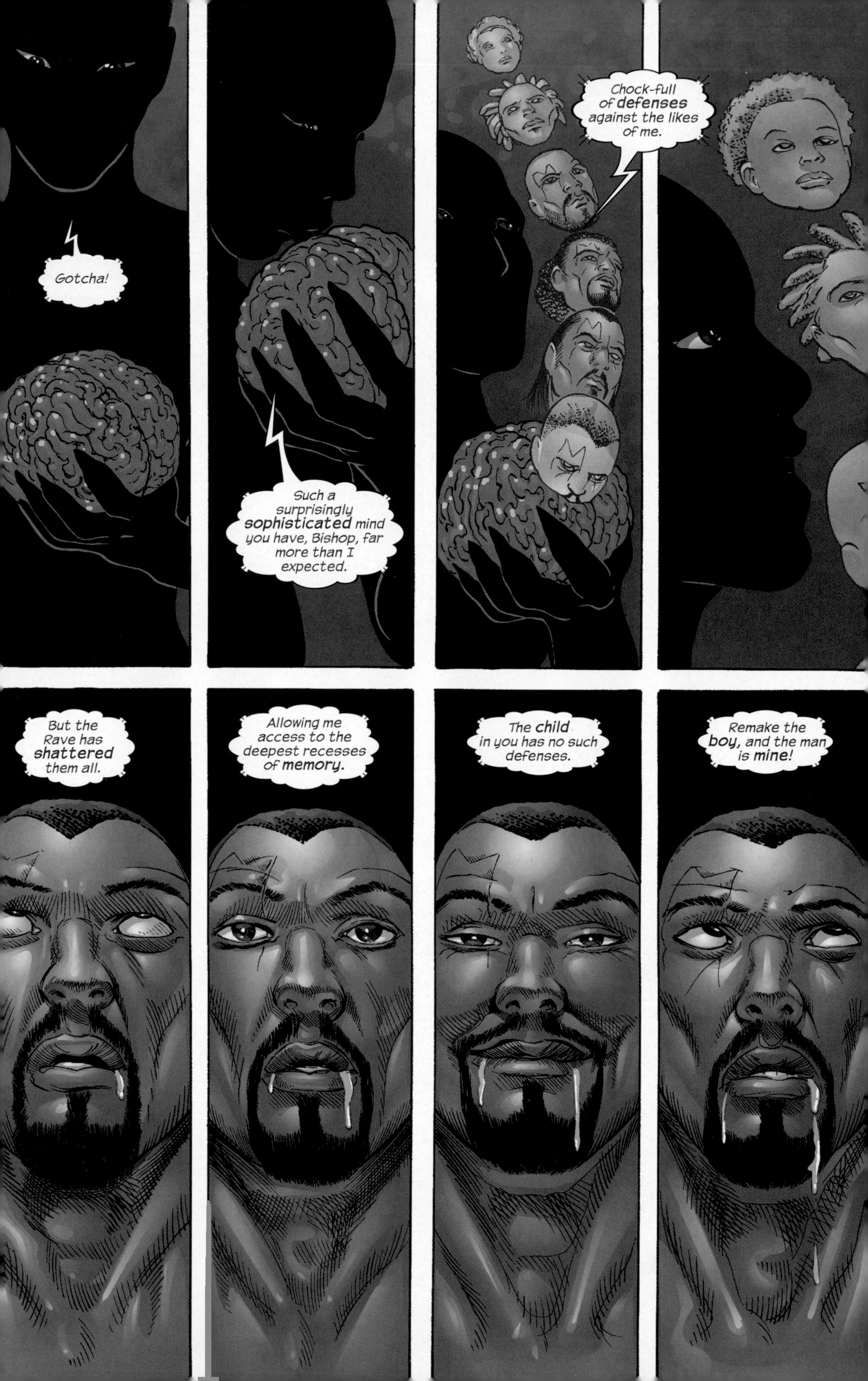
Gotcha!
Such a surprisingly sophisticated mind you have, Bishop, far more than I expected.
Chock-full of defenses against the likes of me.
But the Rave has shattered them all.
Allowing me access to the deepest recesses of memory.
The child in you has no such defenses.
Remake the boy, and the man is mine!

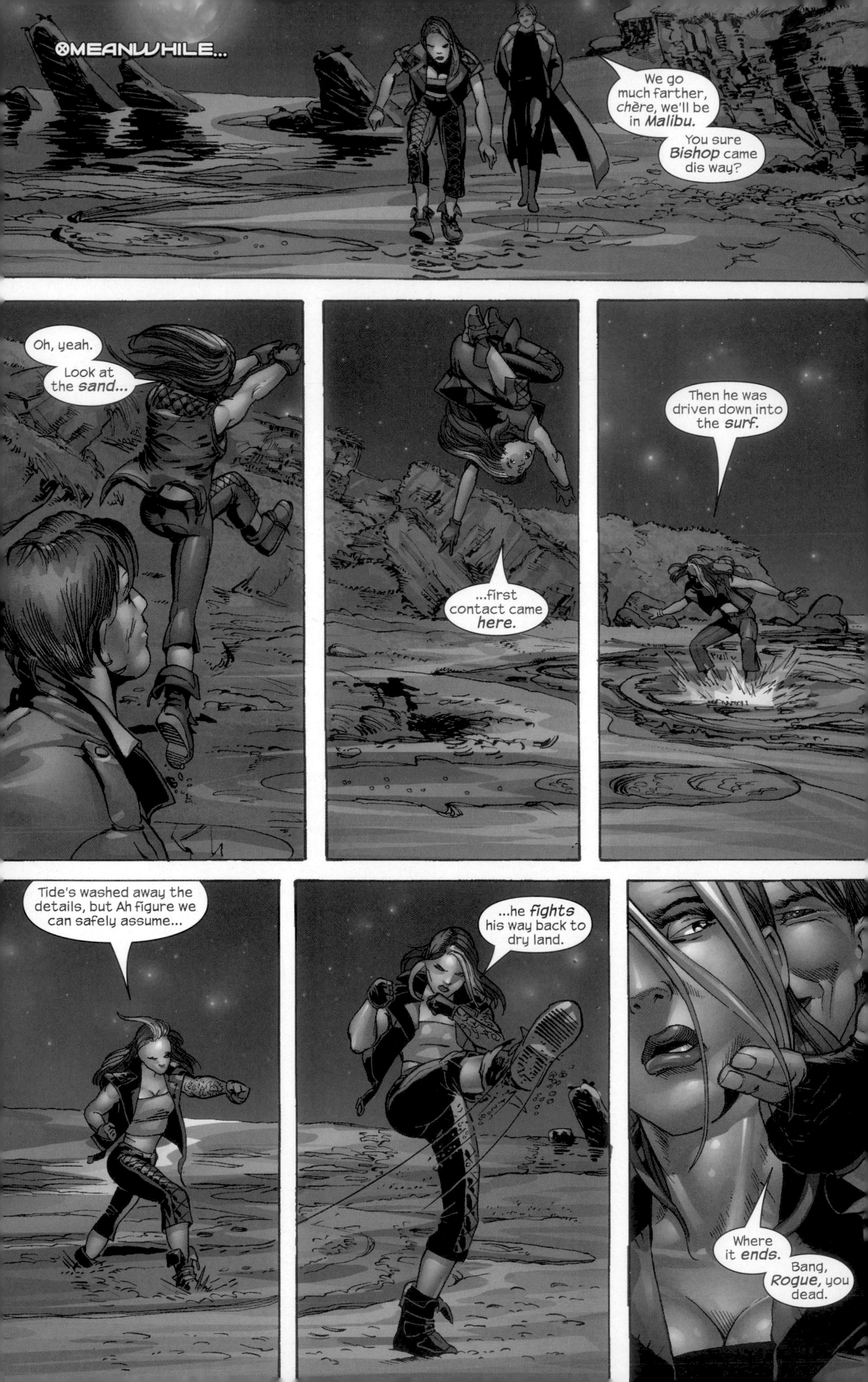
MEANWHILE...
We go much farther, chère, we'll be in Malibu.
You sure Bishop came dis way?
Oh, yeah.
Look at the sand...
...first contact came here.
Then he was driven down into the surf.
Tide's washed away the details, but Ah figure we can safely assume...
...he fights his way back to dry land.
Where it ends.
Bang, Rogue, you dead.

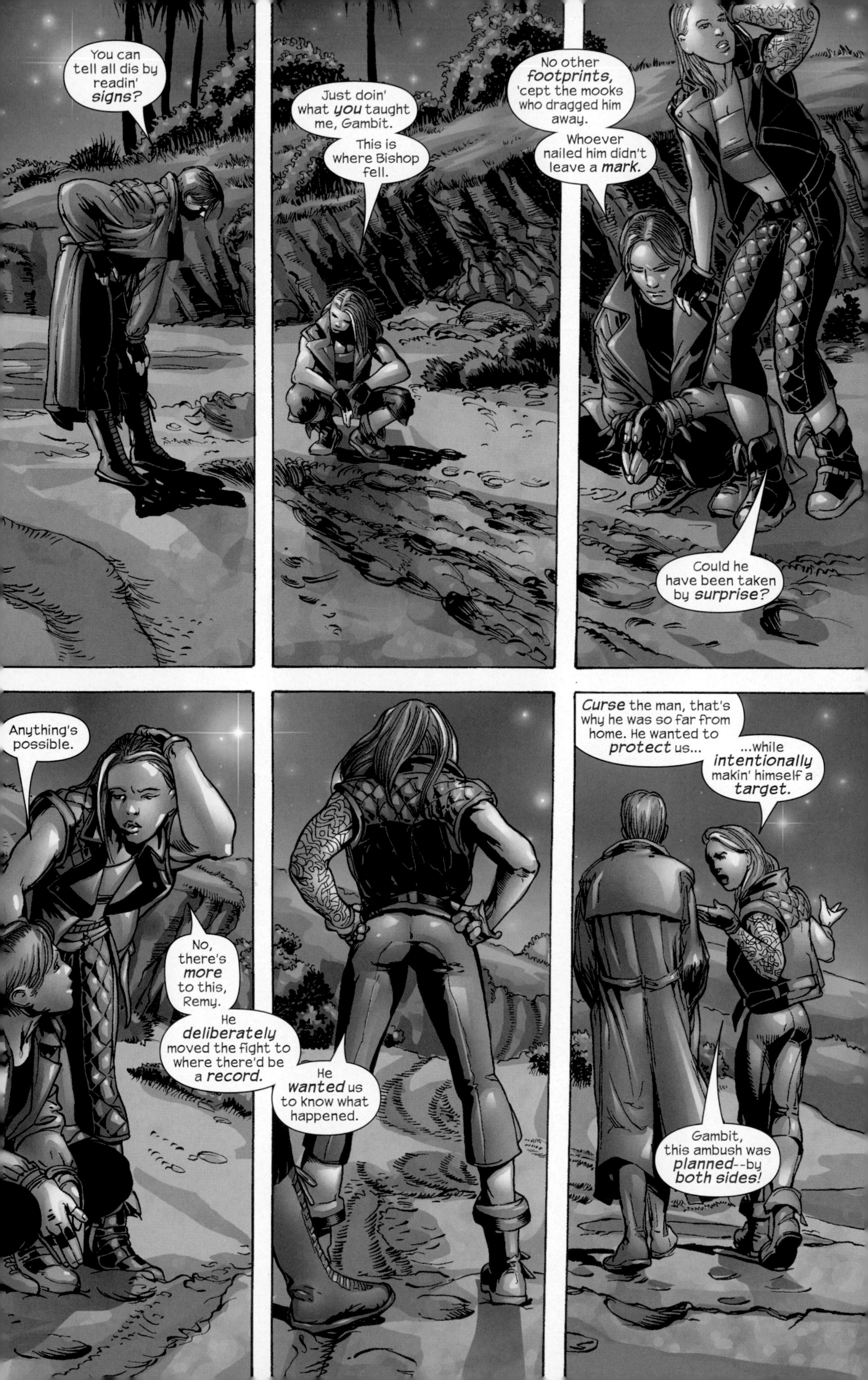

You can tell all dis by readin' signs?
Just doin' what you taught me, Gambit.
This is where Bishop fell.
No other footprints, 'cept the mooks who dragged him away.
Whoever nailed him didn't leave a mark.
Could he have been taken by surprise?
Anything's possible.
No, there's more to this, Remy.
He deliberately moved the fight to where there'd be a record.
He wanted us to know what happened.
Curse the man, that's why he was so far from home. He wanted to protect us...
...while intentionally makin' himself a target.
Gambit, this ambush was planned--by both sides!

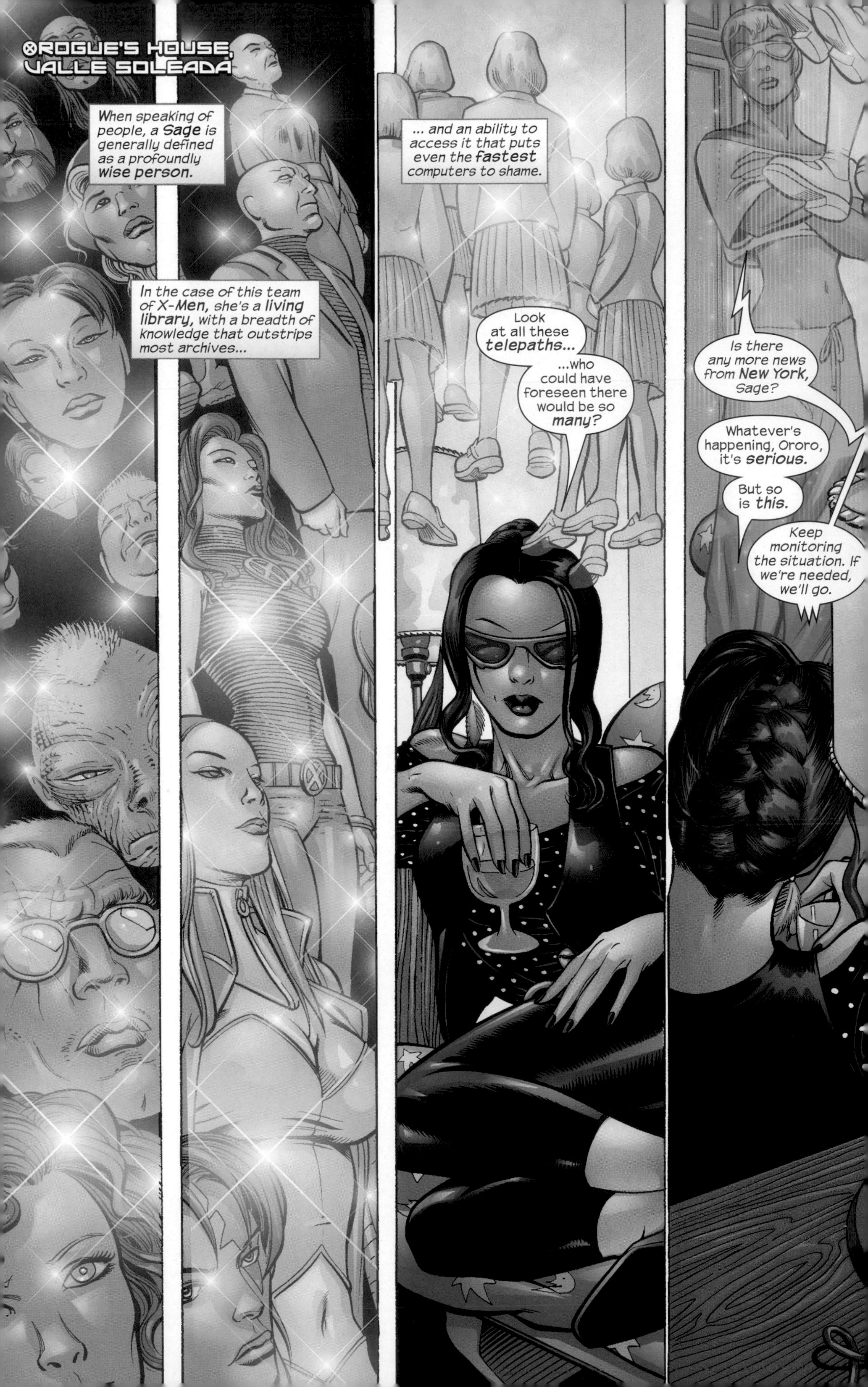
ROGUE'S HOUSE, VALLE SOLEADA
When speaking of people, a Sage is generally defined as a profoundly wise person.
In the case of this team of X-Men, she's a living library, with a breadth of knowledge that outstrips most archives...
... and an ability to access it that puts even the fastest computers to shame.
Look at all these telepaths...
...who could have foreseen there would be so many?
Is there any more news from New York, Sage?
Whatever's happening, Ororo, it's serious.
But so is this.
Keep monitoring the situation. If we're needed, we'll go.

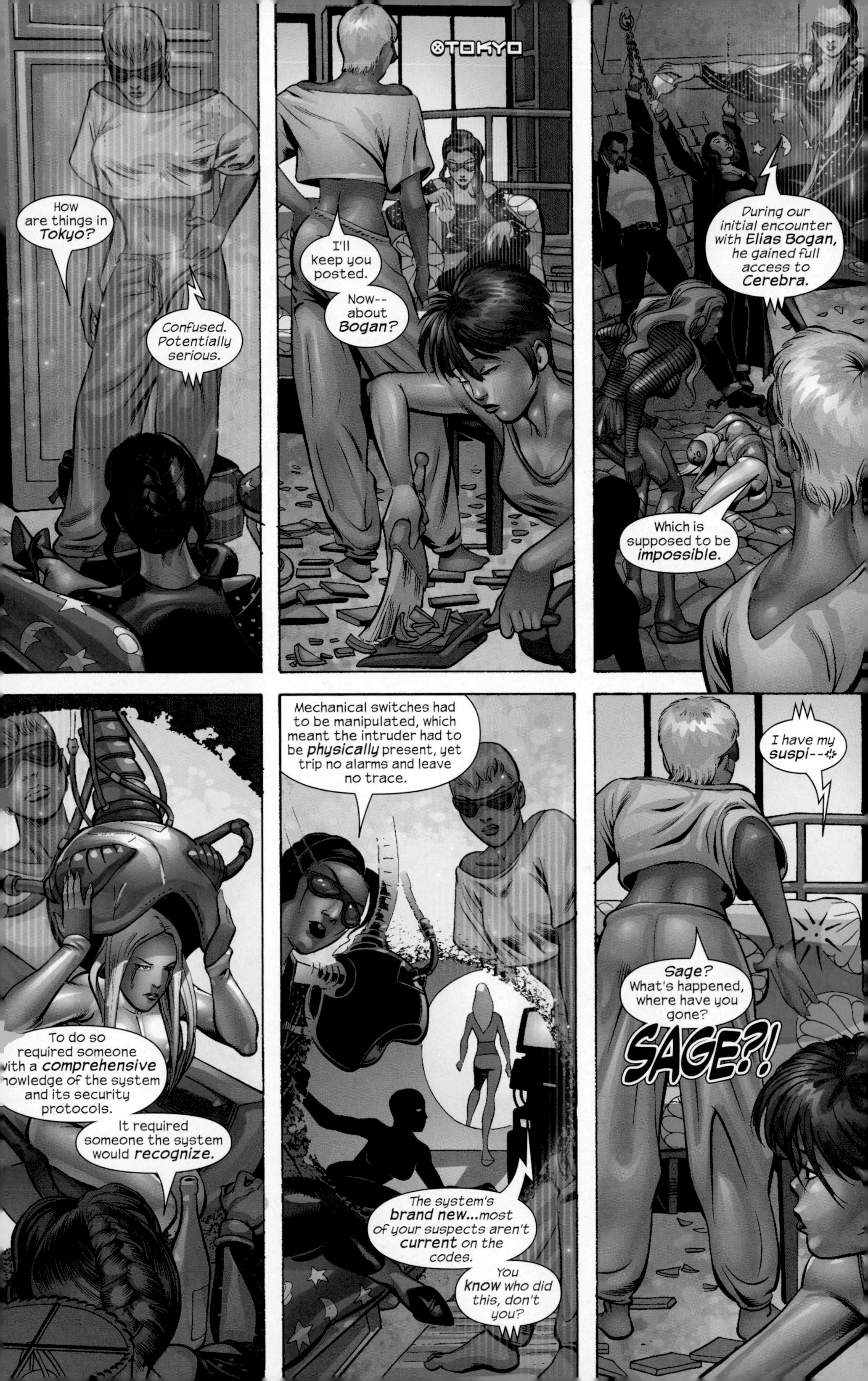
TOKYO
How are things in Tokyo?
Confused. Potentially serious.
I'll keep you posted.
Now--about Bogan?
During our initial encounter with Elias Bogan, he gained full access to Cerebra.
Which is supposed to be impossible.
To do so required someone with a comprehensive nowledge of the system and its security protocols.
It required someone the system would recognize.
Mechanical switches had to be manipulated, which meant the intruder had to be physically present, yet trip no alarms and leave no trace.
The system's brand new...most of your suspects aren't current on the codes.
You know who did this, don't you?
I have my suspi--
Sage? What's happened, where have you gone?
SAGE?!

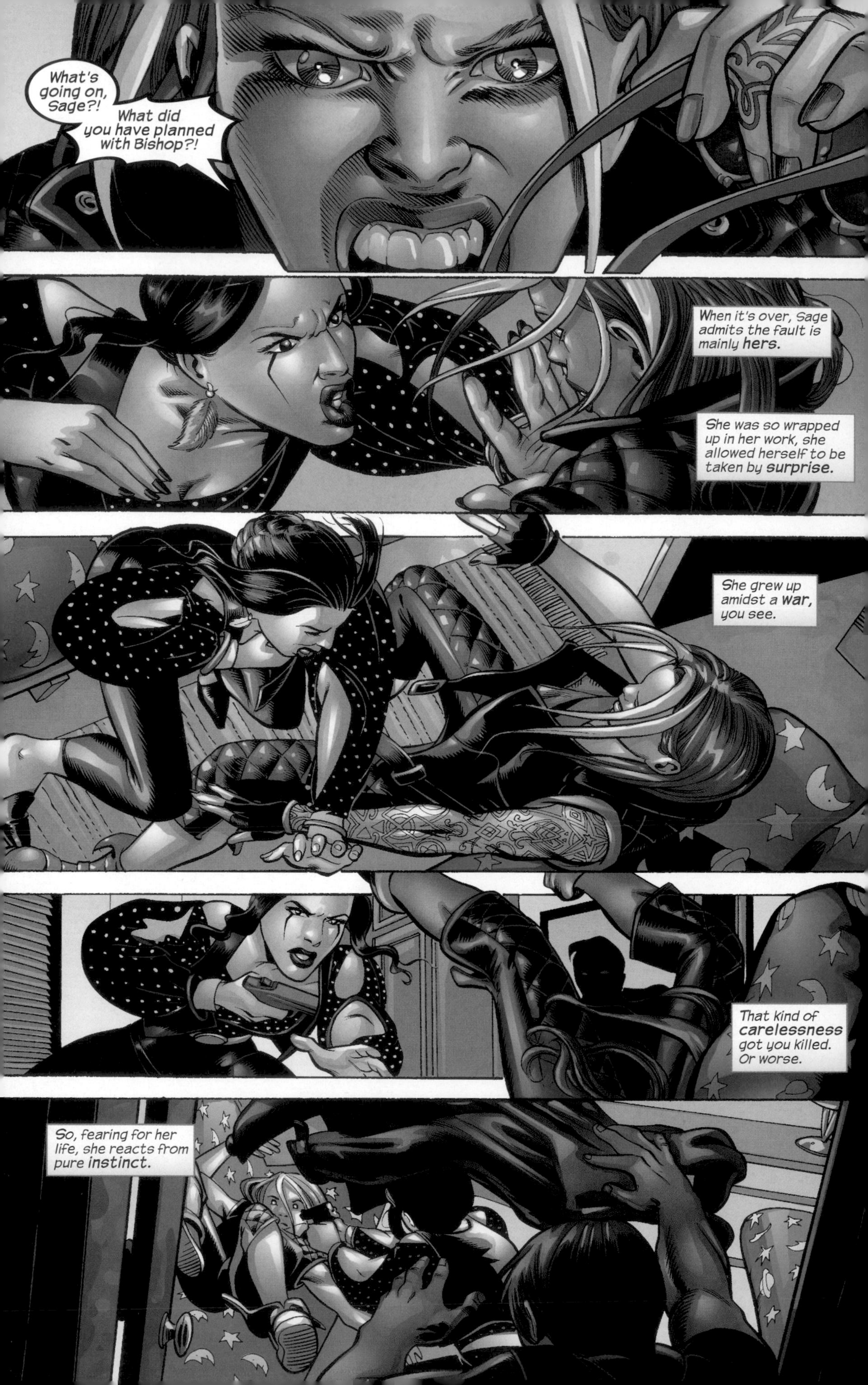

What's going on, Sage?!
What did you have planned with Bishop?!
When it's over, Sage admits the fault is mainly **hers**.
She was so wrapped up in her work, she allowed herself to be taken by **surprise**.
She grew up amidst a **war**, you see.
That kind of **carelessness** got you killed. Or worse.
So, fearing for her life, she reacts from pure **instinct**.

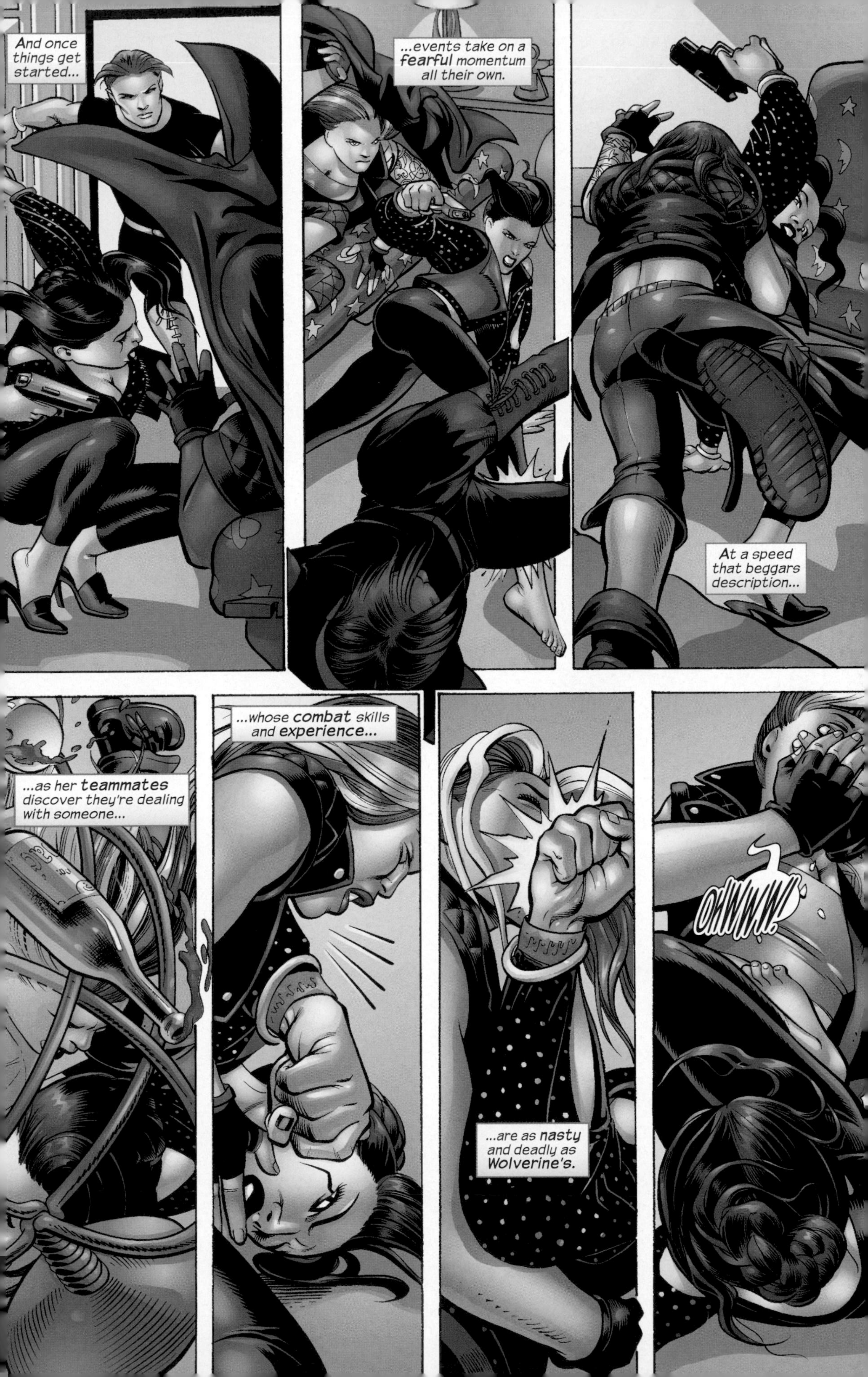

And once things get started...
...events take on a fearful momentum all their own.
At a speed that beggars description...
...as her teammates discover they're dealing with someone...
...whose combat skills and experience...
...are as nasty and deadly as Wolverine's.
OWWW!

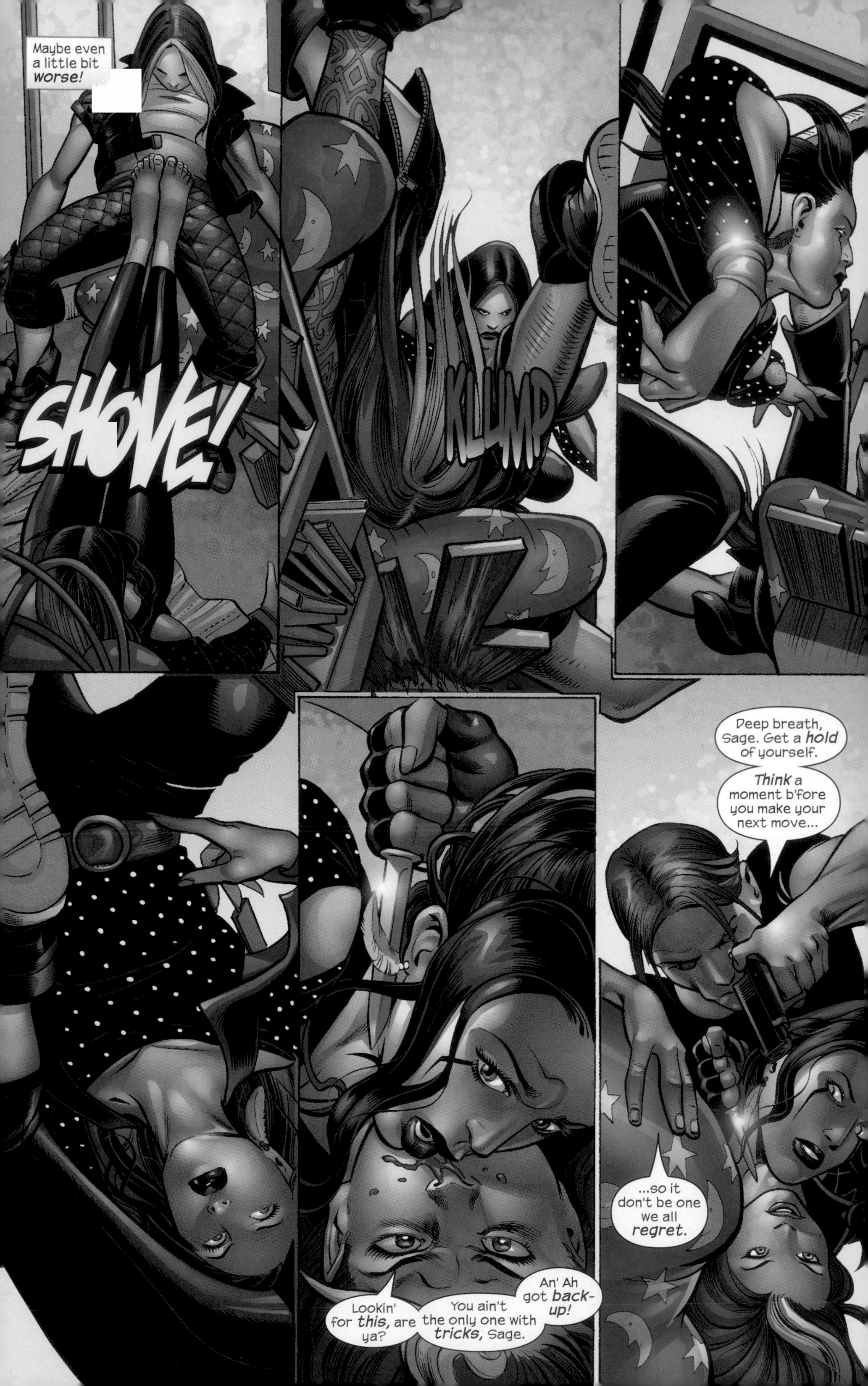
Maybe even a little bit *worse!*
SHOVE!
KLUMP
Deep breath, Sage. Get a *hold* of yourself.
Think a moment b'fore you make your next move...
...so it don't be one we all *regret.*
Lookin' for *this,* are ya?
You ain't the only one with *tricks,* Sage.
An' Ah got *back-up!*

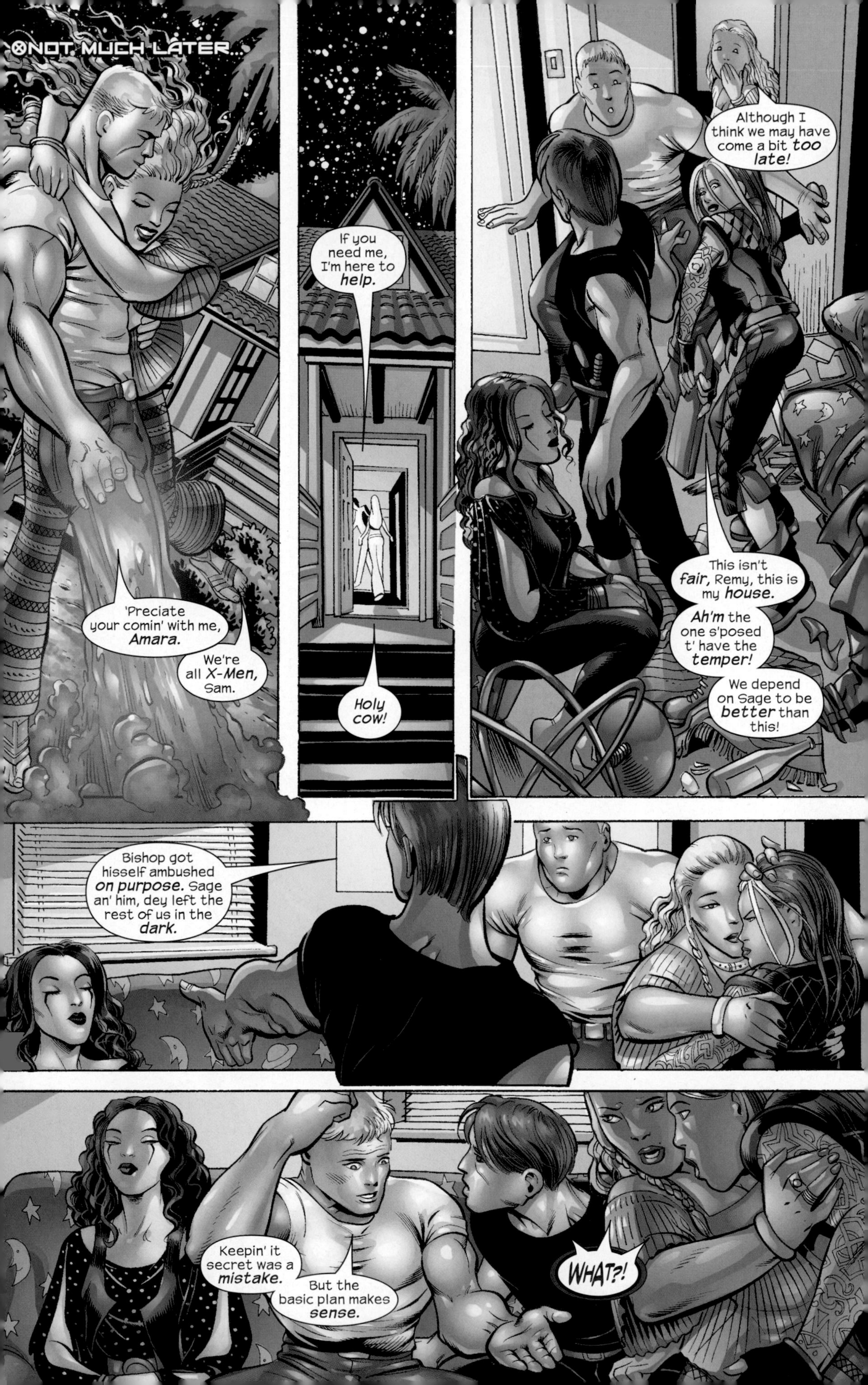
NOT MUCH LATER...
'Preciate your comin' with me, Amara.
We're all X-Men, Sam.
If you need me, I'm here to help.
Holy cow!
Although I think we may have come a bit too late!
This isn't fair, Remy, this is my house.
Ah'm the one s'posed t' have the temper!
We depend on Sage to be better than this!
Bishop got hisself ambushed on purpose. Sage an' him, dey left the rest of us in the dark.
Keepin' it secret was a mistake.
But the basic plan makes sense.
WHAT?!

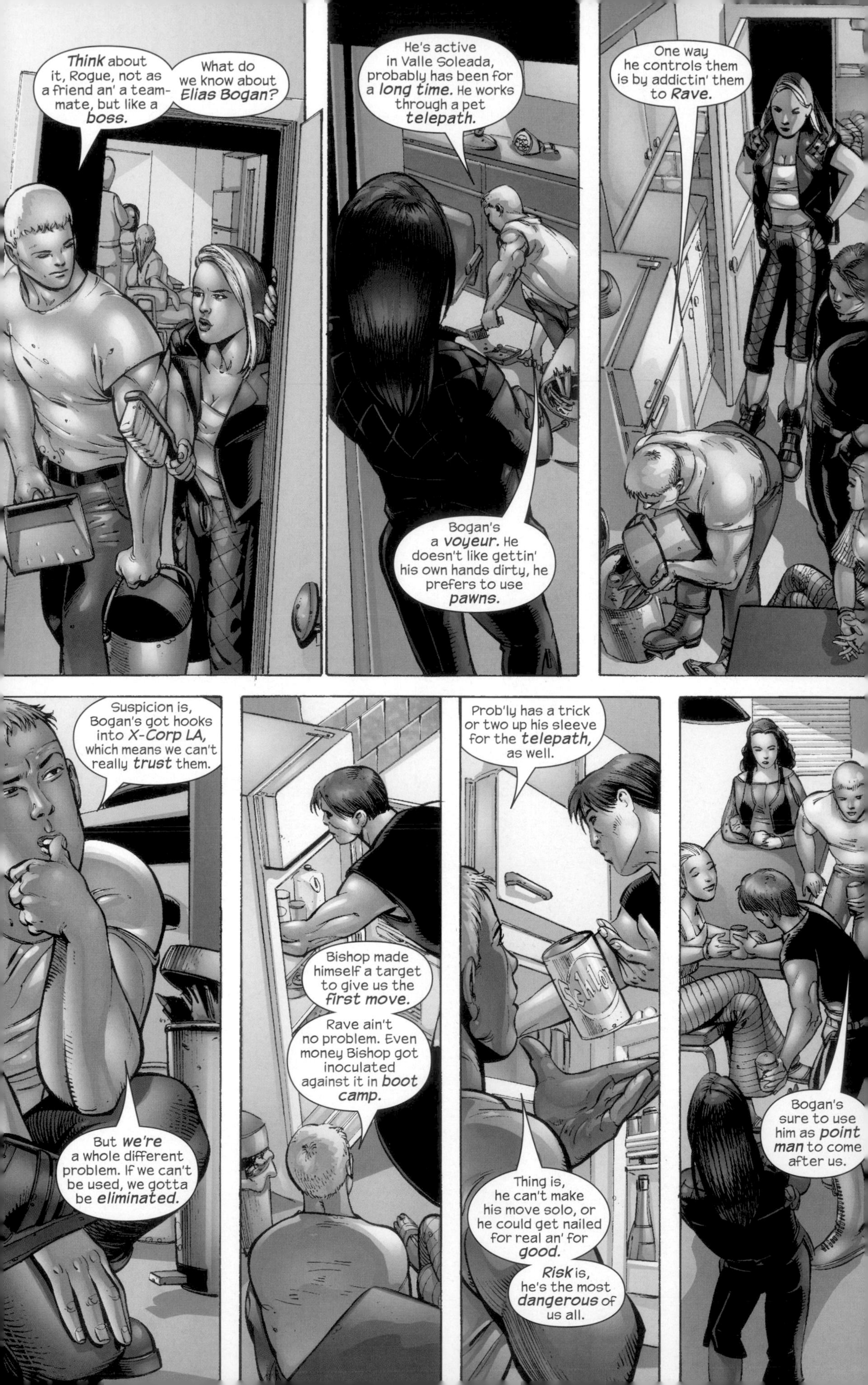

Think about it, Rogue, not as a friend an' a team-mate, but like a boss.
What do we know about Elias Bogan?
He's active in Valle Soleada, probably has been for a long time. He works through a pet telepath.
Bogan's a voyeur. He doesn't like gettin' his own hands dirty, he prefers to use pawns.
One way he controls them is by addictin' them to Rave.
Suspicion is, Bogan's got hooks into X-Corp LA, which means we can't really trust them.
But we're a whole different problem. If we can't be used, we gotta be eliminated.
Bishop made himself a target to give us the first move.
Rave ain't no problem. Even money Bishop got inoculated against it in boot camp.
Prob'ly has a trick or two up his sleeve for the telepath, as well.
Thing is, he can't make his move solo, or he could get nailed for real an' for good.
Risk is, he's the most dangerous of us all.
Bogan's sure to use him as point man to come after us.

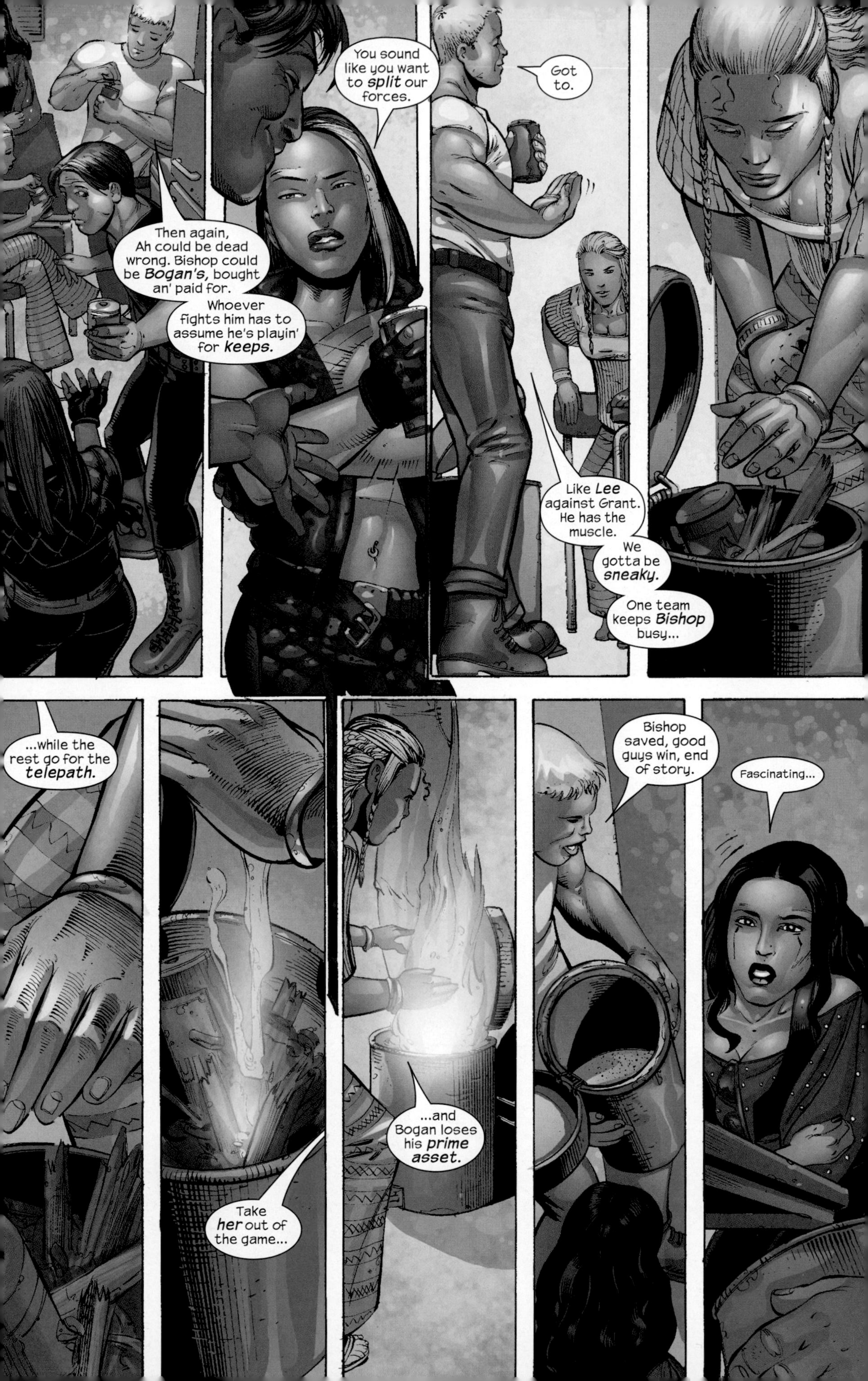
Then again, Ah could be dead wrong. Bishop could be Bogan's, bought an' paid for.
Whoever fights him has to assume he's playin' for keeps.
You sound like you want to split our forces.
Got to.
Like Lee against Grant. He has the muscle.
We gotta be sneaky.
One team keeps Bishop busy...
...while the rest go for the telepath.
Take her out of the game...
...and Bogan loses his prime asset.
Bishop saved, good guys win, end of story.
Fascinating...

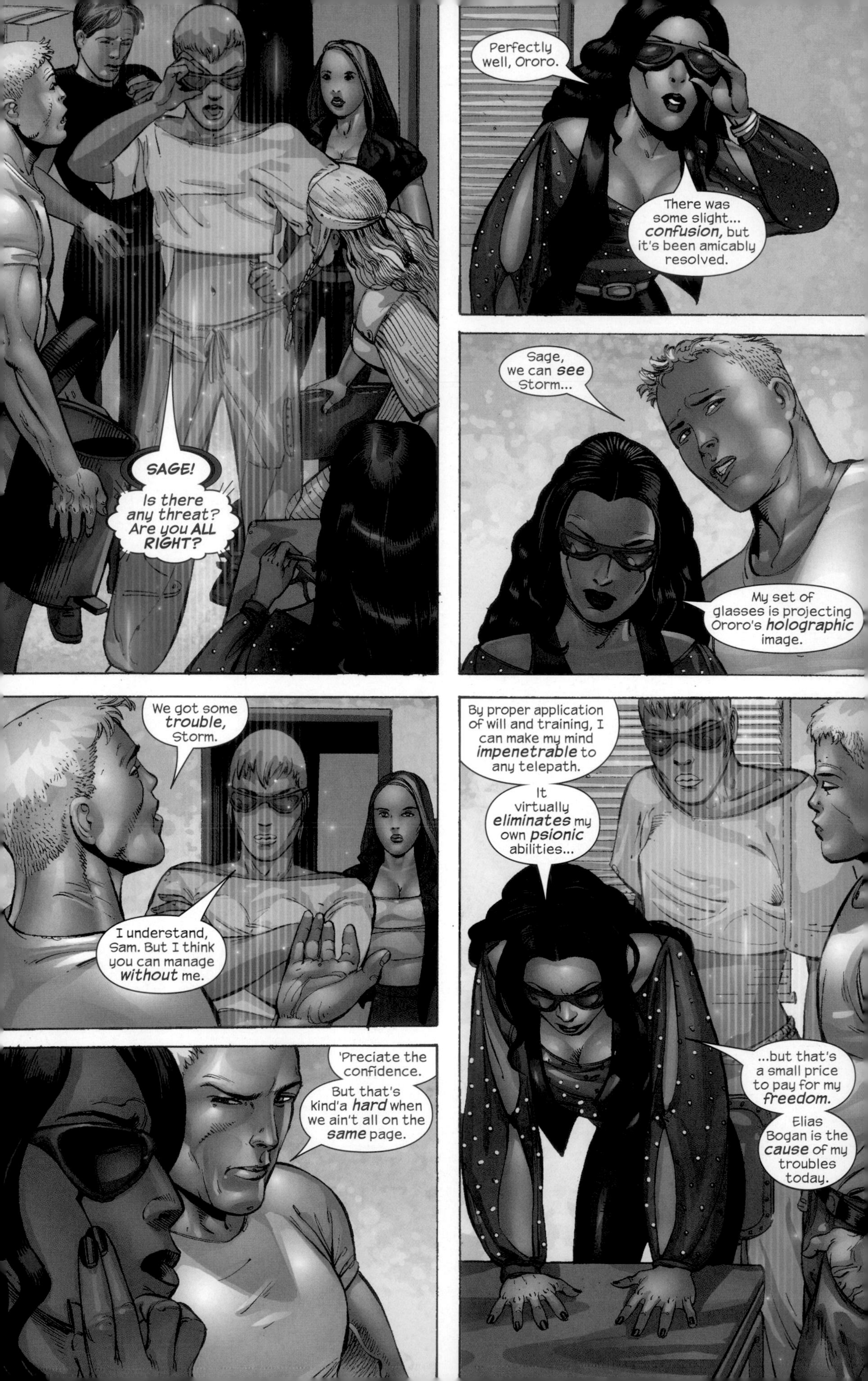
SAGE!
Is there any threat? Are you ALL RIGHT?
Perfectly well, Ororo.
There was some slight... confusion, but it's been amicably resolved.
Sage, we can see Storm...
My set of glasses is projecting Ororo's holographic image.
We got some trouble, Storm.
I understand, Sam. But I think you can manage without me.
'Preciate the confidence.
But that's kind'a hard when we ain't all on the same page.
By proper application of will and training, I can make my mind impenetrable to any telepath.
It virtually eliminates my own psionic abilities...
...but that's a small price to pay for my freedom.
Elias Bogan is the cause of my troubles today.

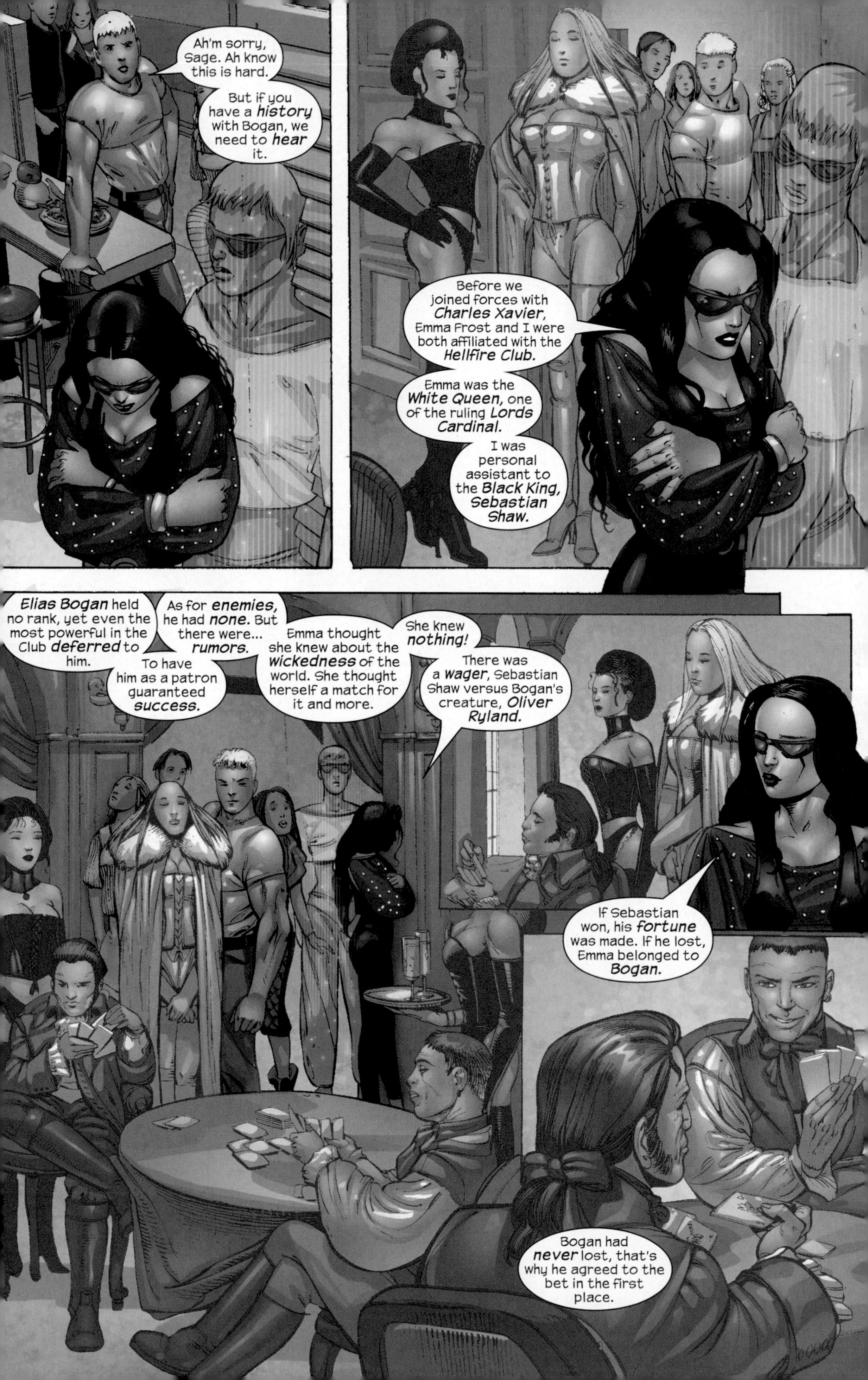
Ah'm sorry, Sage. Ah know this is hard.
But if you have a *history* with Bogan, we need to *hear* it.
Before we joined forces with *Charles Xavier*, Emma Frost and I were both affiliated with the *Hellfire Club*.
Emma was the *White Queen*, one of the ruling *Lords Cardinal*.
I was personal assistant to the *Black King, Sebastian Shaw*.
Elias Bogan held no rank, yet even the most powerful in the Club *deferred* to him.
To have him as a patron guaranteed *success*.
As for *enemies*, he had *none*. But there were... *rumors*.
Emma thought she knew about the *wickedness* of the world. She thought herself a match for it and more.
She knew *nothing!*
There was a *wager*, Sebastian Shaw versus Bogan's creature, *Oliver Ryland*.
If Sebastian won, his *fortune* was made. If he lost, Emma belonged to *Bogan*.
Bogan had *never* lost, that's why he agreed to the bet in the first place.

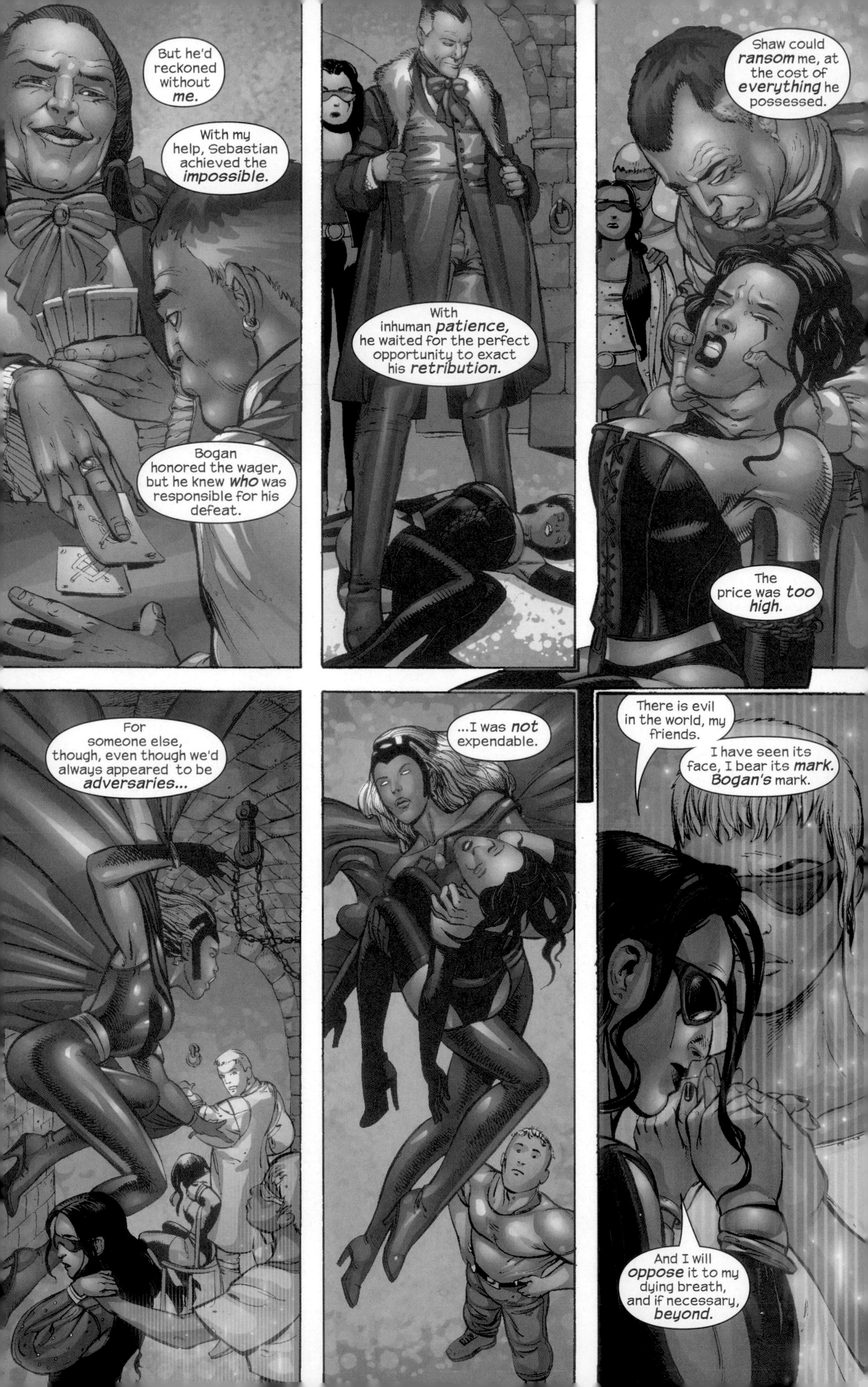

But he'd reckoned without *me.*
With my help, Sebastian achieved the *impossible.*
Bogan honored the wager, but he knew *who* was responsible for his defeat.
With inhuman *patience,* he waited for the perfect opportunity to exact his *retribution.*
Shaw could *ransom* me, at the cost of *everything* he possessed.
The price was *too high.*
For someone else, though, even though we'd always appeared to be *adversaries...*
...I was *not* expendable.
There is evil in the world, my friends.
I have seen its face, I bear its *mark.* *Bogan's* mark.
And I will *oppose* it to my dying breath, and if necessary, *beyond.*

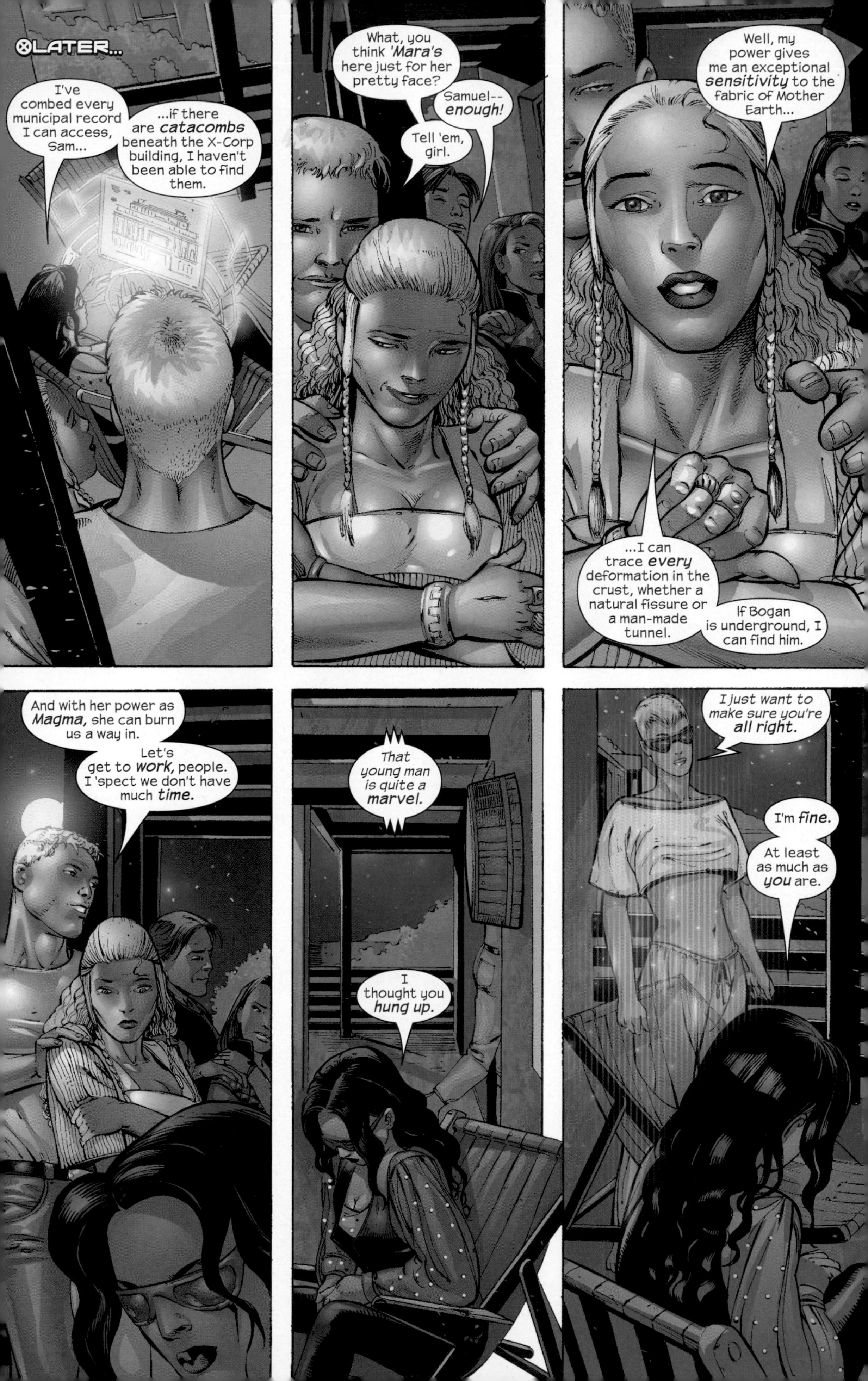
LATER...
I've combed every municipal record I can access, Sam...
...if there are catacombs beneath the X-Corp building, I haven't been able to find them.
What, you think 'Mara's here just for her pretty face?
Samuel-- enough!
Tell 'em, girl.
Well, my power gives me an exceptional sensitivity to the fabric of Mother Earth...
...I can trace every deformation in the crust, whether a natural fissure or a man-made tunnel.
If Bogan is underground, I can find him.
And with her power as Magma, she can burn us a way in.
Let's get to work, people. I 'spect we don't have much time.
That young man is quite a marvel.
I thought you hung up.
I just want to make sure you're all right.
I'm fine.
At least as much as you are.

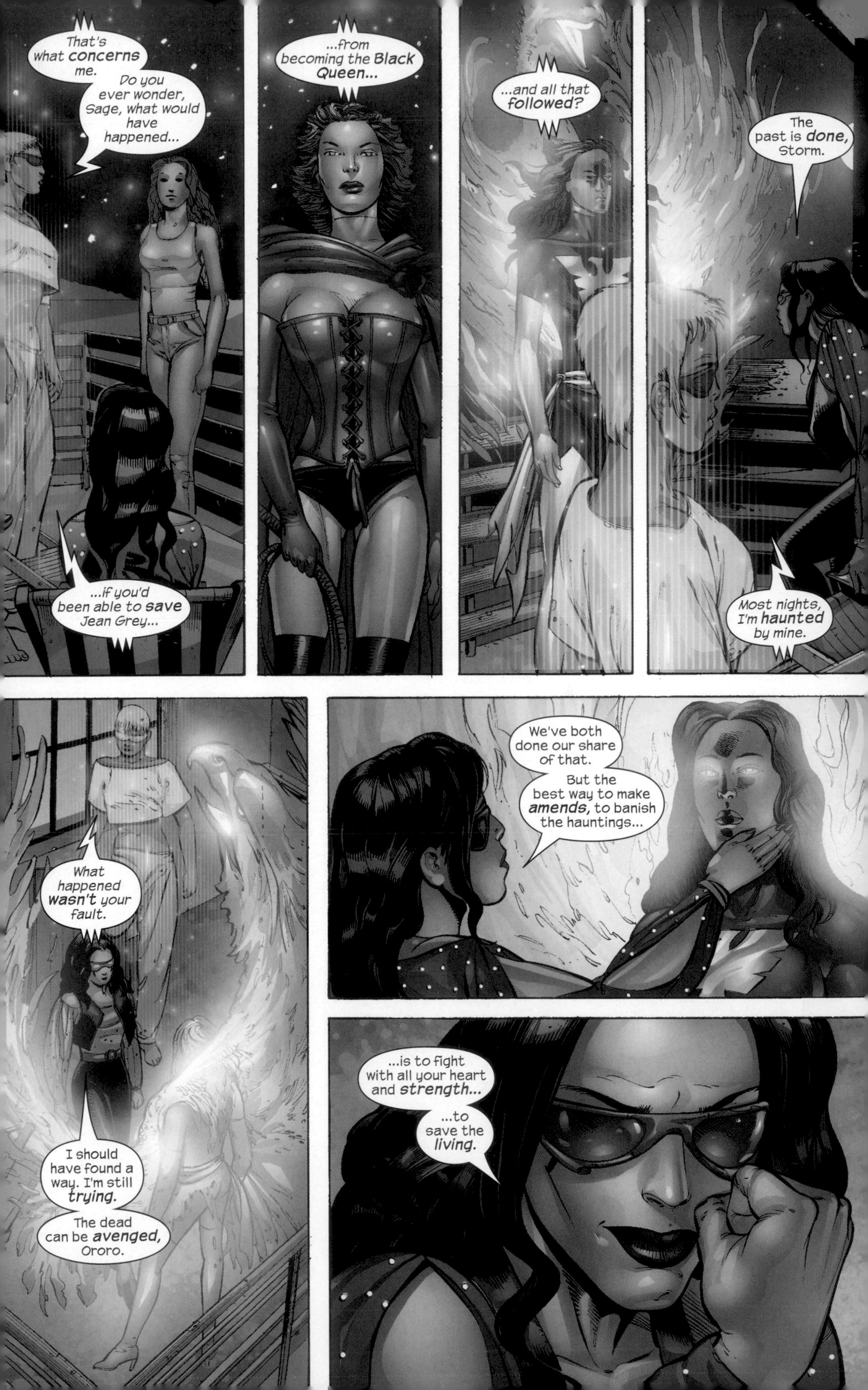
That's what concerns me.
Do you ever wonder, Sage, what would have happened...
...if you'd been able to save Jean Grey...
...from becoming the Black Queen...
...and all that followed?
The past is done, Storm.
Most nights, I'm haunted by mine.
What happened wasn't your fault.
I should have found a way. I'm still trying.
The dead can be avenged, Ororo.
We've both done our share of that.
But the best way to make amends, to banish the hauntings...
...is to fight with all your heart and strength...
...to save the living.

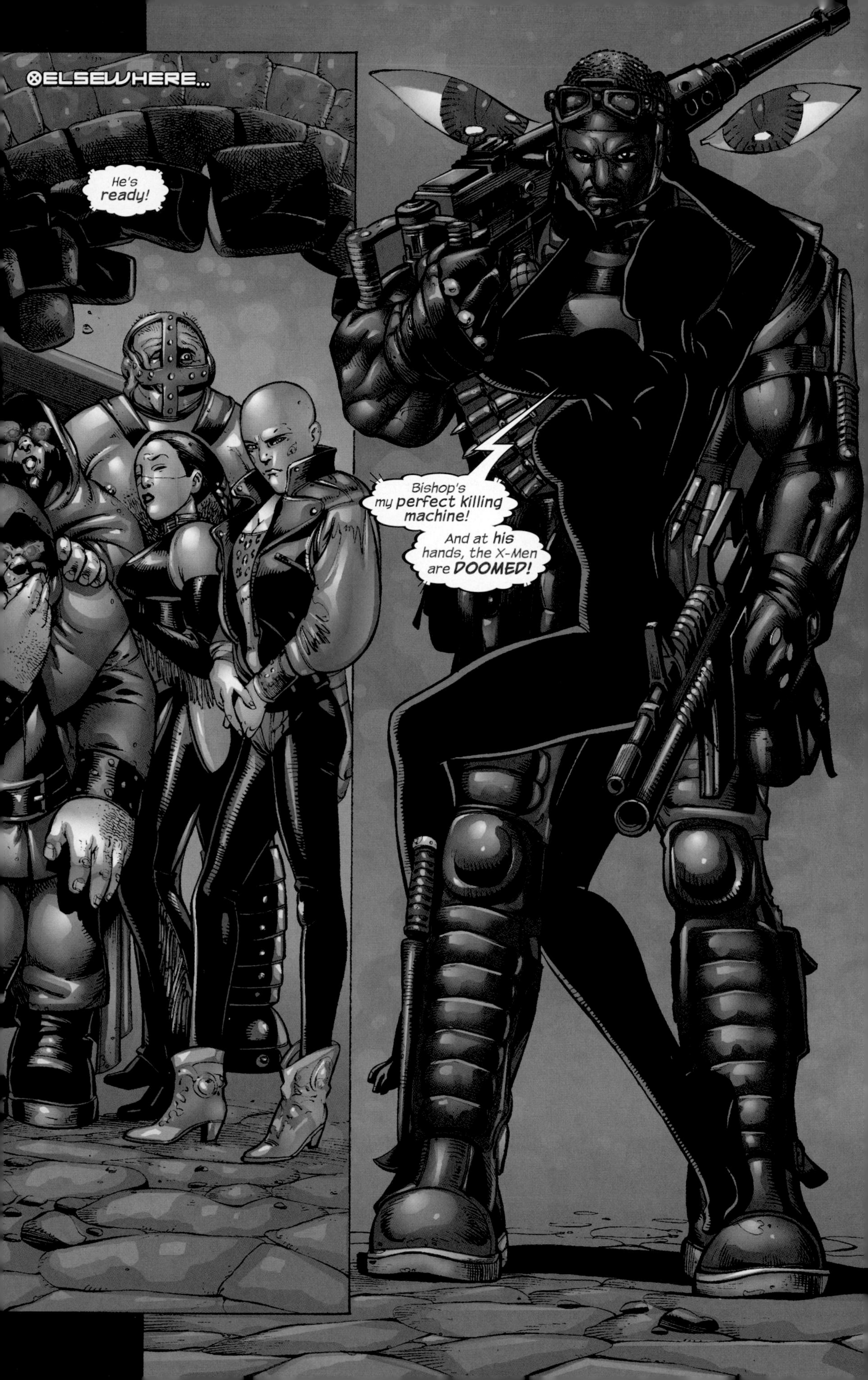
ELSEWHERE...
He's ready!
Bishop's my perfect killing machine!
And at his hands, the X-Men are DOOMED!

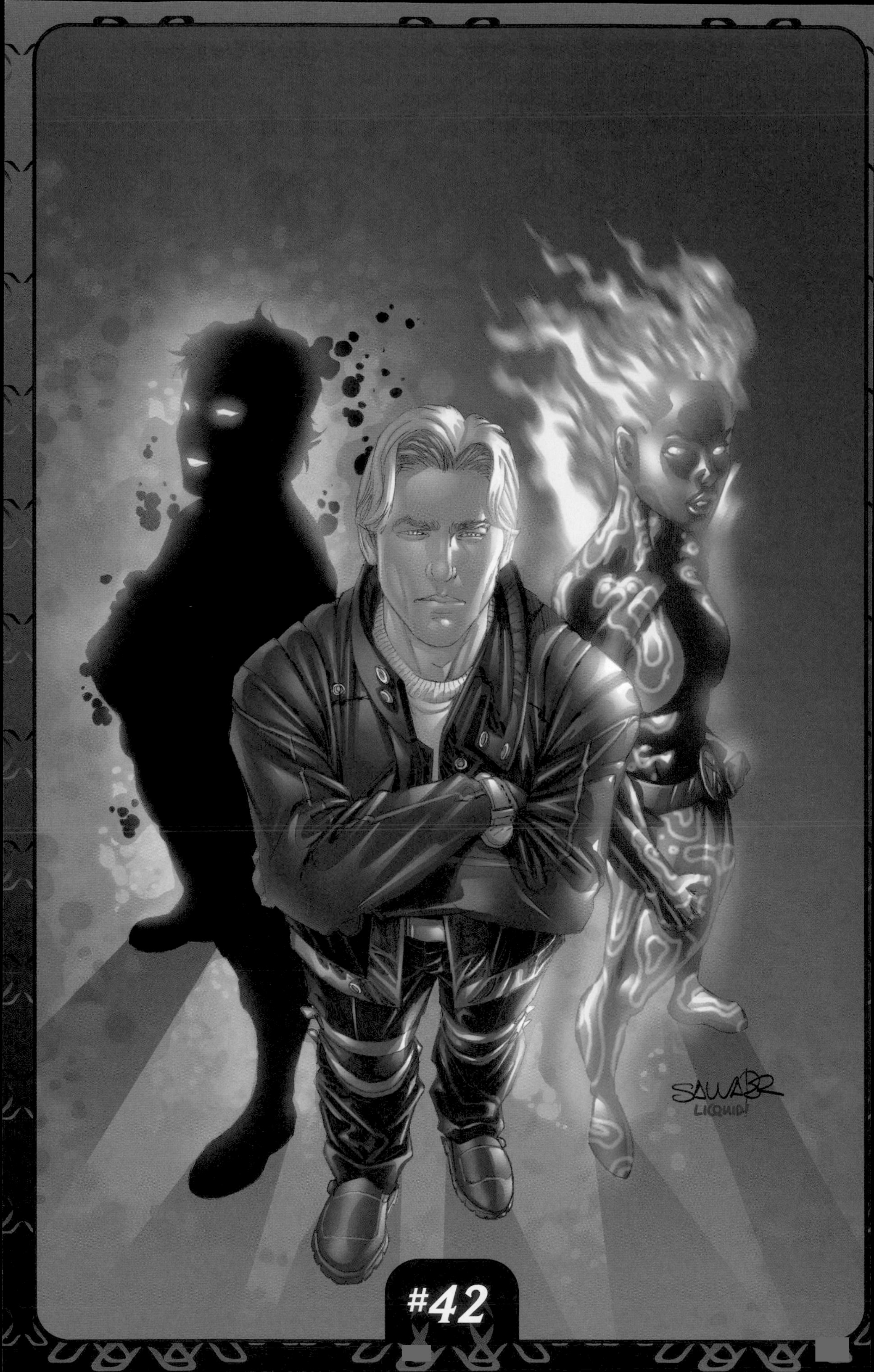
SAWABR
LIQUID!
#42

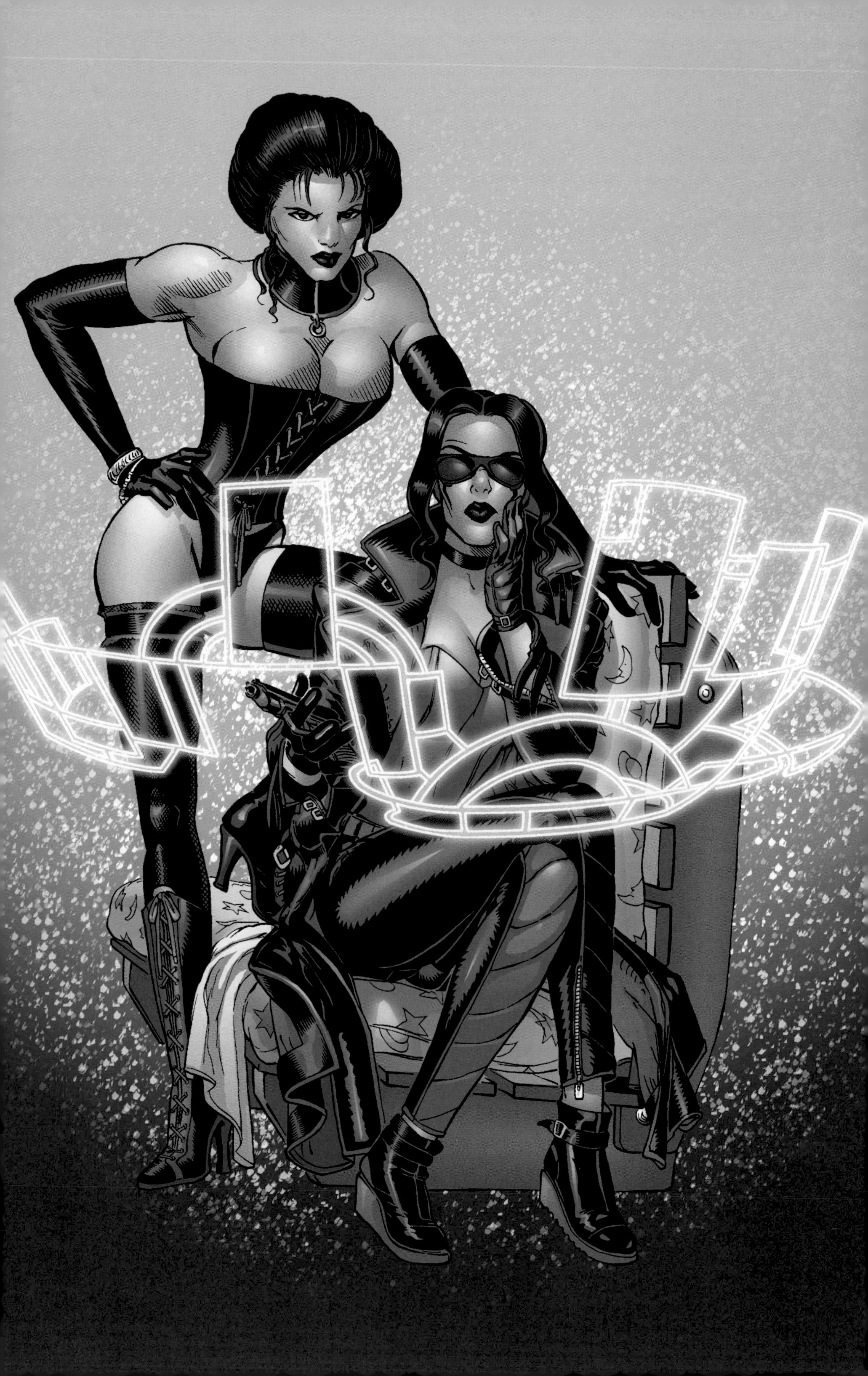

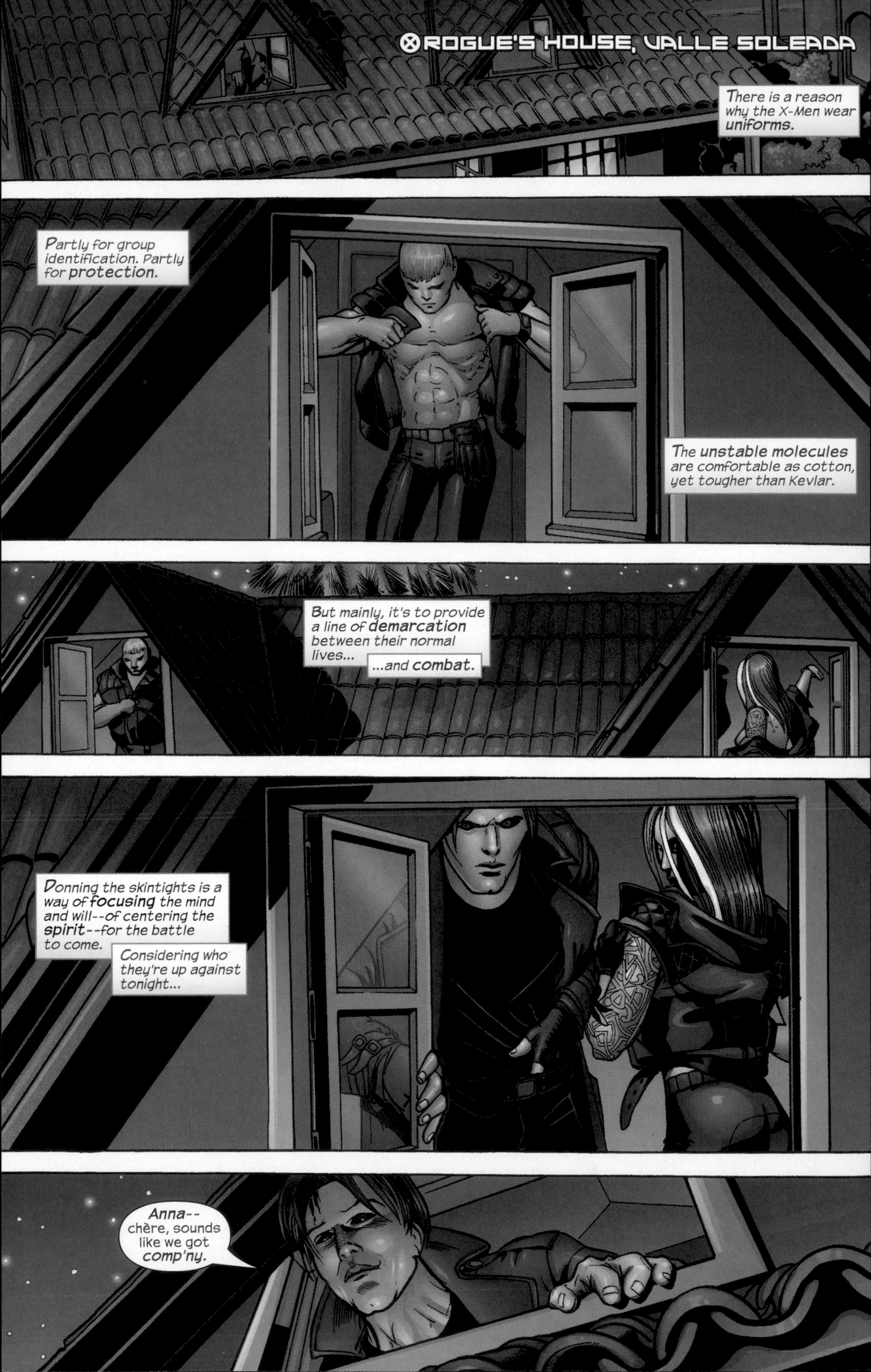

ROGUE'S HOUSE, VALLE SOLEADA
There is a reason why the X-Men wear uniforms.
Partly for group identification. Partly for protection.
The unstable molecules are comfortable as cotton, yet tougher than Kevlar.
But mainly, it's to provide a line of demarcation between their normal lives...
...and combat.
Donning the skintights is a way of focusing the mind and will--of centering the spirit--for the battle to come.
Considering who they're up against tonight...
Anna-- chère, sounds like we got comp'ny.

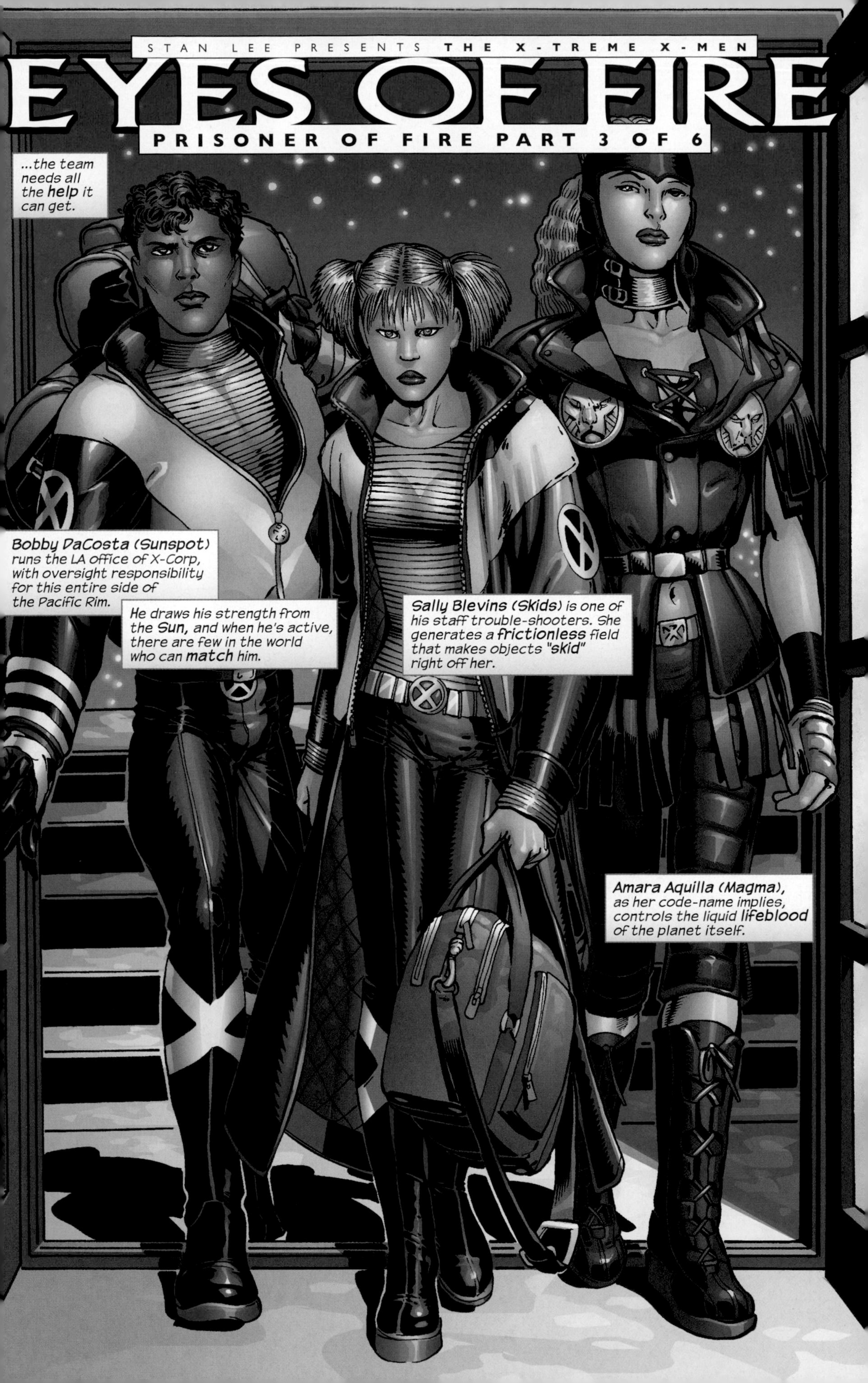
STAN LEE PRESENTS THE X-TREME X-MEN
EYES OF FIRE
PRISONER OF FIRE PART 3 OF 6
...the team needs all the help it can get.
Bobby DaCosta (Sunspot) runs the LA office of X-Corp, with oversight responsibility for this entire side of the Pacific Rim.
He draws his strength from the Sun, and when he's active, there are few in the world who can match him.
Sally Blevins (Skids) is one of his staff trouble-shooters. She generates a frictionless field that makes objects "skid" right off her.
Amara Aquilla (Magma), as her code-name implies, controls the liquid lifeblood of the planet itself.

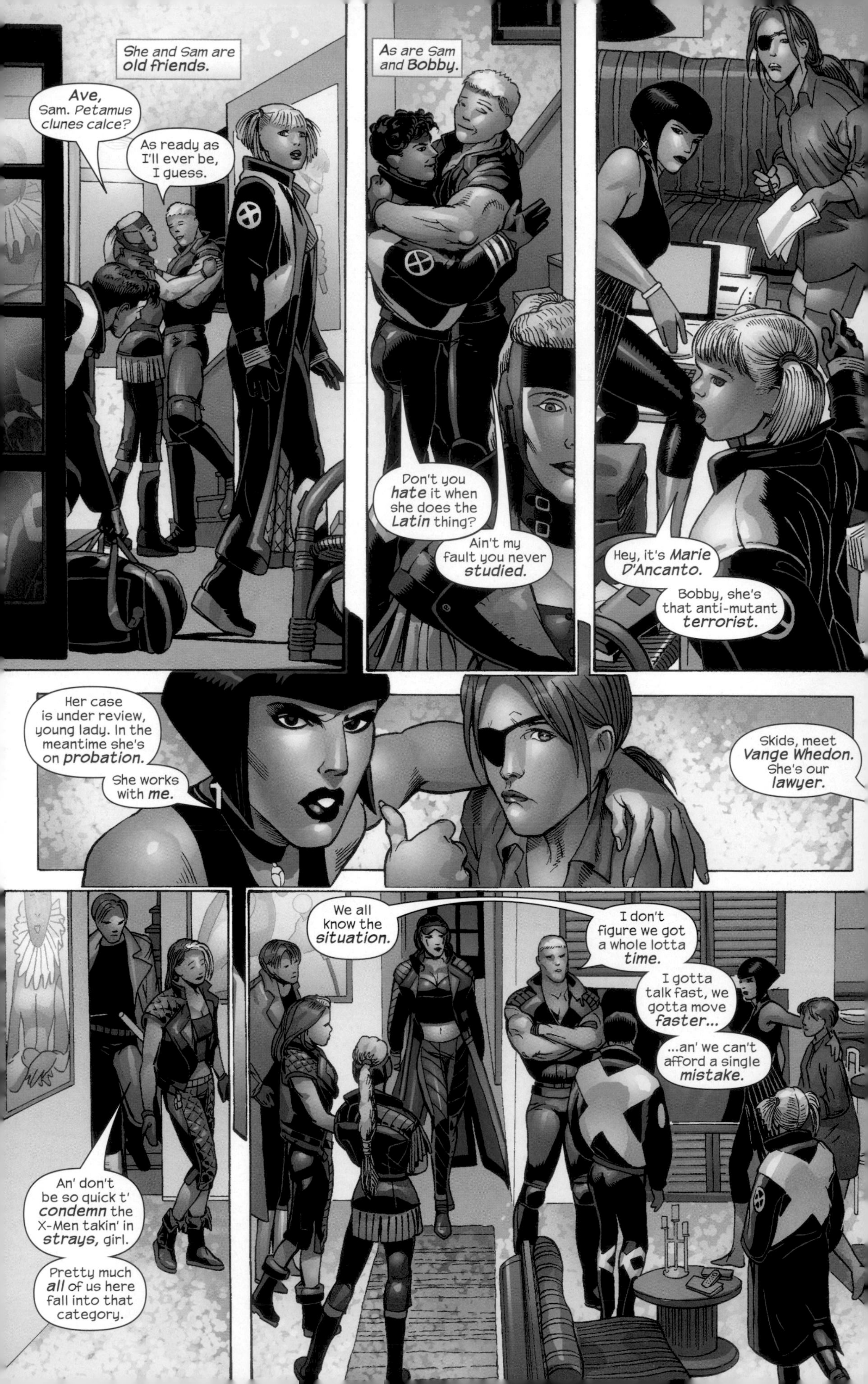
She and Sam are old friends.
Ave, Sam. Petamus clunes calce?
As ready as I'll ever be, I guess.
As are Sam and Bobby.
Don't you hate it when she does the Latin thing?
Ain't my fault you never studied.
Hey, it's Marie D'Ancanto.
Bobby, she's that anti-mutant terrorist.
Her case is under review, young lady. In the meantime she's on probation.
She works with me.
Skids, meet Vange Whedon. She's our lawyer.
An' don't be so quick t' condemn the X-Men takin' in strays, girl.
Pretty much all of us here fall into that category.
We all know the situation.
I don't figure we got a whole lotta time.
I gotta talk fast, we gotta move faster...
...an' we can't afford a single mistake.

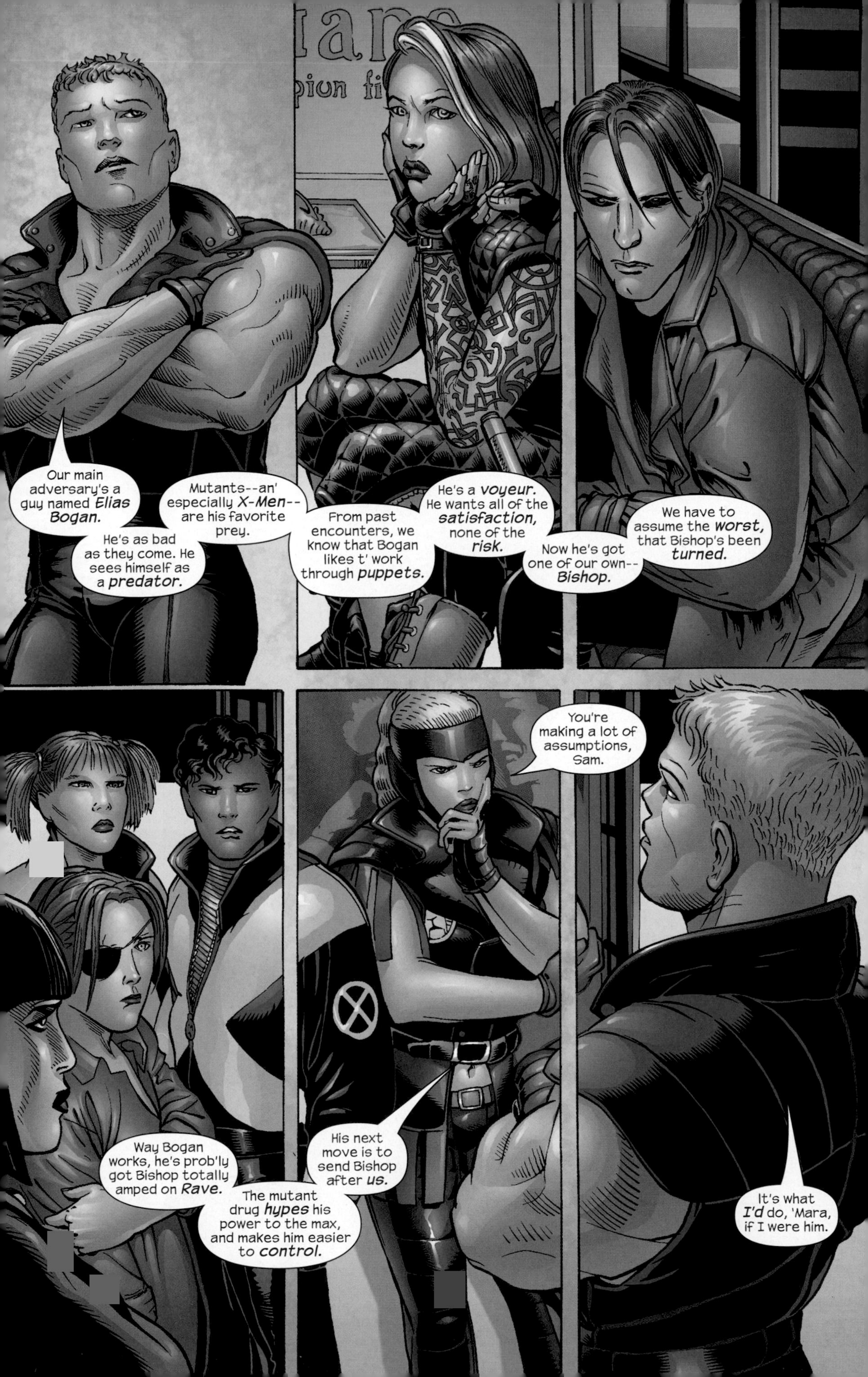
Our main adversary's a guy named Elias Bogan.
He's as bad as they come. He sees himself as a predator.
Mutants--an' especially X-Men--are his favorite prey.
From past encounters, we know that Bogan likes t' work through puppets.
He's a voyeur. He wants all of the satisfaction, none of the risk.
Now he's got one of our own--Bishop.
We have to assume the worst, that Bishop's been turned.
Way Bogan works, he's prob'ly got Bishop totally amped on Rave.
The mutant drug hypes his power to the max, and makes him easier to control.
His next move is to send Bishop after us.
You're making a lot of assumptions, Sam.
It's what I'd do, 'Mara, if I were him.

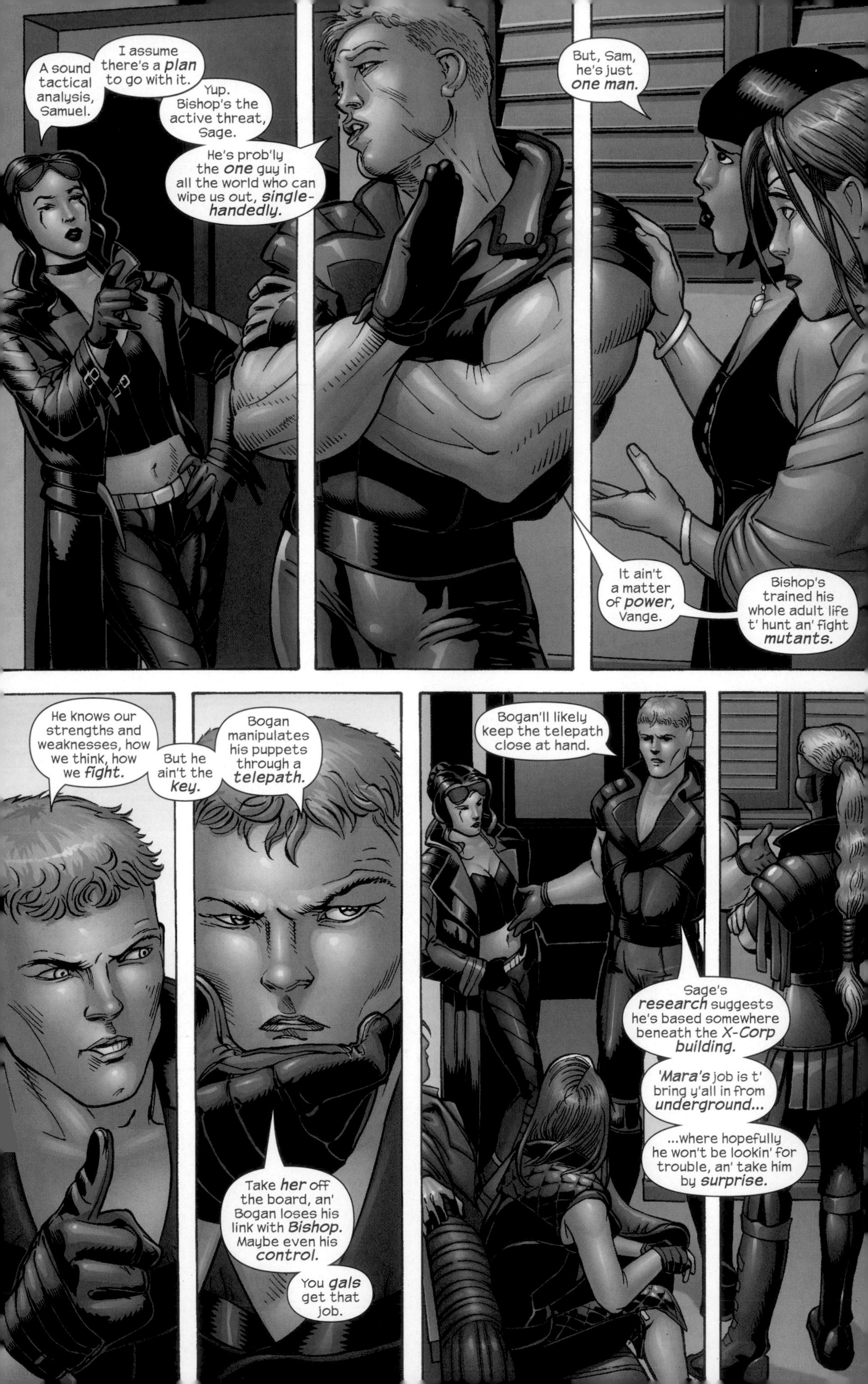
A sound tactical analysis, Samuel.
I assume there's a plan to go with it.
Yup. Bishop's the active threat, Sage.
He's prob'ly the one guy in all the world who can wipe us out, single-handedly.
But, Sam, he's just one man.
It ain't a matter of power, Vange.
Bishop's trained his whole adult life t' hunt an' fight mutants.
He knows our strengths and weaknesses, how we think, how we fight.
But he ain't the key.
Bogan manipulates his puppets through a telepath.
Take her off the board, an' Bogan loses his link with Bishop. Maybe even his control.
You gals get that job.
Bogan'll likely keep the telepath close at hand.
Sage's research suggests he's based somewhere beneath the X-Corp building.
'Mara's job is t' bring y'all in from underground...
...where hopefully he won't be lookin' for trouble, an' take him by surprise.

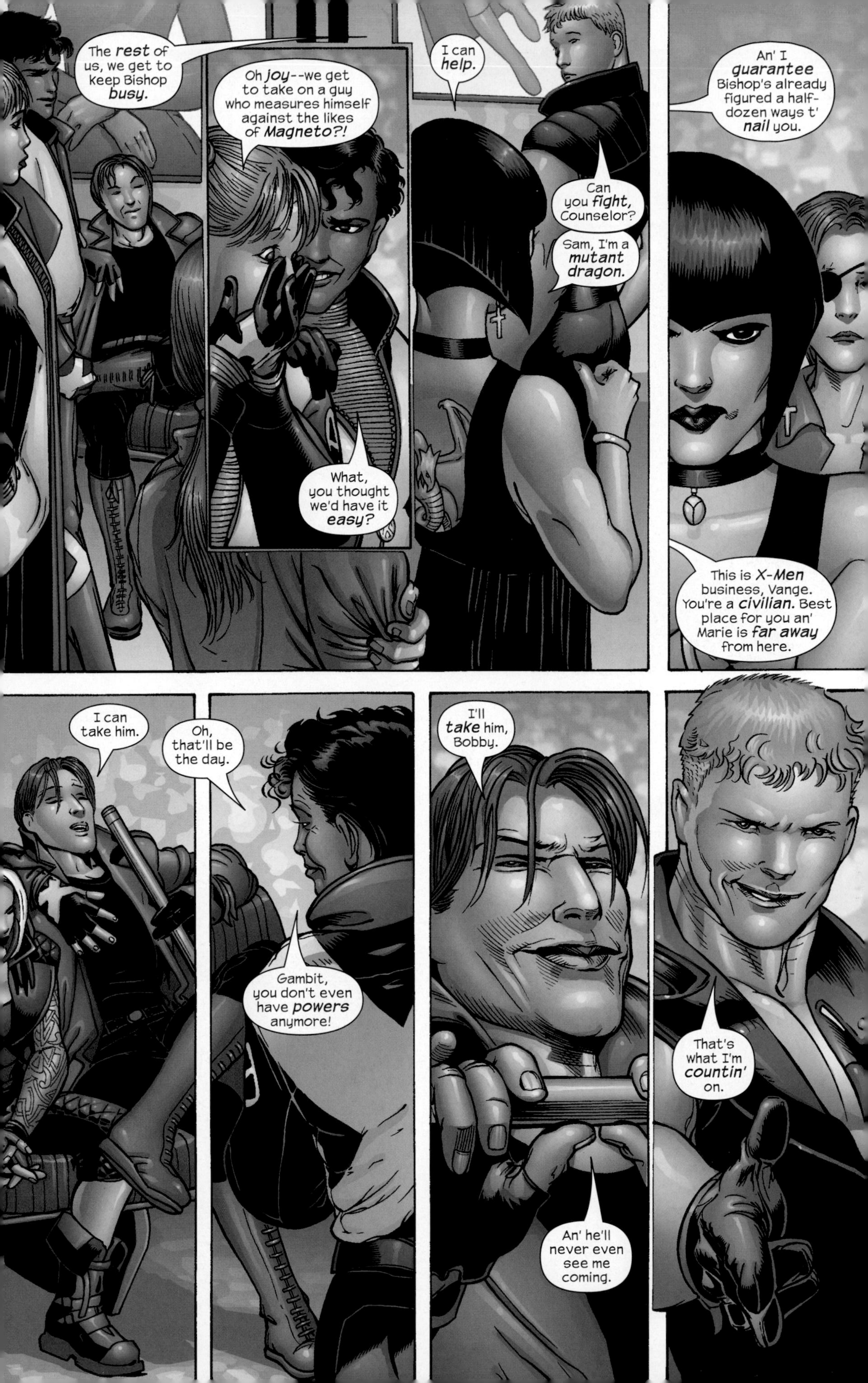
The rest of us, we get to keep Bishop busy.
Oh joy--we get to take on a guy who measures himself against the likes of Magneto?!
What, you thought we'd have it easy?
I can help.
Can you fight, Counselor?
Sam, I'm a mutant dragon.
An' I guarantee Bishop's already figured a half-dozen ways t' nail you.
This is X-Men business, Vange. You're a civilian. Best place for you an' Marie is far away from here.
I can take him.
Oh, that'll be the day.
Gambit, you don't even have powers anymore!
I'll take him, Bobby.
An' he'll never even see me coming.
That's what I'm countin' on.

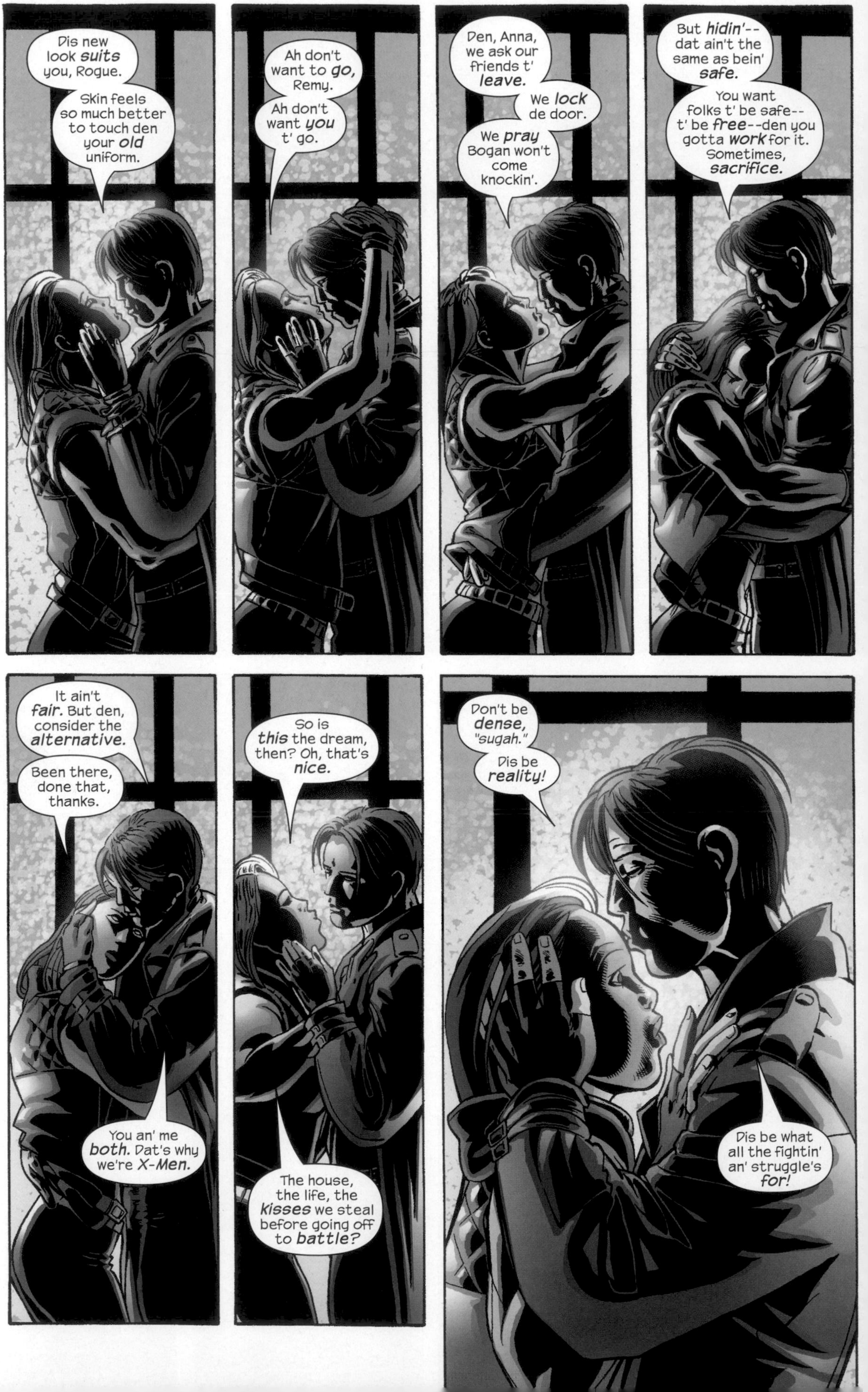

Dis new look suits you, Rogue.
Skin feels so much better to touch den your old uniform.
Ah don't want to go, Remy.
Ah don't want you t' go.
Den, Anna, we ask our friends t' leave.
We lock de door.
We pray Bogan won't come knockin'.
But hidin'--dat ain't the same as bein' safe.
You want folks t' be safe--t' be free--den you gotta work for it. Sometimes, sacrifice.
It ain't fair. But den, consider the alternative.
Been there, done that, thanks.
You an' me both. Dat's why we're X-Men.
So is this the dream, then? Oh, that's nice.
The house, the life, the kisses we steal before going off to battle?
Don't be dense, "sugah."
Dis be reality!
Dis be what all the fightin' an' struggle's for!

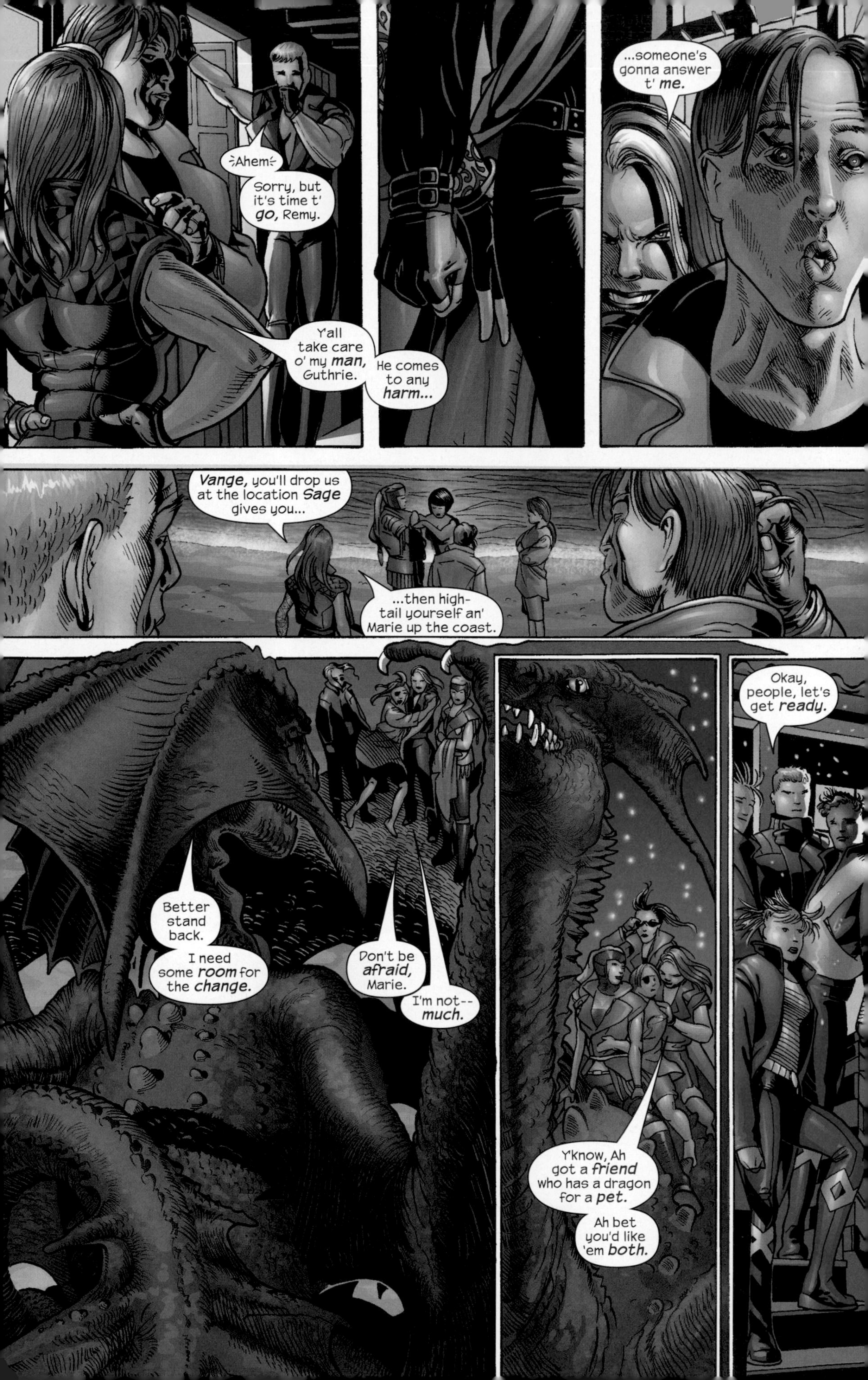

-Ahem-
Sorry, but it's time t' go, Remy.
Y'all take care o' my man, Guthrie.
He comes to any harm...
...someone's gonna answer t' me.
Vange, you'll drop us at the location Sage gives you...
...then high-tail yourself an' Marie up the coast.
Better stand back.
I need some room for the change.
Don't be afraid, Marie.
I'm not--much.
Y'know, Ah got a friend who has a dragon for a pet.
Ah bet you'd like 'em both.
Okay, people, let's get ready.

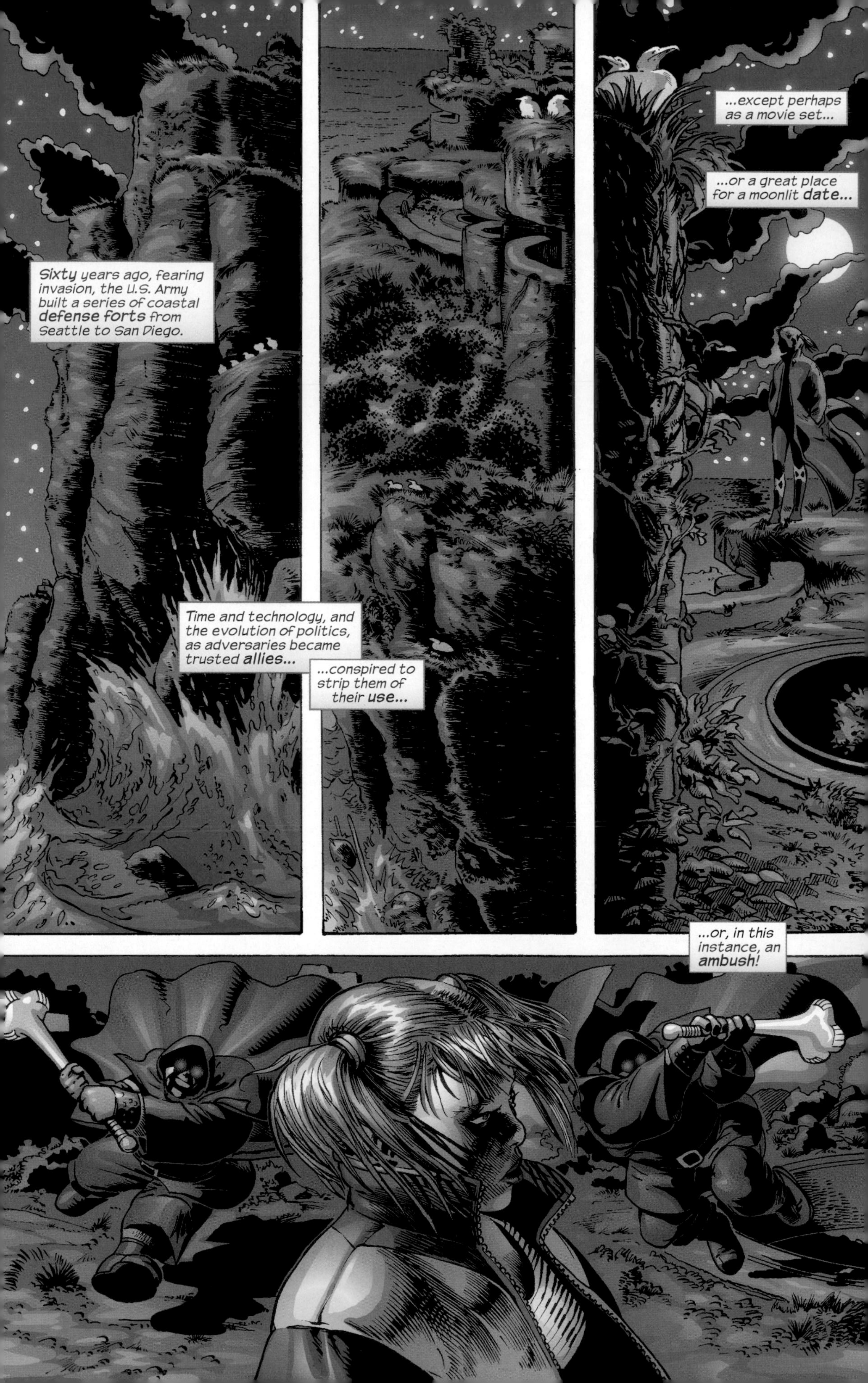

Sixty years ago, fearing invasion, the U.S. Army built a series of coastal defense forts from Seattle to San Diego.
Time and technology, and the evolution of politics, as adversaries became trusted allies...
...conspired to strip them of their use...
...except perhaps as a movie set...
...or a great place for a moonlit date...
...or, in this instance, an ambush!

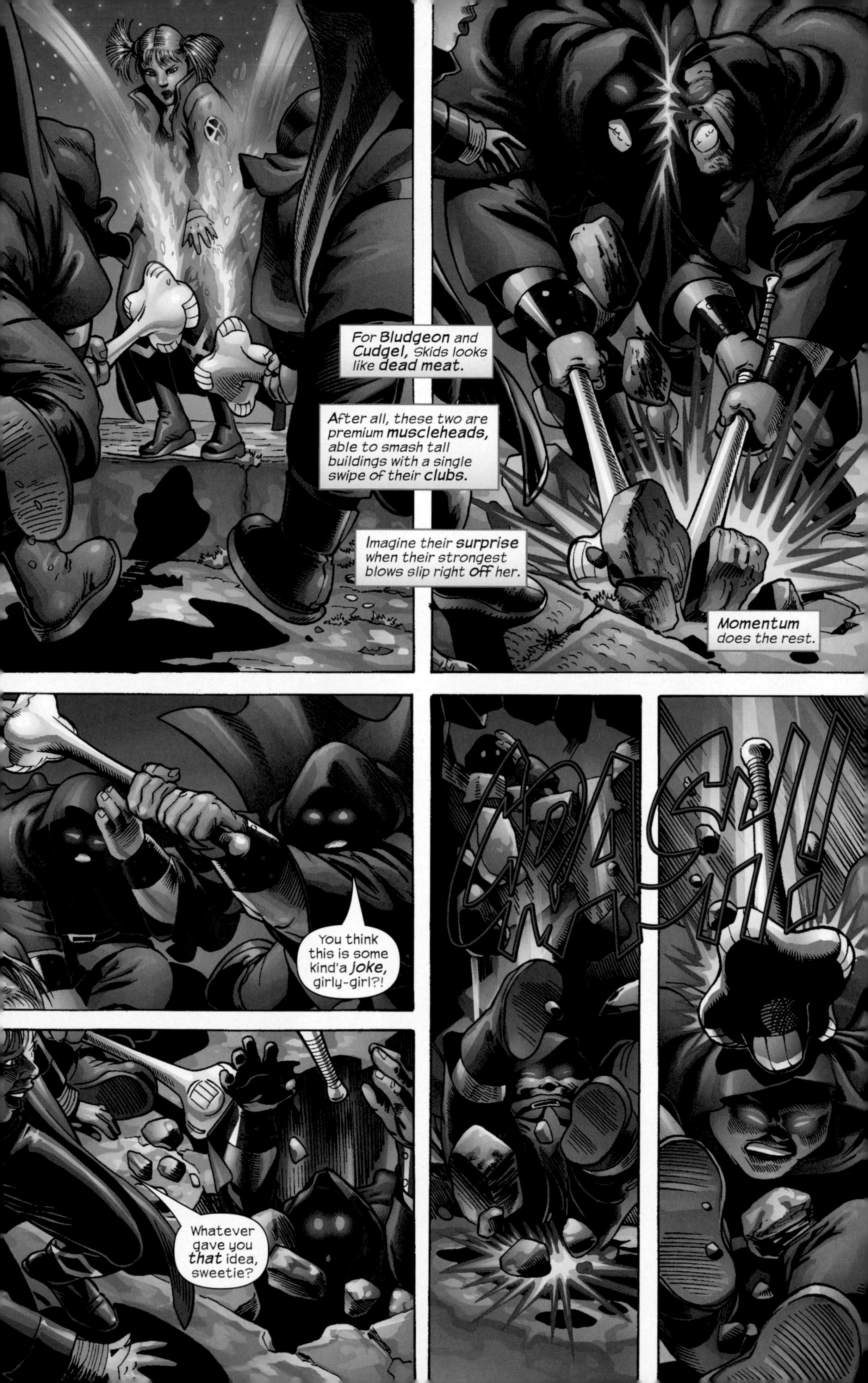
For **Bludgeon** and **Cudgel,** Skids looks like **dead meat.**
After all, these two are premium **muscleheads,** able to smash tall buildings with a single swipe of their **clubs.**
Imagine their **surprise** when their strongest blows slip right **off** her.
Momentum does the rest.
You think this is some kind'a ***joke,*** girly-girl?!
Whatever gave you ***that*** idea, sweetie?

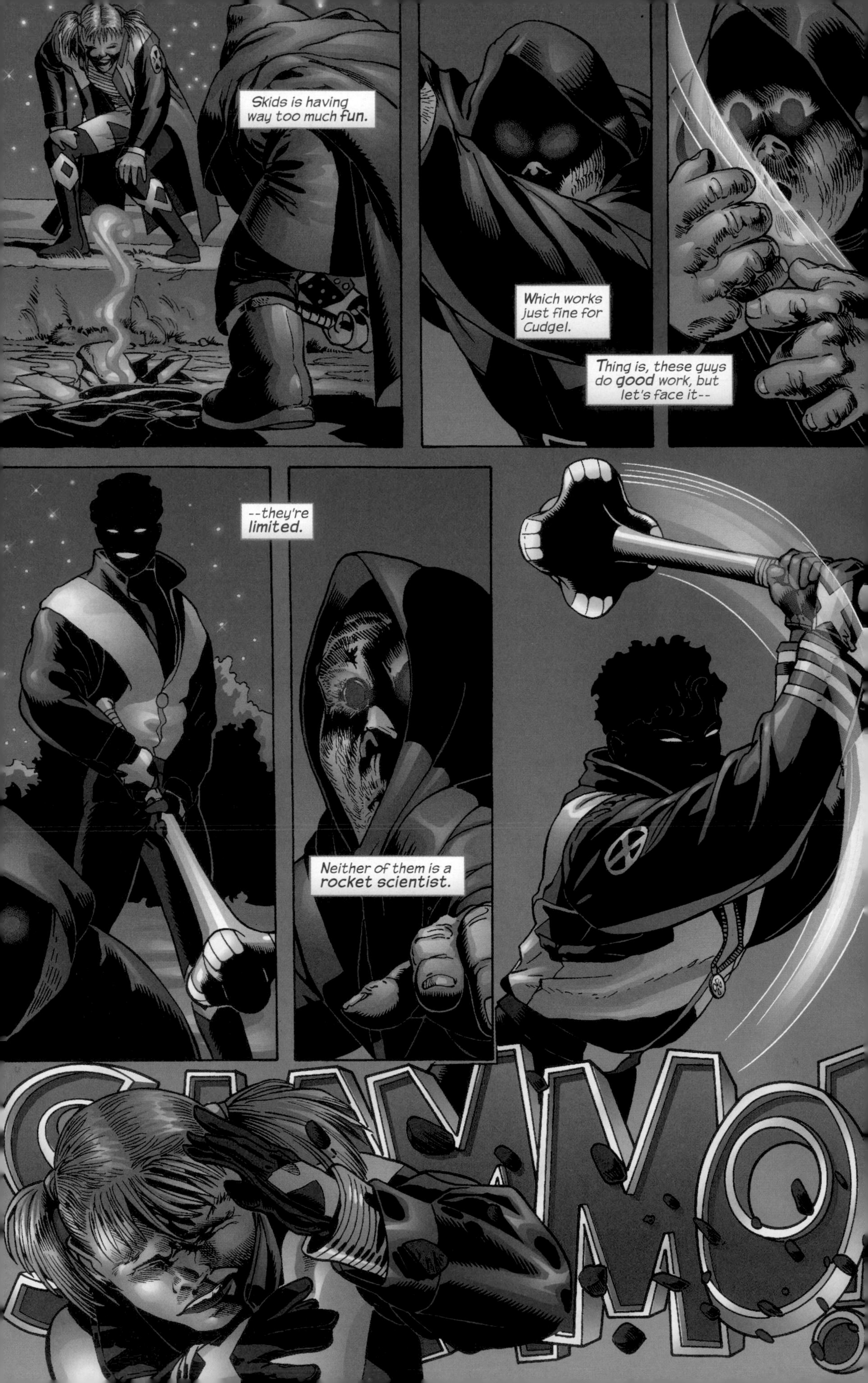
Skids is having way too much fun.
Which works just fine for Cudgel.
Thing is, these guys do good work, but let's face it--
--they're limited.
Neither of them is a rocket scientist.

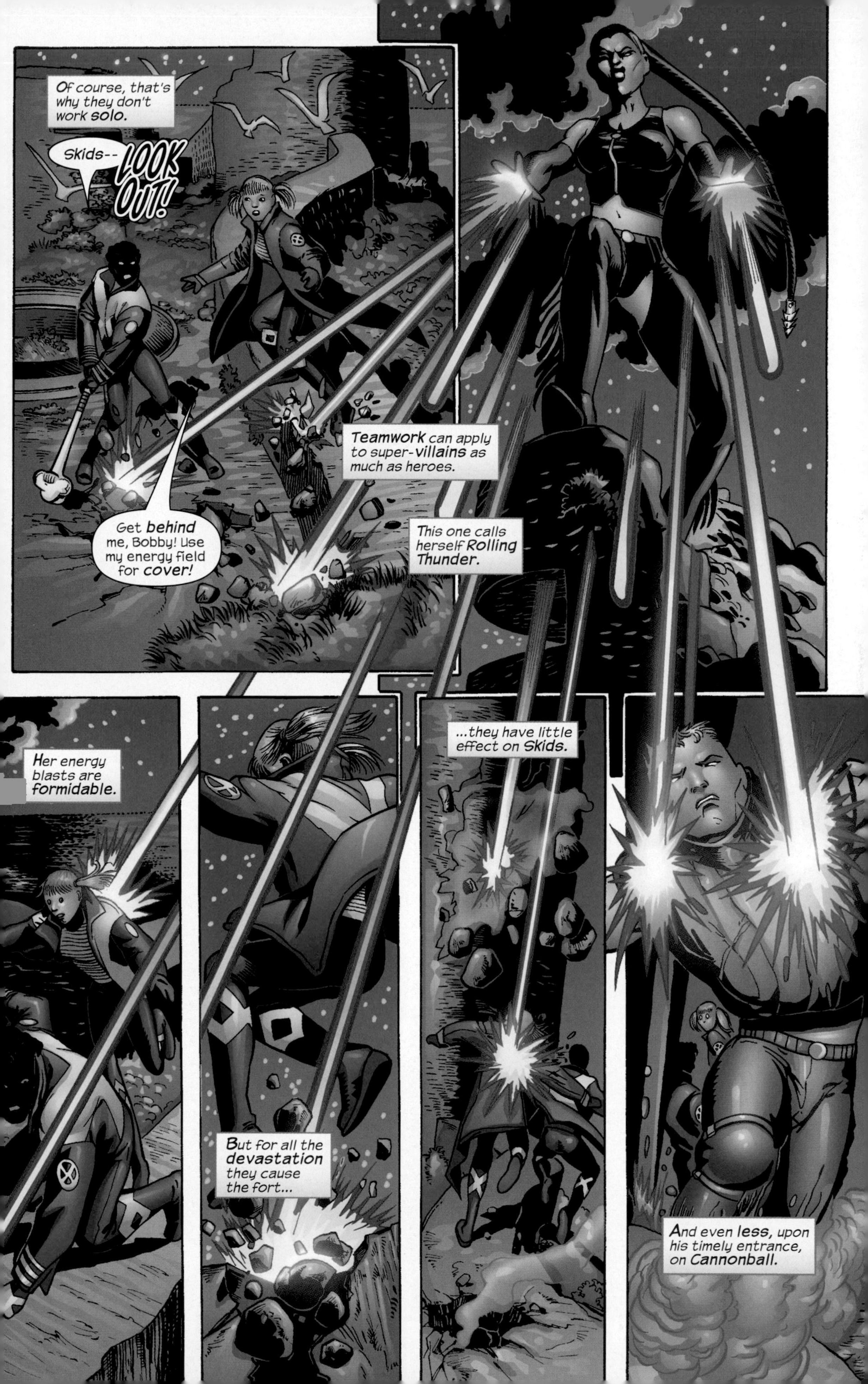
Of course, that's why they don't work solo.
Skids-- LOOK OUT!
Get behind me, Bobby! Use my energy field for cover!
Teamwork can apply to super-villains as much as heroes.
This one calls herself Rolling Thunder.
Her energy blasts are formidable.
But for all the devastation they cause the fort...
...they have little effect on Skids.
And even less, upon his timely entrance, on Cannonball.

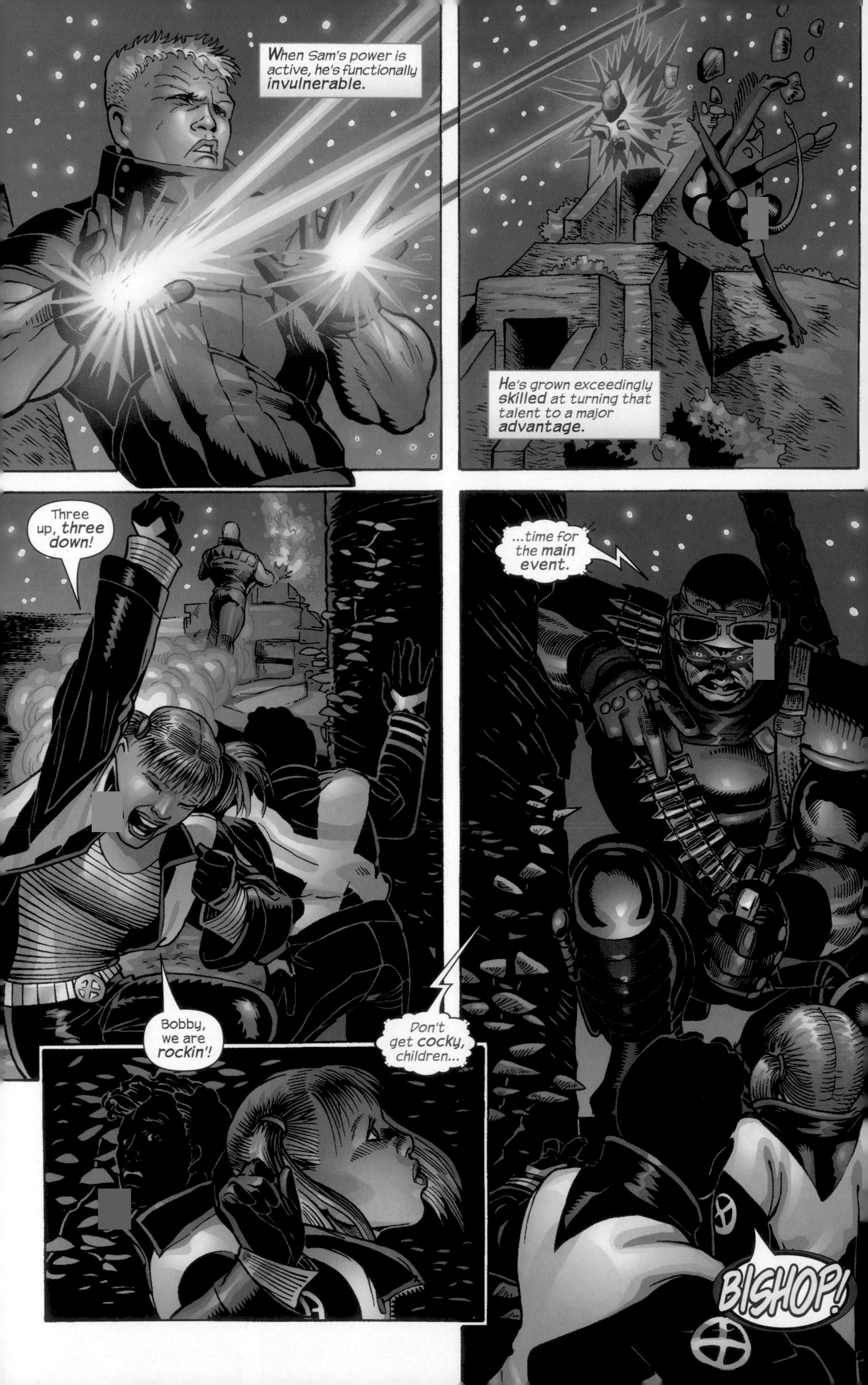
When Sam's power is active, he's functionally invulnerable.
He's grown exceedingly skilled at turning that talent to a major advantage.
Three up, three down!
Bobby, we are rockin'!
Don't get cocky, children...
...time for the main event.
BISHOP!

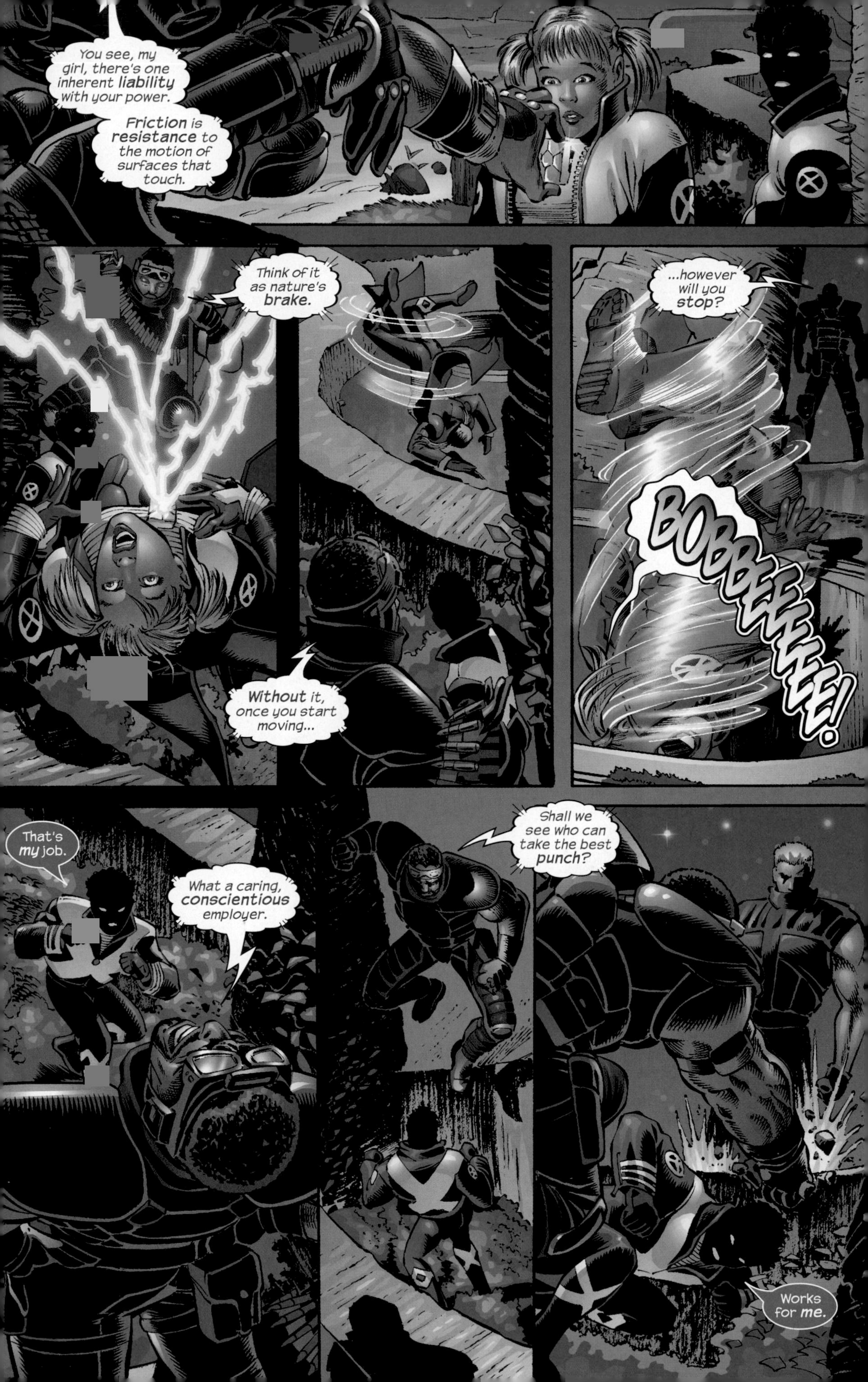
You see, my girl, there's one inherent liability with your power.
Friction is resistance to the motion of surfaces that touch.
Think of it as nature's brake.
Without it, once you start moving...
...however will you stop?
BOBBEEEEEE!
That's my job.
What a caring, conscientious employer.
Shall we see who can take the best punch?
Works for me.

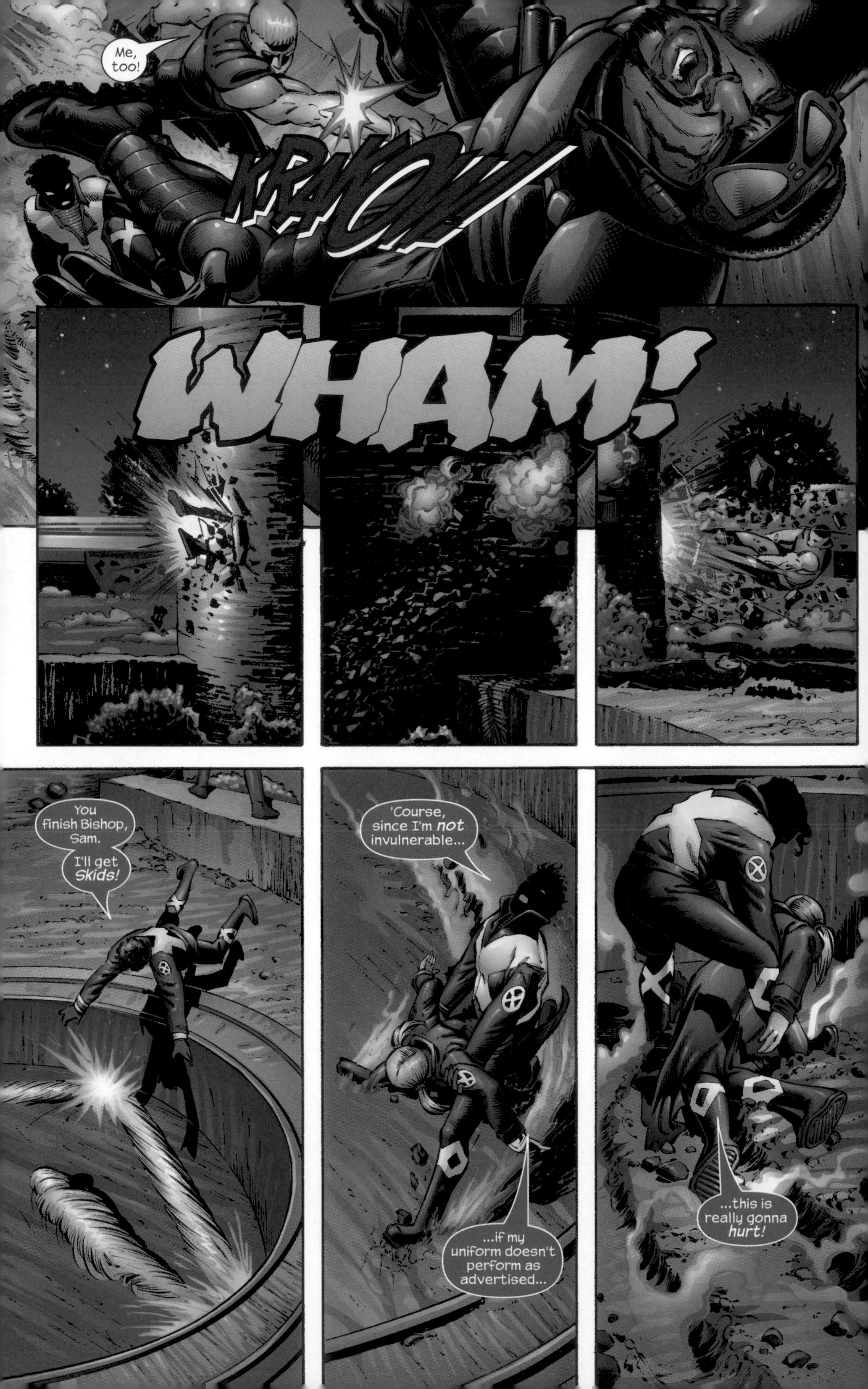
Me, too!
KRAKOW!
WHAM!
You finish Bishop, Sam.
I'll get Skids!
'Course, since I'm not invulnerable...
...if my uniform doesn't perform as advertised...
...this is really gonna hurt!

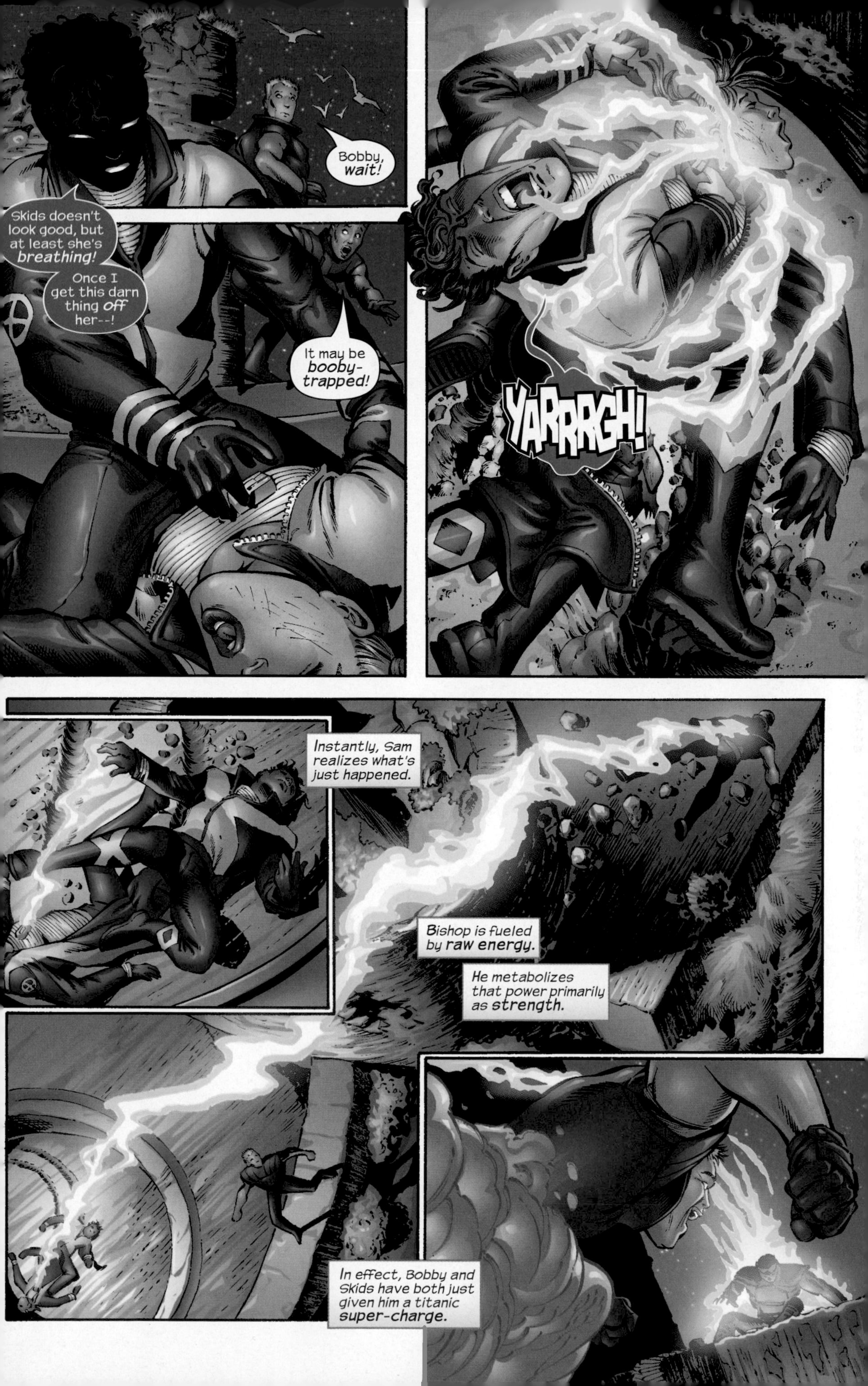
Bobby, wait!
Skids doesn't look good, but at least she's breathing!
Once I get this darn thing off her--!
It may be booby-trapped!
YARRRGH!
Instantly, Sam realizes what's just happened.
Bishop is fueled by raw energy.
He metabolizes that power primarily as strength.
In effect, Bobby and Skids have both just given him a titanic super-charge.

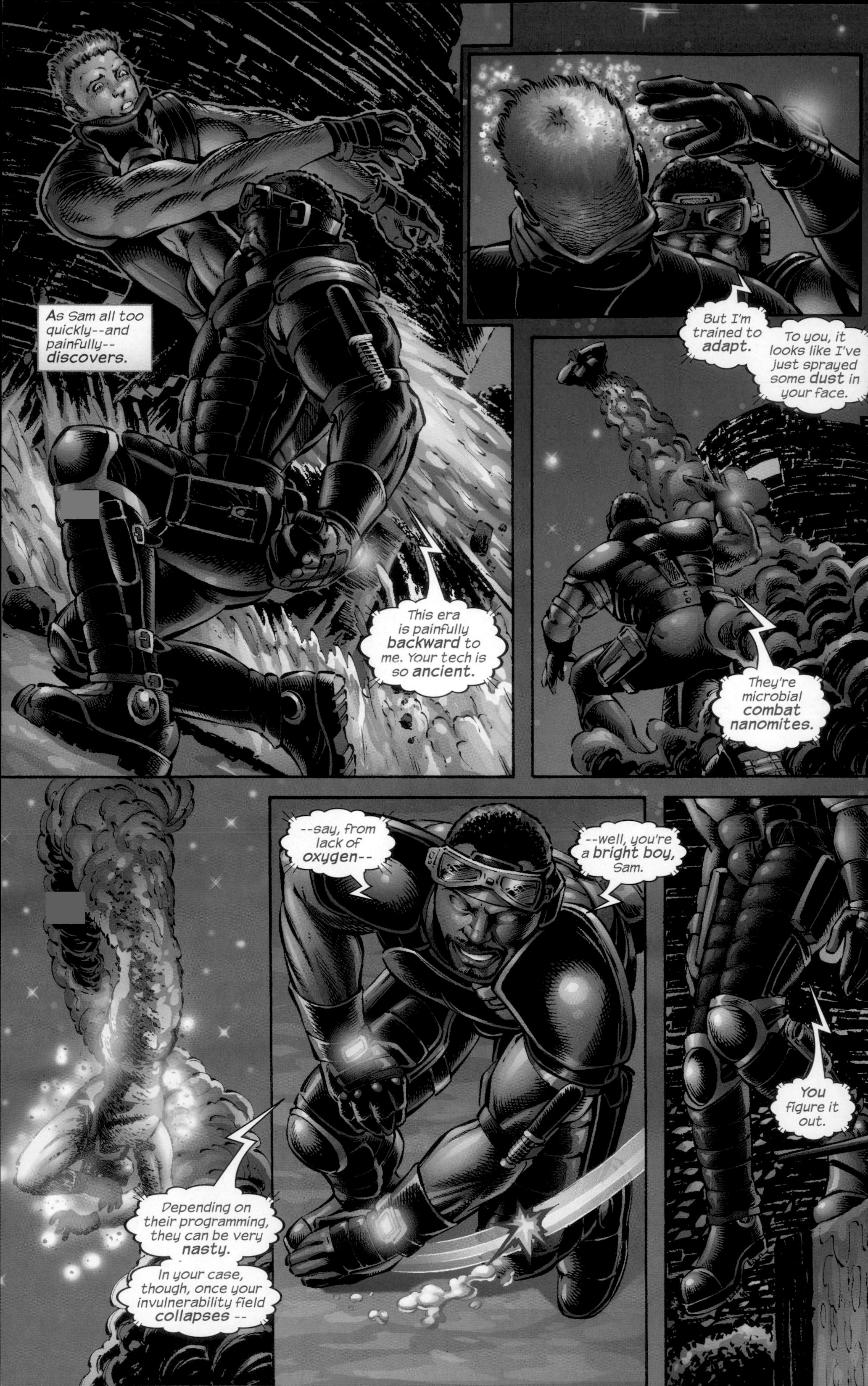
As Sam all too quickly--and painfully--discovers.
This era is painfully backward to me. Your tech is so ancient.
But I'm trained to adapt.
To you, it looks like I've just sprayed some dust in your face.
They're microbial combat nanomites.
Depending on their programming, they can be very nasty.
In your case, though, once your invulnerability field collapses --
--say, from lack of oxygen--
--well, you're a bright boy, Sam.
You figure it out.

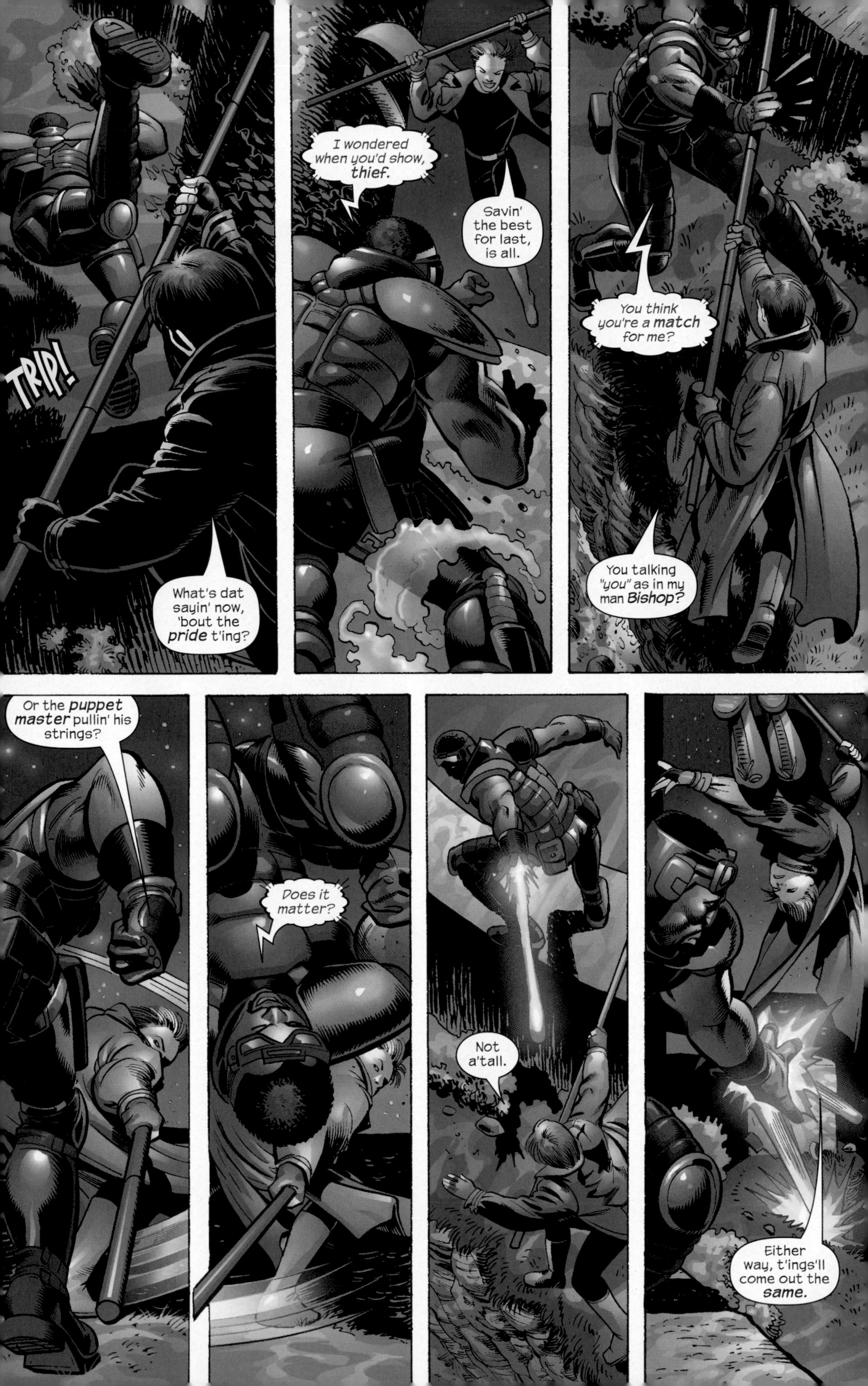
TRIP!
What's dat sayin' now, 'bout the *pride* t'ing?
I wondered when you'd show, *thief.*
Savin' the best for last, is all.
You think you're a *match* for me?
You talking *"you"* as in my man *Bishop?*
Or the *puppet master* pullin' his strings?
Does it matter?
Not a'tall.
Either way, t'ings'll come out the *same.*

What, you think I'm all *sass*, no *sizzle*?

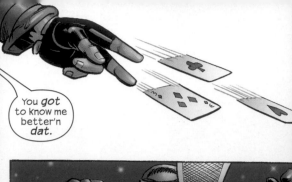

You *got* to know me better'n *dat.*

You absorbed *my* energies b'fore, you 'member how dat felt?

Maybe some *other* time.

Faked you out, homme. Still no powers.

Get *used* to dat. I have.

You may consider yourself the *best.*

But I'm *magic!*

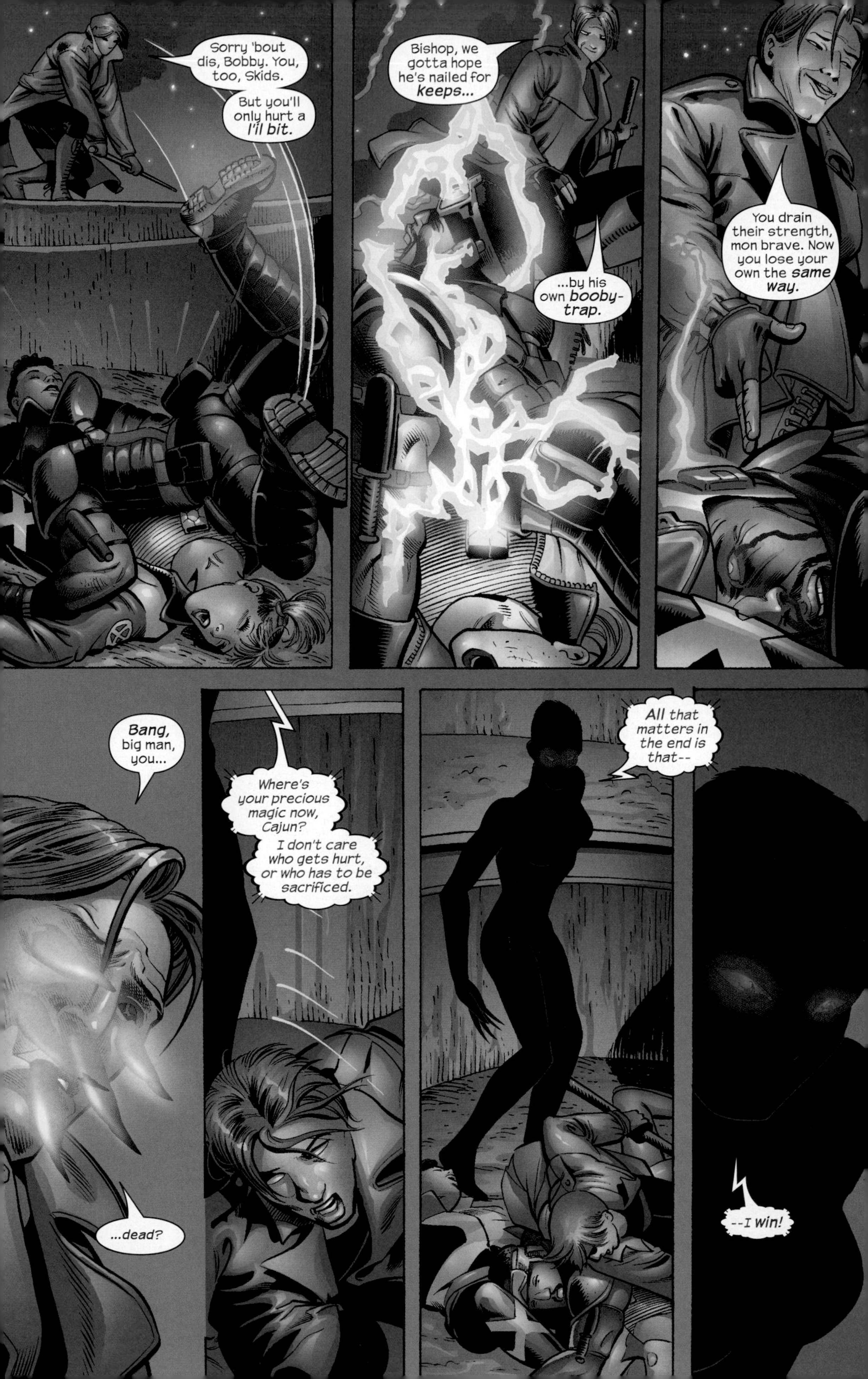
Sorry 'bout dis, Bobby. You, too, Skids.
But you'll only hurt a l'il bit.
Bishop, we gotta hope he's nailed for keeps...
...by his own booby-trap.
You drain their strength, mon brave. Now you lose your own the same way.
Bang, big man, you...
...dead?
Where's your precious magic now, Cajun?
I don't care who gets hurt, or who has to be sacrificed.
All that matters in the end is that--
--I win!

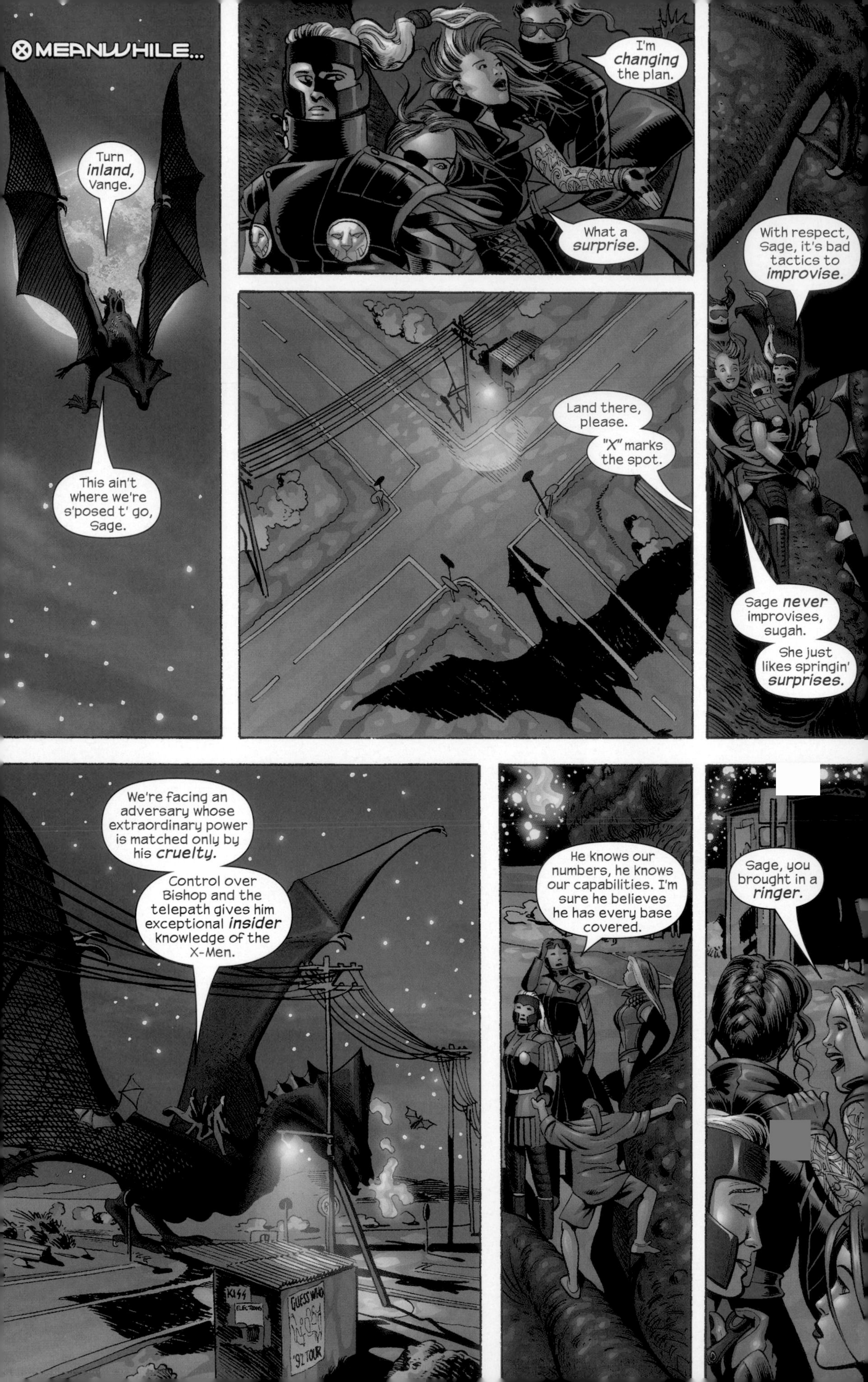
MEANWHILE...
Turn *inland,* Vange.
This ain't where we're s'posed t' go, Sage.
I'm *changing* the plan.
What a *surprise.*
With respect, Sage, it's bad tactics to *improvise.*
Land there, please.
"X" marks the spot.
Sage *never* improvises, sugah.
She just likes springin' *surprises.*
We're facing an adversary whose extraordinary power is matched only by his *cruelty.*
Control over Bishop and the telepath gives him exceptional *insider* knowledge of the X-Men.
He knows our numbers, he knows our capabilities. I'm sure he believes he has every base covered.
Sage, you brought in a *ringer.*

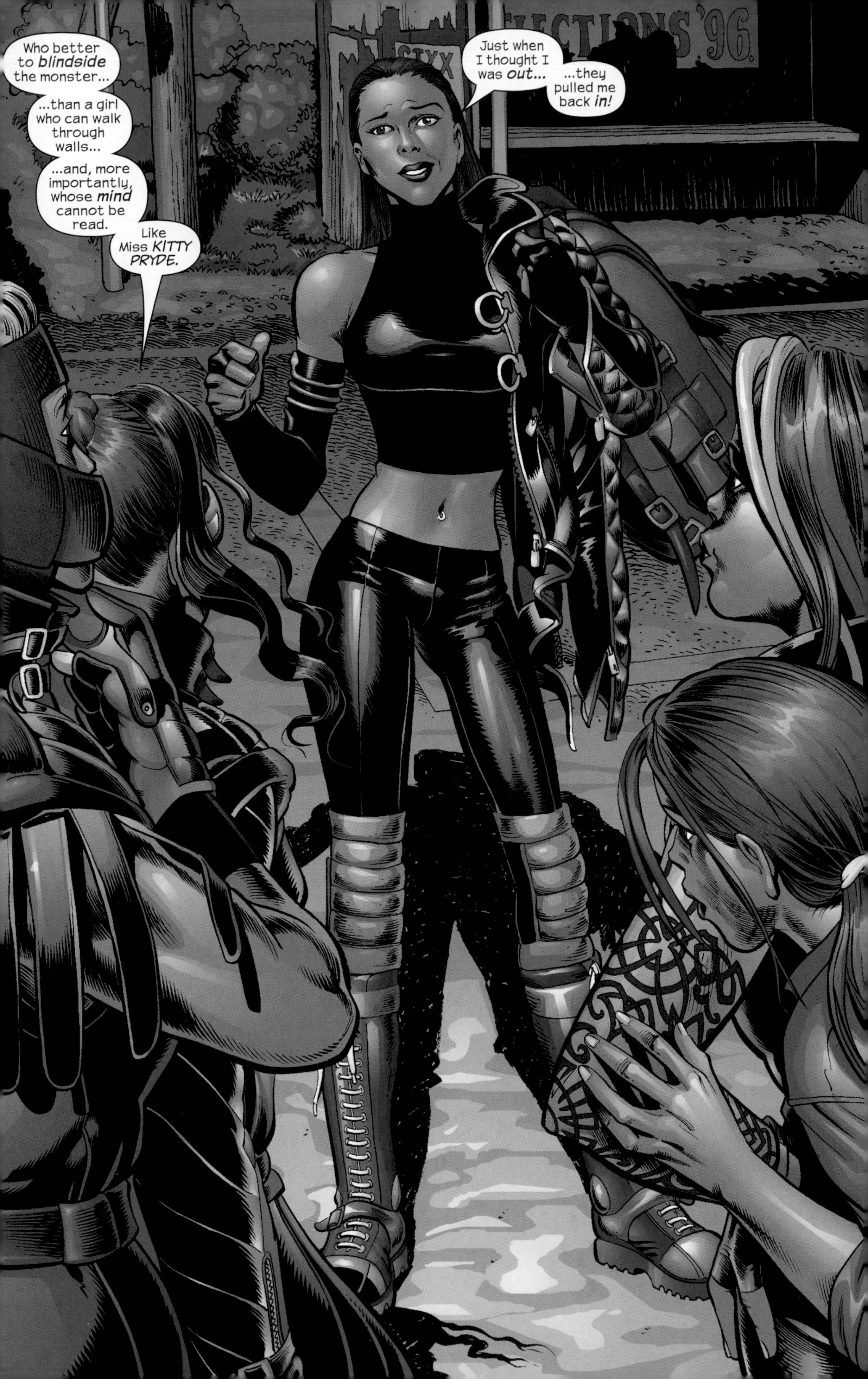

ELECTIONS '96
SIXX
Who better to blindside the monster...
...than a girl who can walk through walls...
...and, more importantly, whose mind cannot be read.
Like Miss KITTY PRYDE.
Just when I thought I was out...
...they pulled me back in!

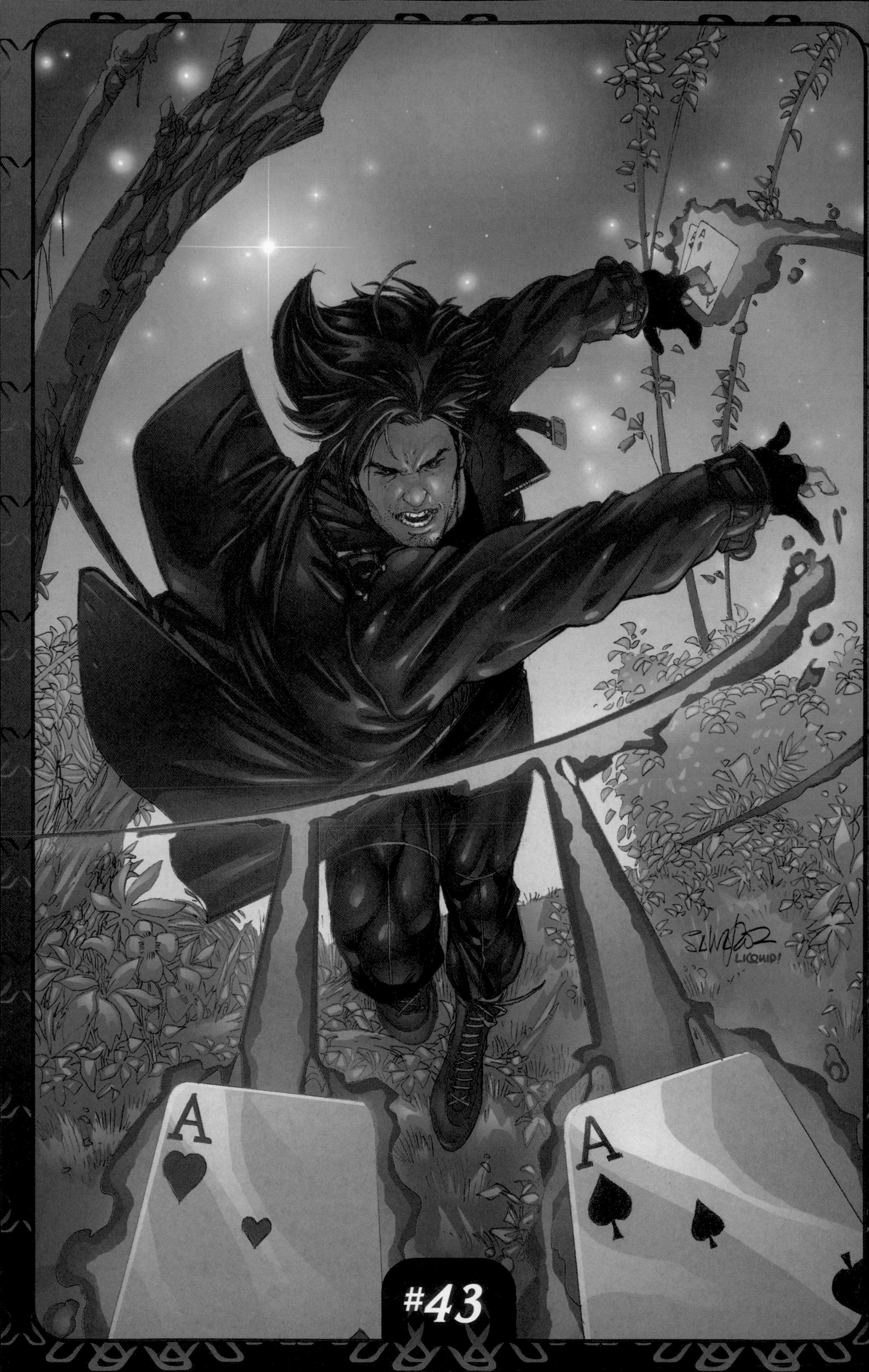
SALVADOR
LIQUID!
#43

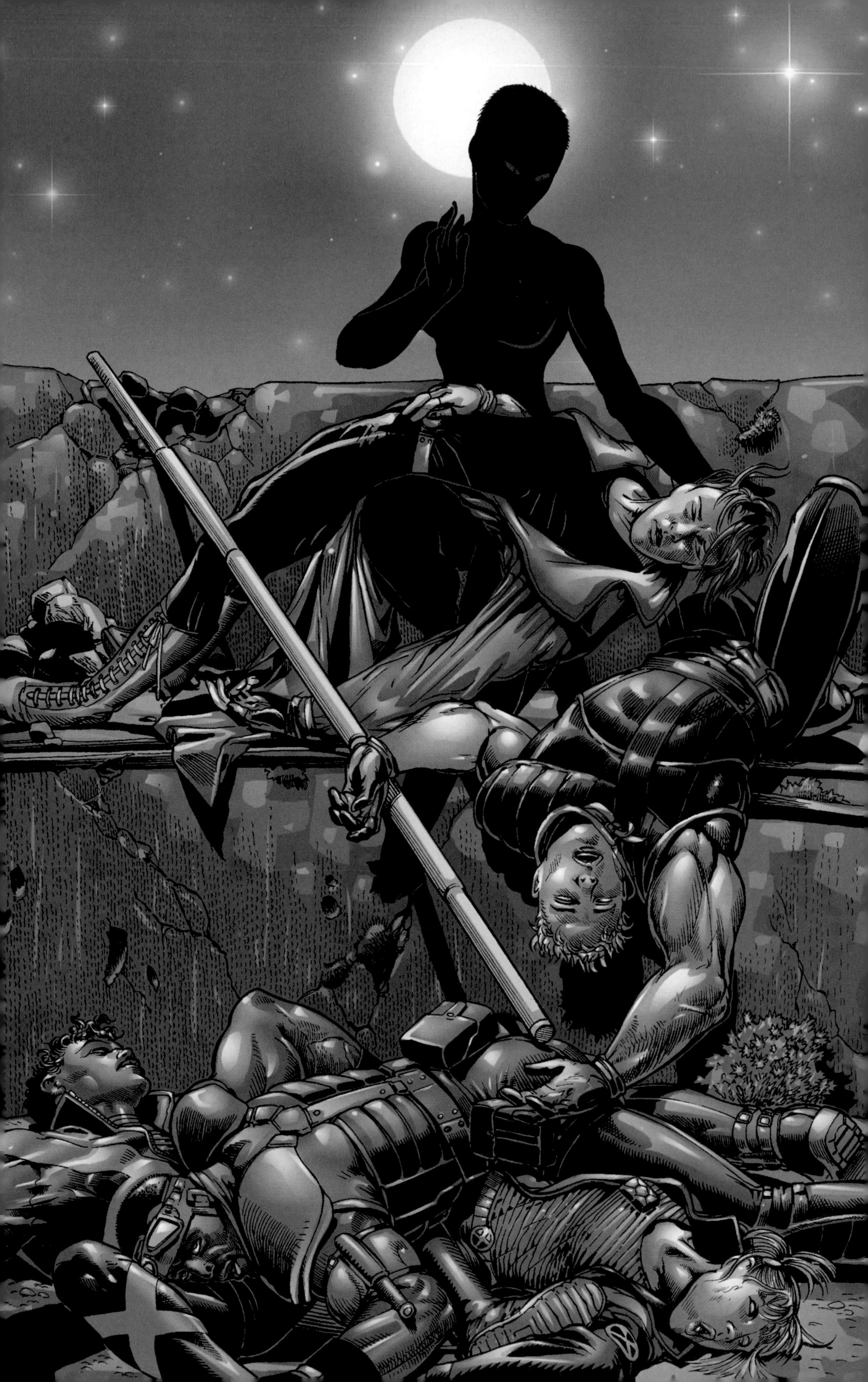

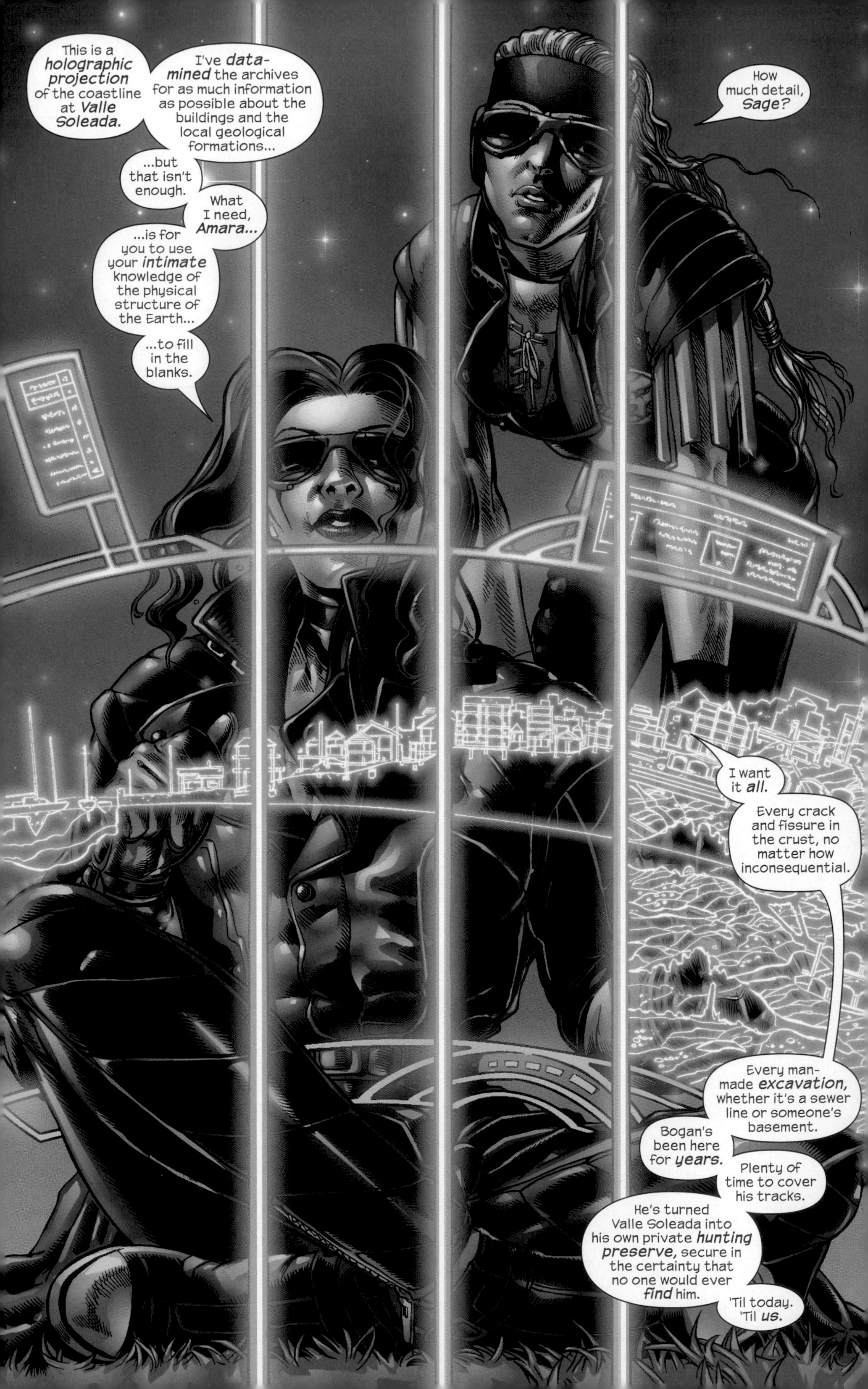
This is a *holographic projection* of the coastline at *Valle Soleada.*
I've *data-mined* the archives for as much information as possible about the buildings and the local geological formations...
...but that isn't enough.
What I need, *Amara...*
...is for you to use your *intimate* knowledge of the physical structure of the Earth...
...to fill in the blanks.
How much detail, *Sage?*
I want it *all.*
Every crack and fissure in the crust, no matter how inconsequential.
Every man-made *excavation,* whether it's a sewer line or someone's basement.
Bogan's been here for *years.*
Plenty of time to cover his tracks.
He's turned Valle Soleada into his own private *hunting preserve,* secure in the certainty that no one would ever *find* him.
'Til today. 'Til *us.*

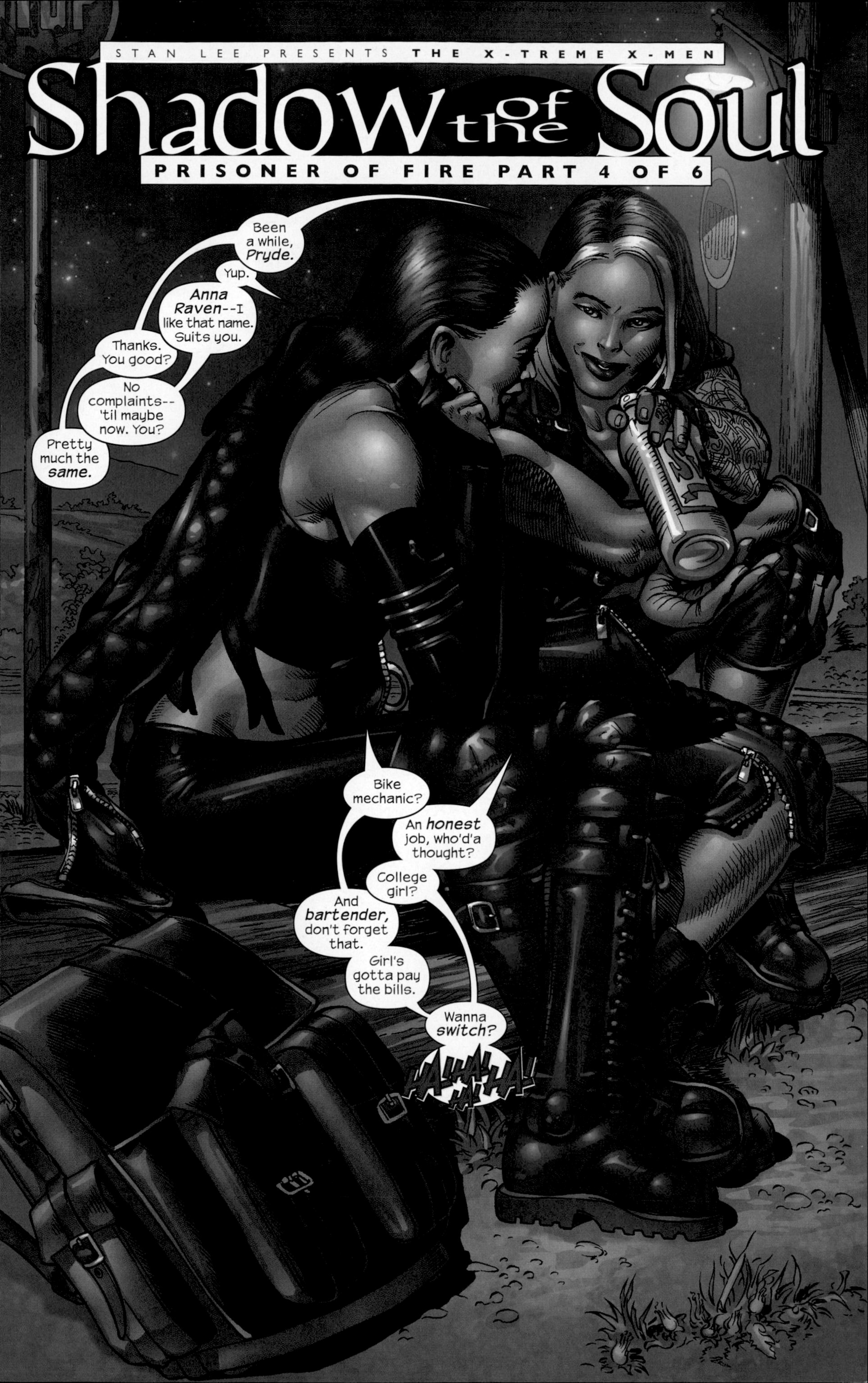
STAN LEE PRESENTS THE X-TREME X-MEN
Shadow of the Soul
PRISONER OF FIRE PART 4 OF 6
Been a while, *Pryde.*
Yup.
Anna Raven--I like that name. Suits you.
Thanks. You good?
No complaints--'til maybe now. You?
Pretty much the *same.*
Bike mechanic?
An *honest* job, who'd'a thought?
College girl?
And *bartender,* don't forget that.
Girl's gotta pay the bills.
Wanna *switch?*
HA!HA!HA! HA!HA!

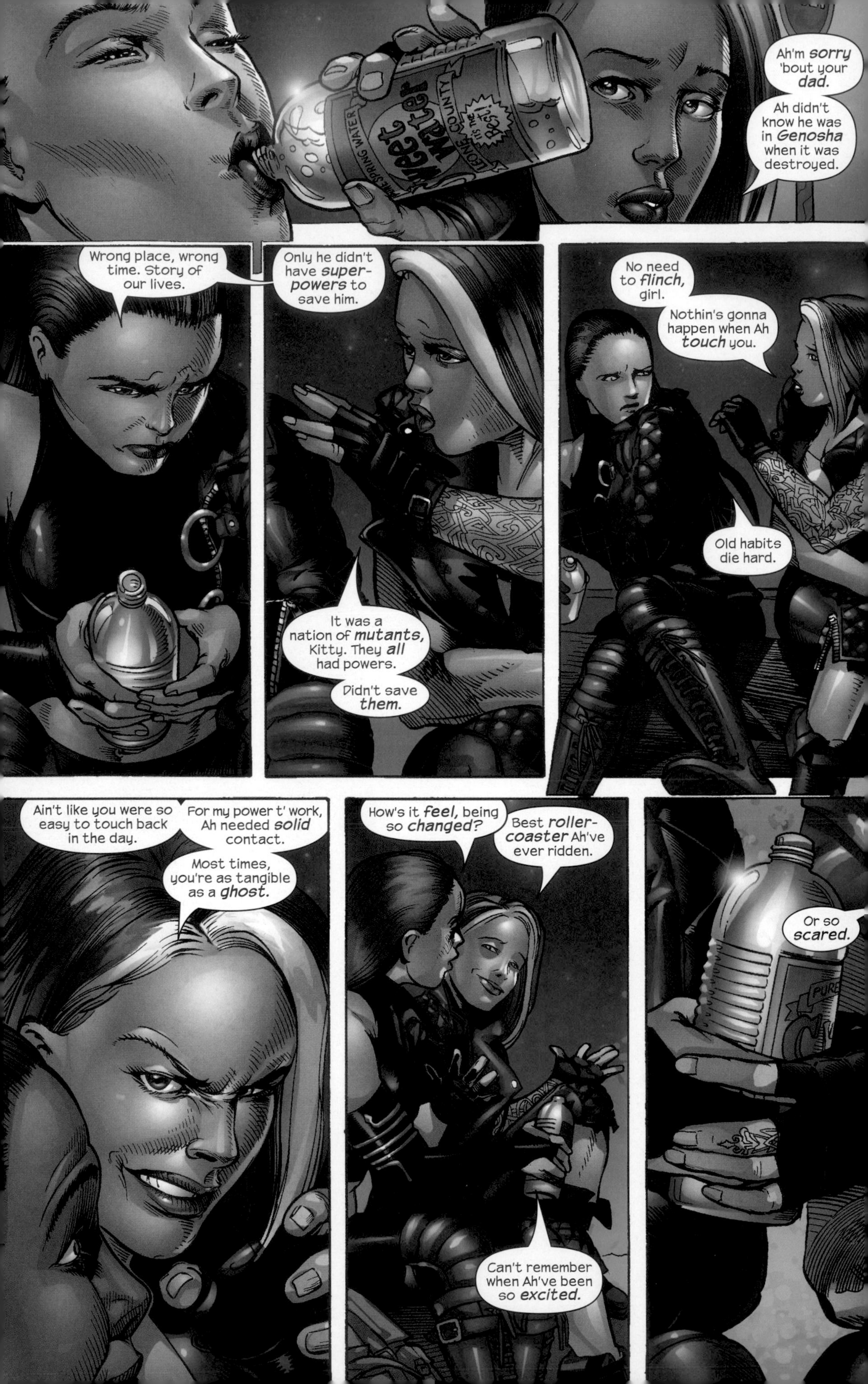

Ah'm sorry 'bout your dad.
Ah didn't know he was in Genosha when it was destroyed.
Wrong place, wrong time. Story of our lives.
Only he didn't have super-powers to save him.
It was a nation of mutants, Kitty. They all had powers.
Didn't save them.
No need to flinch, girl.
Nothin's gonna happen when Ah touch you.
Old habits die hard.
Ain't like you were so easy to touch back in the day.
For my power t' work, Ah needed solid contact.
Most times, you're as tangible as a ghost.
How's it feel, being so changed?
Best roller-coaster Ah've ever ridden.
Can't remember when Ah've been so excited.
Or so scared.

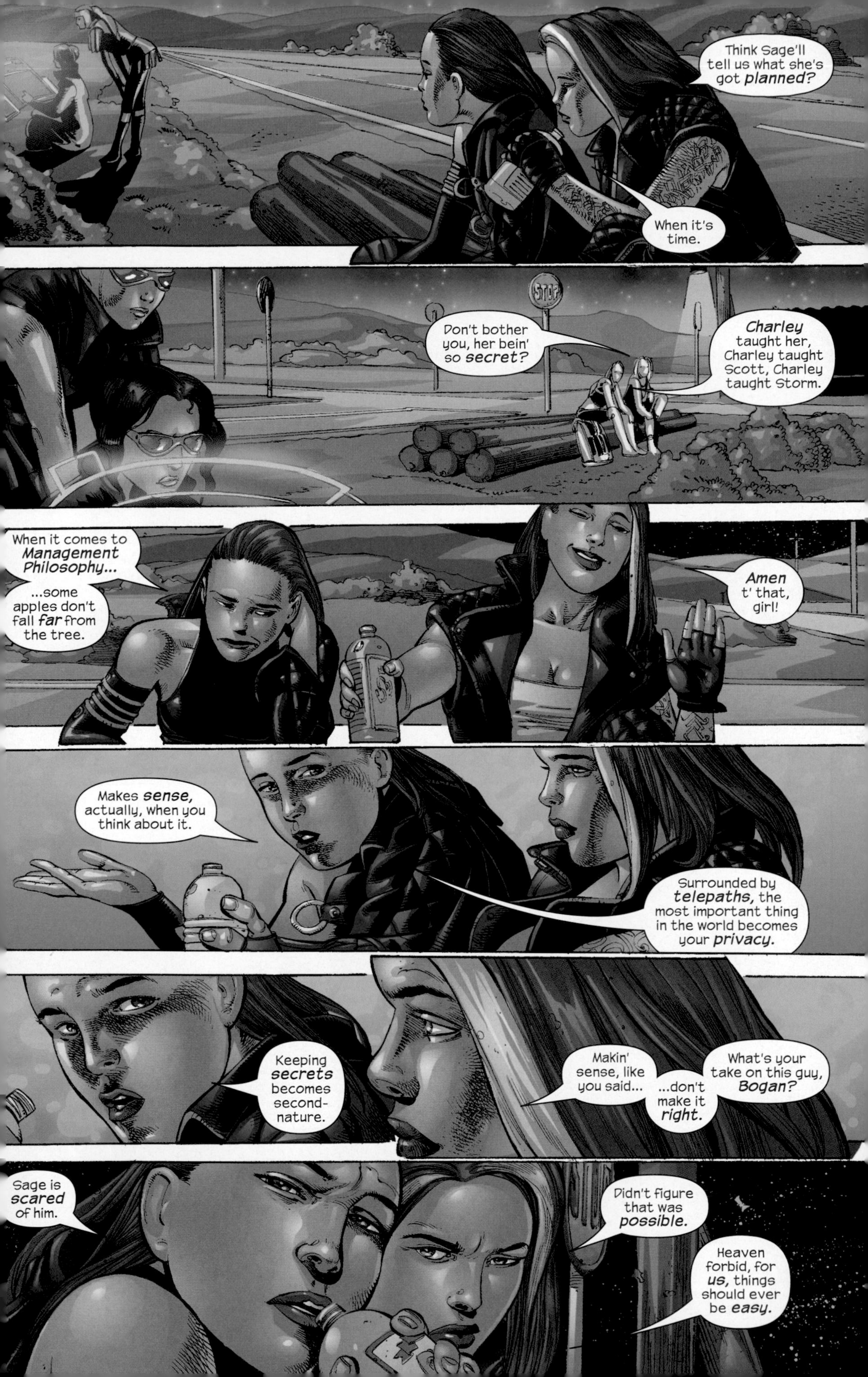
Think Sage'll tell us what she's got *planned?*
When it's time.
Don't bother you, her bein' so *secret?*
Charley taught her, Charley taught Scott, Charley taught Storm.
When it comes to *Management Philosophy...*
...some apples don't fall *far* from the tree.
Amen t' that, girl!
Makes *sense,* actually, when you think about it.
Surrounded by *telepaths,* the most important thing in the world becomes your *privacy.*
Keeping *secrets* becomes second-nature.
Makin' sense, like you said...
...don't make it *right.*
What's your take on this guy, *Bogan?*
Sage is *scared* of him.
Didn't figure that was *possible.*
Heaven forbid, for *us,* things should ever be *easy.*

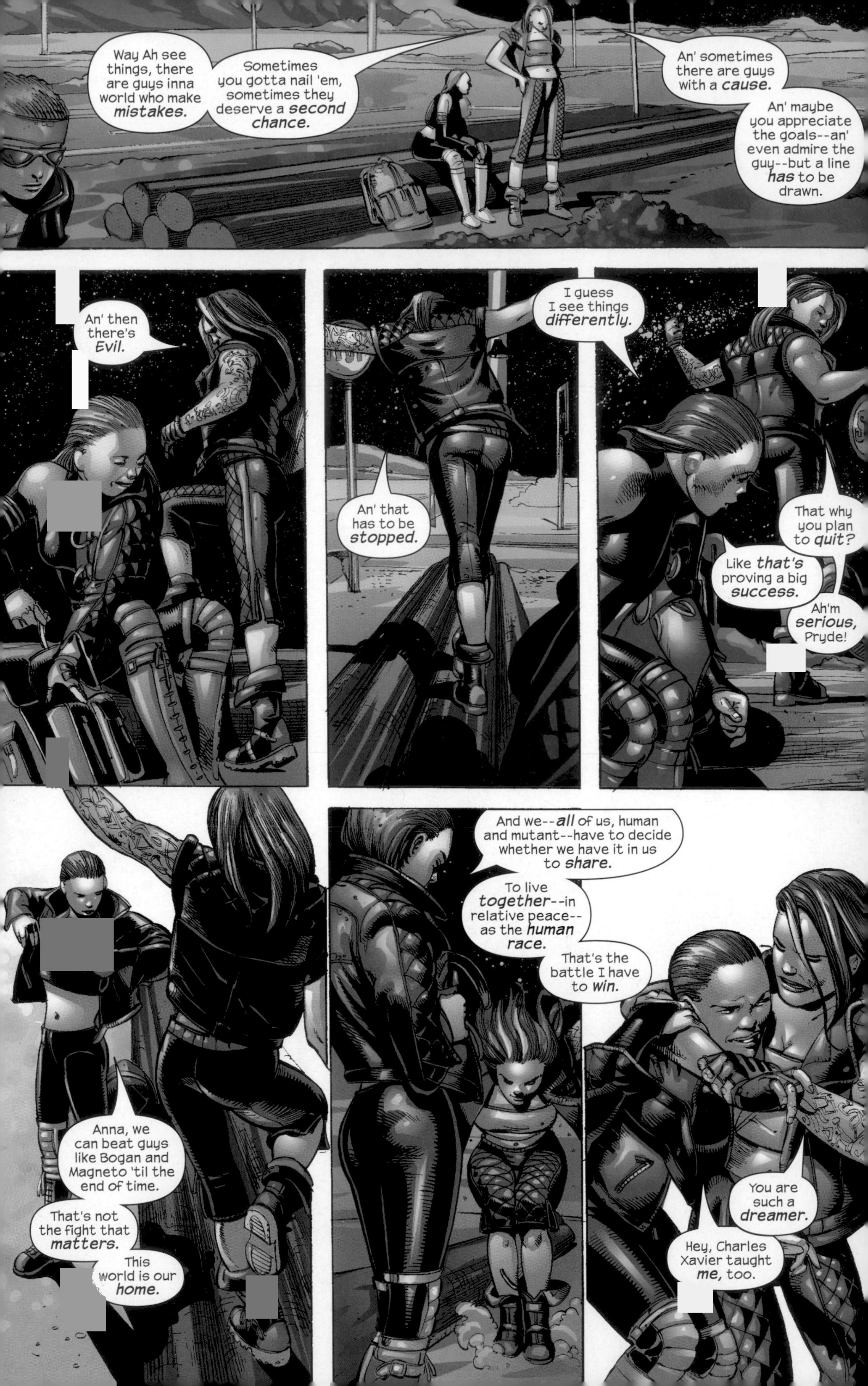
Way Ah see things, there are guys inna world who make mistakes.
Sometimes you gotta nail 'em, sometimes they deserve a second chance.
An' sometimes there are guys with a cause.
An' maybe you appreciate the goals--an' even admire the guy--but a line has to be drawn.
An' then there's Evil.
An' that has to be stopped.
I guess I see things differently.
That why you plan to quit?
Like that's proving a big success.
Ah'm serious, Pryde!
Anna, we can beat guys like Bogan and Magneto 'til the end of time.
That's not the fight that matters.
This world is our home.
And we--all of us, human and mutant--have to decide whether we have it in us to share.
To live together--in relative peace--as the human race.
That's the battle I have to win.
You are such a dreamer.
Hey, Charles Xavier taught me, too.

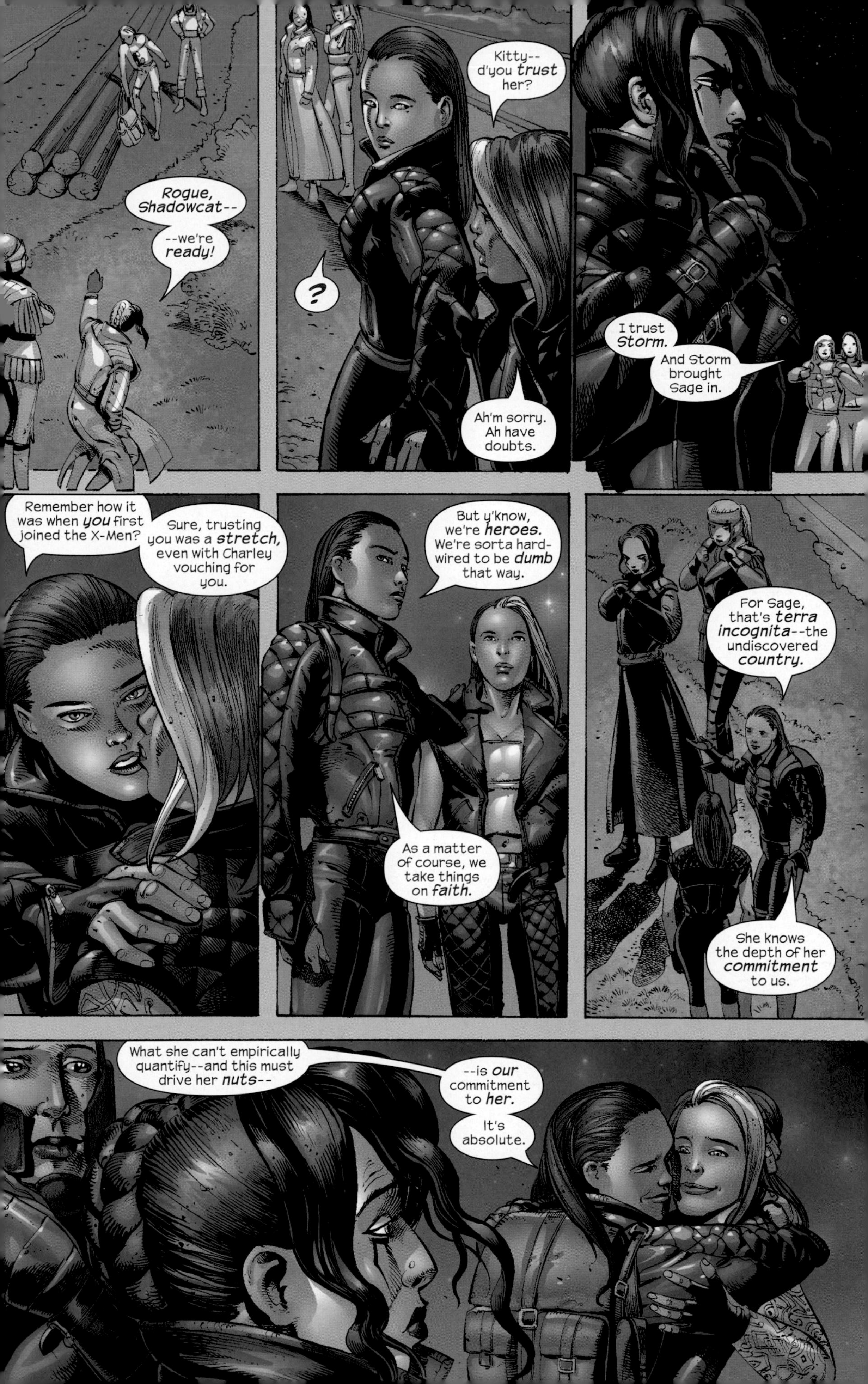
Rogue, Shadowcat--
--we're ready!
Kitty-- d'you trust her?
?
Ah'm sorry. Ah have doubts.
I trust Storm.
And Storm brought Sage in.
Remember how it was when you first joined the X-Men?
Sure, trusting you was a stretch, even with Charley vouching for you.
But y'know, we're heroes. We're sorta hard-wired to be dumb that way.
As a matter of course, we take things on faith.
For Sage, that's terra incognita--the undiscovered country.
She knows the depth of her commitment to us.
What she can't empirically quantify--and this must drive her nuts--
--is our commitment to her.
It's absolute.

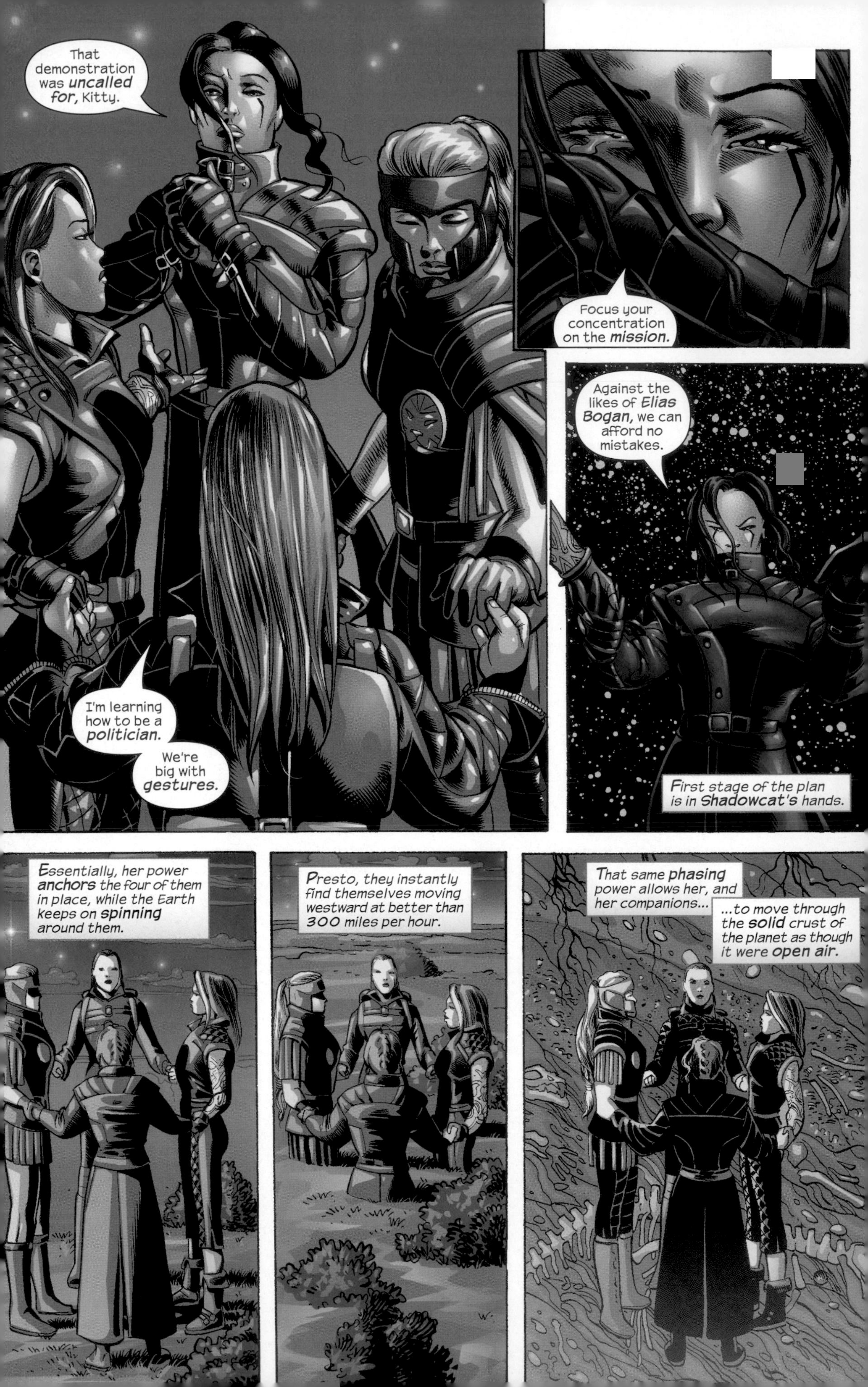
That demonstration was *uncalled for*, Kitty.
I'm learning how to be a *politician*.
We're big with *gestures*.
Focus your concentration on the *mission*.
Against the likes of *Elias Bogan*, we can afford no mistakes.
First stage of the plan is in *Shadowcat's* hands.
Essentially, her power **anchors** the four of them in place, while the Earth keeps on **spinning** around them.
Presto, they instantly find themselves moving westward at better than 300 miles per hour.
That same **phasing** power allows her, and her companions...
...to move through the **solid** crust of the planet as though it were **open air**.

Stay loose, guys. I'm slipping the molecules of *our* bodies through the spaces between those of the mass around us.

If anyone lets *go*, they instantly become *solid*.

That would be very, very *bad*.

I wield the fires of Mother *Gaea*... ...I "know" her body as well as I do my own...

...yet to be *one* with her in such a way--!

Manoman--Ah thought *surfin'* was wicked!

Ohhh, *Remy*-- you are so gonna *hate* that you *missed* this li'l ride.

The *darkness* will pass, the fear is but illusion.

The path to the heart of the *monster* is as hard as the monster is *deadly*.

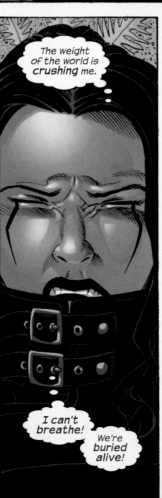

The weight of the world is *crushing* me.

I can't breathe!

We're buried alive!

No.

Buried, yes. Alive, yes. We are in *good* hands. We will *prevail*.

Kitty, Amara--it is *time*!

And just like that, the ride isn't so much *fun* anymore...

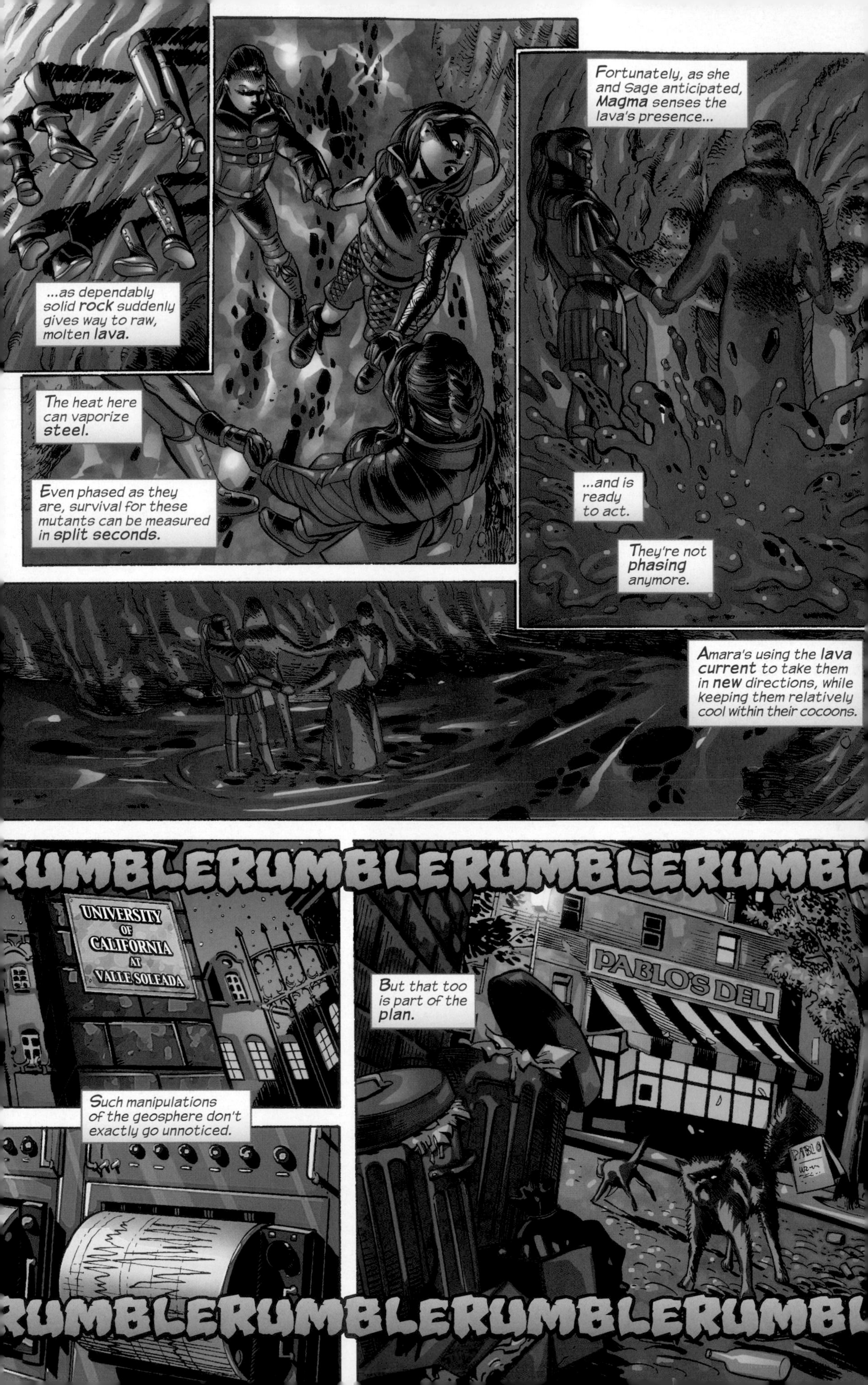
...as dependably solid rock suddenly gives way to raw, molten lava.
The heat here can vaporize steel.
Even phased as they are, survival for these mutants can be measured in split seconds.
Fortunately, as she and Sage anticipated, Magma senses the lava's presence...
...and is ready to act.
They're not phasing anymore.
Amara's using the lava current to take them in new directions, while keeping them relatively cool within their cocoons.
RUMBLERUMBLERUMBLERUMBL
UNIVERSITY OF CALIFORNIA AT VALLE SOLEADA
Such manipulations of the geosphere don't exactly go unnoticed.
PABLO'S DELI
But that too is part of the plan.
RUMBLERUMBLERUMBLERUMBL

Officially, this will be described as a moderate **tremblor**, whose epicenter is deep within the crust and far inland.

No big deal in this part of the world.

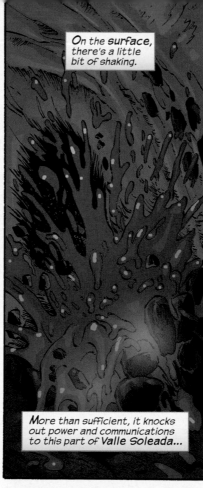

On the **surface**, there's a little bit of shaking.

More than sufficient, it knocks out power and communications to this part of **Valle Soleada**...

...and specifically **disables** the tech-based **security** systems protecting **X-Corp** headquarters.

At the same time, in a **cavern** down below the city...

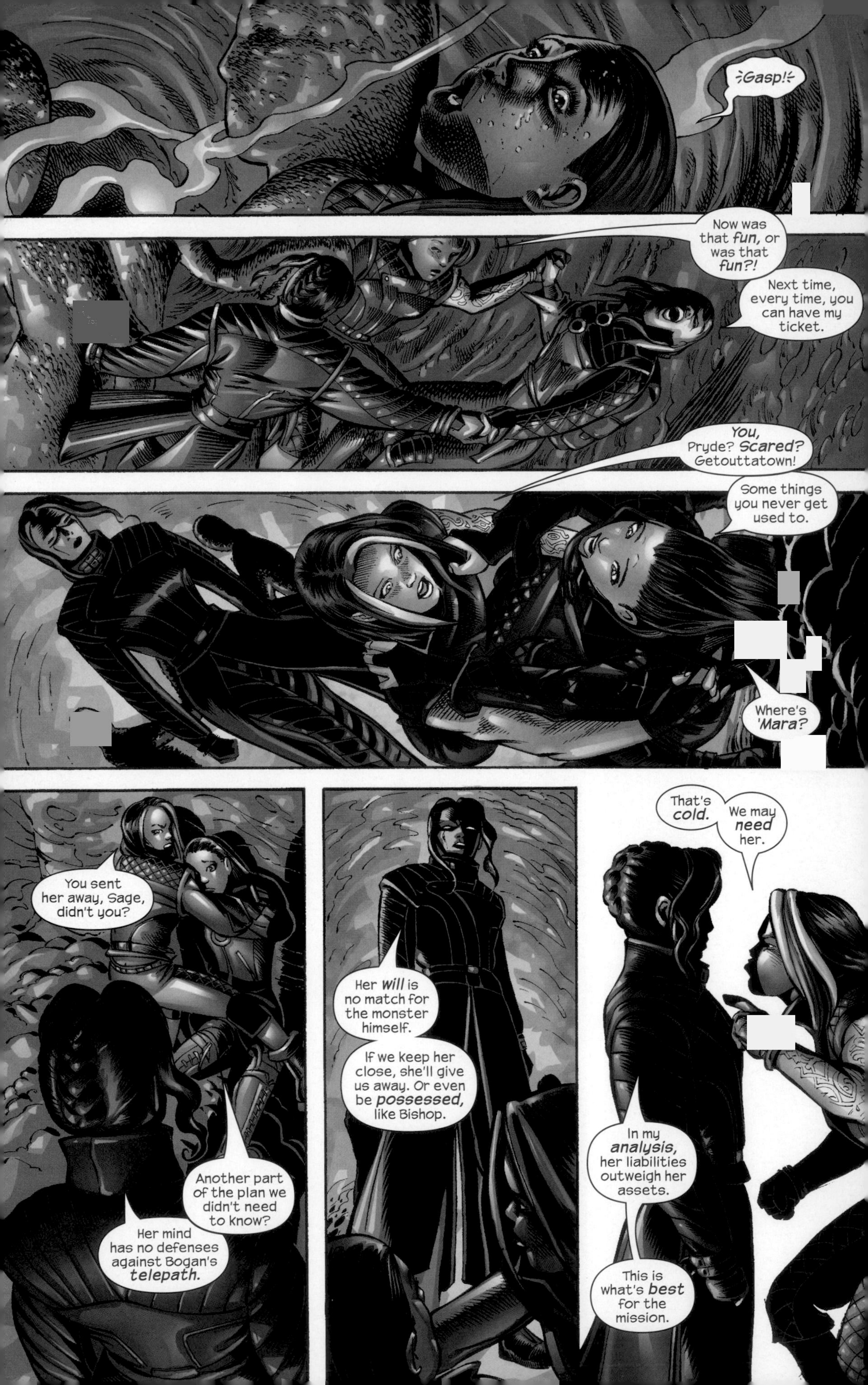
Gasp!
Now was that fun, or was that fun?!
Next time, every time, you can have my ticket.
You, Pryde? Scared? Getouttatown!
Some things you never get used to.
Where's 'Mara?
You sent her away, Sage, didn't you?
Another part of the plan we didn't need to know?
Her mind has no defenses against Bogan's telepath.
Her will is no match for the monster himself.
If we keep her close, she'll give us away. Or even be possessed, like Bishop.
That's cold.
We may need her.
In my analysis, her liabilities outweigh her assets.
This is what's best for the mission.

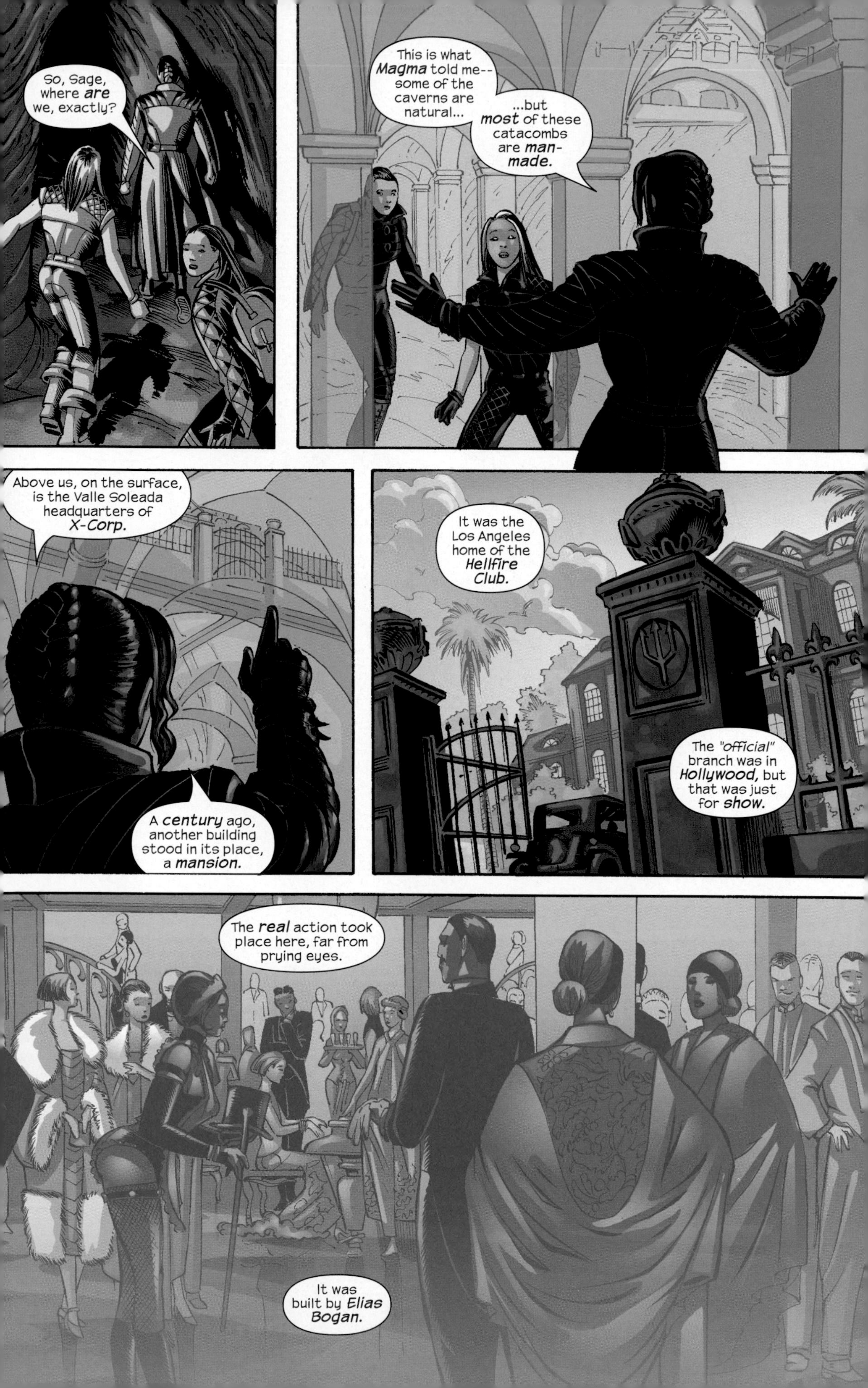
So, Sage, where are we, exactly?
This is what Magma told me-- some of the caverns are natural...
...but most of these catacombs are man-made.
Above us, on the surface, is the Valle Soleada headquarters of X-Corp.
A century ago, another building stood in its place, a mansion.
It was the Los Angeles home of the Hellfire Club.
The "official" branch was in Hollywood, but that was just for show.
The real action took place here, far from prying eyes.
It was built by Elias Bogan.

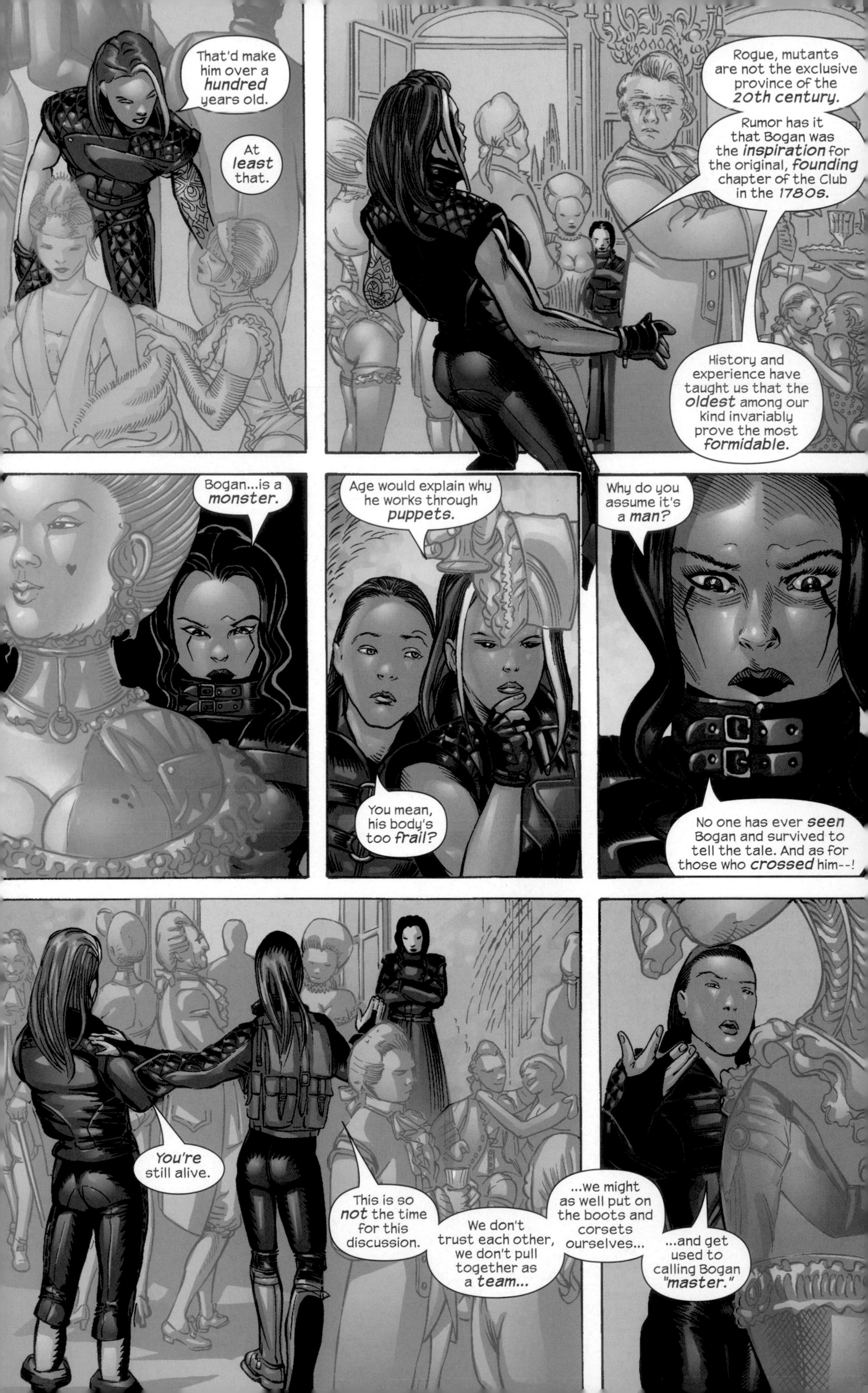
That'd make him over a *hundred* years old.
At *least* that.
Rogue, mutants are not the exclusive province of the *20th century.*
Rumor has it that Bogan was the *inspiration* for the original, *founding* chapter of the Club in the *1780s.*
History and experience have taught us that the *oldest* among our kind invariably prove the most *formidable.*
Bogan...is a *monster.*
Age would explain why he works through *puppets.*
You mean, his body's too *frail?*
Why do you assume it's a *man?*
No one has ever *seen* Bogan and survived to tell the tale. And as for those who *crossed* him--!
You're still alive.
This is so *not* the time for this discussion.
We don't trust each other, we don't pull together as a *team...*
...we might as well put on the boots and corsets ourselves...
...and get used to calling Bogan *"master."*

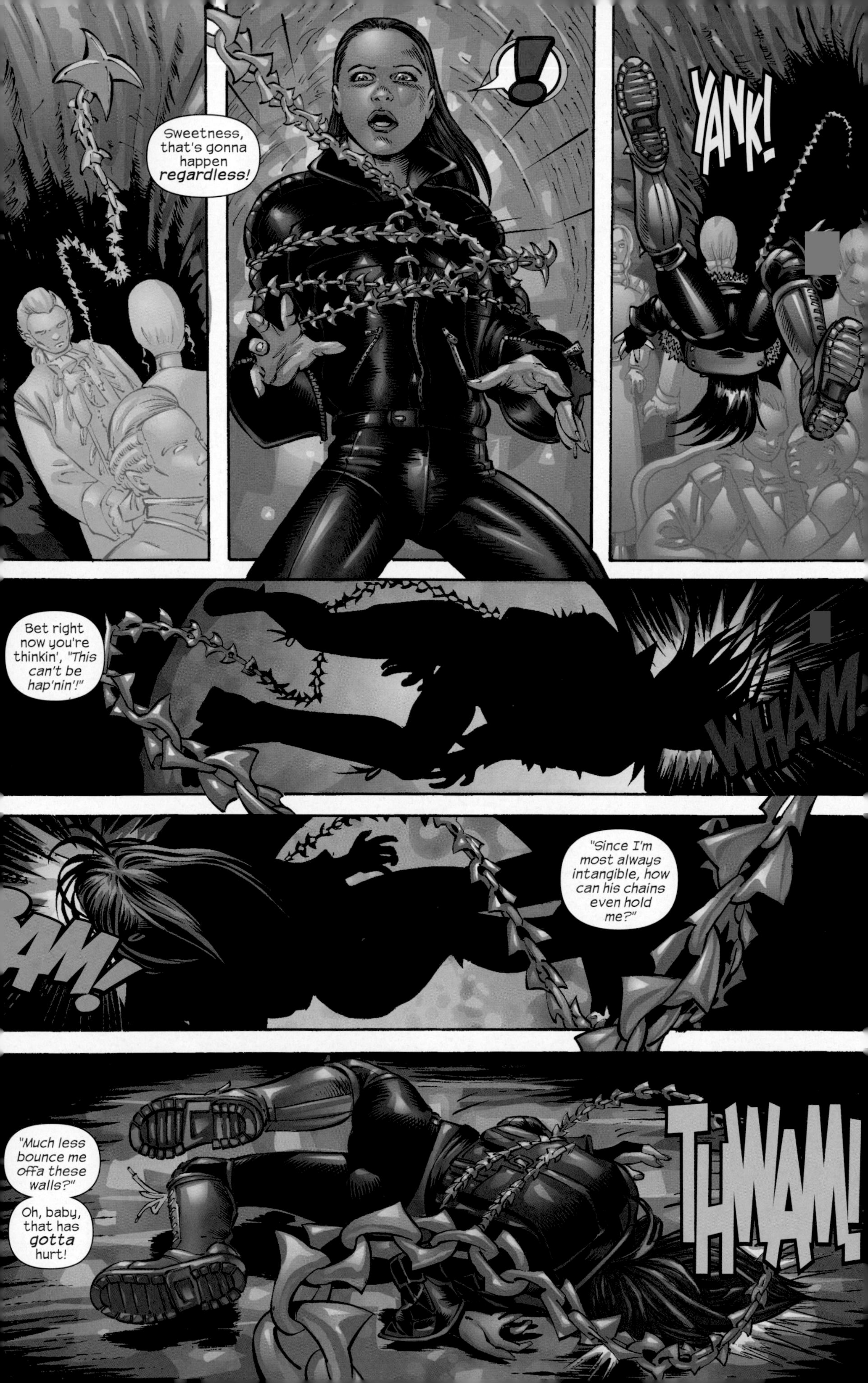
Sweetness, that's gonna happen *regardless!*
!
YANK!
Bet right now you're thinkin', *"This can't be hap'nin'!"*
WHAM
AM!
"Since I'm most always intangible, how can his chains even hold me?"
"Much less bounce me offa these walls?"
Oh, baby, that has ***gotta*** hurt!
THWAM!

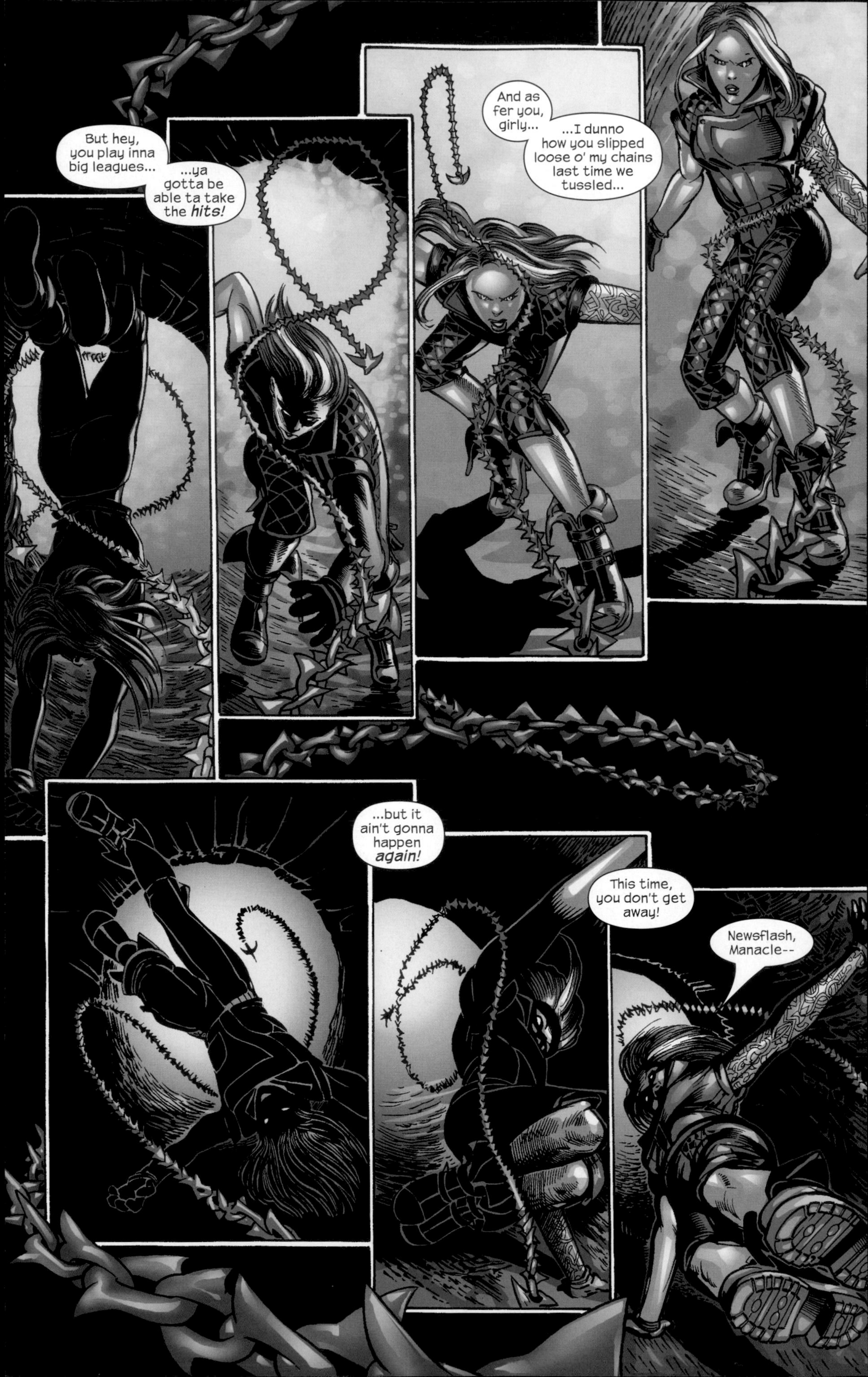
But hey, you play inna big leagues...
...ya gotta be able ta take the *hits!*
And as fer you, girly...
...I dunno how you slipped loose o' my chains last time we tussled...
...but it ain't gonna happen *again!*
This time, you don't get away!
Newsflash, Manacle--

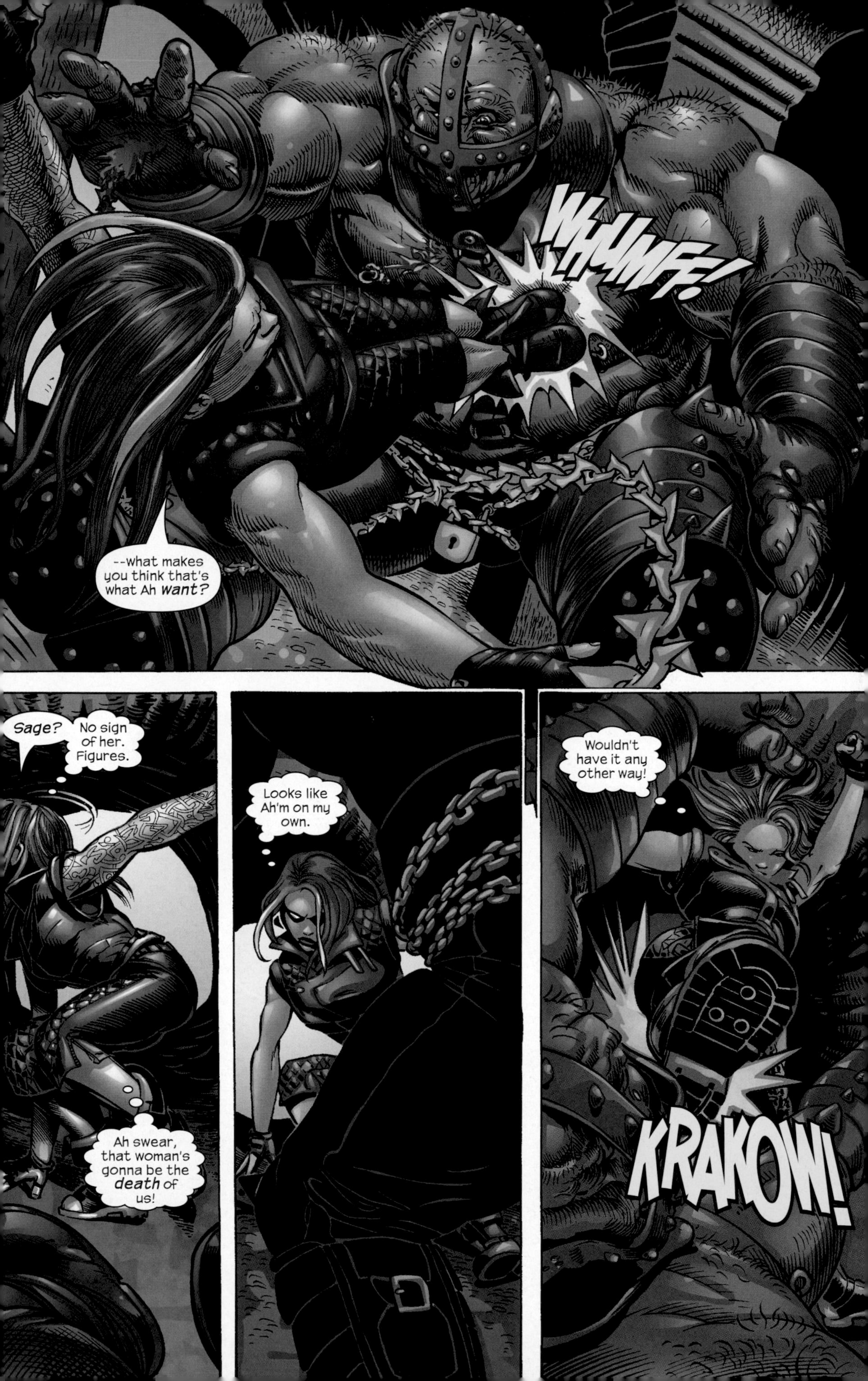

WHUMFF!
--what makes you think that's what Ah *want?*
Sage?
No sign of her. Figures.
Ah swear, that woman's gonna be the *death* of us!
Looks like Ah'm on my own.
Wouldn't have it any other way!
KRAKOW!

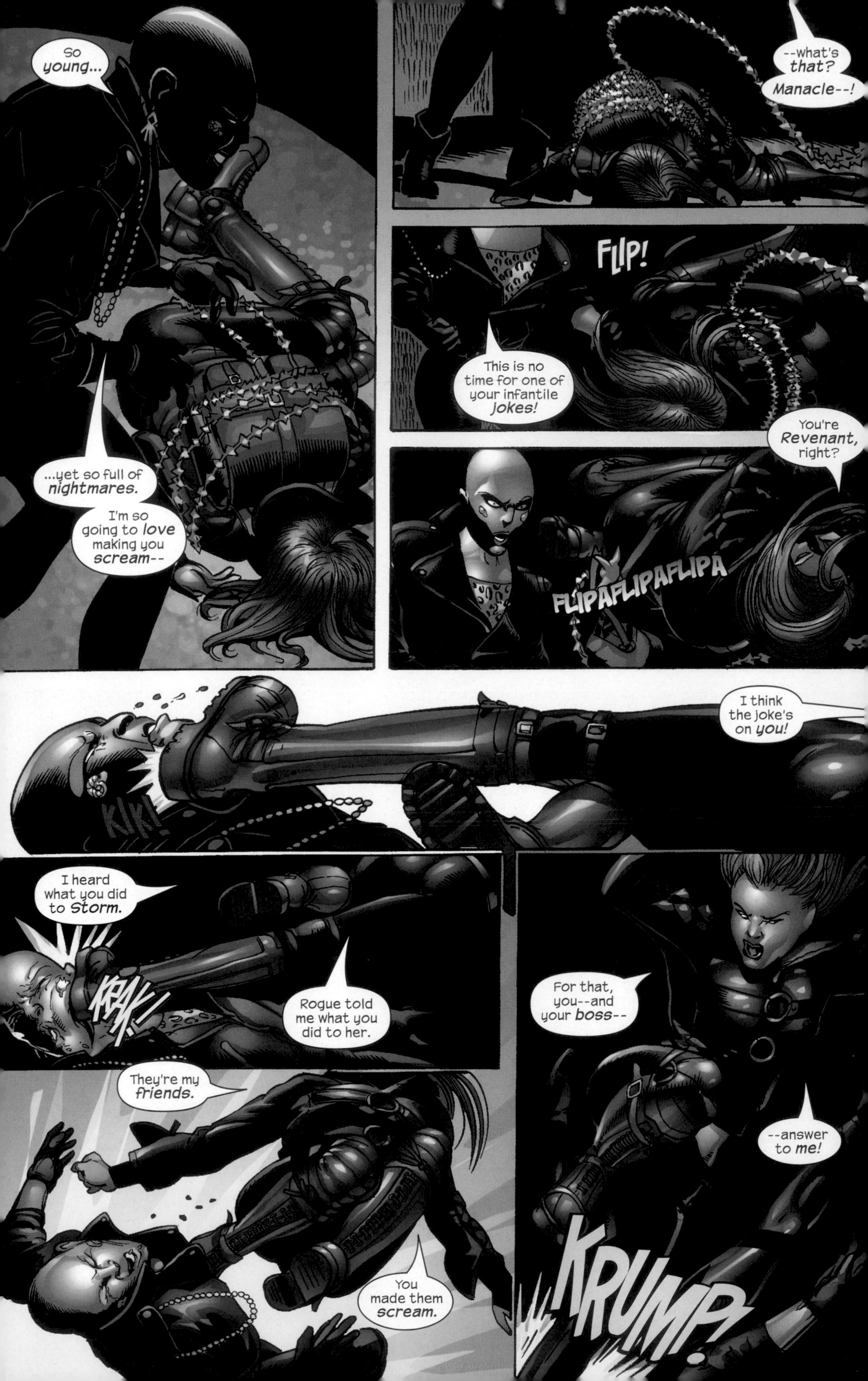
So young...
...yet so full of nightmares.
I'm so going to love making you scream--
--what's that? Manacle--!
FLIP!
This is no time for one of your infantile jokes!
You're Revenant, right?
FLIPAFLIPAFLIPA
I think the joke's on you!
KIK!
I heard what you did to Storm.
KRAK!
Rogue told me what you did to her.
They're my friends.
You made them scream.
For that, you--and your boss--
--answer to me!
KRUMP!

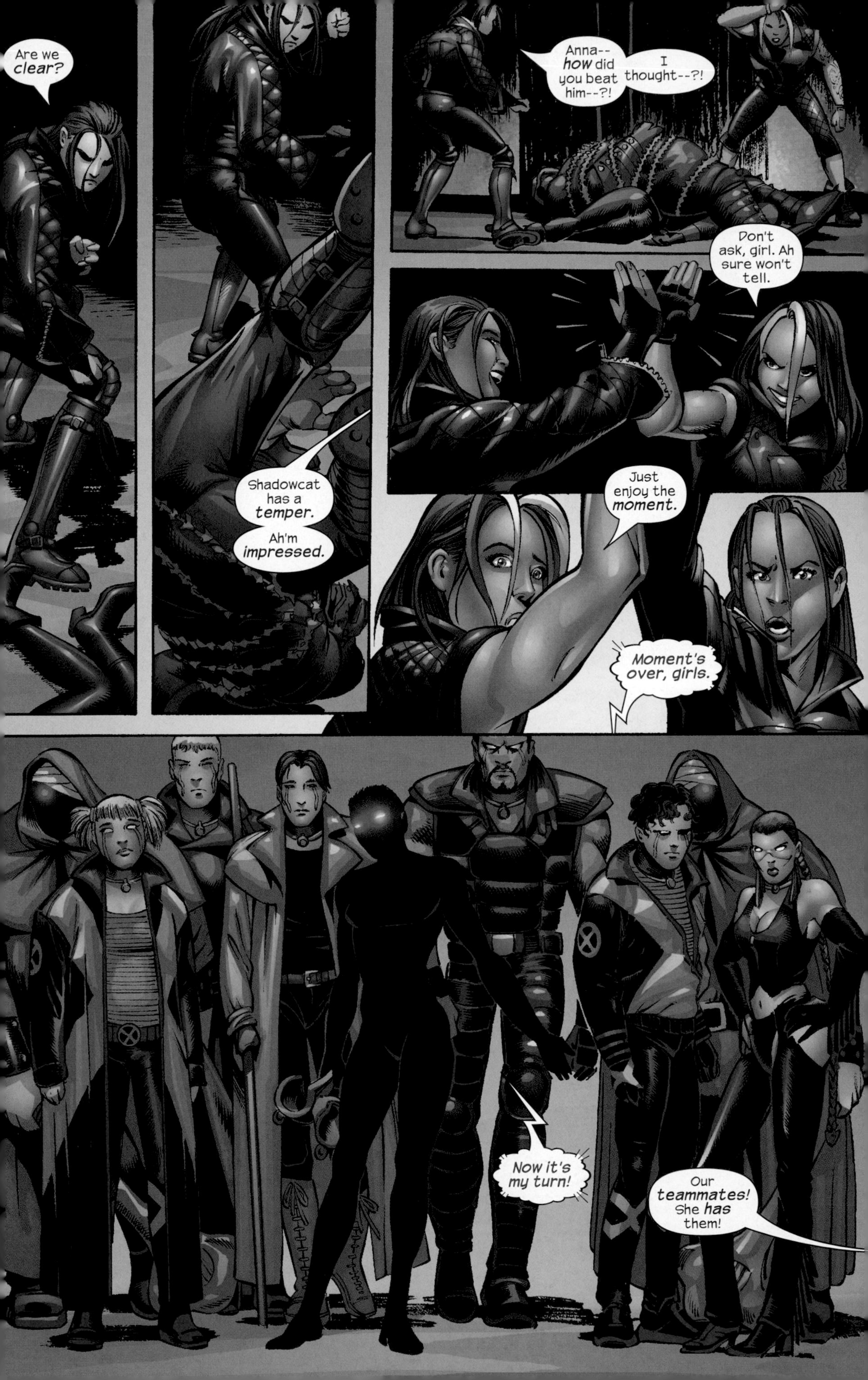
Are we clear?
Anna-- how did you beat him--?!
I thought--?!
Don't ask, girl. Ah sure won't tell.
Shadowcat has a temper.
Ah'm impressed.
Just enjoy the moment.
Moment's over, girls.
Now it's my turn!
Our teammates! She has them!

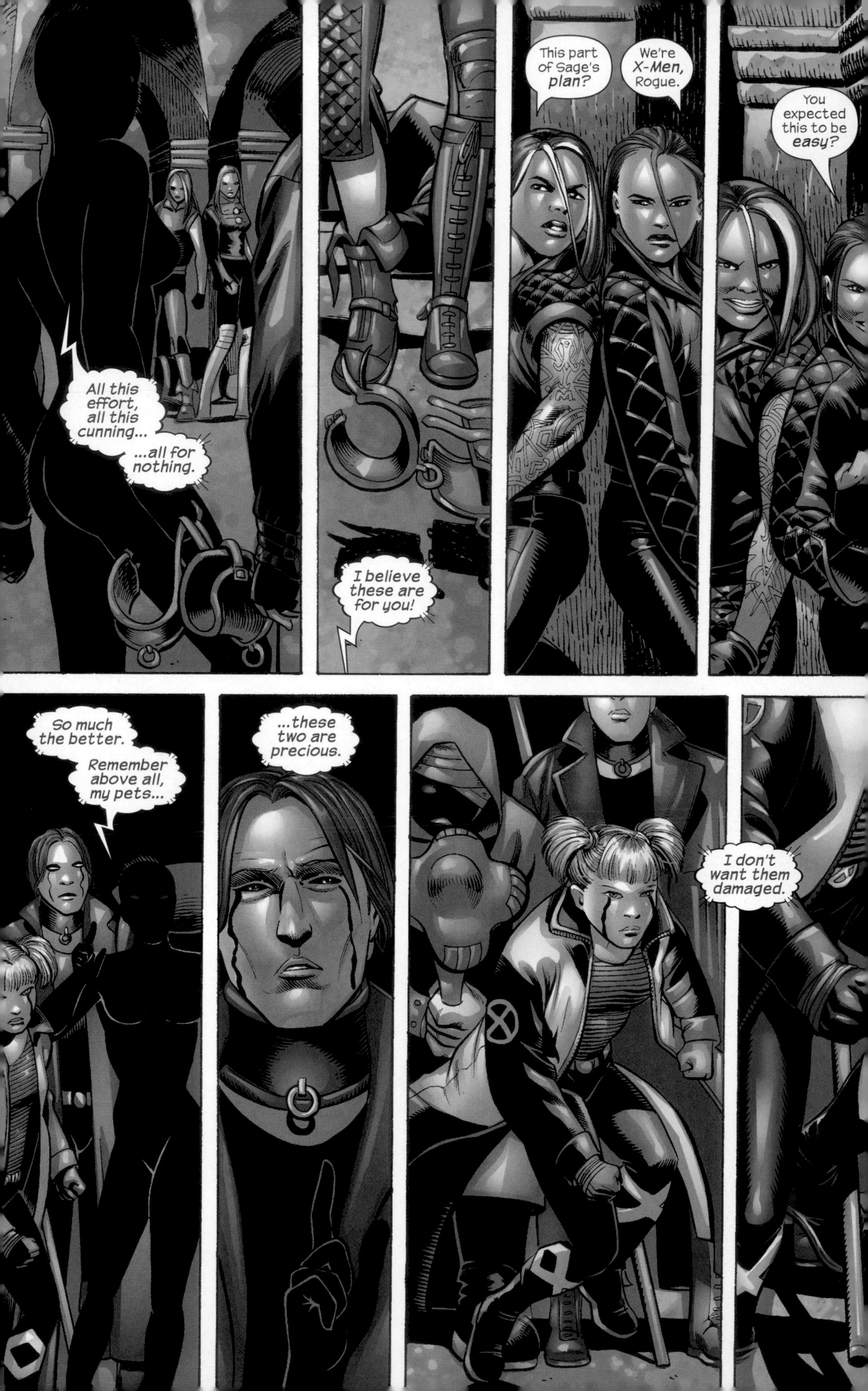
All this effort, all this cunning...
...all for nothing.
I believe these are for you!
This part of Sage's *plan?*
We're *X-Men,* Rogue.
You expected this to be *easy?*
So much the better.
Remember above all, my pets...
...these two are precious.
I don't want them damaged.

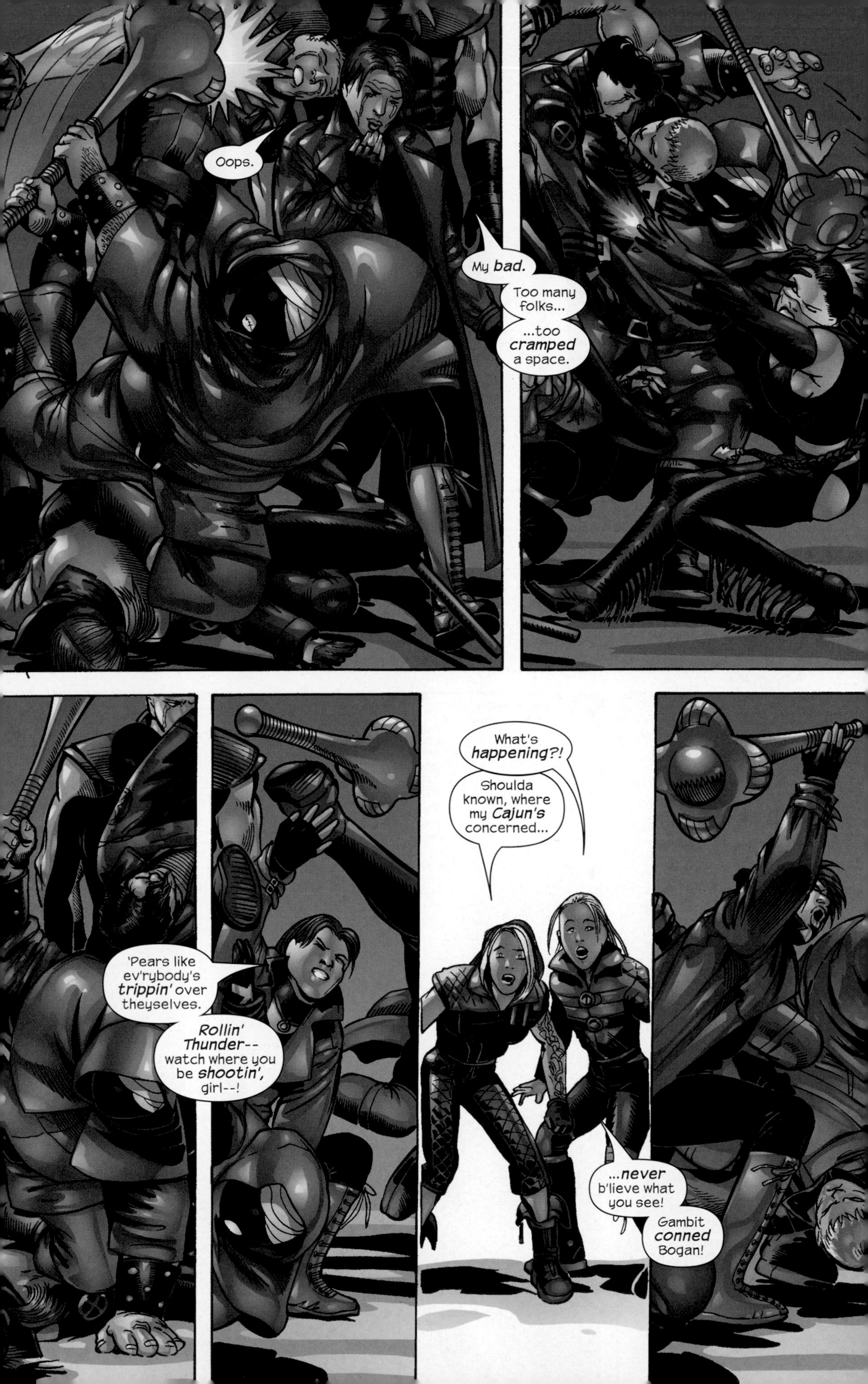
Oops.
My bad.
Too many folks...
...too cramped a space.
'Pears like ev'rybody's trippin' over theyselves.
Rollin' Thunder--watch where you be shootin', girl--!
What's happening?!
Shoulda known, where my Cajun's concerned...
...never b'lieve what you see!
Gambit conned Bogan!

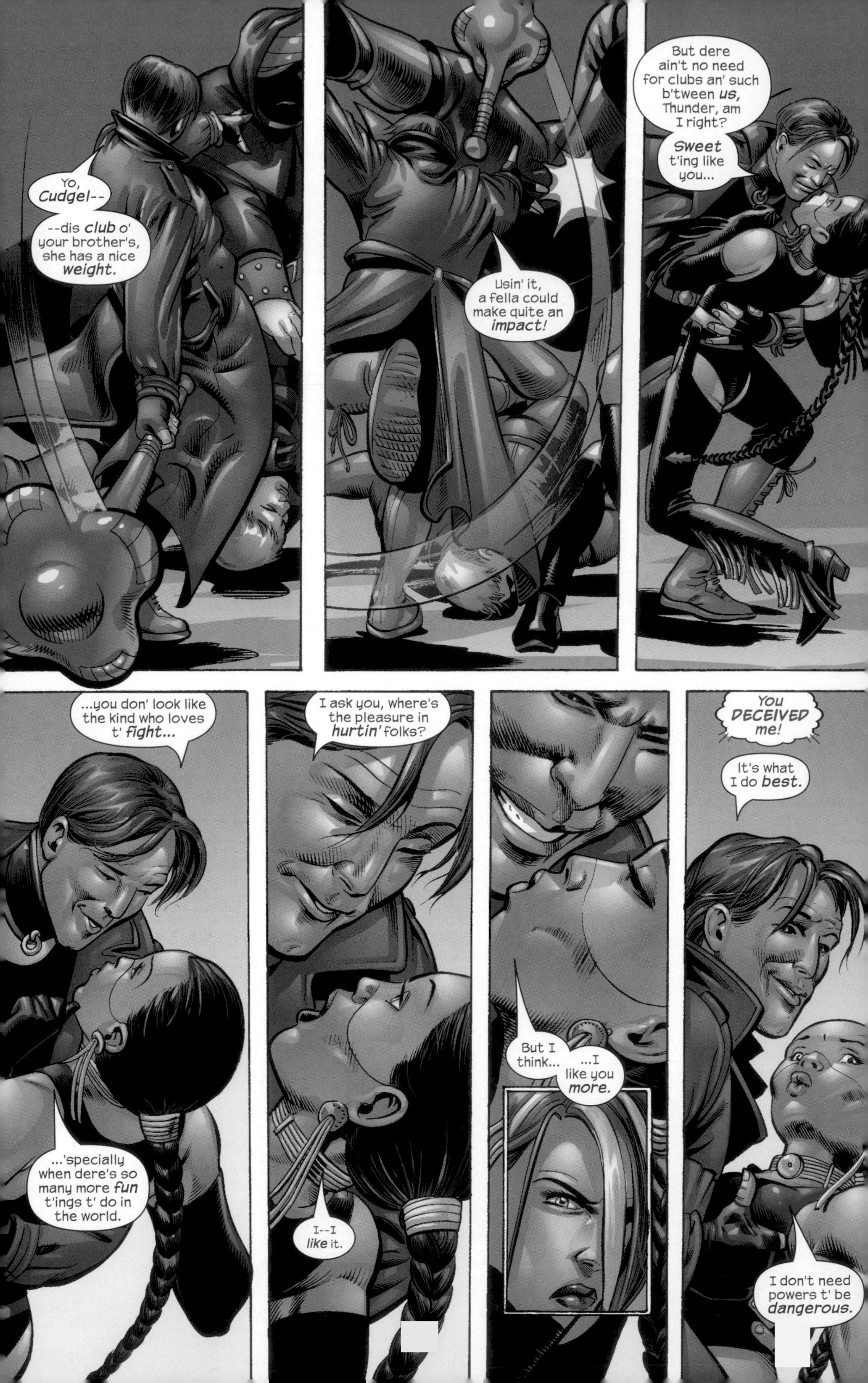
Yo, Cudgel--
--dis club o' your brother's, she has a nice weight.
Usin' it, a fella could make quite an impact!
But dere ain't no need for clubs an' such b'tween us, Thunder, am I right?
Sweet t'ing like you...
...you don' look like the kind who loves t' fight...
...'specially when dere's so many more fun t'ings t' do in the world.
I ask you, where's the pleasure in hurtin' folks?
I--I like it.
But I think...
...I like you more.
You DECEIVED me!
It's what I do best.
I don't need powers t' be dangerous.

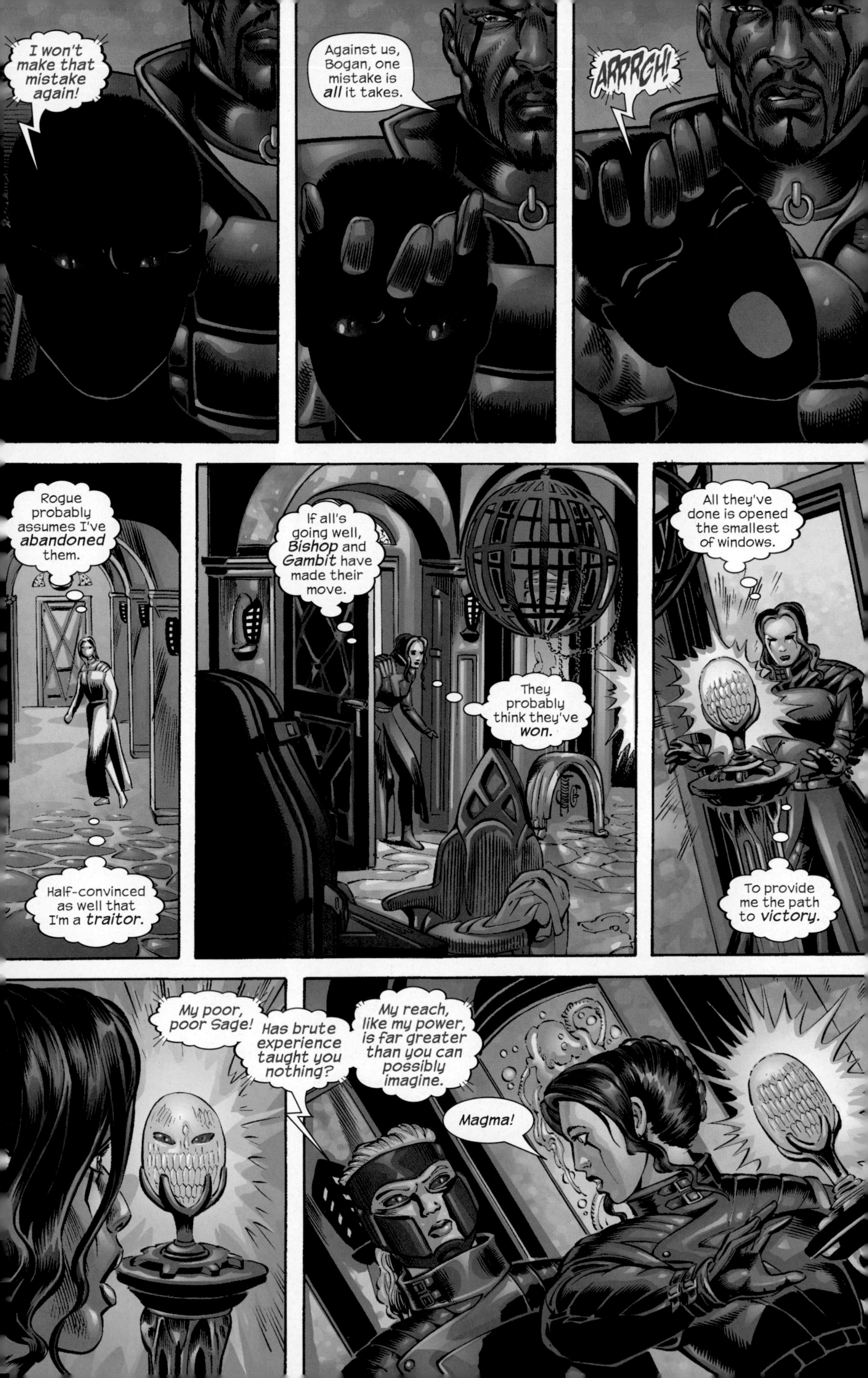
I won't make that mistake again!
Against us, Bogan, one mistake is *all* it takes.
ARRRGH!
Rogue probably assumes I've *abandoned* them.
Half-convinced as well that I'm a *traitor*.
If all's going well, *Bishop* and *Gambit* have made their move.
They probably think they've *won*.
All they've done is opened the smallest of windows.
To provide me the path to *victory*.
My poor, poor Sage!
Has brute experience taught you nothing?
My reach, like my power, is far greater than you can possibly imagine.
Magma!

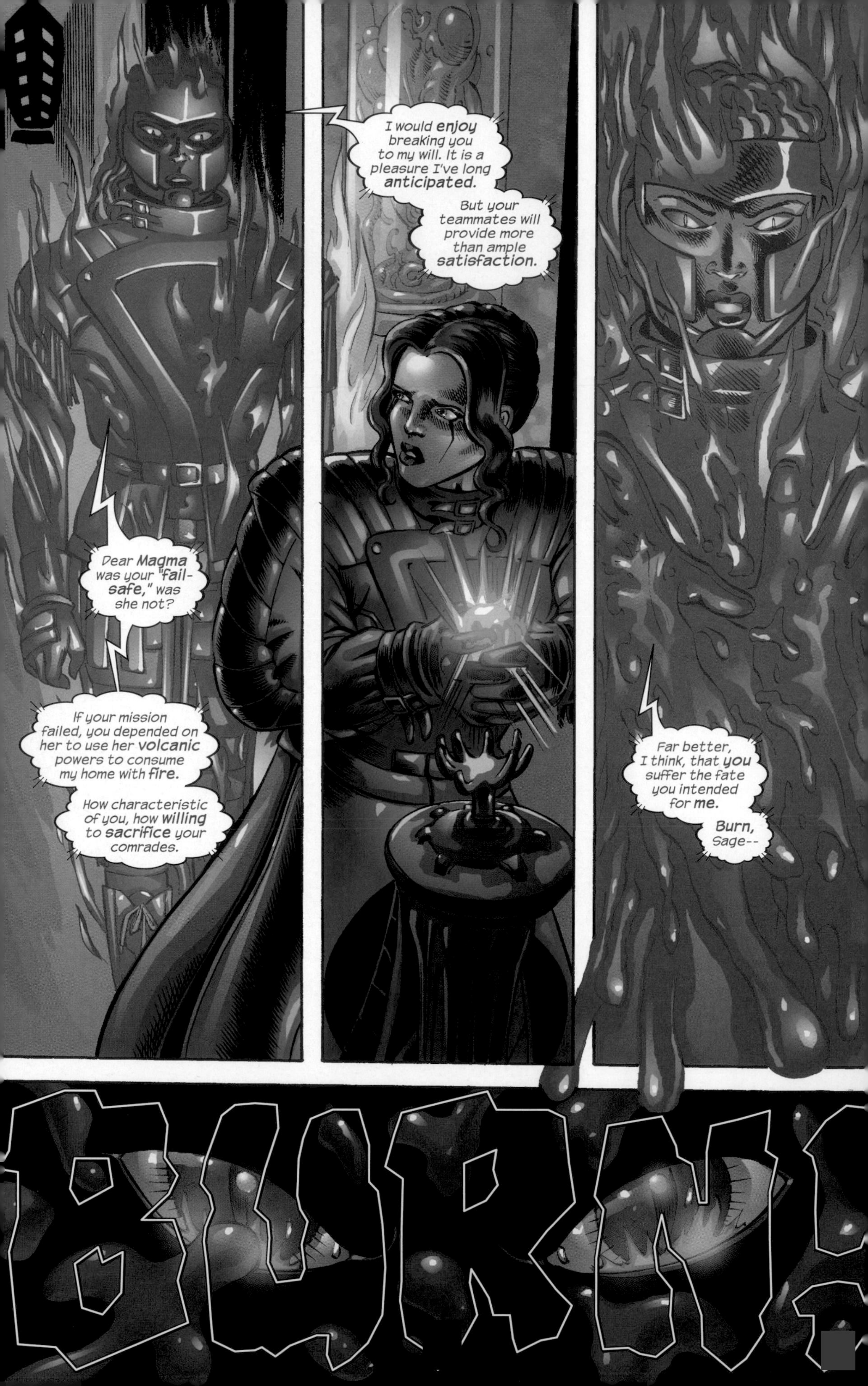
I would enjoy breaking you to my will. It is a pleasure I've long anticipated.
But your teammates will provide more than ample satisfaction.
Dear Magma was your "fail-safe," was she not?
If your mission failed, you depended on her to use her volcanic powers to consume my home with fire.
How characteristic of you, how willing to sacrifice your comrades.
Far better, I think, that you suffer the fate you intended for me.
Burn, Sage--
BURN!

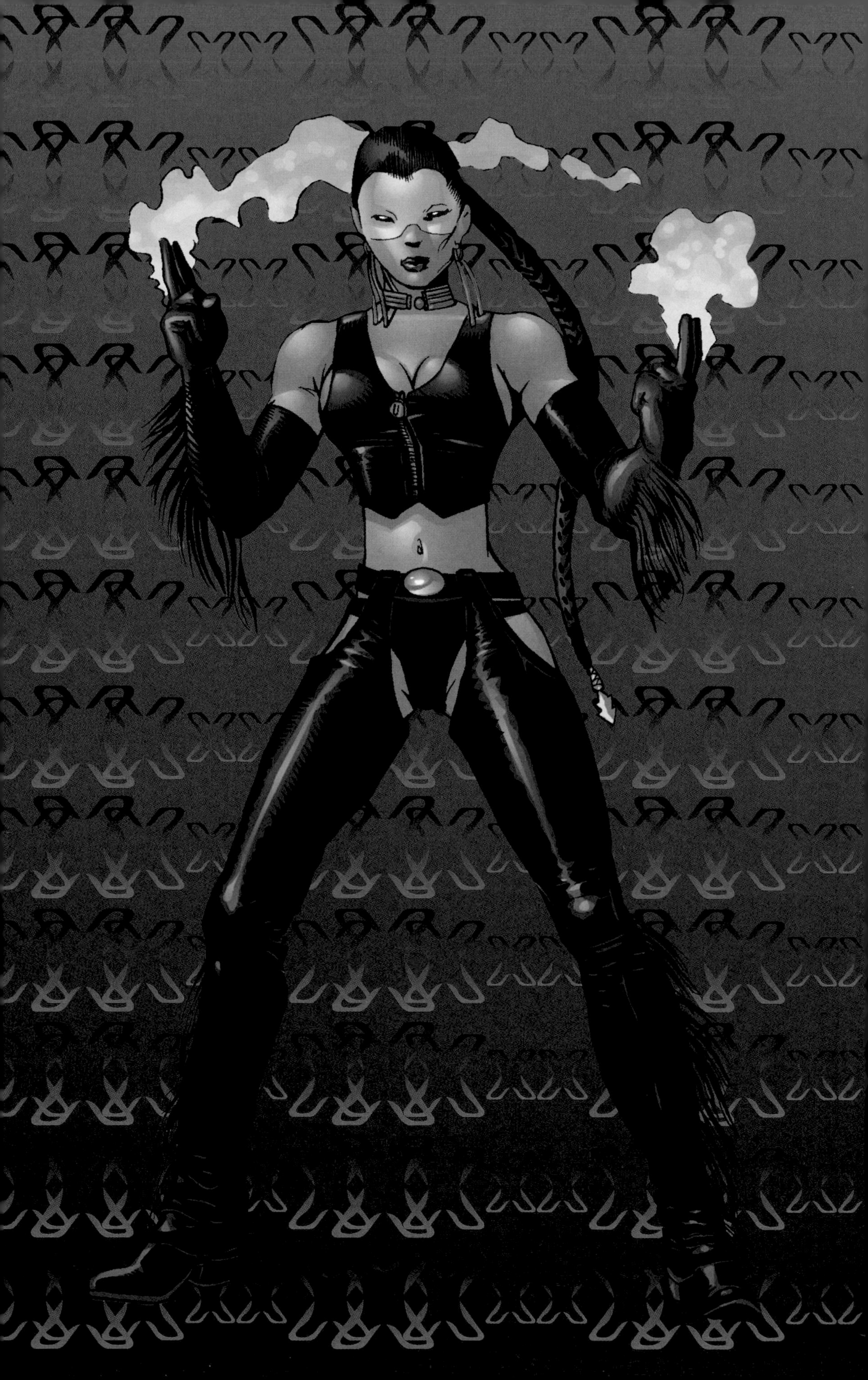

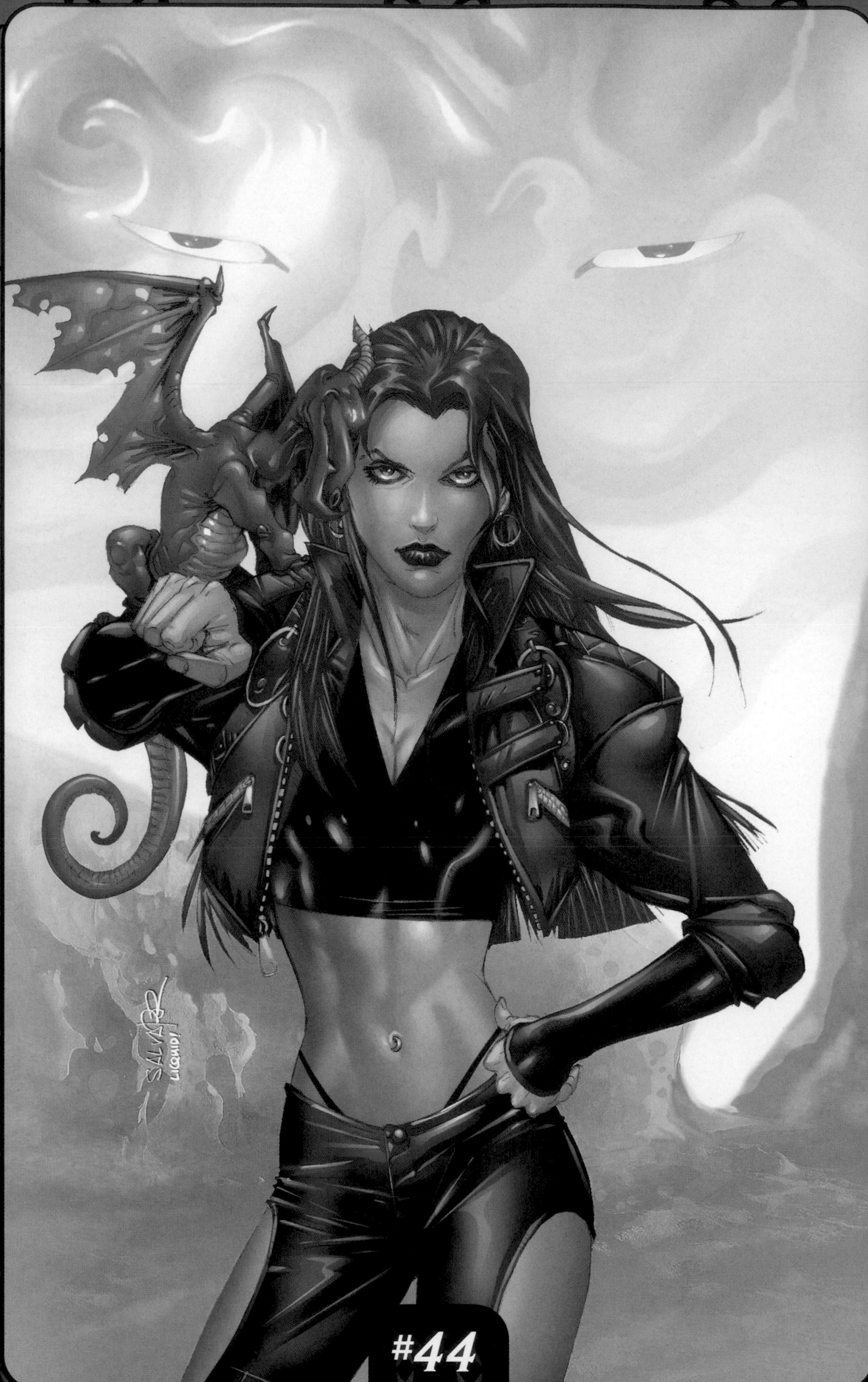
#44

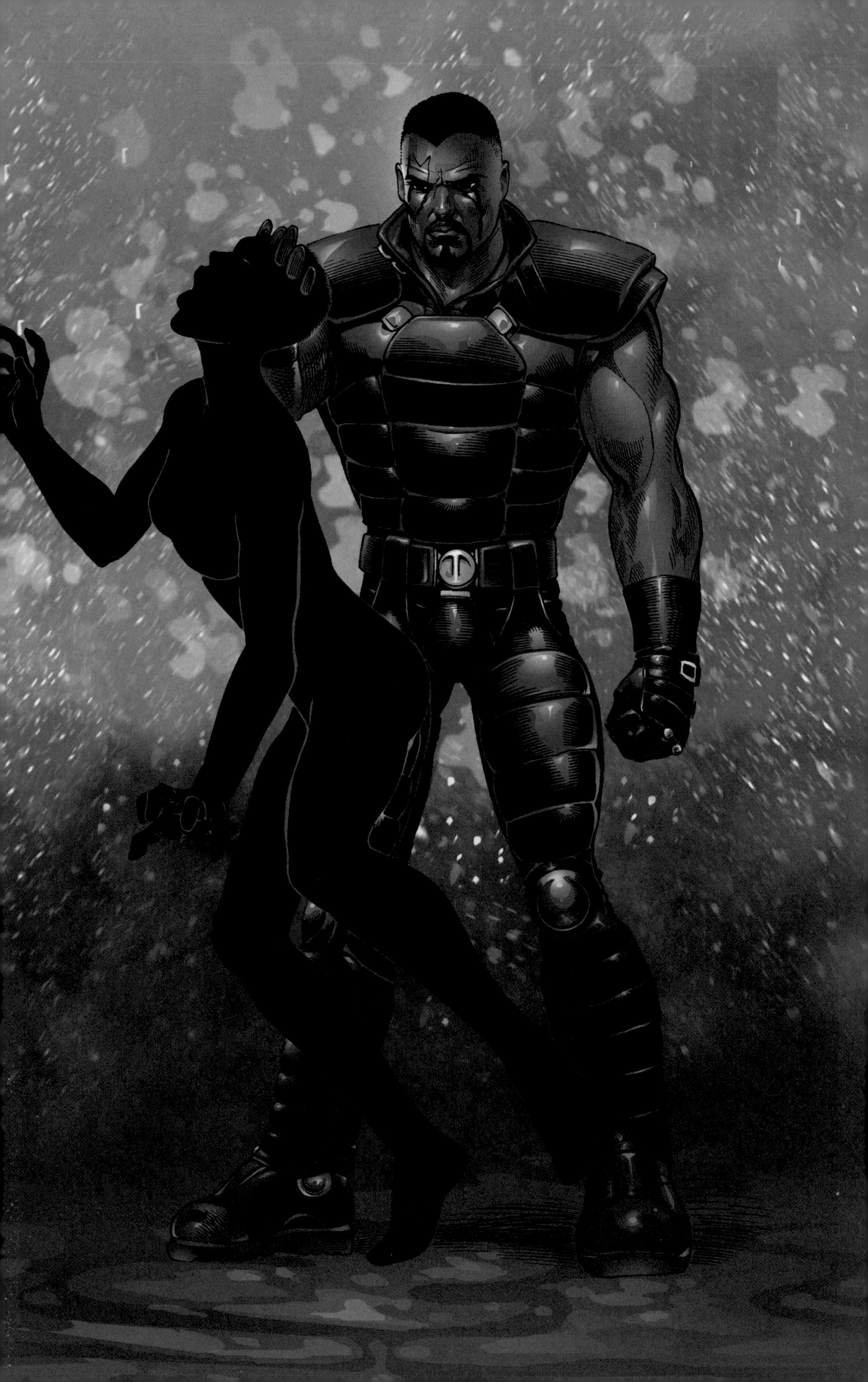

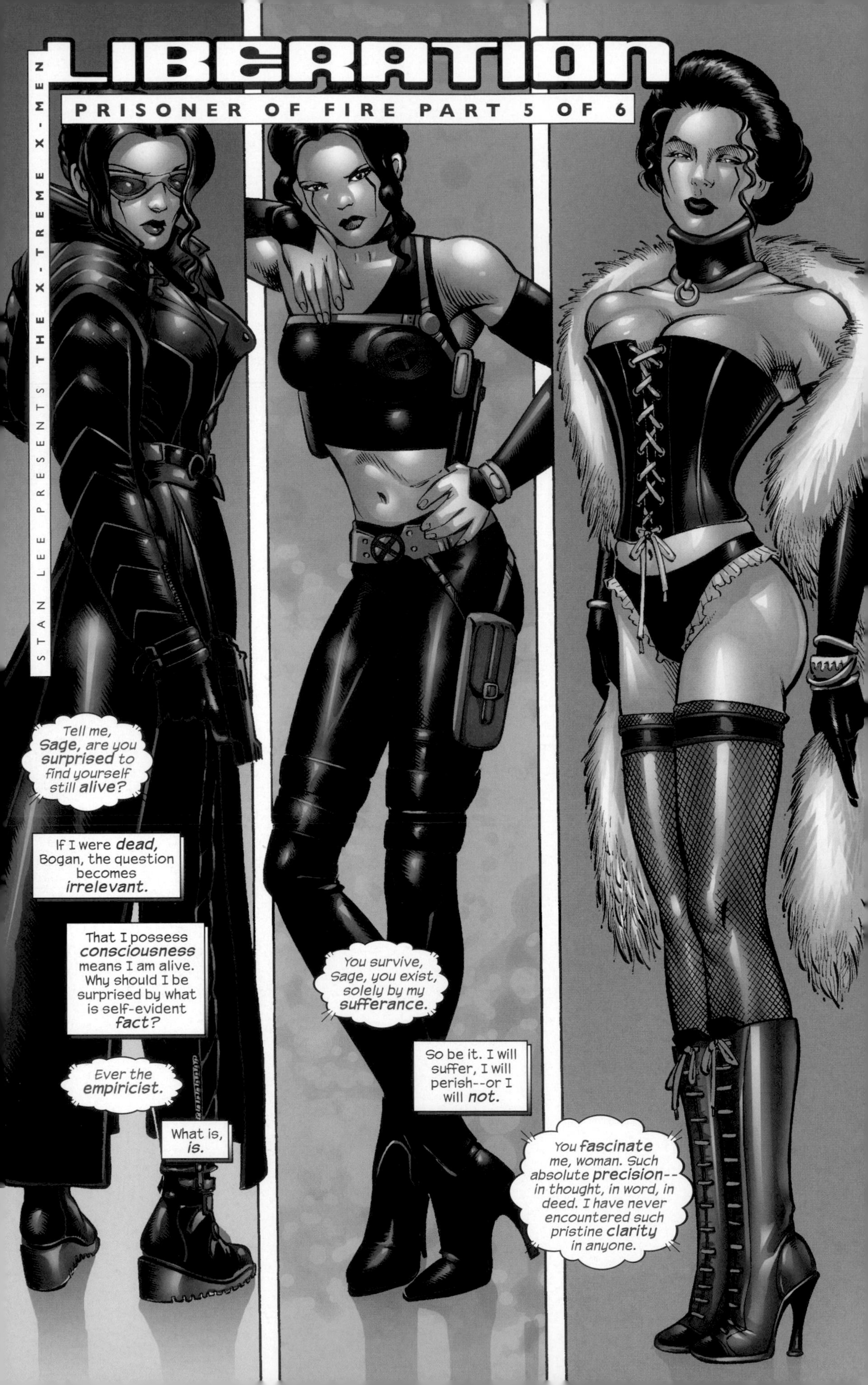
STAN LEE PRESENTS THE X-TREME X-MEN
LIBERATION
PRISONER OF FIRE PART 5 OF 6
Tell me, Sage, are you surprised to find yourself still alive?
If I were dead, Bogan, the question becomes irrelevant.
That I possess consciousness means I am alive. Why should I be surprised by what is self-evident fact?
Ever the empiricist.
What is, is.
You survive, Sage, you exist, solely by my sufferance.
So be it. I will suffer, I will perish--or I will not.
You fascinate me, woman. Such absolute precision--in thought, in word, in deed. I have never encountered such pristine clarity in anyone.

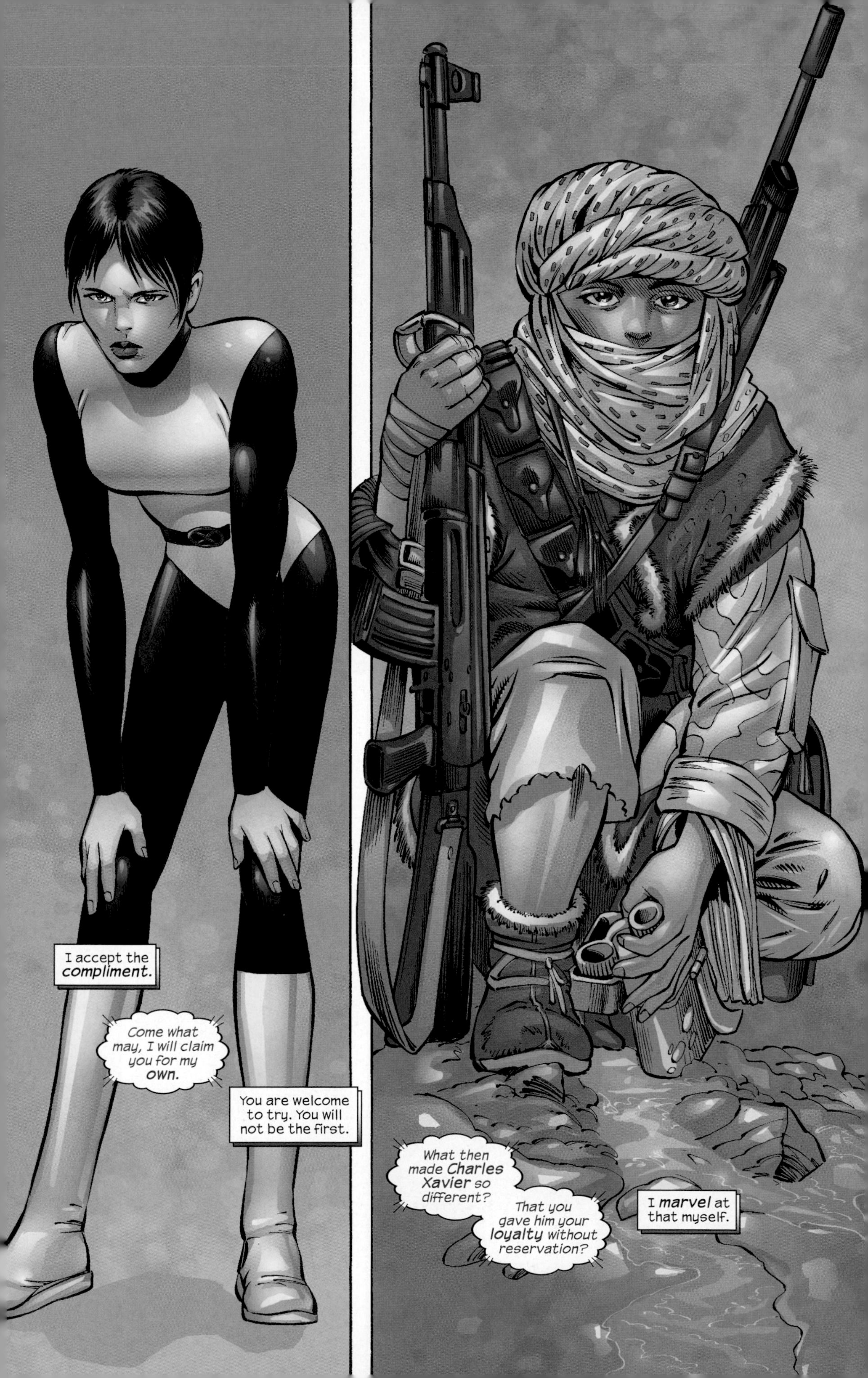

I accept the compliment.
Come what may, I will claim you for my own.
You are welcome to try. You will not be the first.
What then made Charles Xavier so different?
That you gave him your loyalty without reservation?
I marvel at that myself.

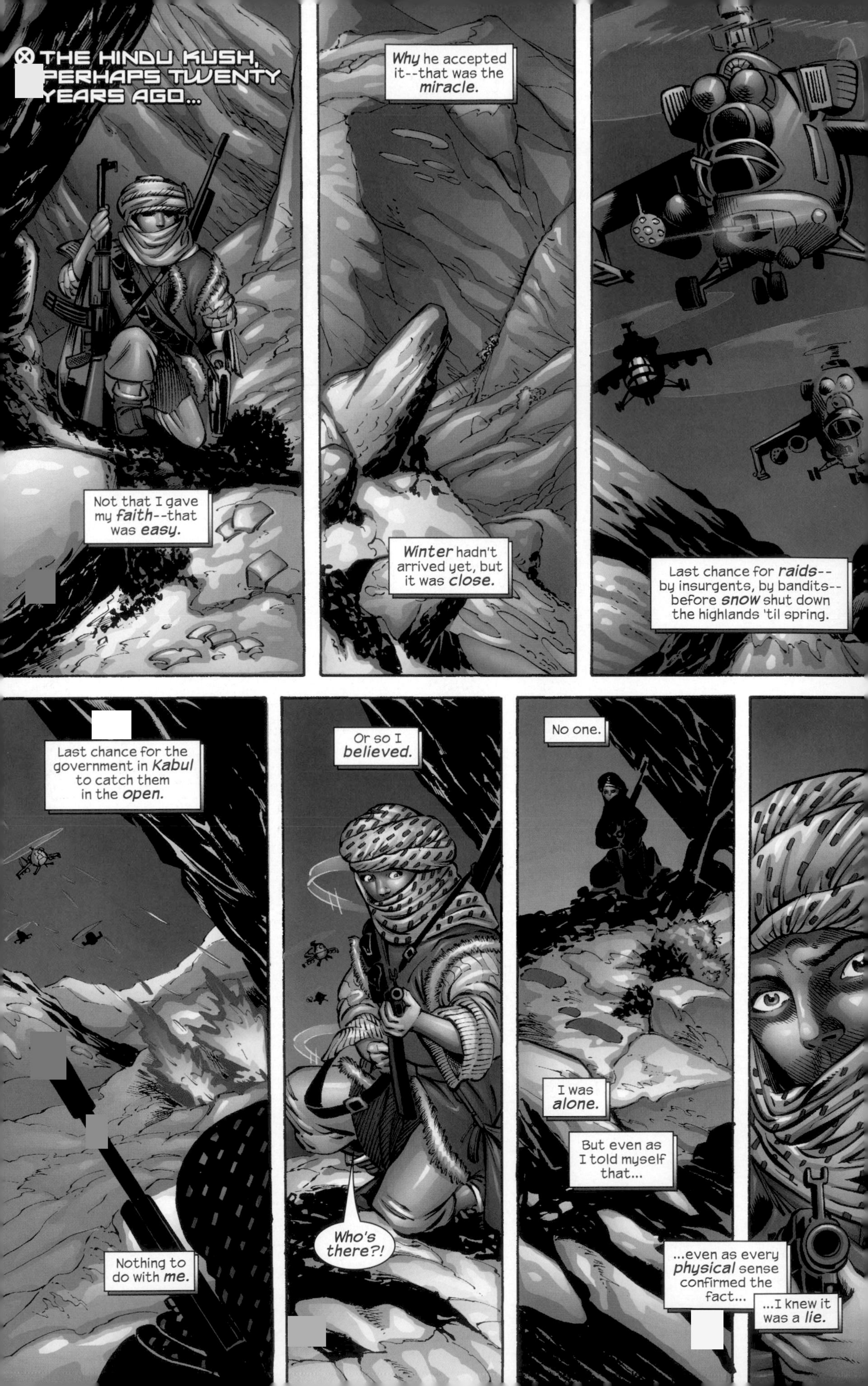
THE HINDU KUSH, PERHAPS TWENTY YEARS AGO...
Not that I gave my faith--that was easy.
Why he accepted it--that was the miracle.
Winter hadn't arrived yet, but it was close.
Last chance for raids--by insurgents, by bandits--before snow shut down the highlands 'til spring.
Last chance for the government in Kabul to catch them in the open.
Nothing to do with me.
Or so I believed.
Who's there?!
No one.
I was alone.
But even as I told myself that...
...even as every physical sense confirmed the fact...
...I knew it was a lie.

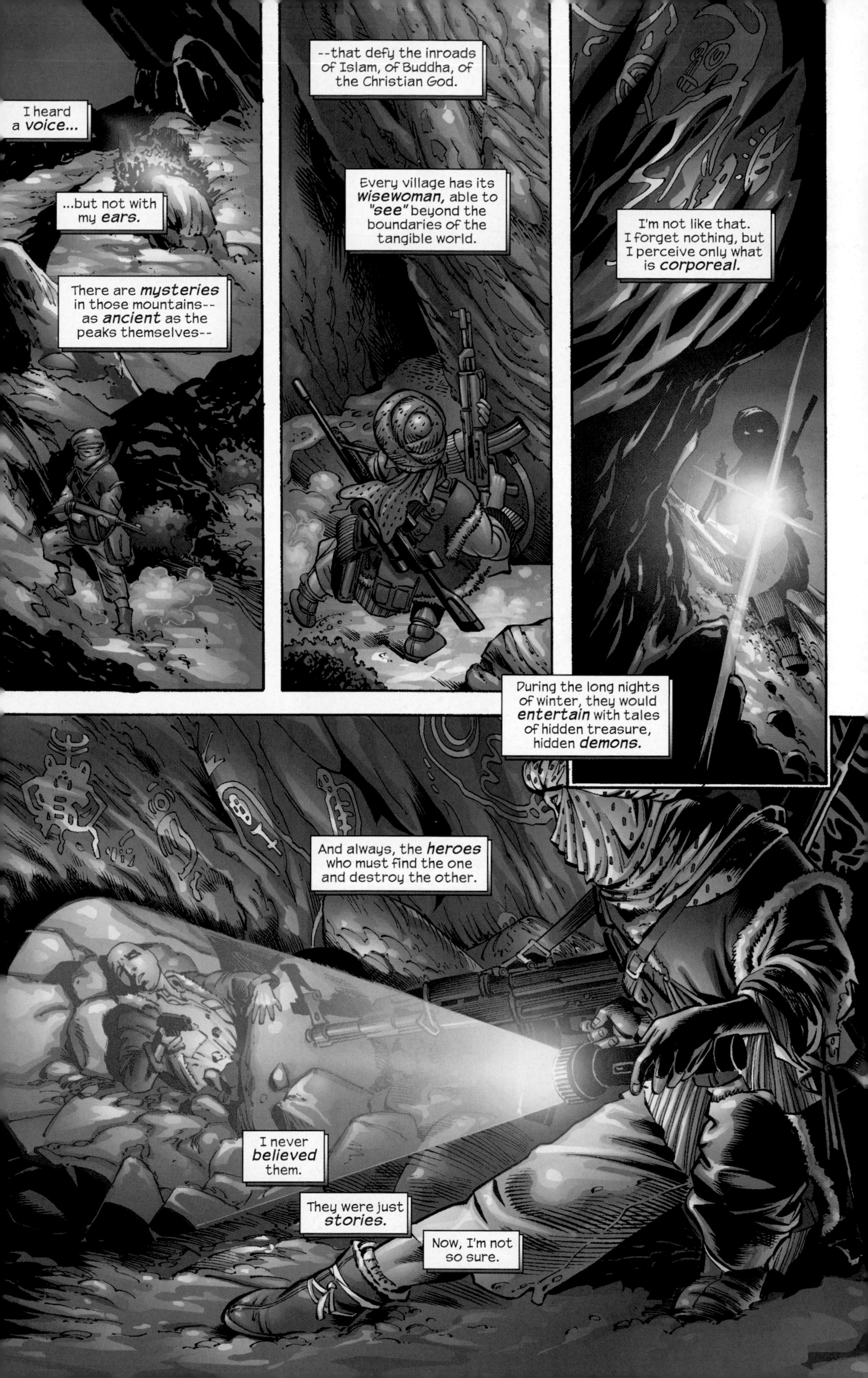

I heard a *voice...*
...but not with my *ears.*
There are *mysteries* in those mountains-- as *ancient* as the peaks themselves--
--that defy the inroads of Islam, of Buddha, of the Christian God.
Every village has its *wisewoman,* able to *"see"* beyond the boundaries of the tangible world.
I'm not like that. I forget nothing, but I perceive only what is *corporeal.*
During the long nights of winter, they would *entertain* with tales of hidden treasure, hidden *demons.*
And always, the *heroes* who must find the one and destroy the other.
I never *believed* them.
They were just *stories.*
Now, I'm not so sure.

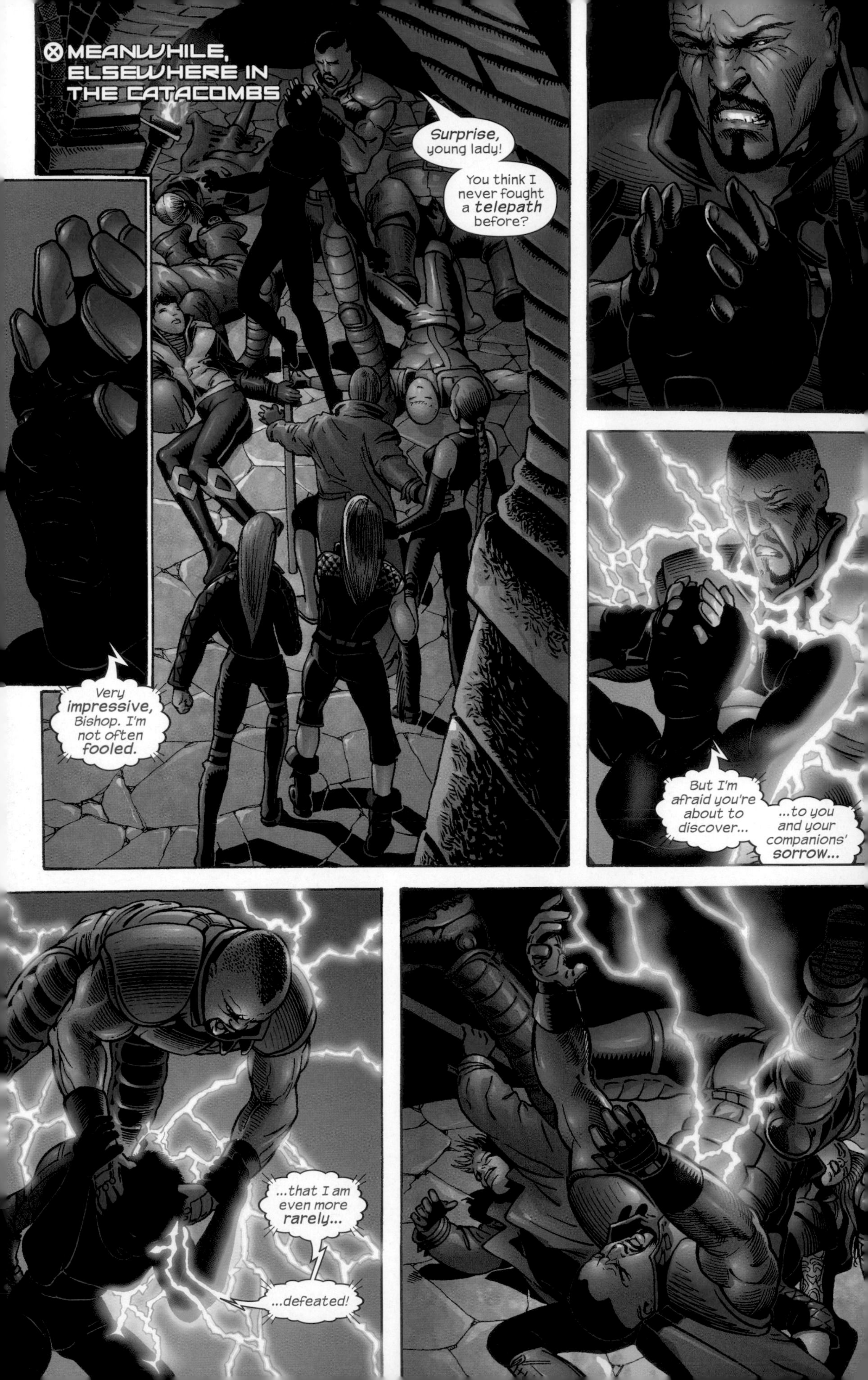
MEANWHILE, ELSEWHERE IN THE CATACOMBS
Surprise, young lady!
You think I never fought a telepath before?
Very impressive, Bishop. I'm not often fooled.
But I'm afraid you're about to discover...
...to you and your companions' sorrow...
...that I am even more rarely...
...defeated!

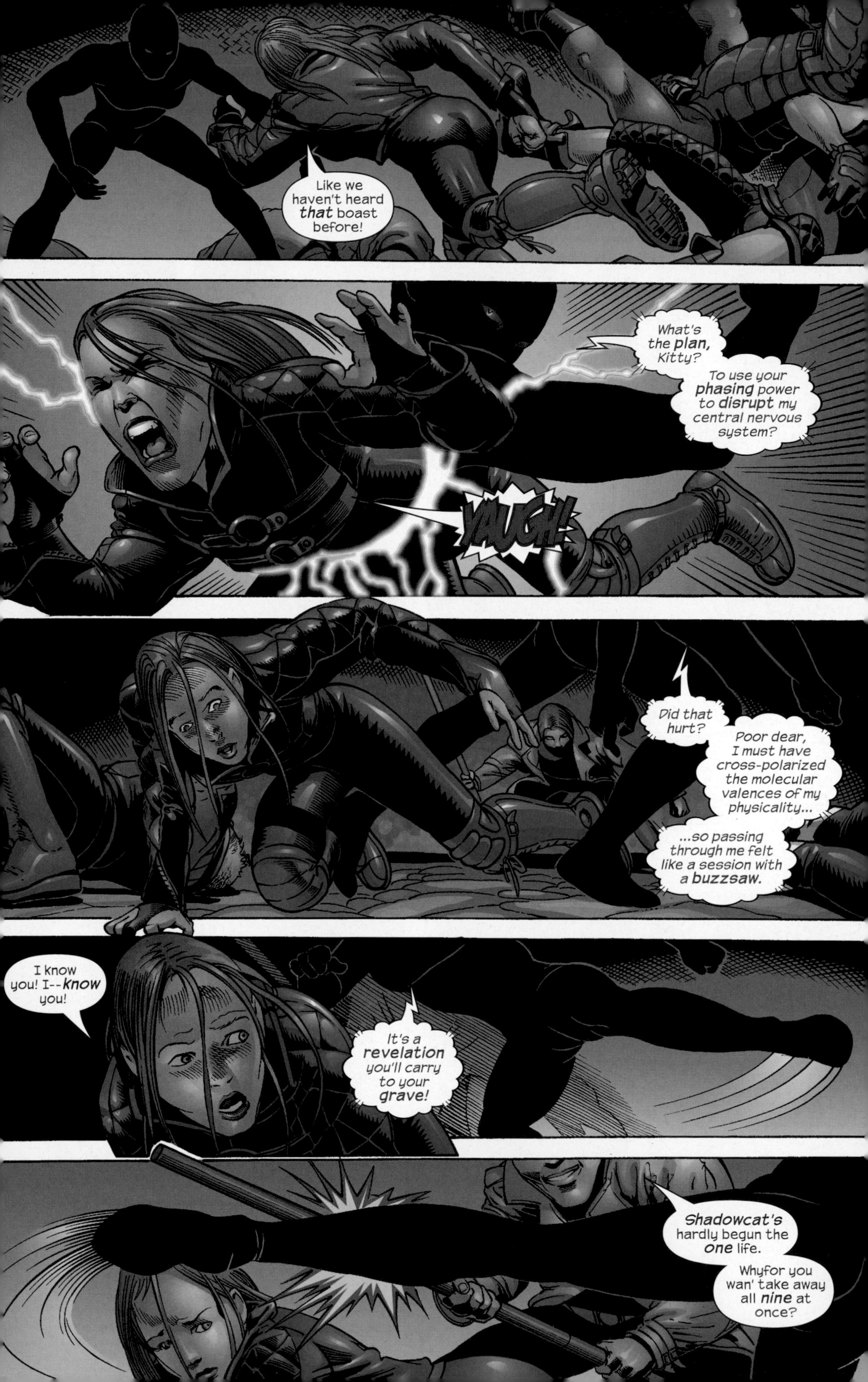

Like we haven't heard *that* boast before!
What's the **plan,** Kitty?
To use your **phasing** power to **disrupt** my central nervous system?
YAUGH!
Did that hurt?
Poor dear, I must have cross-polarized the molecular valences of my physicality...
...so passing through me felt like a session with a **buzzsaw.**
I know you! I--**know** you!
It's a **revelation** you'll carry to your **grave!**
Shadowcat's hardly begun the *one* life.
Whyfor you wan' take away all *nine* at once?

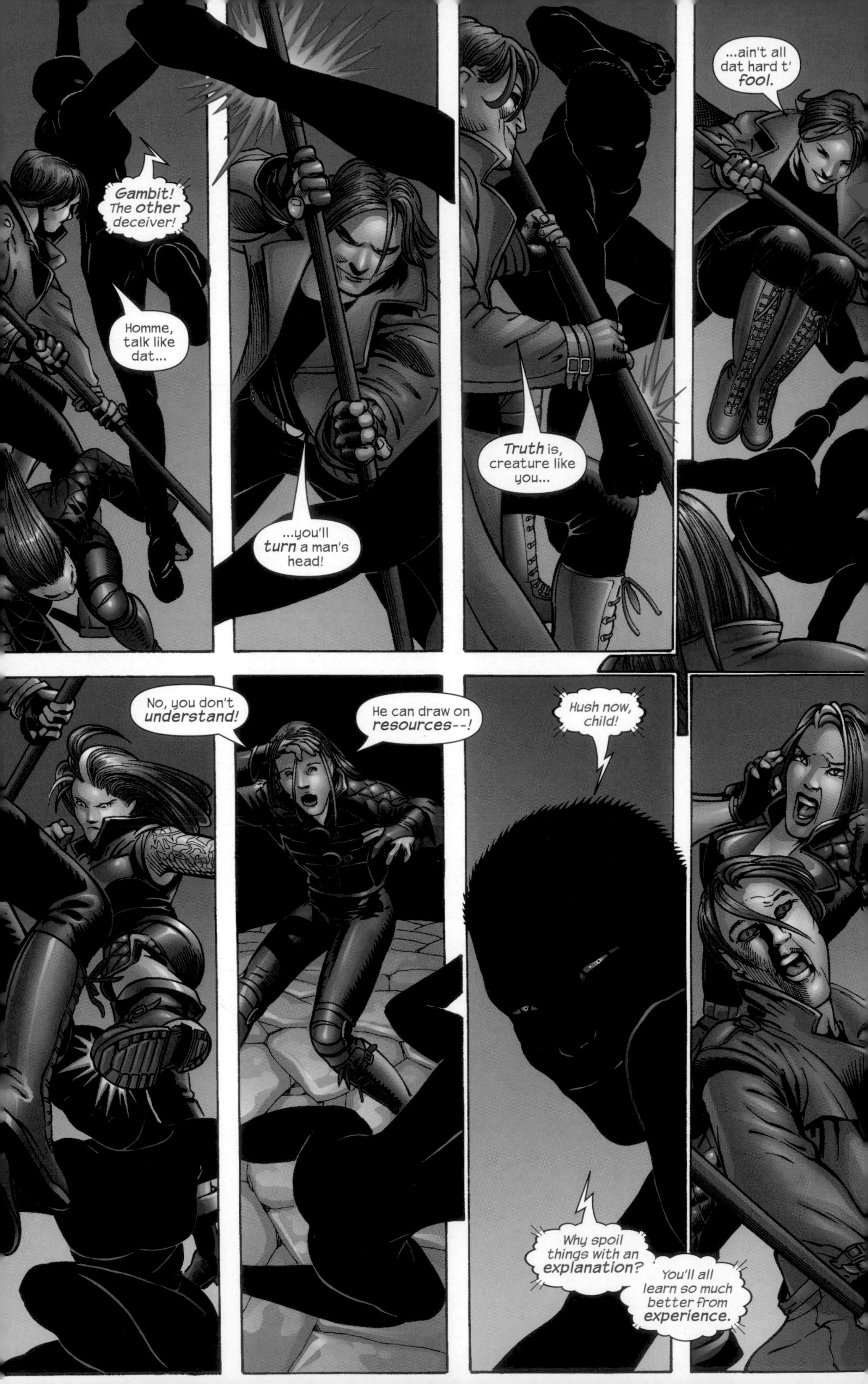
Gambit! The other deceiver!
Homme, talk like dat...
...you'll turn a man's head!
Truth is, creature like you...
...ain't all dat hard t' fool.
No, you don't understand!
He can draw on resources--!
Hush now, child!
Why spoil things with an explanation?
You'll all learn so much better from experience.

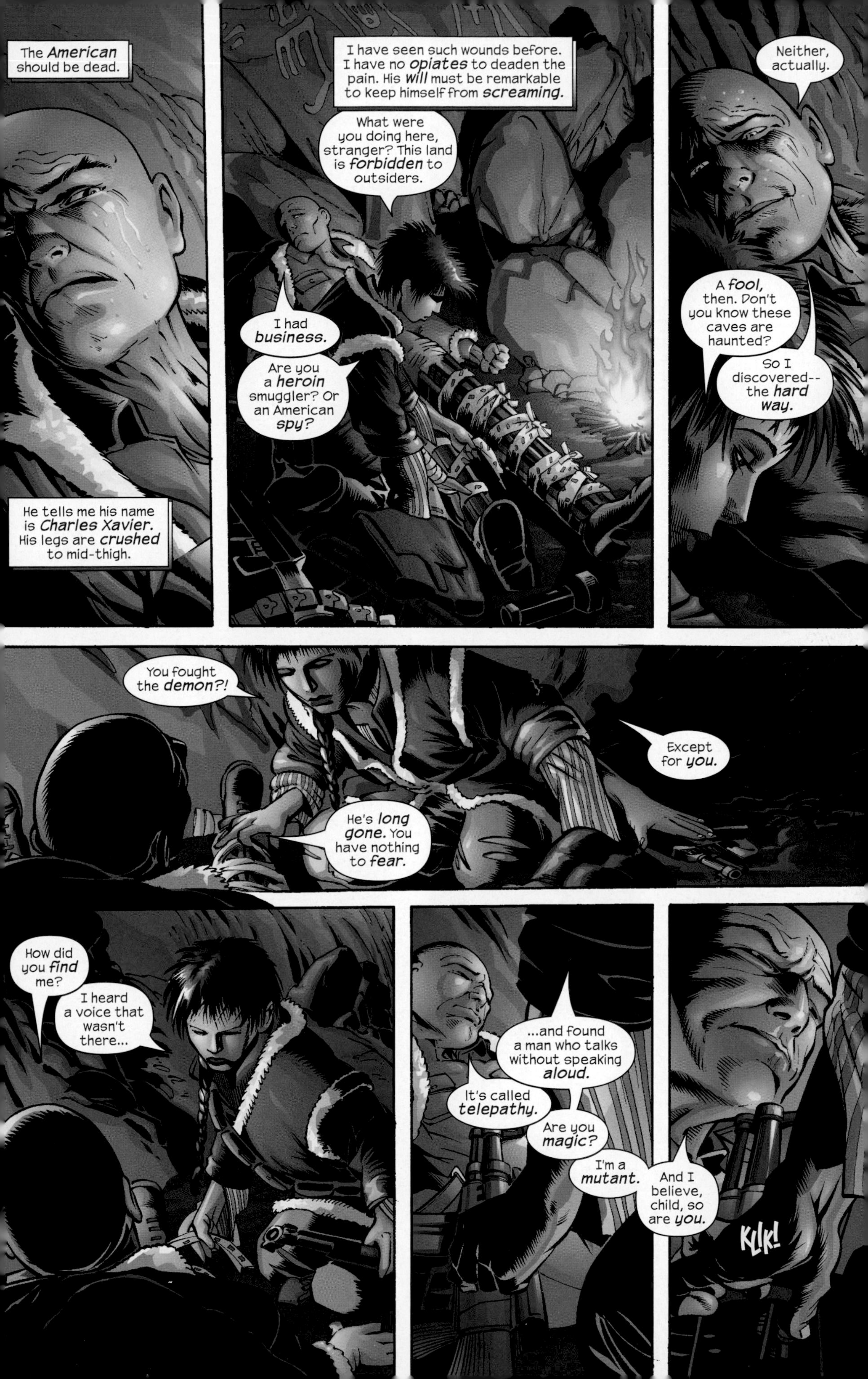
The American should be dead.
He tells me his name is Charles Xavier. His legs are crushed to mid-thigh.
I have seen such wounds before. I have no opiates to deaden the pain. His will must be remarkable to keep himself from screaming.
What were you doing here, stranger? This land is forbidden to outsiders.
I had business.
Are you a heroin smuggler? Or an American spy?
Neither, actually.
A fool, then. Don't you know these caves are haunted?
So I discovered-- the hard way.
You fought the demon?!
Except for you.
He's long gone. You have nothing to fear.
How did you find me?
I heard a voice that wasn't there...
...and found a man who talks without speaking aloud.
It's called telepathy.
Are you magic?
I'm a mutant.
And I believe, child, so are you.
KLIK!

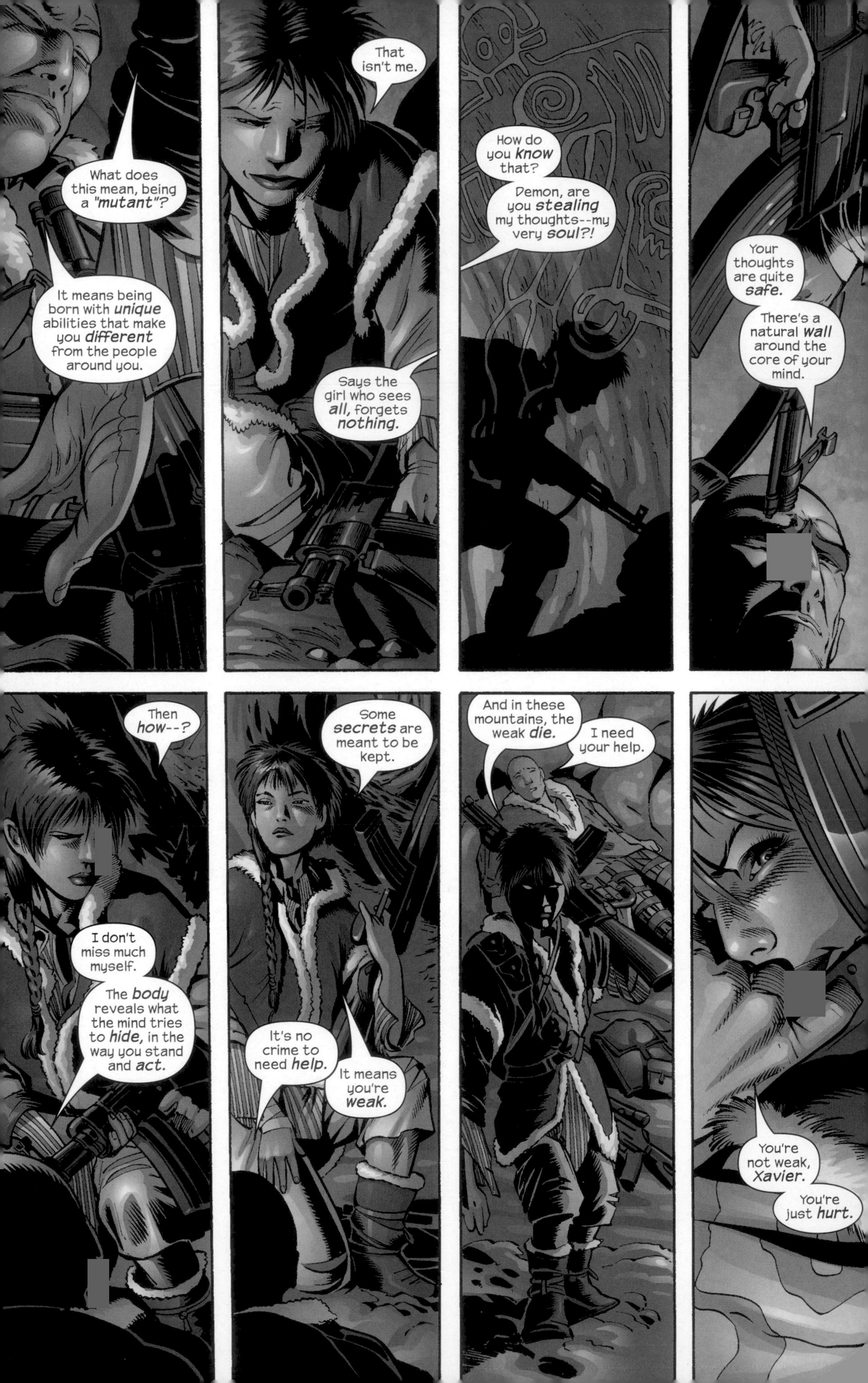
What does this mean, being a "mutant"?
It means being born with unique abilities that make you different from the people around you.
That isn't me.
Says the girl who sees all, forgets nothing.
How do you know that?
Demon, are you stealing my thoughts--my very soul?!
Your thoughts are quite safe.
There's a natural wall around the core of your mind.
Then how--?
I don't miss much myself.
The body reveals what the mind tries to hide, in the way you stand and act.
Some secrets are meant to be kept.
It's no crime to need help.
It means you're weak.
And in these mountains, the weak die.
I need your help.
You're not weak, Xavier.
You're just hurt.

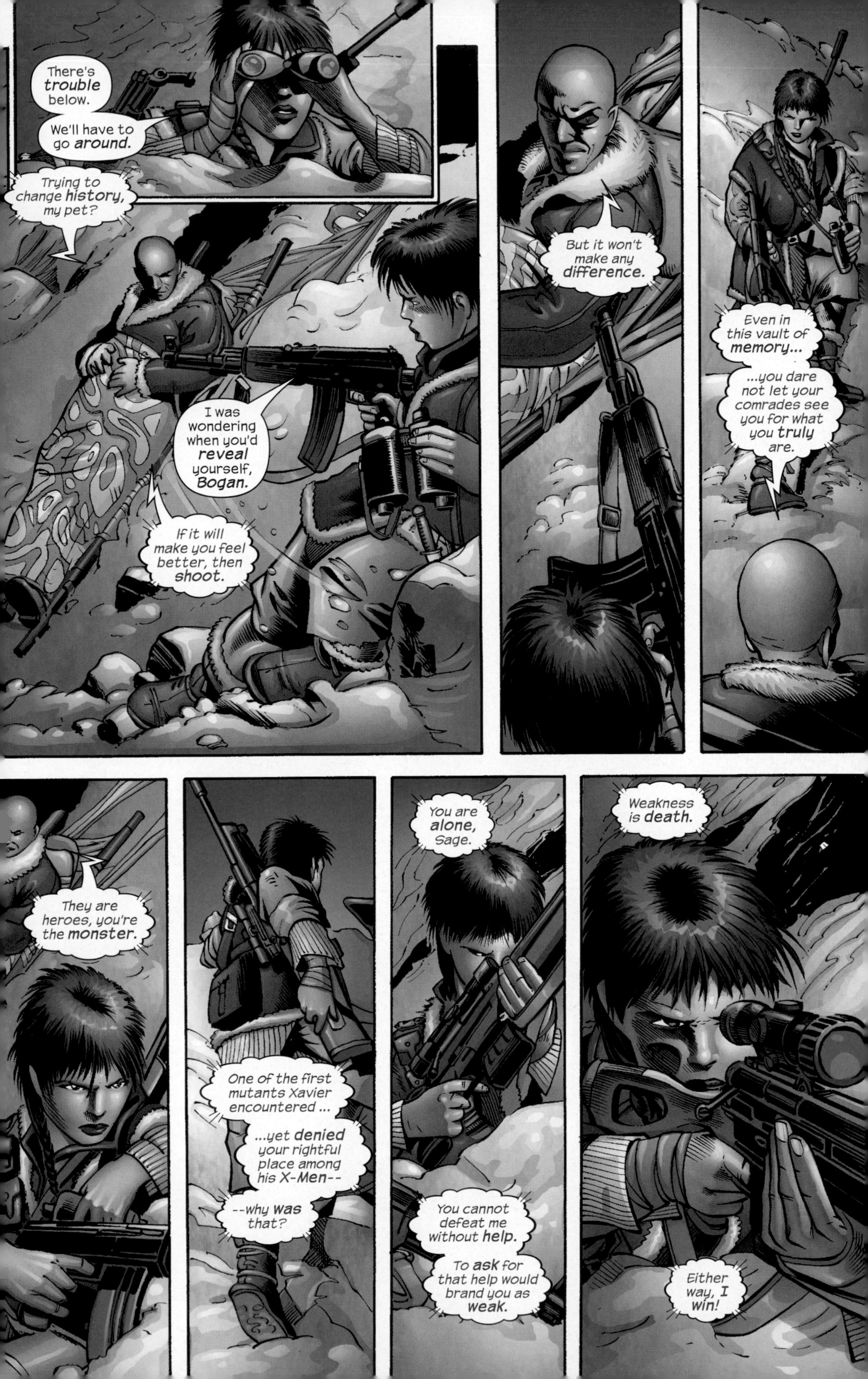
There's trouble below.
We'll have to go around.
Trying to change history, my pet?
I was wondering when you'd reveal yourself, Bogan.
If it will make you feel better, then shoot.
But it won't make any difference.
Even in this vault of memory...
...you dare not let your comrades see you for what you truly are.
They are heroes, you're the monster.
One of the first mutants Xavier encountered ...
...yet denied your rightful place among his X-Men--
--why was that?
You are alone, Sage.
You cannot defeat me without help.
To ask for that help would brand you as weak.
Weakness is death.
Either way, I win!

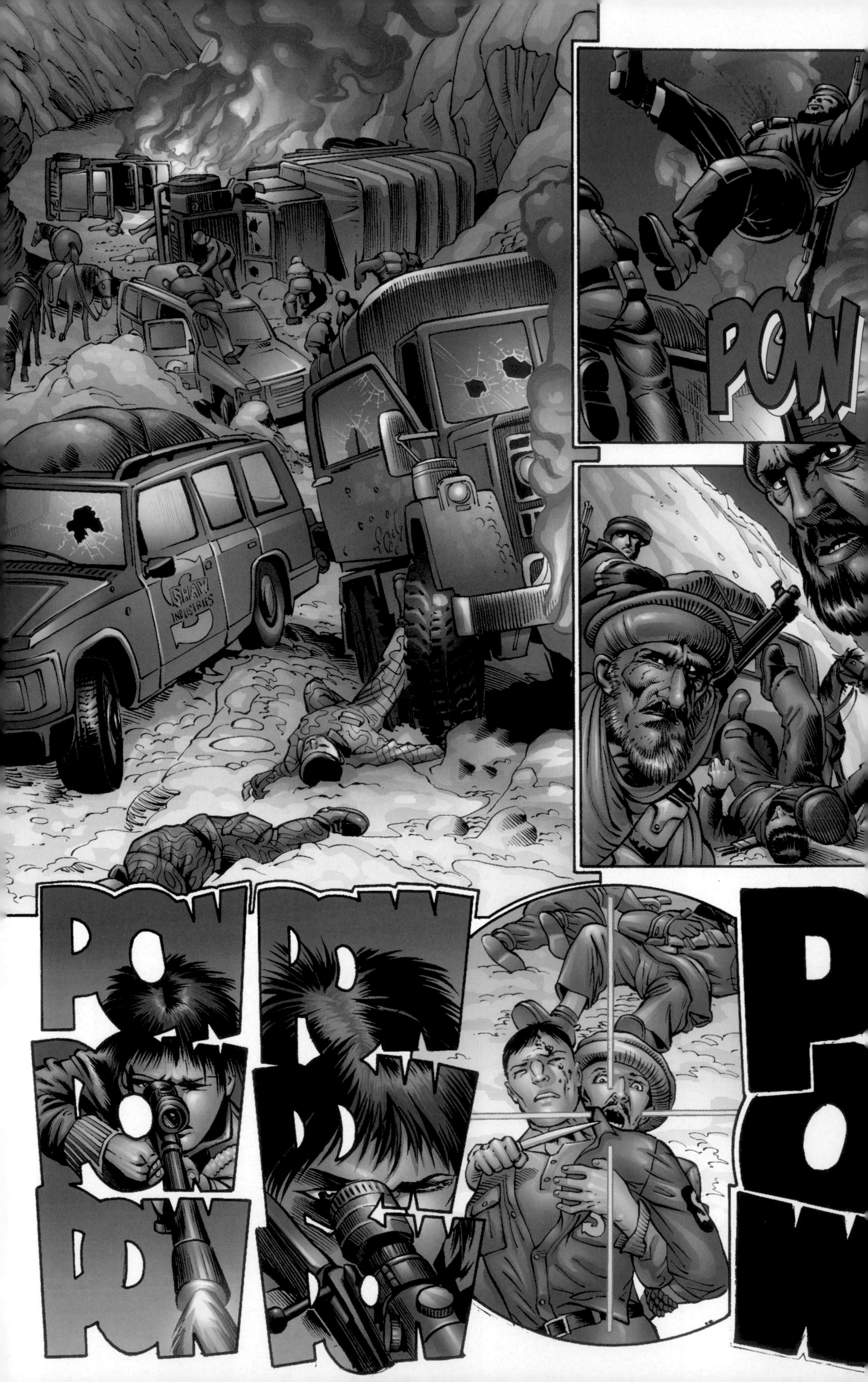

SHAW INDUSTRIES
POW
POW
POW
POW
POW
POW
POW

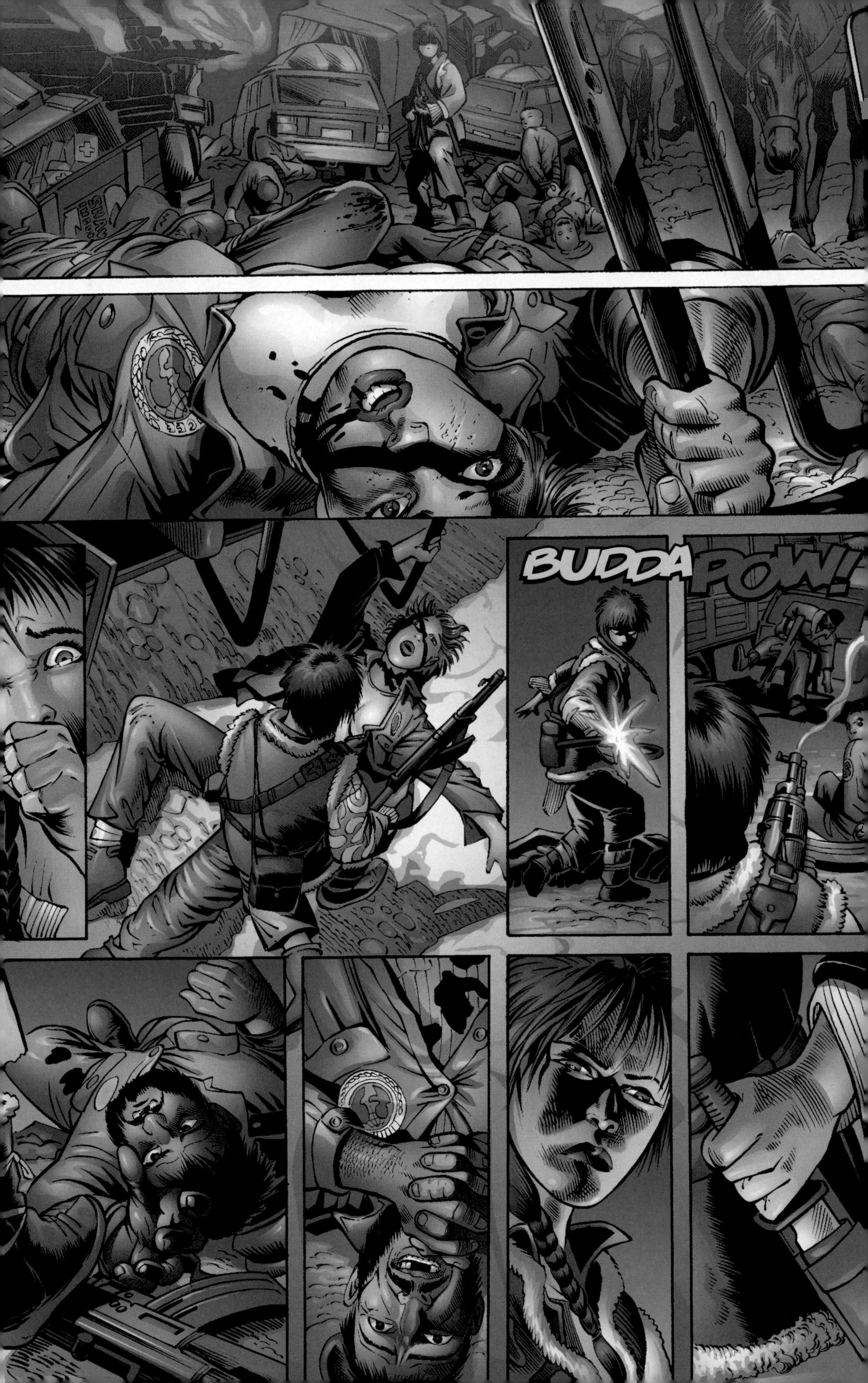
BUDDA POW!

So, X-Men, what's the **verdict**--

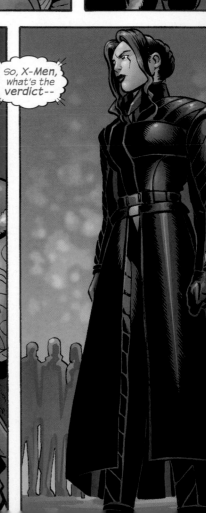

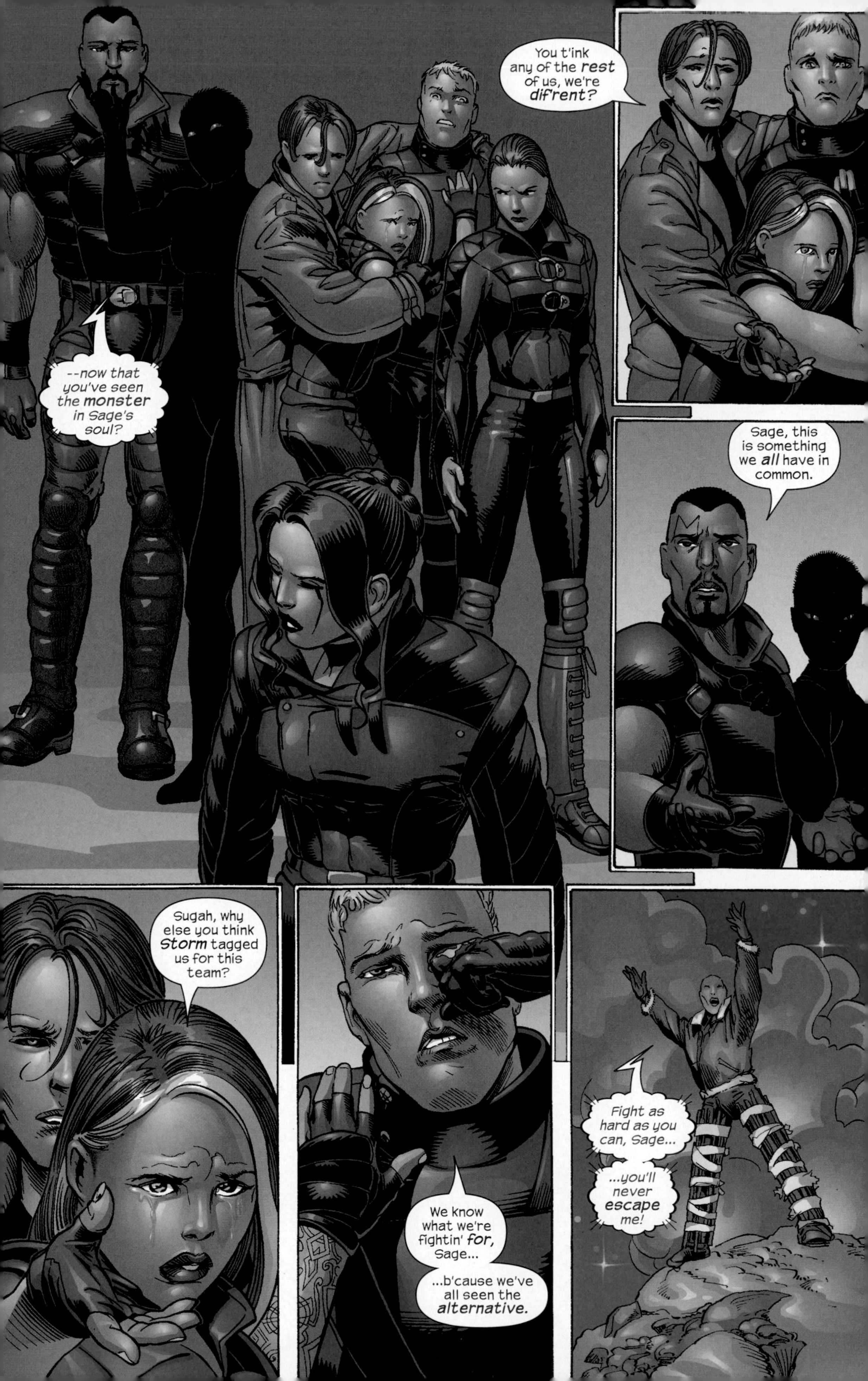

You t'ink any of the rest of us, we're dif'rent?
--now that you've seen the monster in Sage's soul?
Sage, this is something we all have in common.
Sugah, why else you think Storm tagged us for this team?
We know what we're fightin' for, Sage...
...b'cause we've all seen the alternative.
Fight as hard as you can, Sage...
...you'll never escape me!

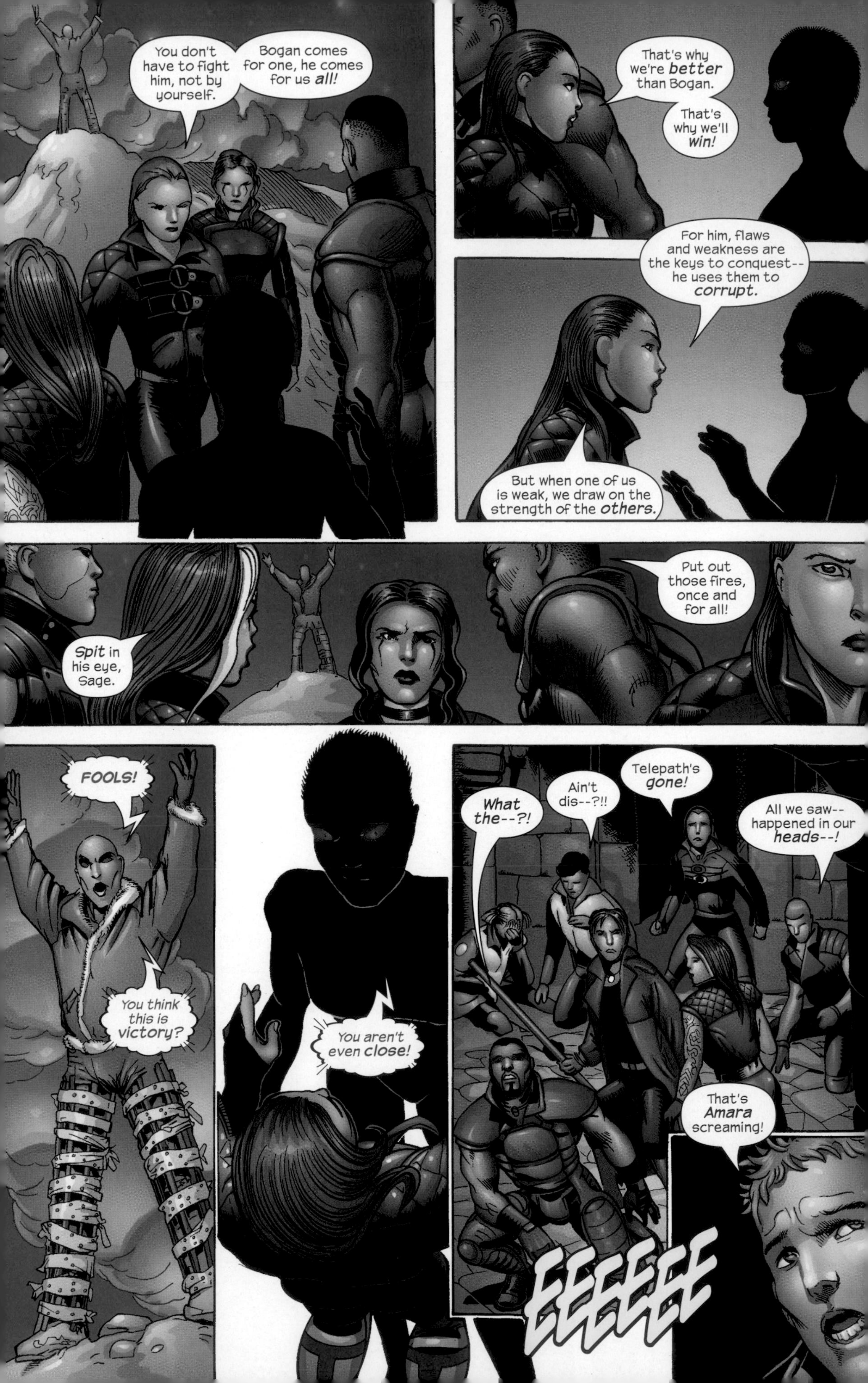

You don't have to fight him, not by yourself.
Bogan comes for one, he comes for us all!
That's why we're better than Bogan.
That's why we'll win!
For him, flaws and weakness are the keys to conquest-- he uses them to corrupt.
But when one of us is weak, we draw on the strength of the others.
Spit in his eye, Sage.
Put out those fires, once and for all!
FOOLS!
You think this is victory?
You aren't even close!
What the--?!
Ain't dis--?!!
Telepath's gone!
All we saw-- happened in our heads--!
That's Amara screaming!
EEEEEE

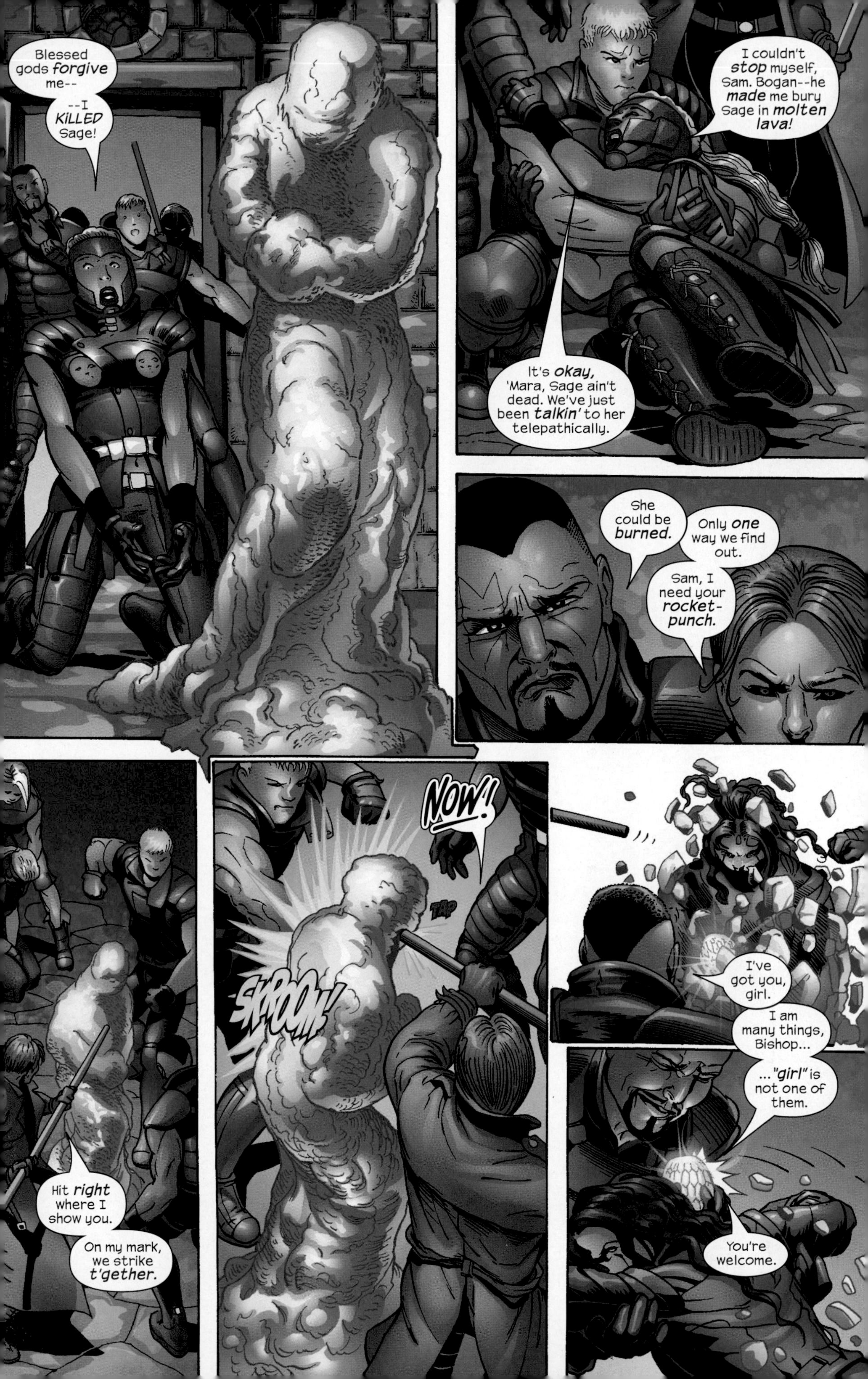
Blessed gods *forgive* me--
--I *KILLED* Sage!
I couldn't *stop* myself, Sam. Bogan--he *made* me bury Sage in *molten lava!*
It's *okay,* 'Mara, Sage ain't dead. We've just been *talkin'* to her telepathically.
She could be *burned.*
Only *one* way we find out.
Sam, I need your *rocket-punch.*
Hit *right* where I show you.
On my mark, we strike *t'gether.*
NOW!
SKROOM!
TAP
I've got you, girl.
I am many things, Bishop...
..."*girl*" is not one of them.
You're welcome.

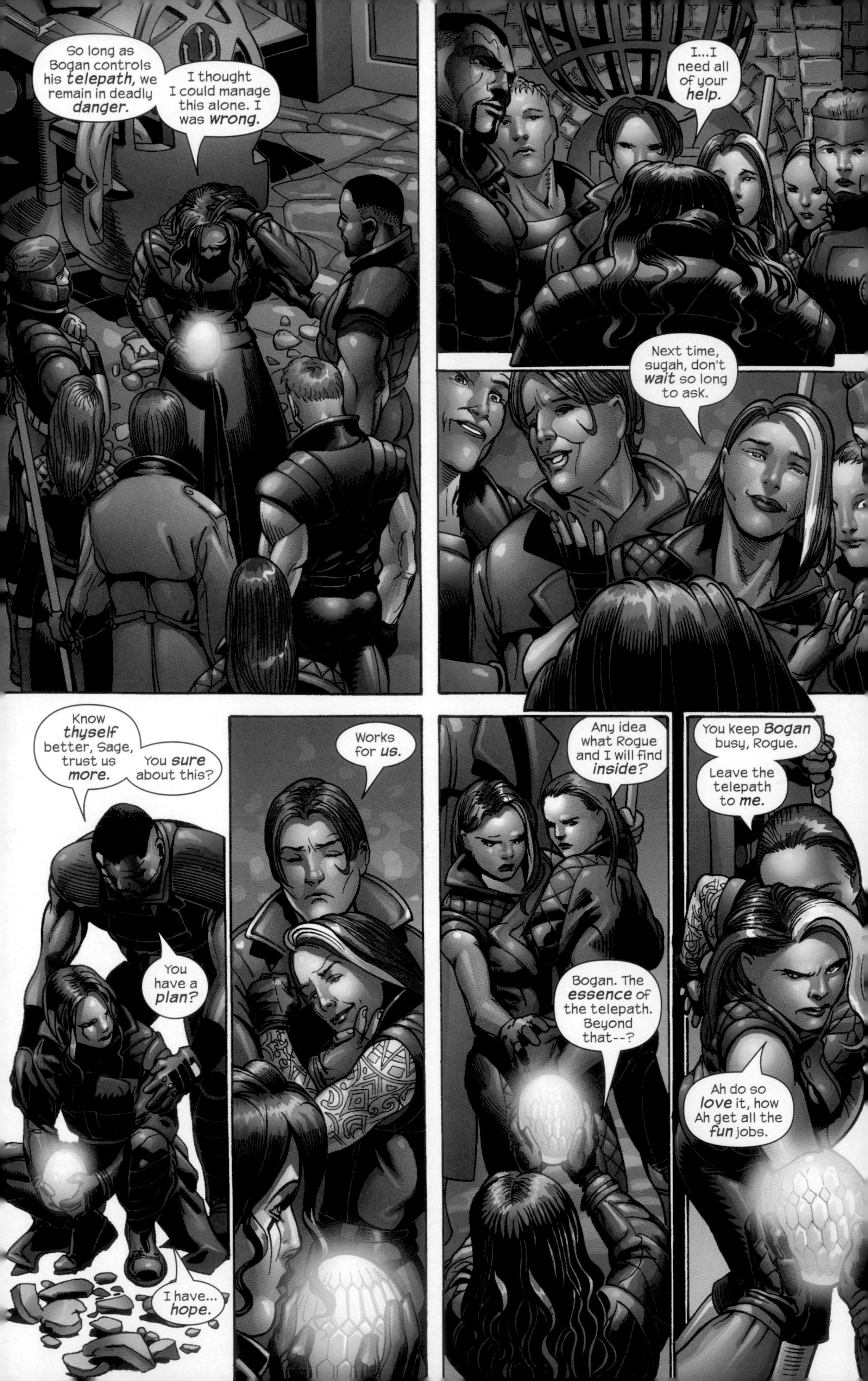
So long as Bogan controls his *telepath*, we remain in deadly *danger*.
I thought I could manage this alone. I was *wrong*.
I...I need all of your *help*.
Next time, sugah, don't *wait* so long to ask.
Know *thyself* better, Sage, trust us *more*.
You *sure* about this?
You have a *plan*?
I have... *hope*.
Works for *us*.
Any idea what Rogue and I will find *inside*?
Bogan. The *essence* of the telepath. Beyond that--?
You keep *Bogan* busy, Rogue.
Leave the telepath to *me*.
Ah do so *love* it, how Ah get all the *fun* jobs.

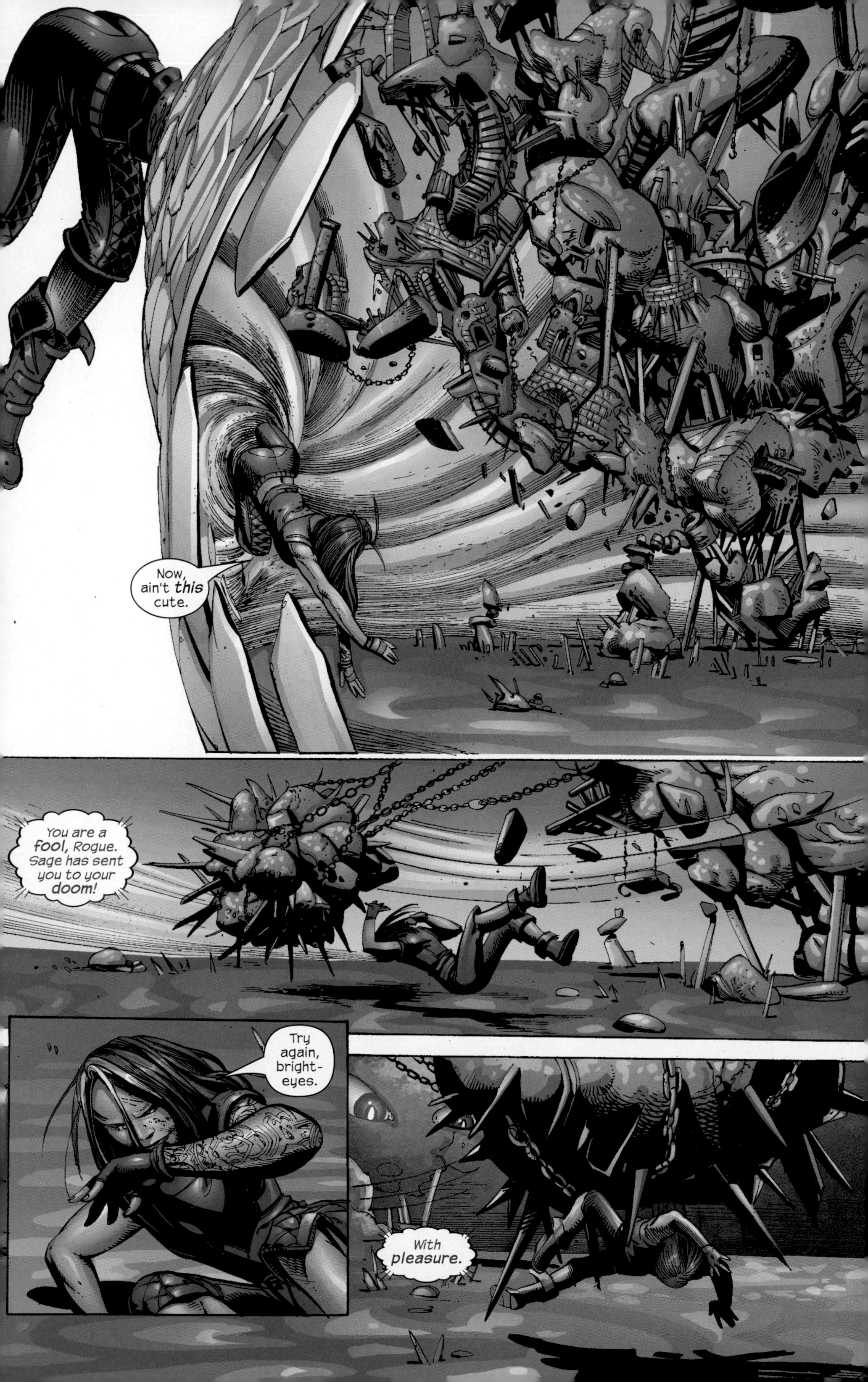
Now, ain't this cute.
You are a fool, Rogue. Sage has sent you to your doom!
Try again, bright-eyes.
With pleasure.

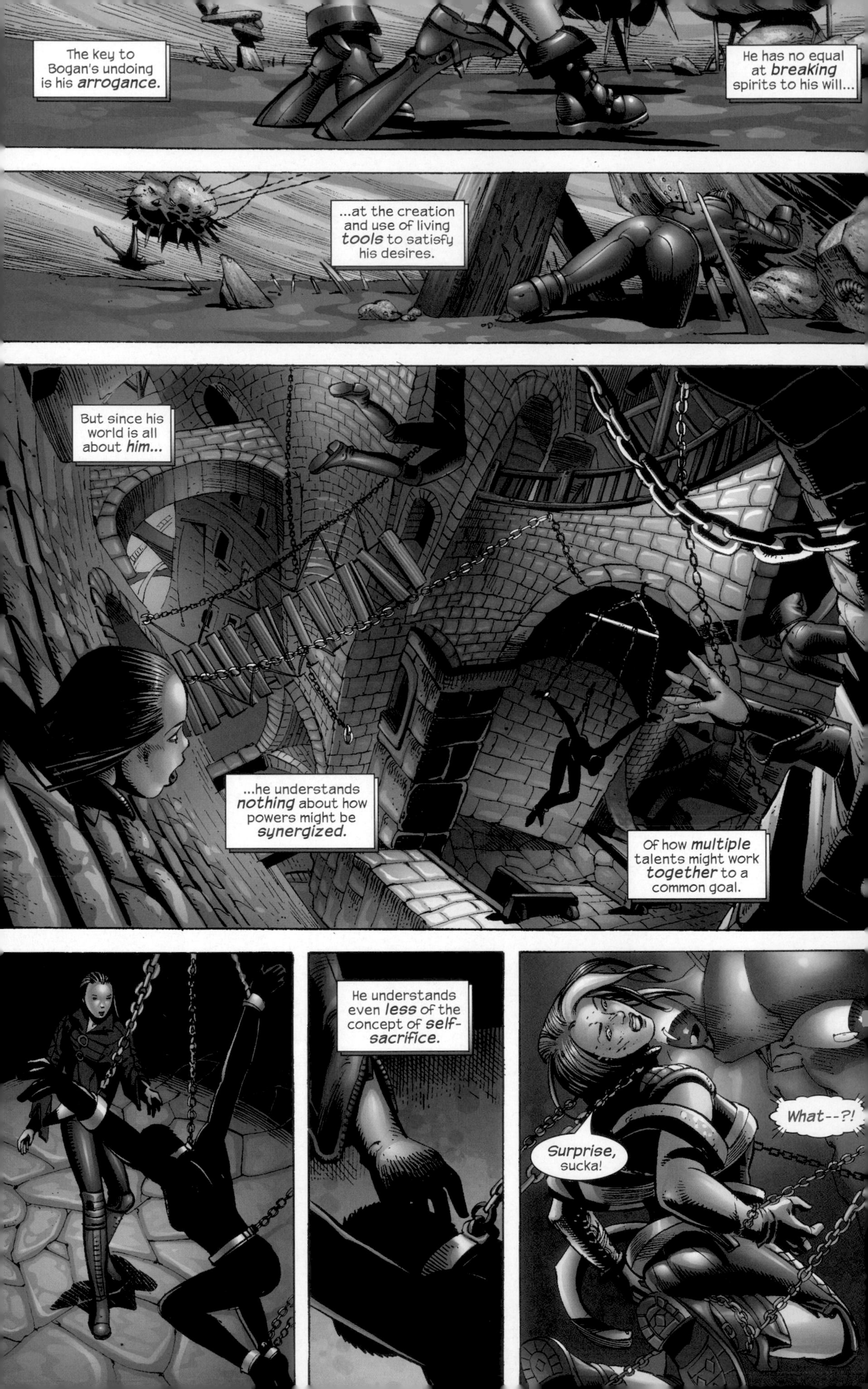

The key to Bogan's undoing is his *arrogance.*
He has no equal at *breaking* spirits to his will...
...at the creation and use of living *tools* to satisfy his desires.
But since his world is all about *him*...
...he understands *nothing* about how powers might be *synergized.*
Of how *multiple* talents might work *together* to a common goal.
He understands even *less* of the concept of *self-sacrifice.*
Surprise, sucka!
What--?!

I offered faith and *loyalty* to Charles Xavier...

...because after all he had seen of me...

...he considered me *worthy* of his.

Bishop-- all the *energy* you possess-- give it to me--

NOW!

You're pretty good at dishin' out *punishment*, Bogan.

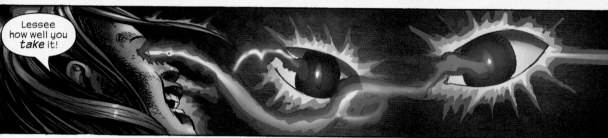

Lessee how well you *take* it!

My stratagem is borrowed from *Xavier* himself, first used years ago against *alien* invaders.

Bishop provides the raw power.

A *telepath*-- myself--regulates and *amplifies* the energy flow.

Rogue provides the targeting lens.

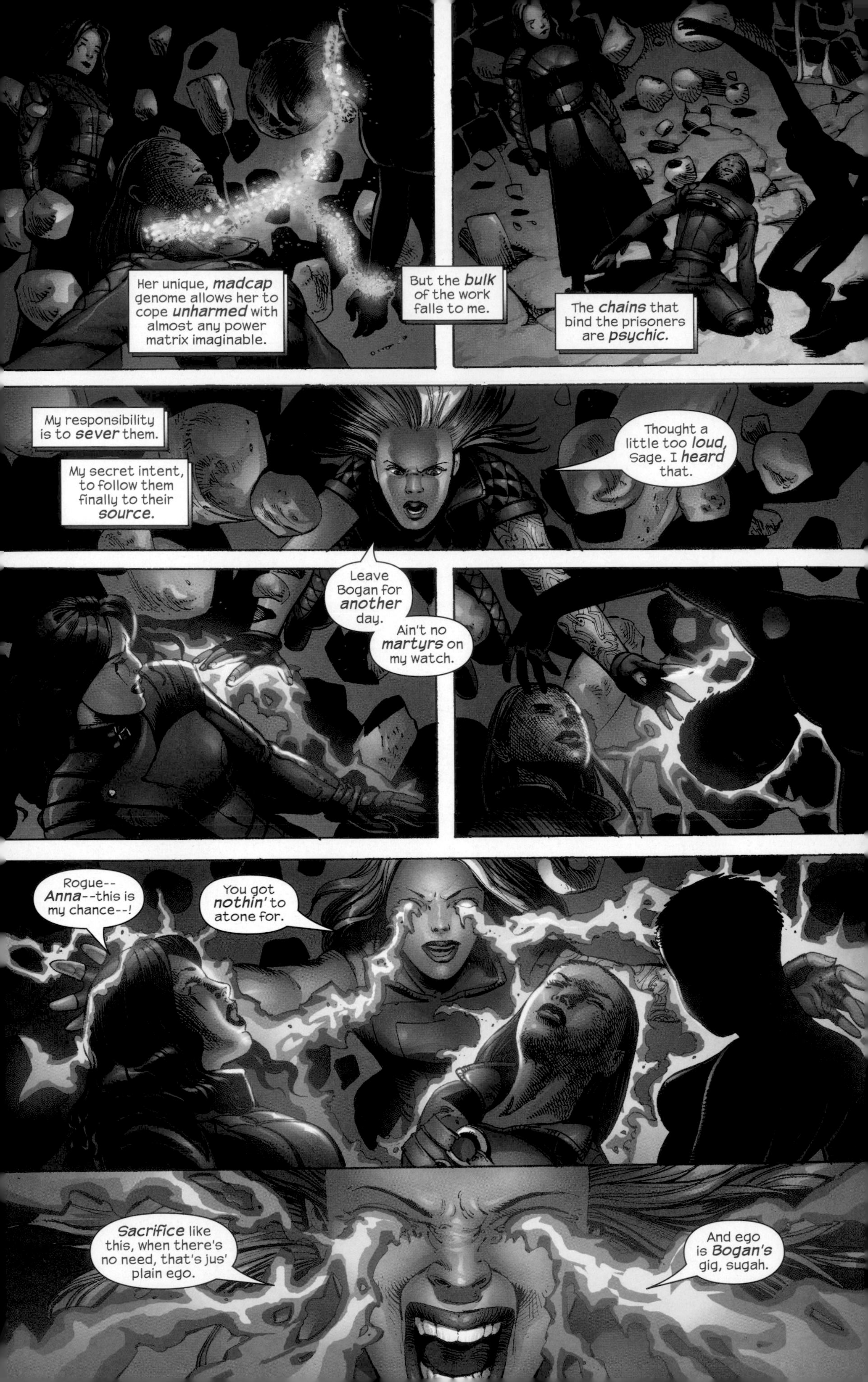
Her unique, *madcap* genome allows her to cope *unharmed* with almost any power matrix imaginable.
But the *bulk* of the work falls to me.
The *chains* that bind the prisoners are *psychic.*
My responsibility is to *sever* them.
My secret intent, to follow them finally to their *source.*
Thought a little too *loud,* Sage. I *heard* that.
Leave Bogan for *another* day.
Ain't no *martyrs* on my watch.
Rogue-- *Anna*--this is my chance--!
You got *nothin'* to atone for.
Sacrifice like this, when there's no need, that's jus' plain ego.
And ego is *Bogan's* gig, sugah.

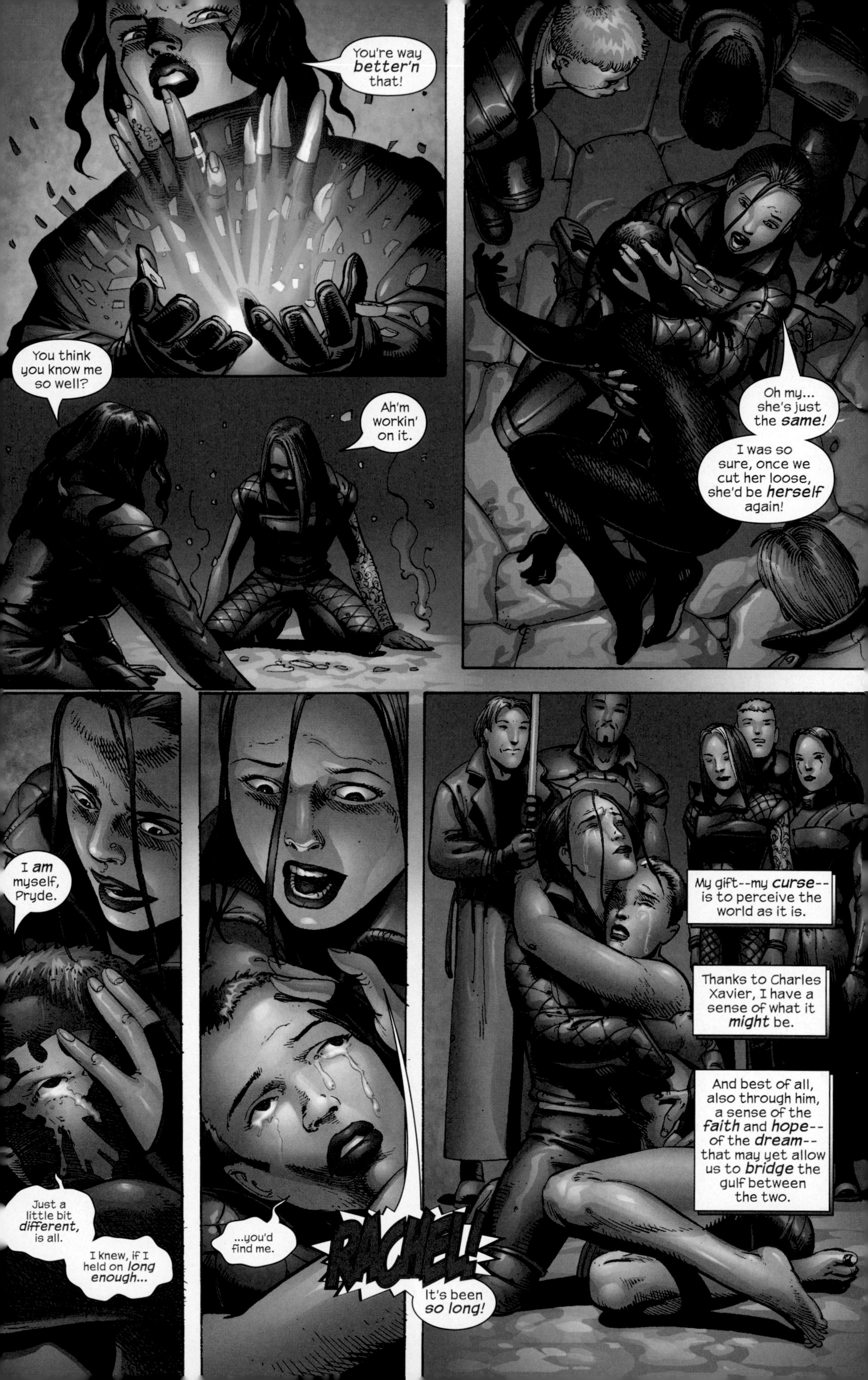
You're way better'n that!
You think you know me so well?
Ah'm workin' on it.
Oh my... she's just the same!
I was so sure, once we cut her loose, she'd be herself again!
I am myself, Pryde.
Just a little bit different, is all.
I knew, if I held on long enough...
...you'd find me.
RACHEL!
It's been so long!
My gift--my curse--is to perceive the world as it is.
Thanks to Charles Xavier, I have a sense of what it might be.
And best of all, also through him, a sense of the faith and hope--of the dream--that may yet allow us to bridge the gulf between the two.

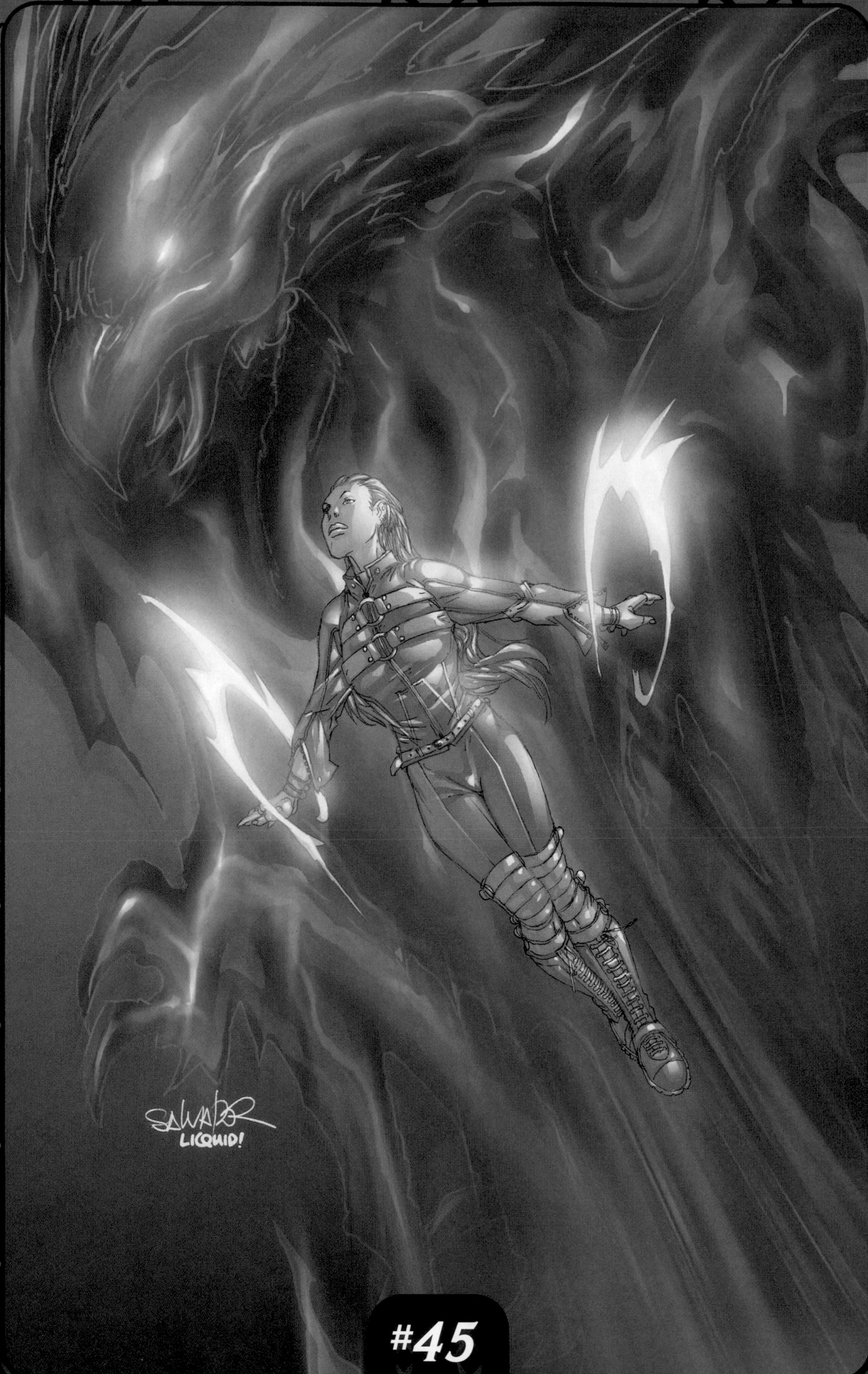
LIQUID!

#45

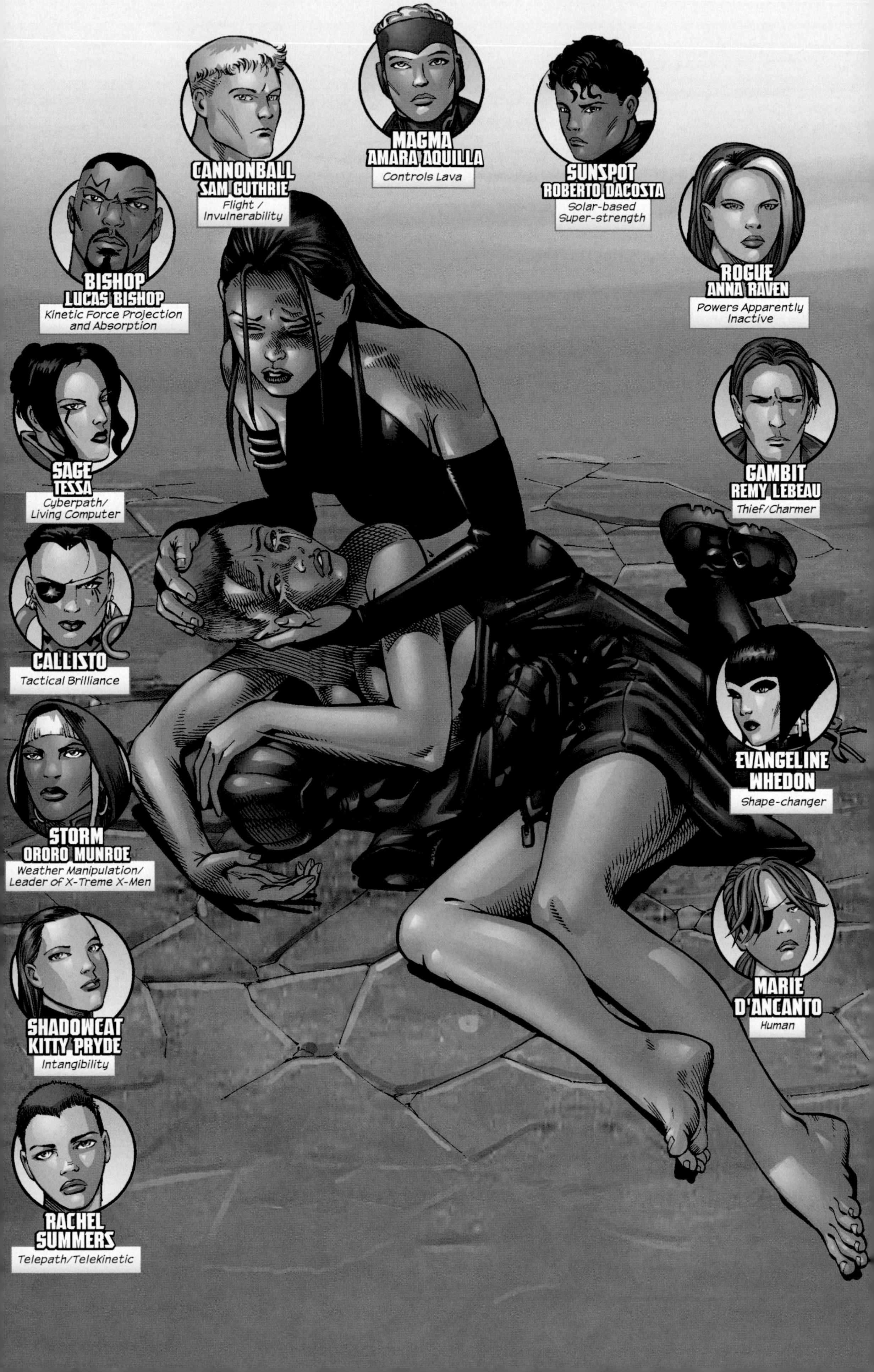
CANNONBALL
SAM GUTHRIE
Flight / Invulnerability
MAGMA
AMARA AQUILLA
Controls Lava
SUNSPOT
ROBERTO DACOSTA
Solar-based Super-strength
BISHOP
LUCAS BISHOP
Kinetic Force Projection and Absorption
ROGUE
ANNA RAVEN
Powers Apparently Inactive
SAGE
TESSA
Cyberpath/ Living Computer
GAMBIT
REMY LEBEAU
Thief/Charmer
CALLISTO
Tactical Brilliance
EVANGELINE WHEDON
Shape-changer
STORM
ORORO MUNROE
Weather Manipulation/ Leader of X-Treme X-Men
MARIE D'ANCANTO
Human
SHADOWCAT
KITTY PRYDE
Intangibility
RACHEL SUMMERS
Telepath/Telekinetic

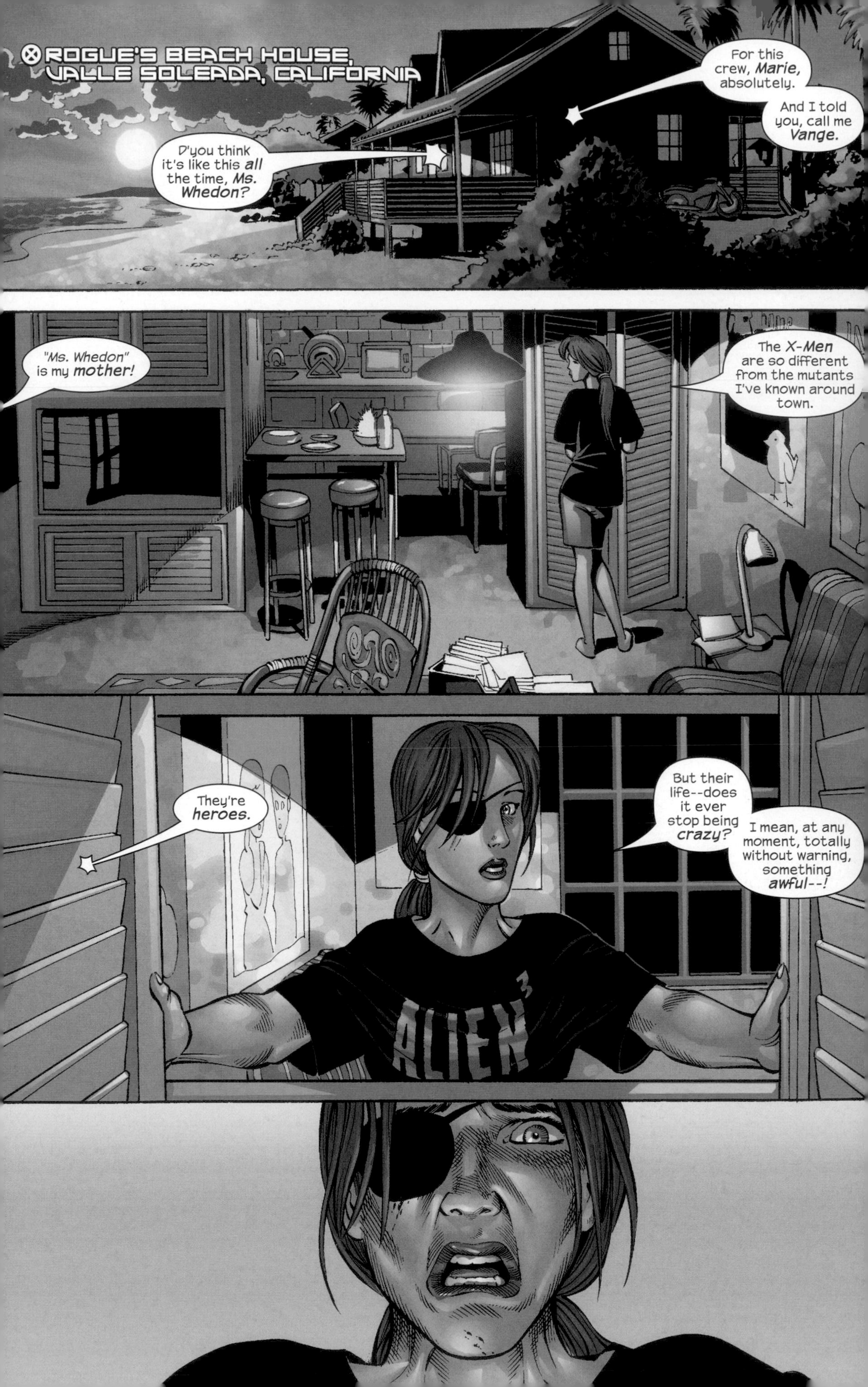

ROGUE'S BEACH HOUSE, VALLE SOLEADA, CALIFORNIA
D'you think it's like this all the time, Ms. Whedon?
For this crew, Marie, absolutely.
And I told you, call me Vange.
"Ms. Whedon" is my mother!
The X-Men are so different from the mutants I've known around town.
They're heroes.
But their life--does it ever stop being crazy?
I mean, at any moment, totally without warning, something awful--!
ALIEN 3

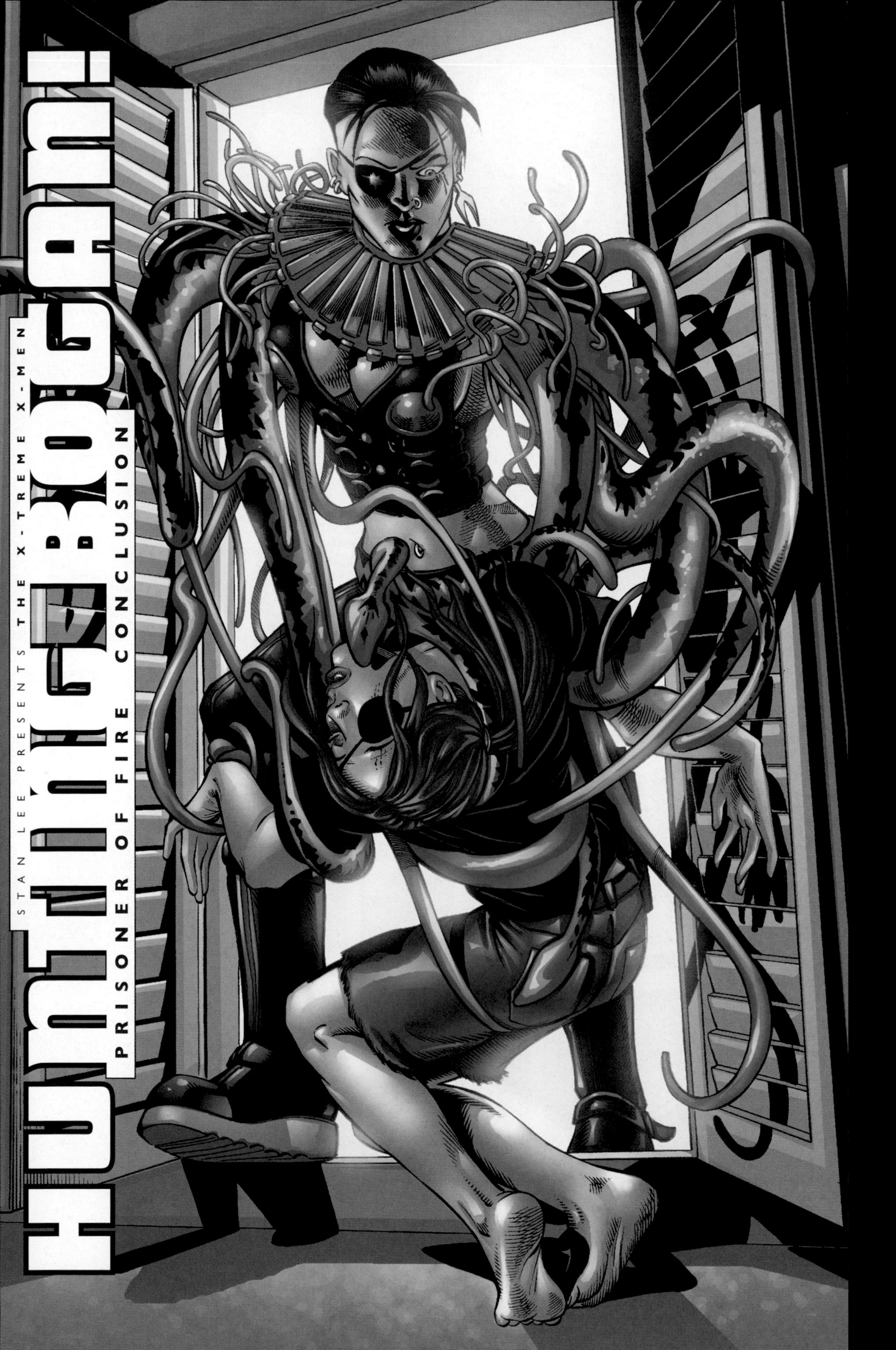
STAN LEE PRESENTS THE X-TREME X-MEN
PRISONER OF FIRE CONCLUSION

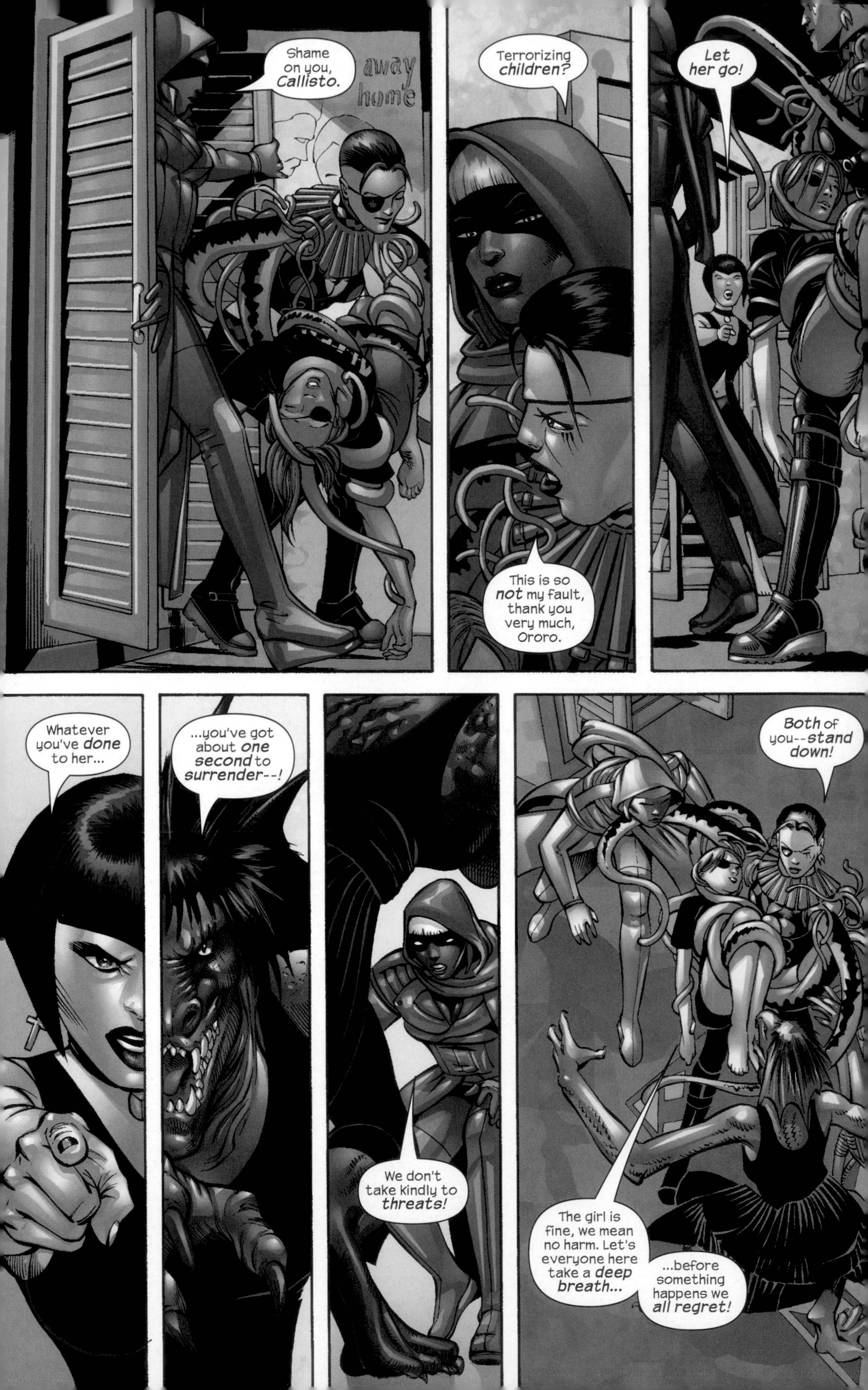
Shame on you, Callisto.
away home
Terrorizing children?
This is so not my fault, thank you very much, Ororo.
Let her go!
Whatever you've done to her...
...you've got about one second to surrender--!
We don't take kindly to threats!
Both of you--stand down!
The girl is fine, we mean no harm. Let's everyone here take a deep breath...
...before something happens we all regret!

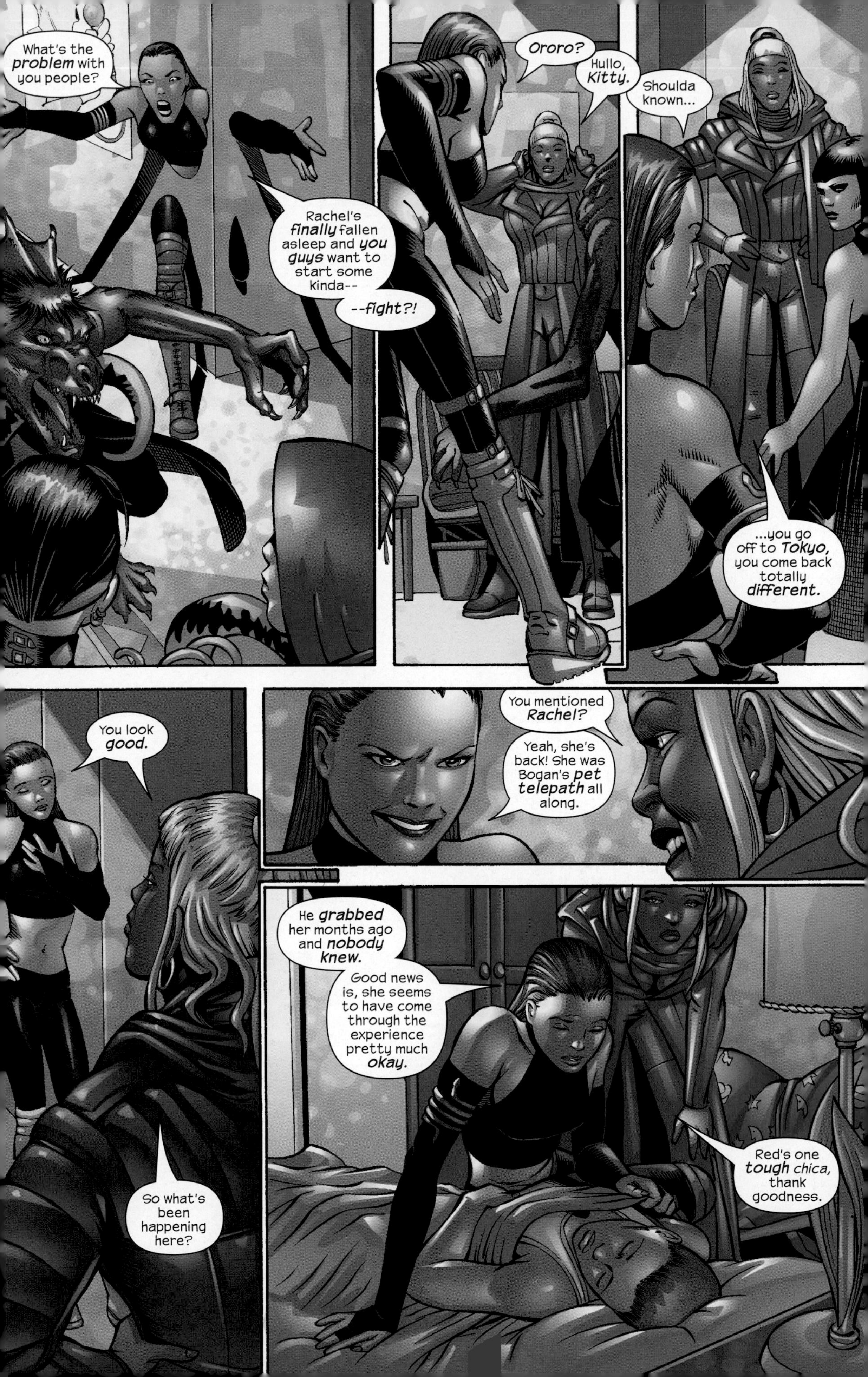
What's the problem with you people?
Rachel's finally fallen asleep and you guys want to start some kinda--
--fight?!
Ororo?
Hullo, Kitty.
Shoulda known...
...you go off to Tokyo, you come back totally different.
You look good.
So what's been happening here?
You mentioned Rachel?
Yeah, she's back! She was Bogan's pet telepath all along.
He grabbed her months ago and nobody knew.
Good news is, she seems to have come through the experience pretty much okay.
Red's one tough chica, thank goodness.

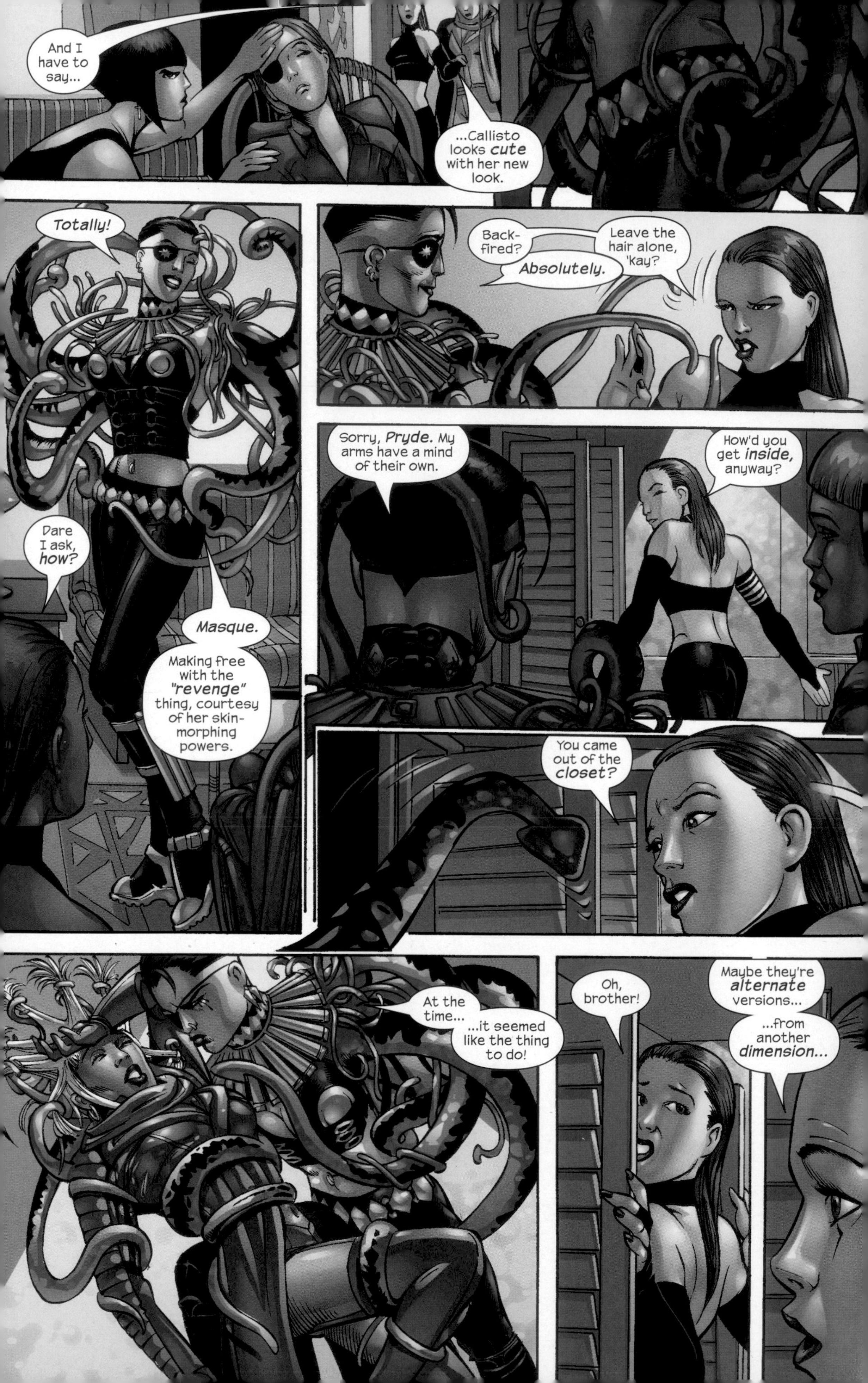
And I have to say...
...Callisto looks cute with her new look.
Totally!
Back-fired?
Absolutely.
Leave the hair alone, 'kay?
Dare I ask, how?
Masque.
Making free with the "revenge" thing, courtesy of her skin-morphing powers.
Sorry, Pryde. My arms have a mind of their own.
How'd you get inside, anyway?
You came out of the closet?
At the time...
...it seemed like the thing to do!
Oh, brother!
Maybe they're alternate versions...
...from another dimension...

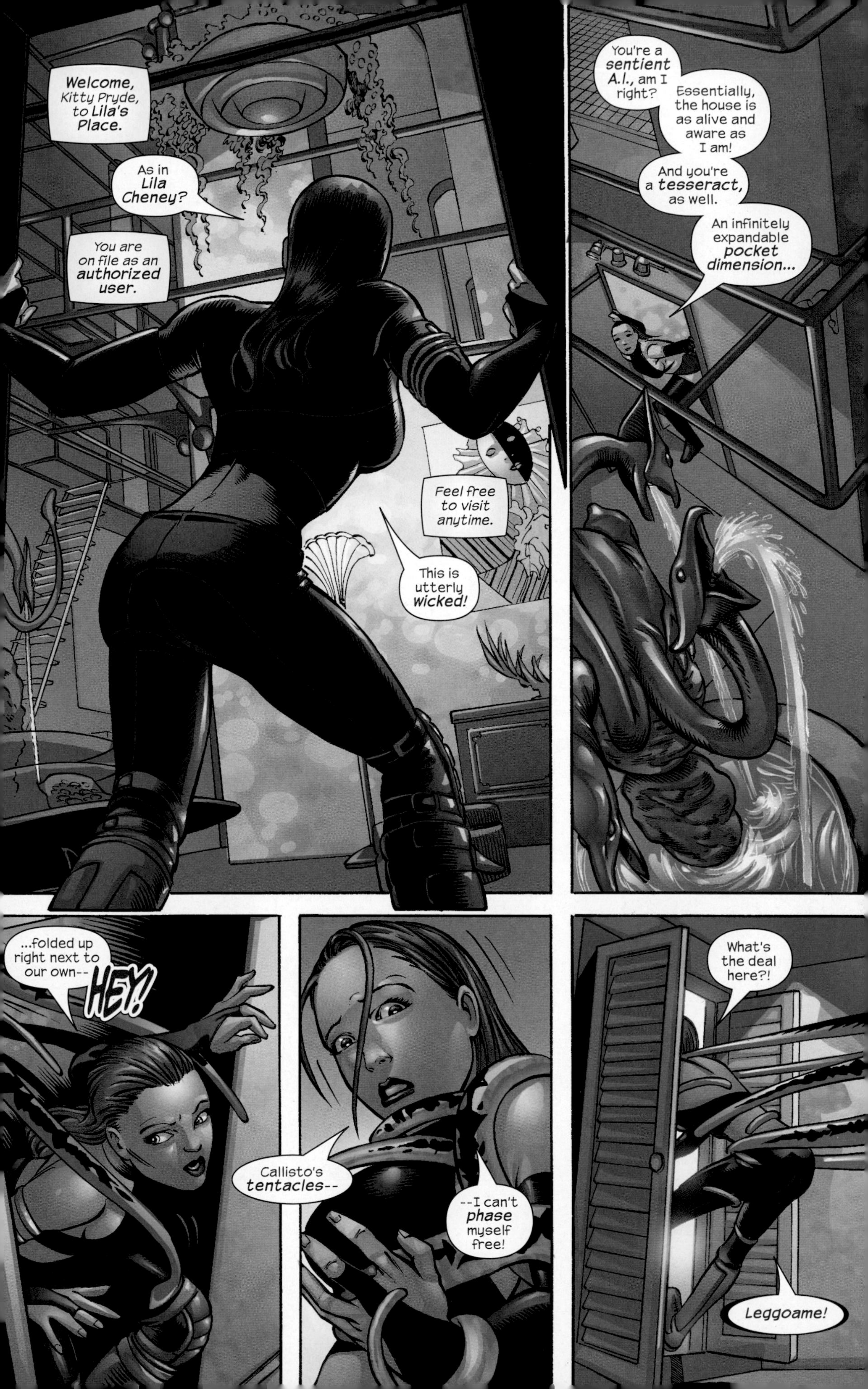

Welcome, Kitty Pryde, to Lila's Place.
As in Lila Cheney?
You are on file as an authorized user.
Feel free to visit anytime.
This is utterly wicked!
You're a sentient A.I., am I right?
Essentially, the house is as alive and aware as I am!
And you're a tesseract, as well.
An infinitely expandable pocket dimension...
...folded up right next to our own--
HEY!
Callisto's tentacles--
--I can't phase myself free!
What's the deal here?!
Leggoame!

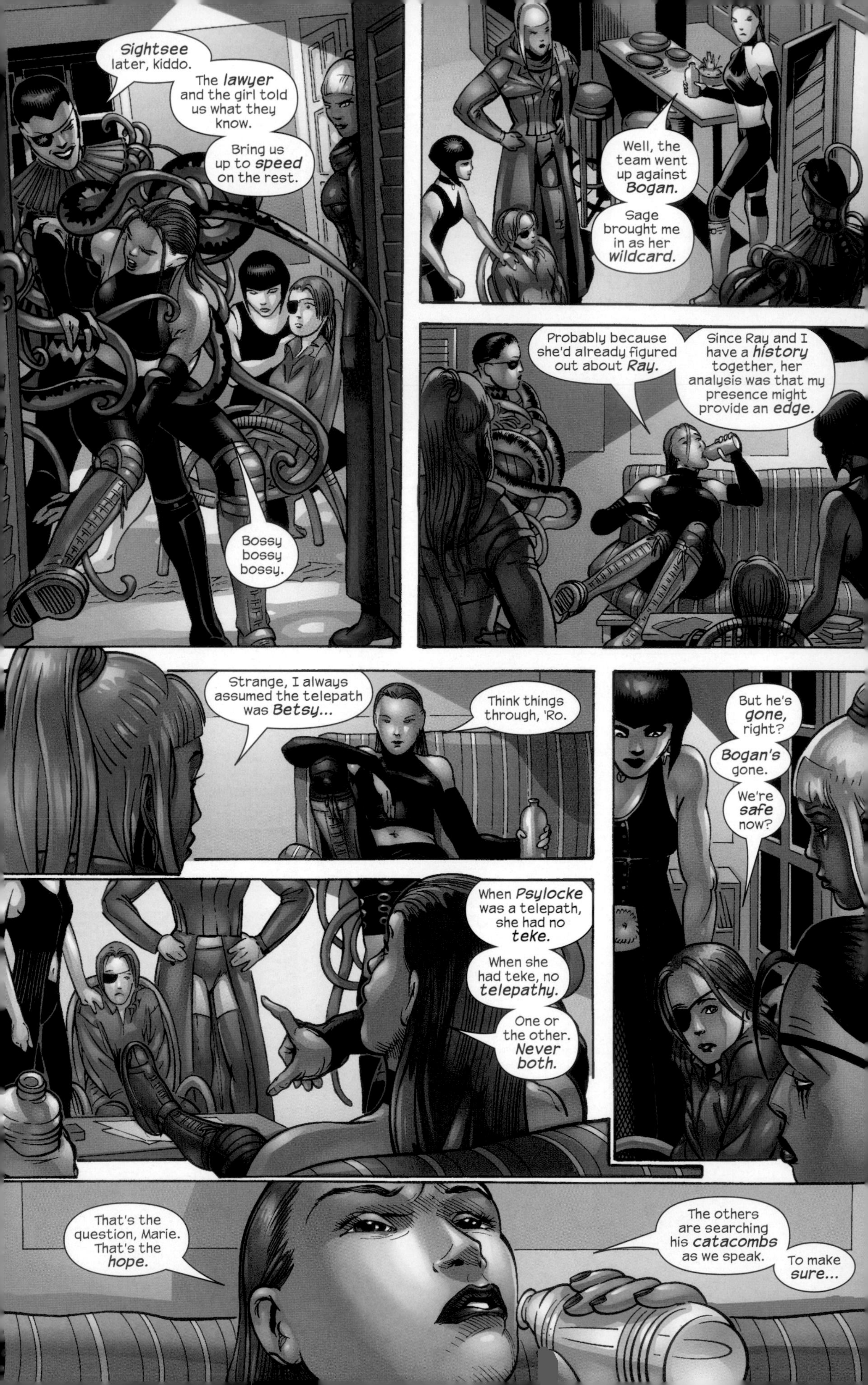
Sightsee later, kiddo.
The lawyer and the girl told us what they know.
Bring us up to speed on the rest.
Bossy bossy bossy.
Well, the team went up against Bogan.
Sage brought me in as her wildcard.
Probably because she'd already figured out about Ray.
Since Ray and I have a history together, her analysis was that my presence might provide an edge.
Strange, I always assumed the telepath was Betsy...
Think things through, 'Ro.
When Psylocke was a telepath, she had no teke.
When she had teke, no telepathy.
One or the other. Never both.
But he's gone, right?
Bogan's gone.
We're safe now?
That's the question, Marie. That's the hope.
The others are searching his catacombs as we speak.
To make sure...

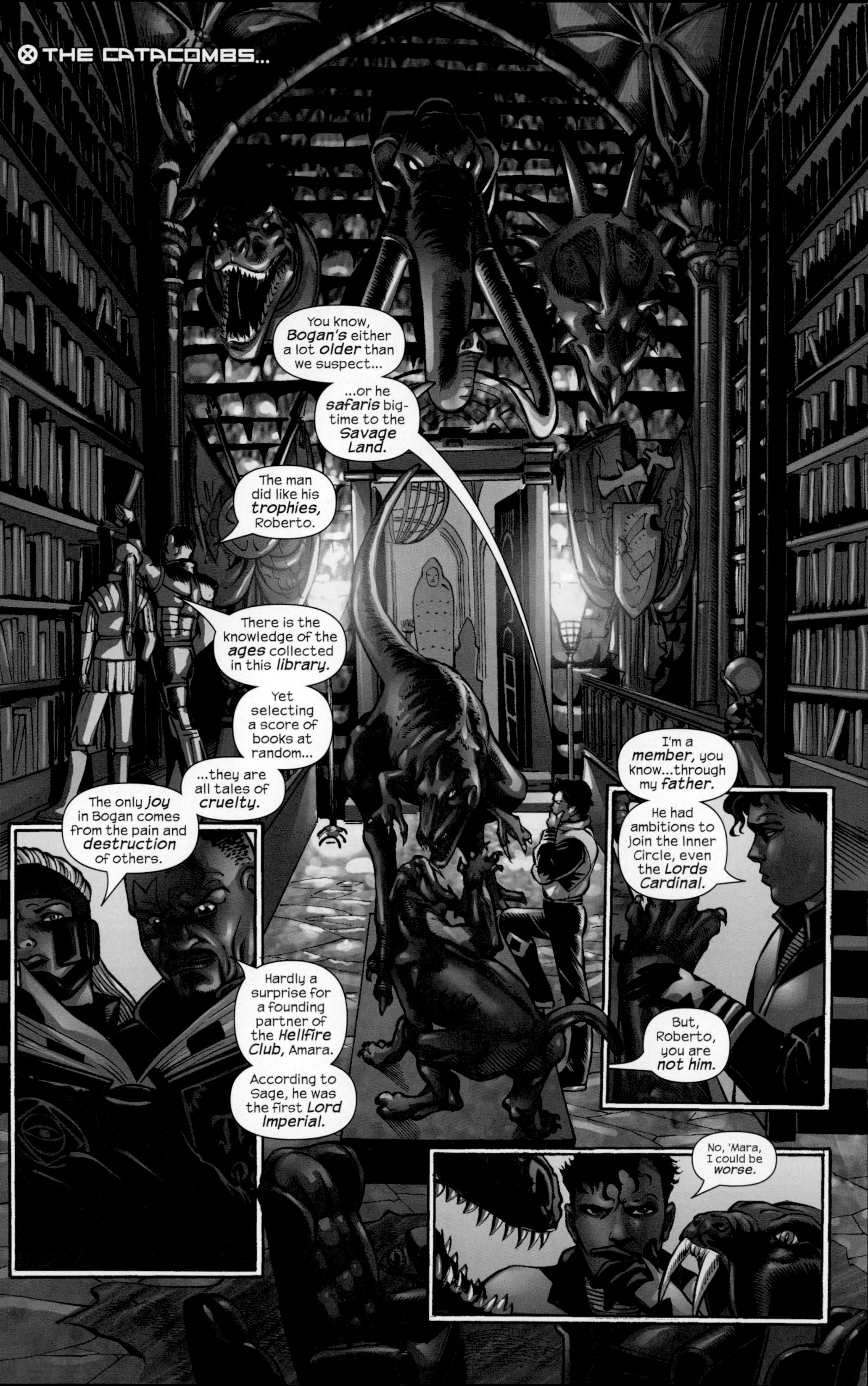
THE CATACOMBS...
You know, Bogan's either a lot older than we suspect...
...or he safaris big-time to the Savage Land.
The man did like his trophies, Roberto.
There is the knowledge of the ages collected in this library.
Yet selecting a score of books at random...
...they are all tales of cruelty.
The only joy in Bogan comes from the pain and destruction of others.
Hardly a surprise for a founding partner of the Hellfire Club, Amara.
According to Sage, he was the first Lord Imperial.
I'm a member, you know...through my father.
He had ambitions to join the Inner Circle, even the Lords Cardinal.
But, Roberto, you are not him.
No, 'Mara, I could be worse.

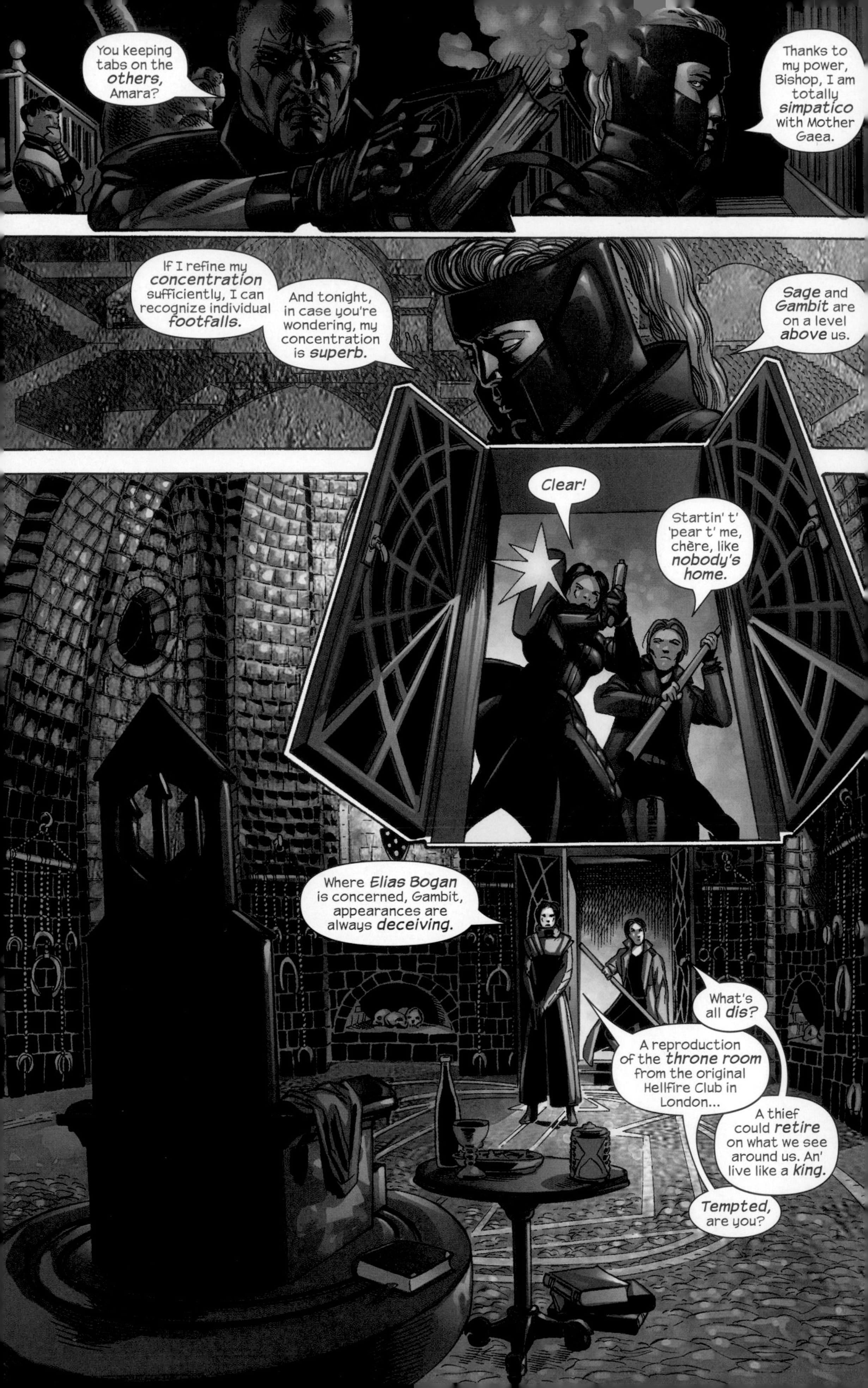
You keeping tabs on the others, Amara?
Thanks to my power, Bishop, I am totally simpatico with Mother Gaea.
If I refine my concentration sufficiently, I can recognize individual footfalls.
And tonight, in case you're wondering, my concentration is superb.
Sage and Gambit are on a level above us.
Clear!
Startin' t' 'pear t' me, chère, like nobody's home.
Where Elias Bogan is concerned, Gambit, appearances are always deceiving.
What's all dis?
A reproduction of the throne room from the original Hellfire Club in London...
A thief could retire on what we see around us. An' live like a king.
Tempted, are you?

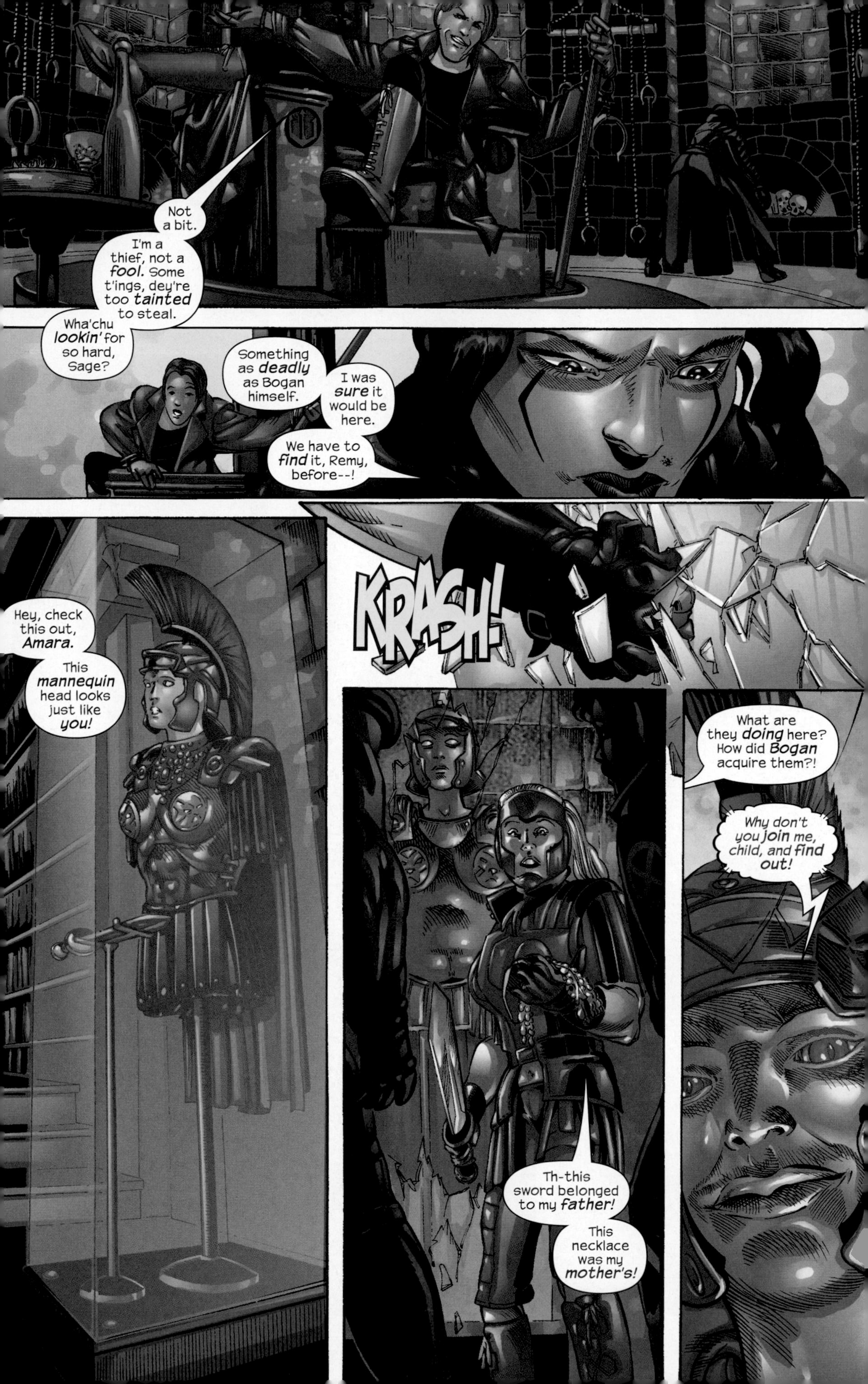
Not a bit.
I'm a thief, not a fool. Some t'ings, dey're too tainted to steal.
Wha'chu lookin' for so hard, Sage?
Something as deadly as Bogan himself.
I was sure it would be here.
We have to find it, Remy, before--!
Hey, check this out, Amara.
This mannequin head looks just like you!
KRASH!
Th-this sword belonged to my father!
This necklace was my mother's!
What are they doing here? How did Bogan acquire them?!
Why don't you join me, child, and find out!

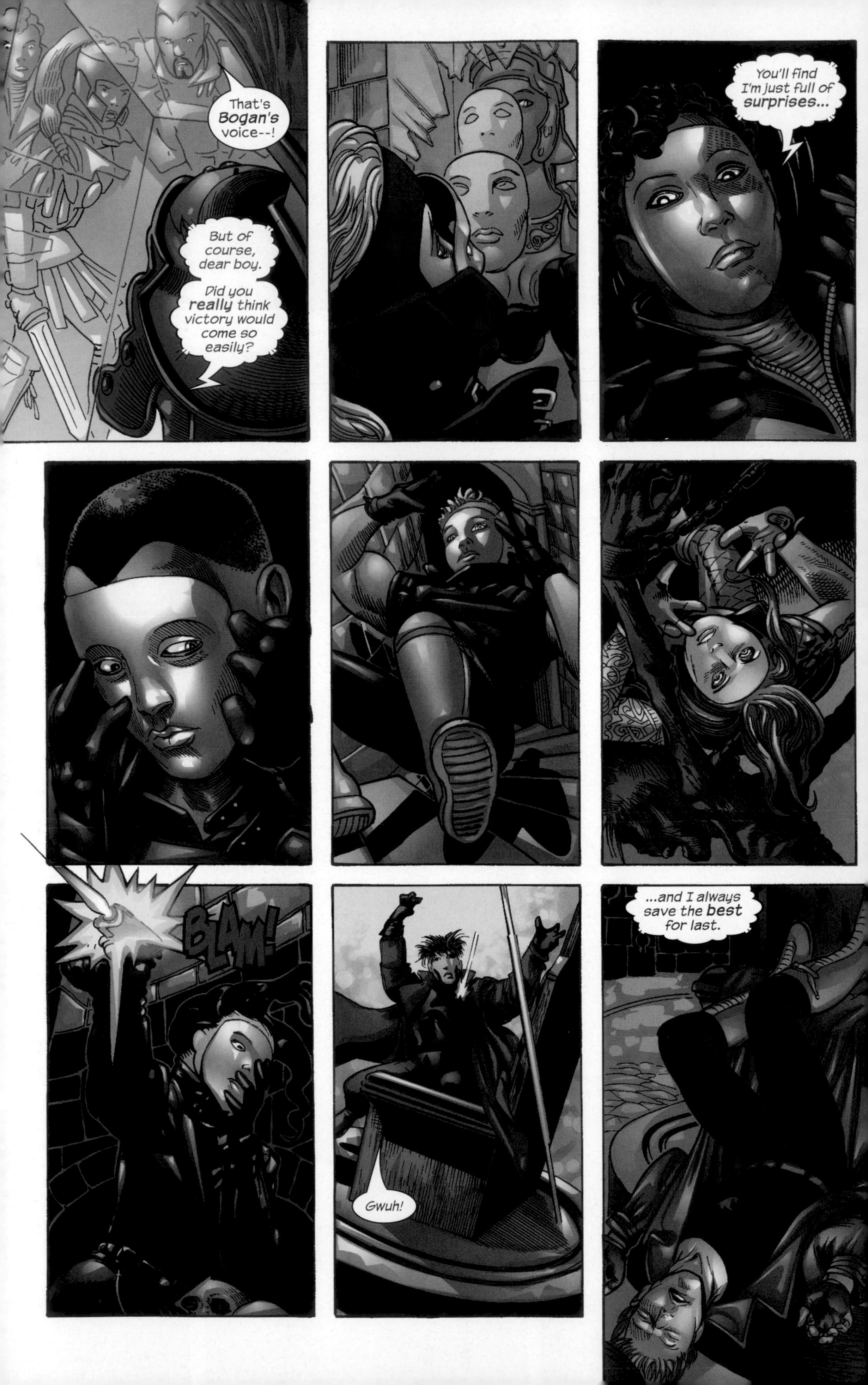
That's Bogan's voice--!
But of course, dear boy.
Did you really think victory would come so easily?
You'll find I'm just full of surprises...
BLAM!
Gwuh!
...and I always save the best for last.

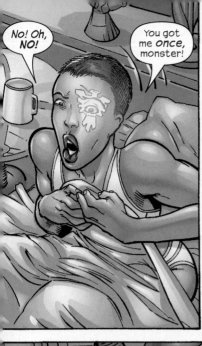

No! Oh, NO!

You got me *once*, monster!

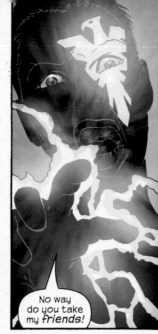

No way do you take my *friends*!

What the--?!

It's Rachel!

Is this an *attack*?! Is she still working for Bogan?!

It's an attack, *yes*!

But she's trying to *save* us!

I'm sorry I'm sorry I'm sorry, no time to *explain*...

SLAM!

...only to *act*!

Inside Lila's house, Bogan can't *reach* us.

But Ray--

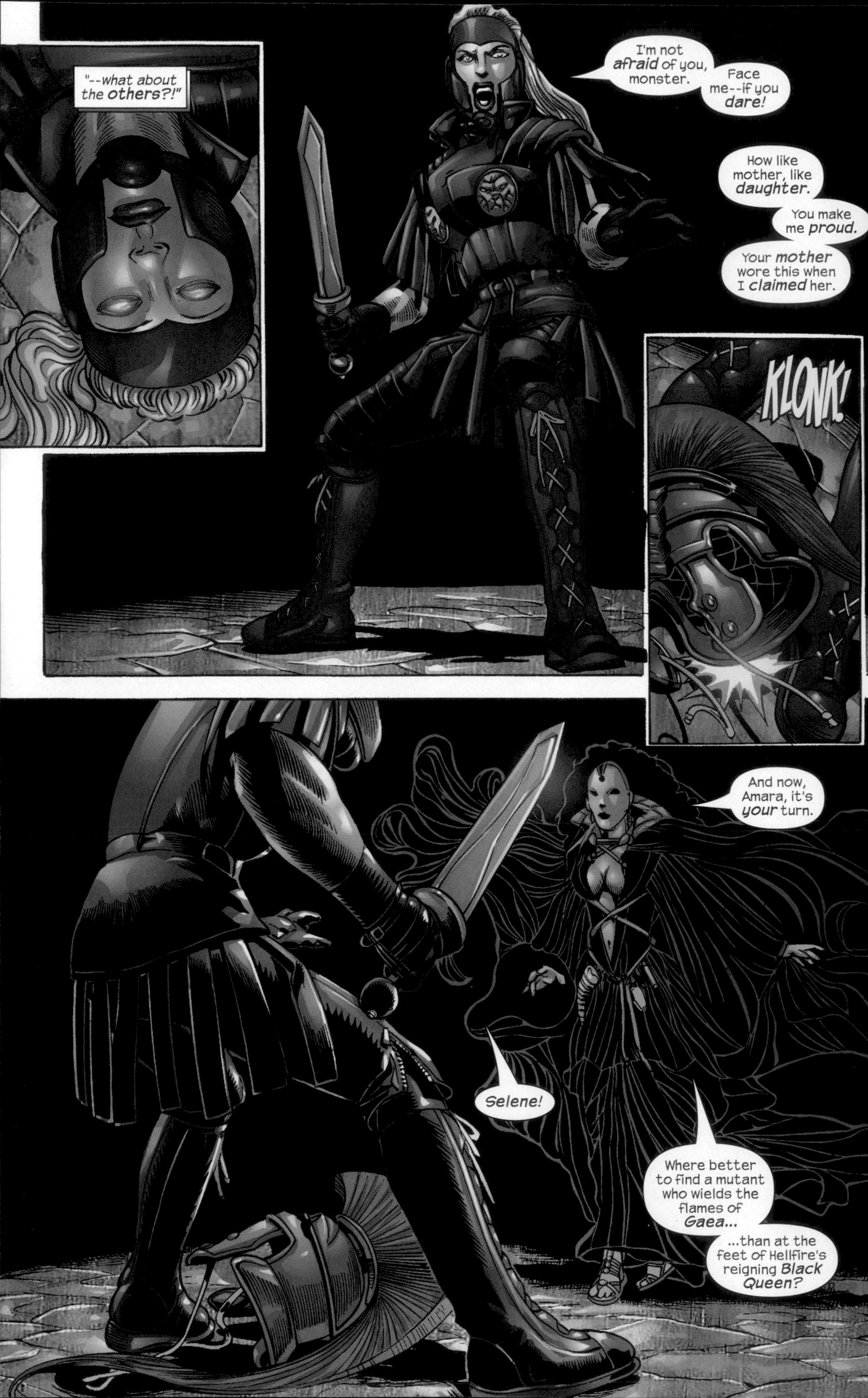
"--what about the *others?!*"
I'm not *afraid* of you, monster.
Face me--if you *dare!*
How like mother, like *daughter.*
You make me *proud.*
Your *mother* wore this when I *claimed* her.
KLONK!
And now, Amara, it's *your* turn.
Selene!
Where better to find a mutant who wields the flames of *Gaea...*
...than at the feet of Hellfire's reigning *Black Queen?*

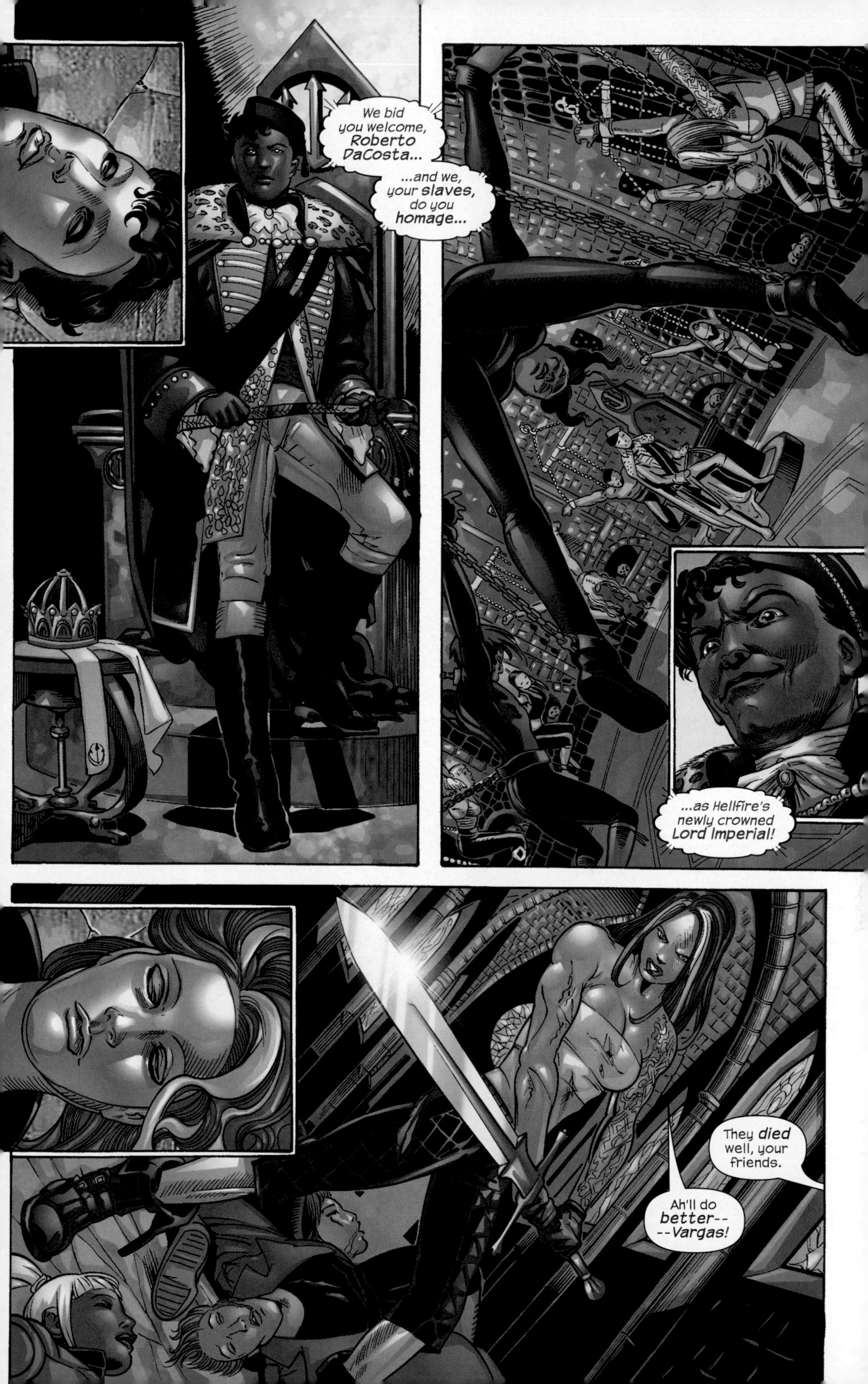
We bid you welcome, Roberto DaCosta...
...and we, your slaves, do you homage...
...as Hellfire's newly crowned Lord Imperial!
They died well, your friends.
Ah'll do better--
--Vargas!

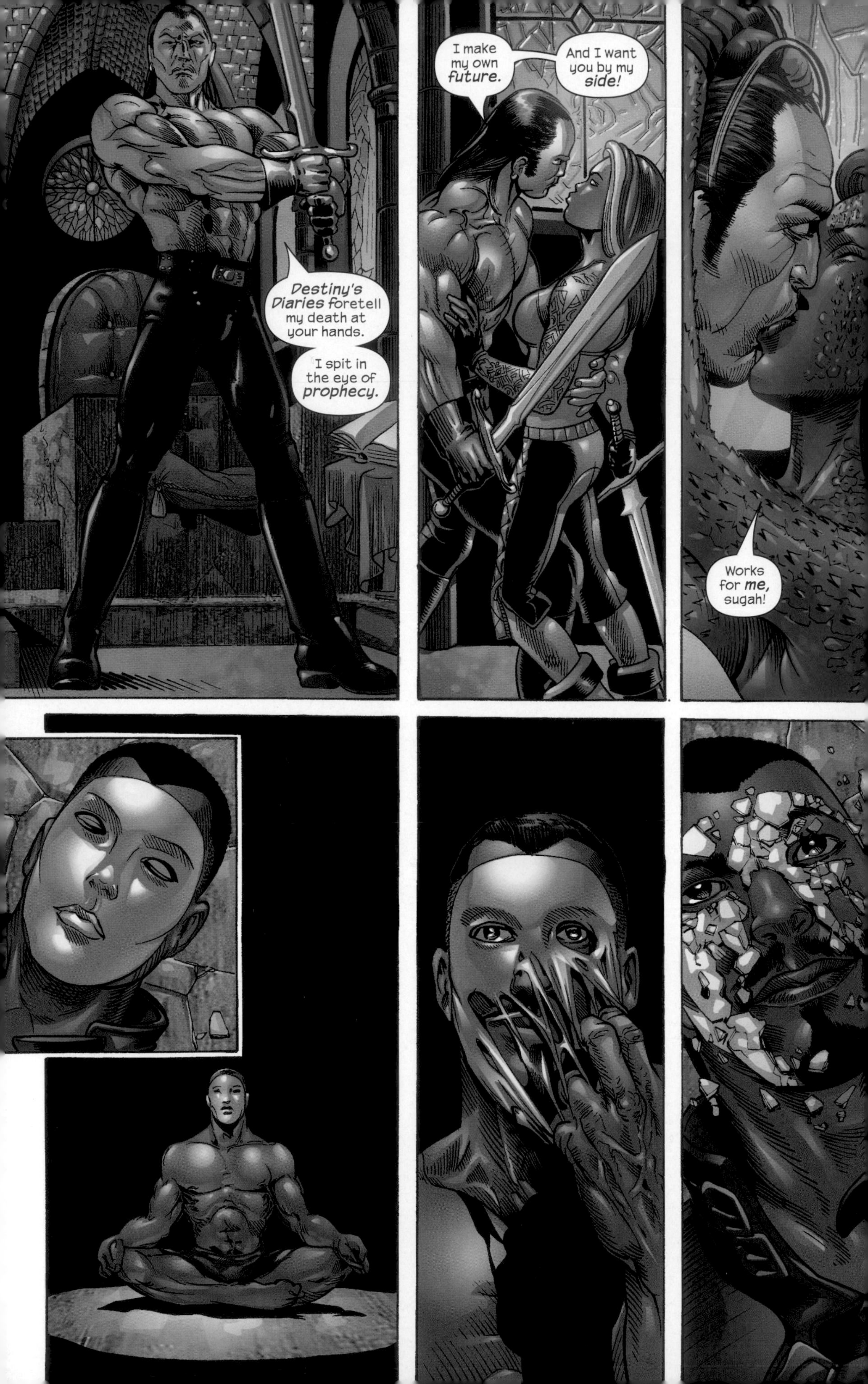
Destiny's Diaries foretell my death at your hands.
I spit in the eye of prophecy.
I make my own future.
And I want you by my side!
Works for me, sugah!

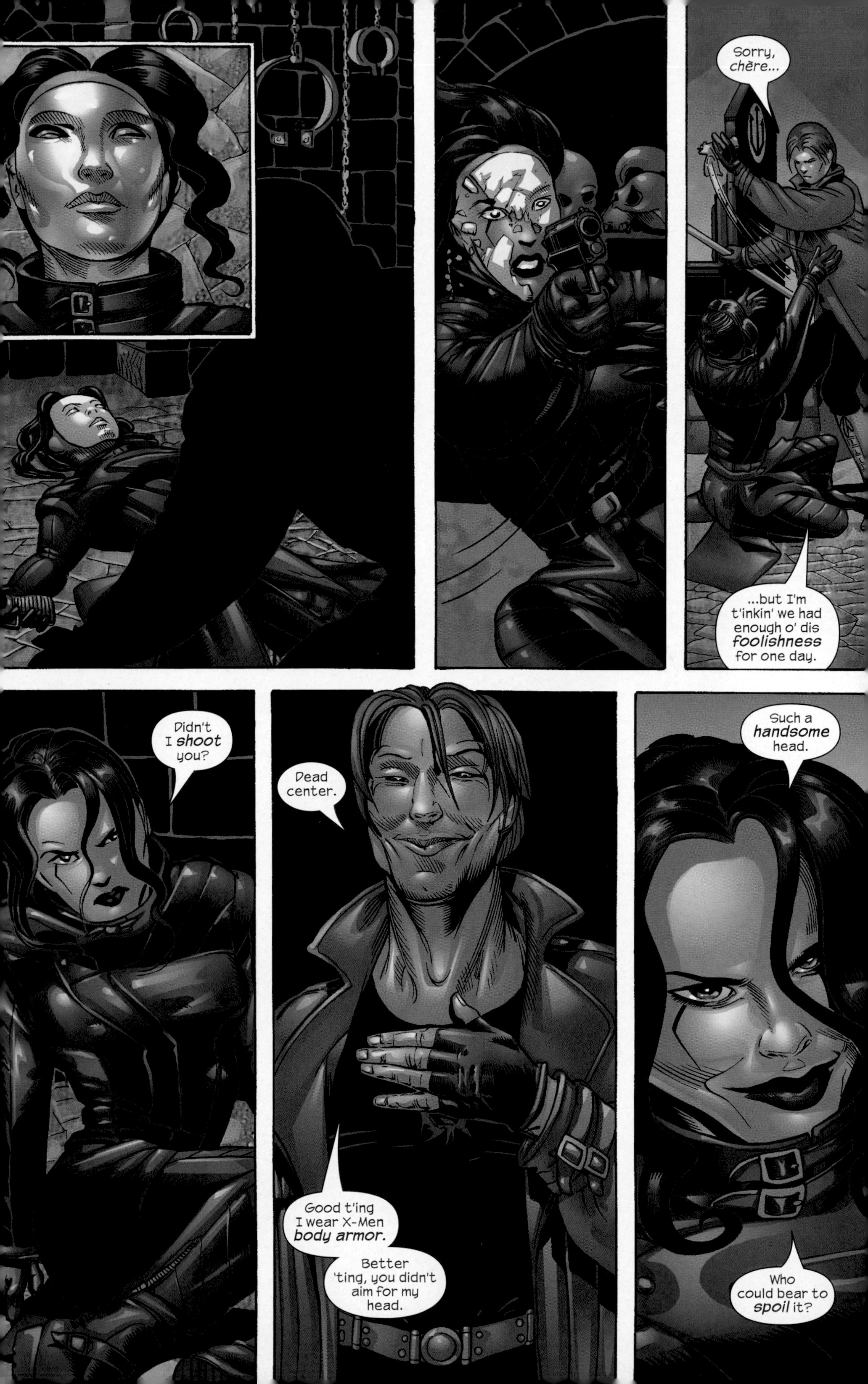
Sorry, chère...
...but I'm t'inkin' we had enough o' dis *foolishness* for one day.
Didn't I *shoot* you?
Dead center.
Good t'ing I wear X-Men *body armor.*
Better 'ting, you didn't aim for my head.
Such a *handsome* head.
Who could bear to *spoil* it?

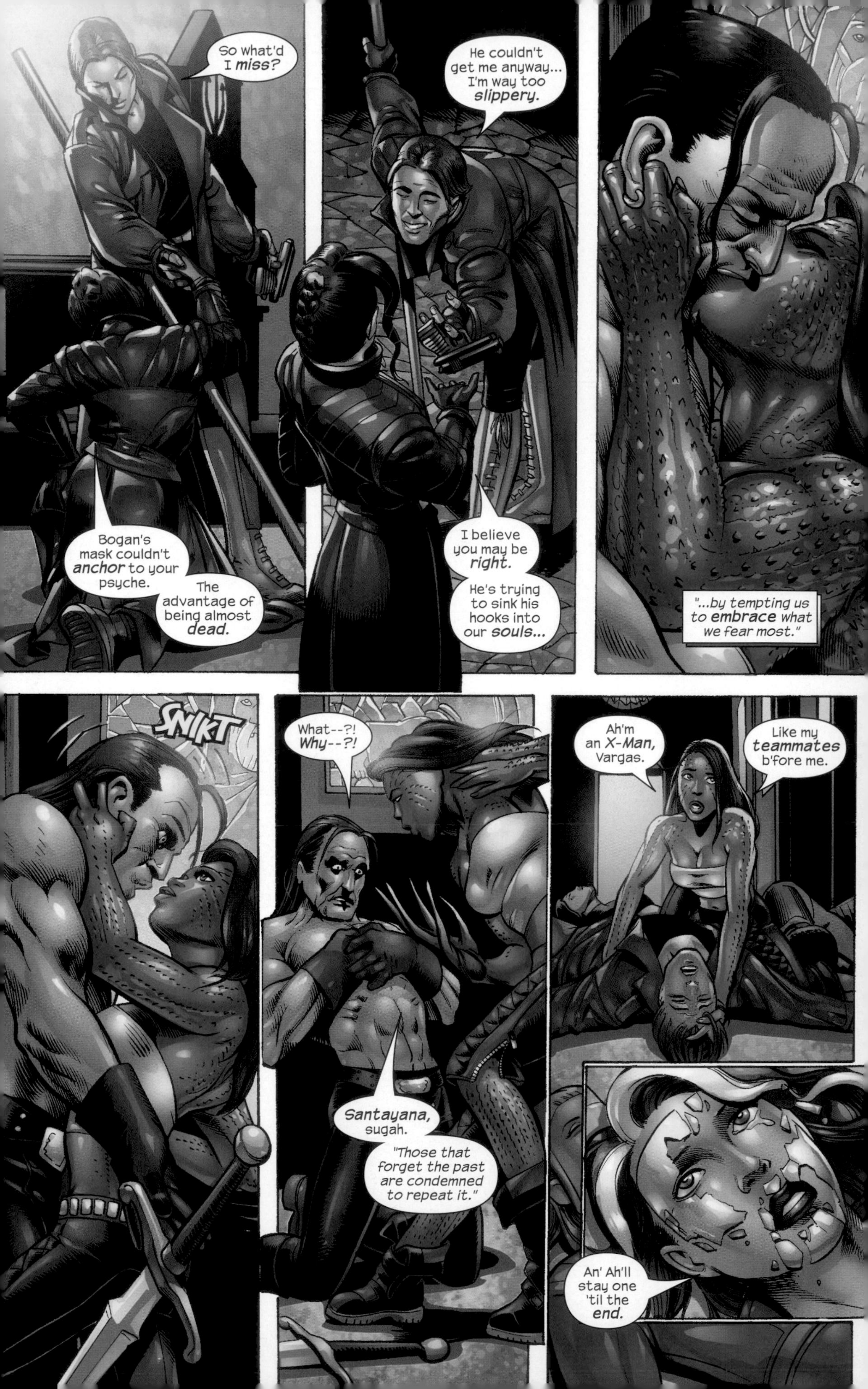
So what'd I miss?
Bogan's mask couldn't anchor to your psyche.
The advantage of being almost dead.
He couldn't get me anyway... I'm way too slippery.
I believe you may be right.
He's trying to sink his hooks into our souls...
"...by tempting us to embrace what we fear most."
SNIKT
What--?! Why--?!
Santayana, sugah.
"Those that forget the past are condemned to repeat it."
Ah'm an X-Man, Vargas.
Like my teammates b'fore me.
An' Ah'll stay one 'til the end.

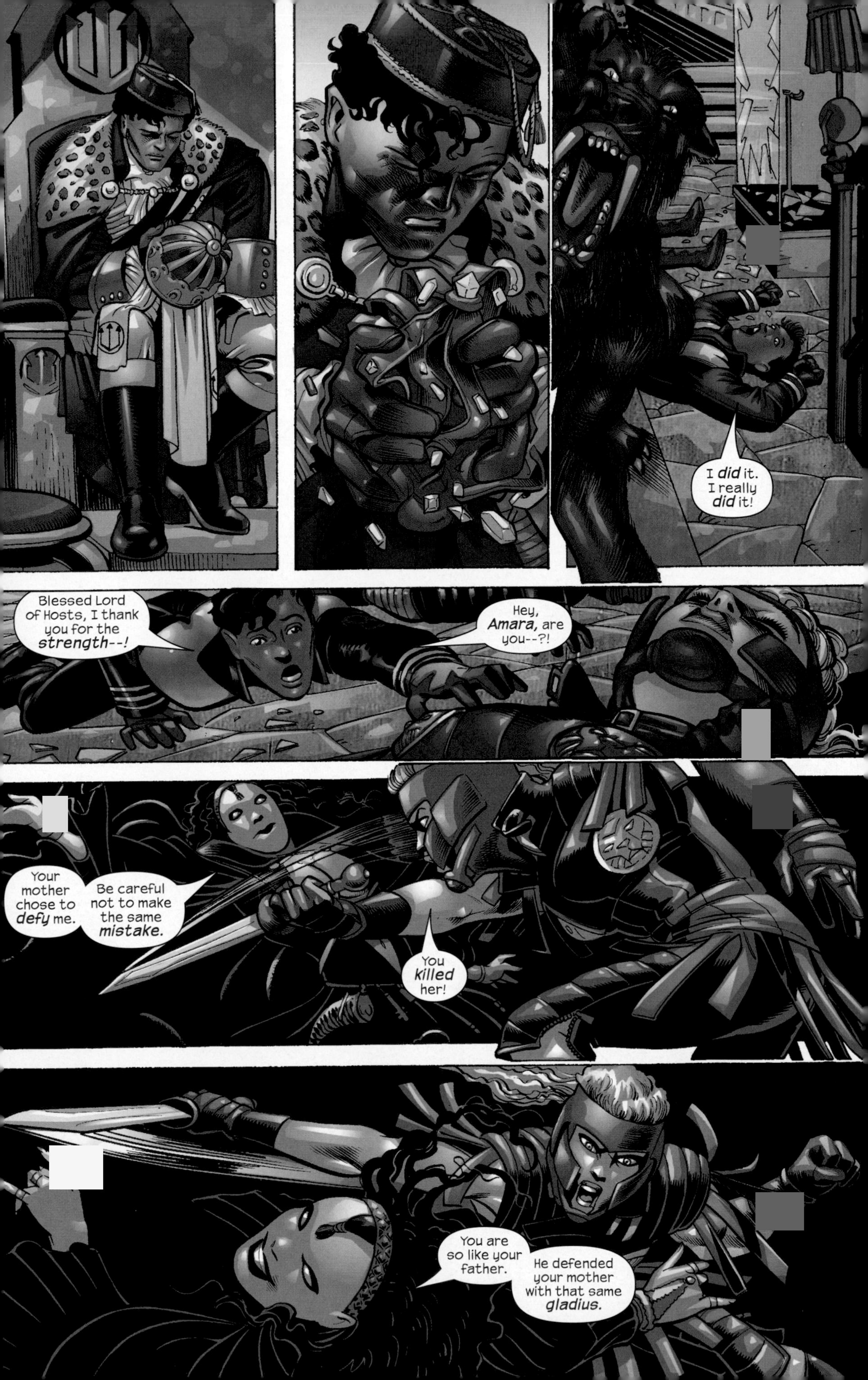
I did it. I really did it!
Blessed Lord of Hosts, I thank you for the strength--!
Hey, Amara, are you--?!
Your mother chose to defy me.
Be careful not to make the same mistake.
You killed her!
You are so like your father.
He defended your mother with that same gladius.

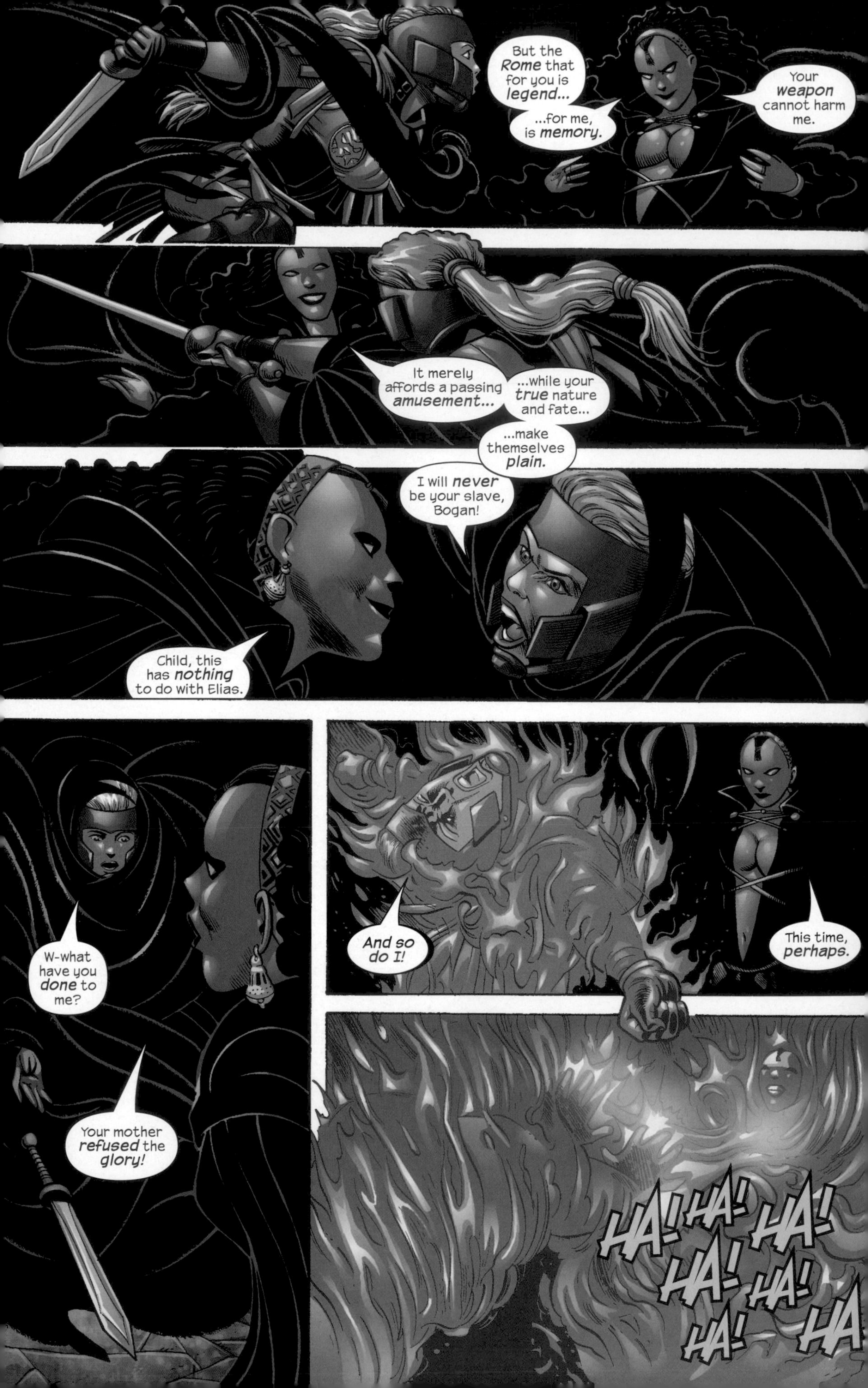

But the Rome that for you is legend...
...for me, is memory.
Your weapon cannot harm me.
It merely affords a passing amusement...
...while your true nature and fate...
...make themselves plain.
I will never be your slave, Bogan!
Child, this has nothing to do with Elias.
W-what have you done to me?
Your mother refused the glory!
And so do I!
This time, perhaps.
HA! HA! HA! HA! HA! HA! HA

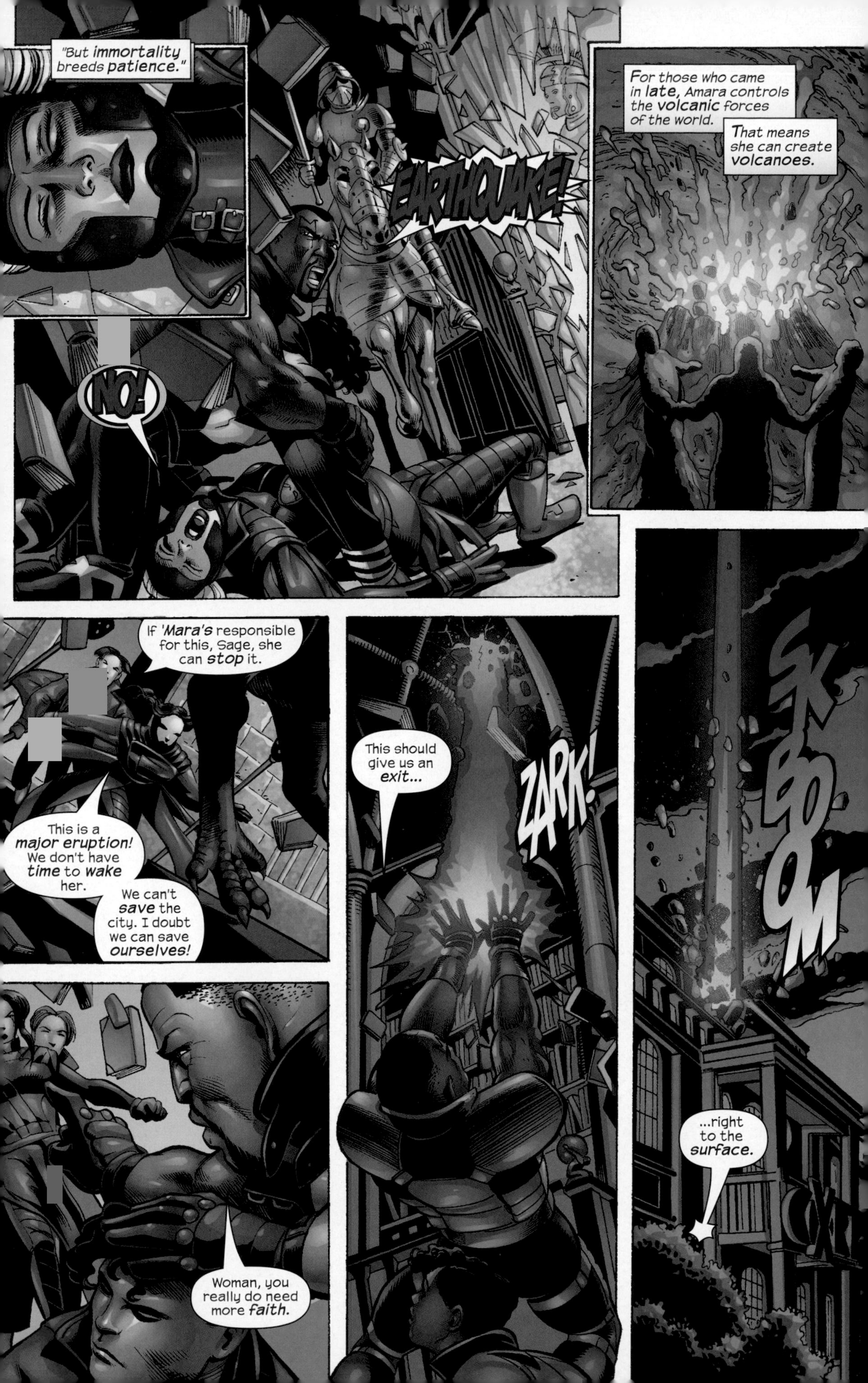
"But immortality breeds patience."
EARTHQUAKE!
NO!
For those who came in late, Amara controls the volcanic forces of the world.
That means she can create volcanoes.
If 'Mara's responsible for this, Sage, she can stop it.
This is a major eruption! We don't have time to wake her.
We can't save the city. I doubt we can save ourselves!
Woman, you really do need more faith.
This should give us an exit...
ZARK!
SKBOOM
...right to the surface.

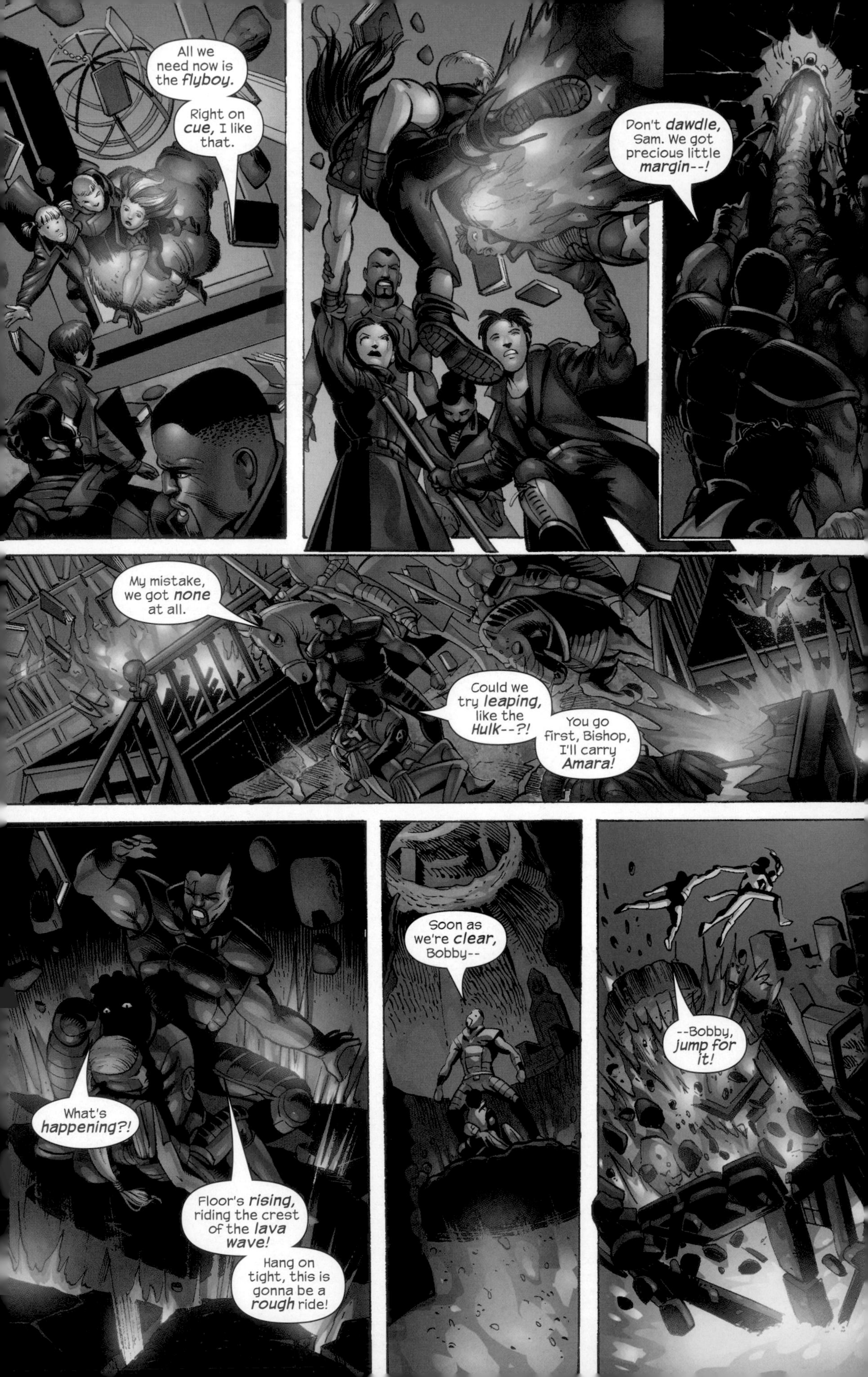
All we need now is the flyboy.
Right on cue, I like that.
Don't dawdle, Sam. We got precious little margin--!
My mistake, we got none at all.
Could we try leaping, like the Hulk--?!
You go first, Bishop, I'll carry Amara!
What's happening?!
Floor's rising, riding the crest of the lava wave!
Hang on tight, this is gonna be a rough ride!
Soon as we're clear, Bobby--
--Bobby, jump for it!

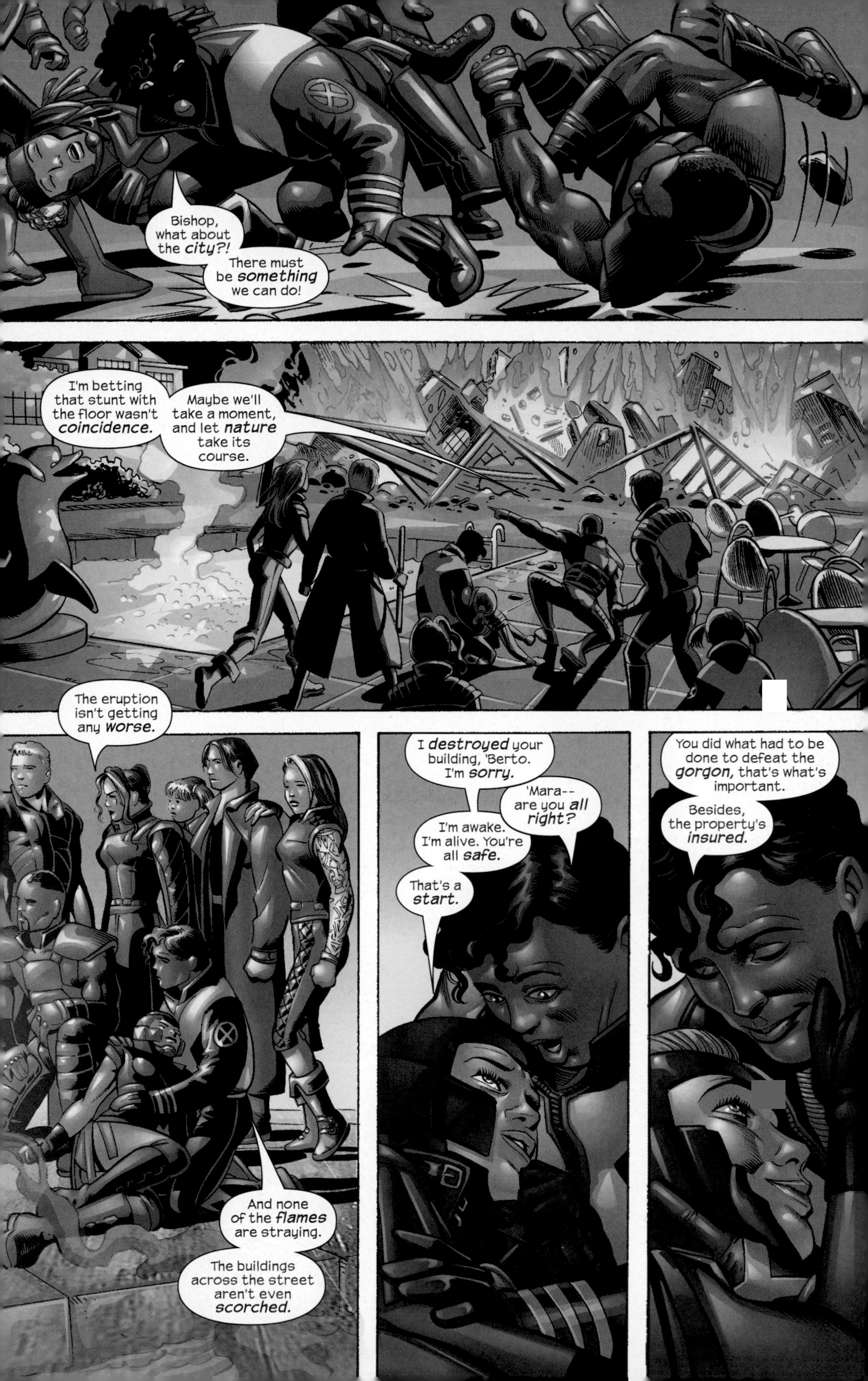
Bishop, what about the *city?!*
There must be *something* we can do!
I'm betting that stunt with the floor wasn't *coincidence.*
Maybe we'll take a moment, and let *nature* take its course.
The eruption isn't getting any *worse.*
And none of the *flames* are straying.
The buildings across the street aren't even *scorched.*
I *destroyed* your building, 'Berto. I'm *sorry.*
'Mara-- are you *all right?*
I'm awake. I'm alive. You're all *safe.*
That's a *start.*
You did what had to be done to defeat the *gorgon,* that's what's important.
Besides, the property's *insured.*

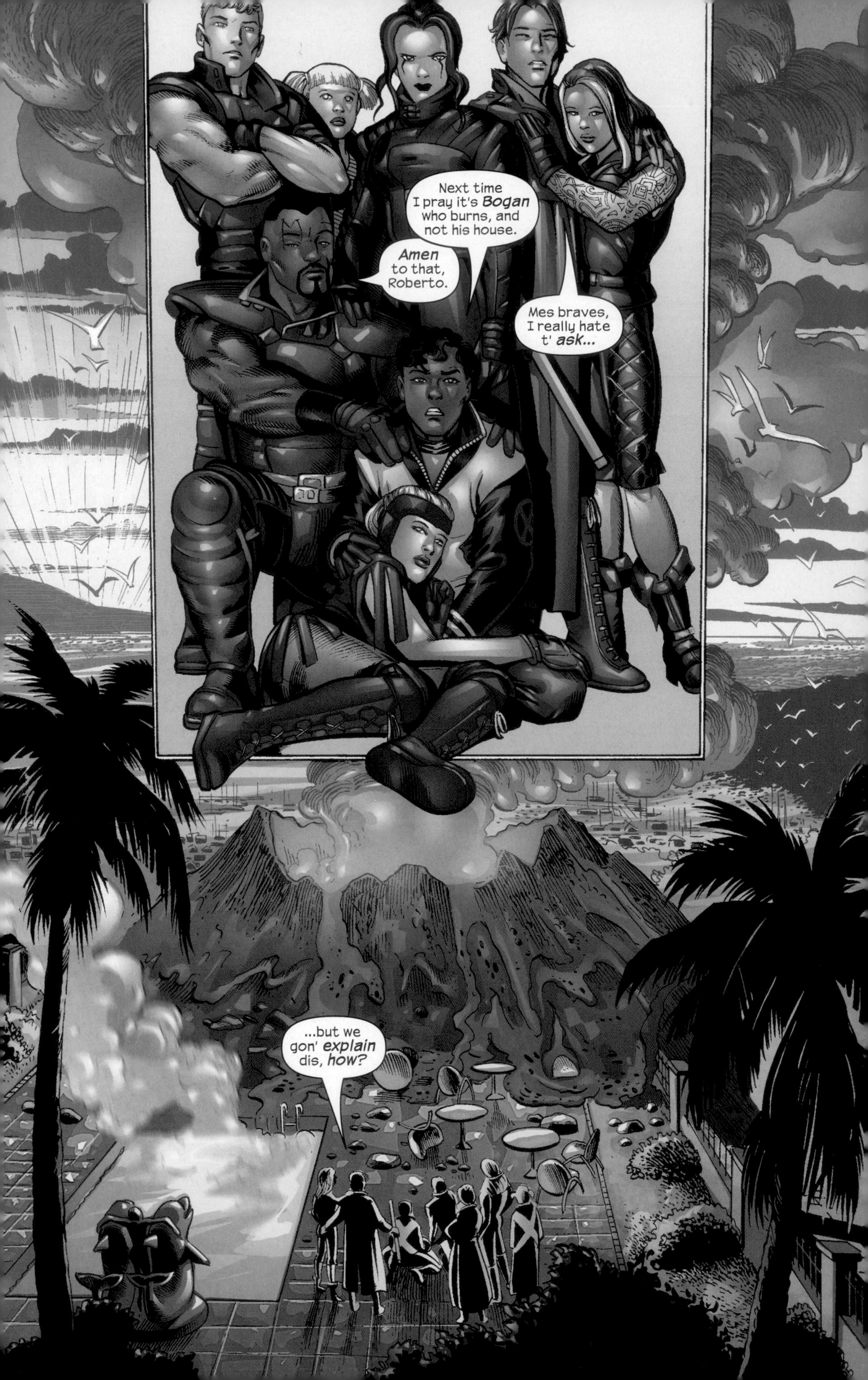
Next time I pray it's Bogan who burns, and not his house.
Amen to that, Roberto.
Mes braves, I really hate t' ask...
...but we gon' explain dis, how?

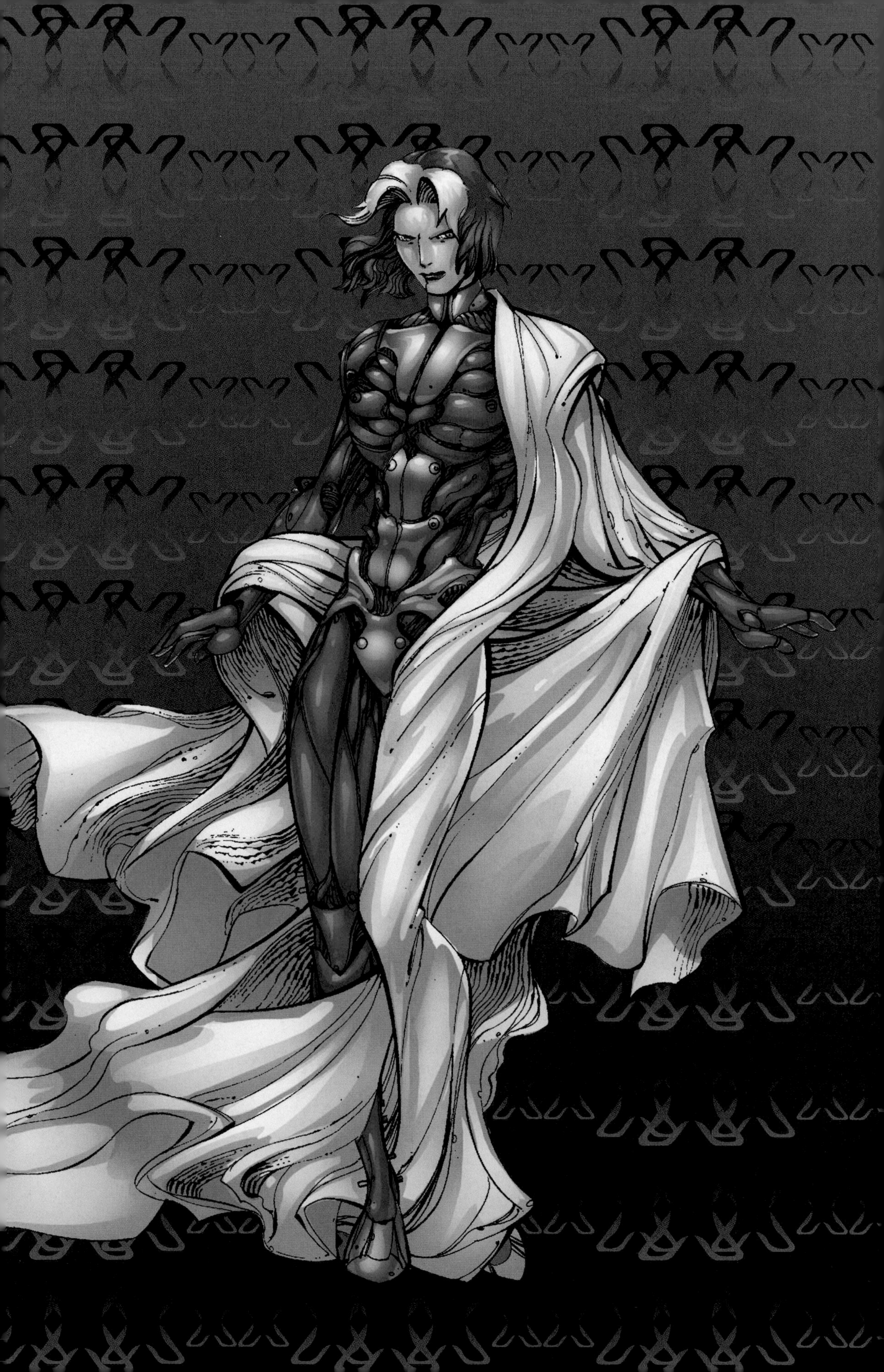

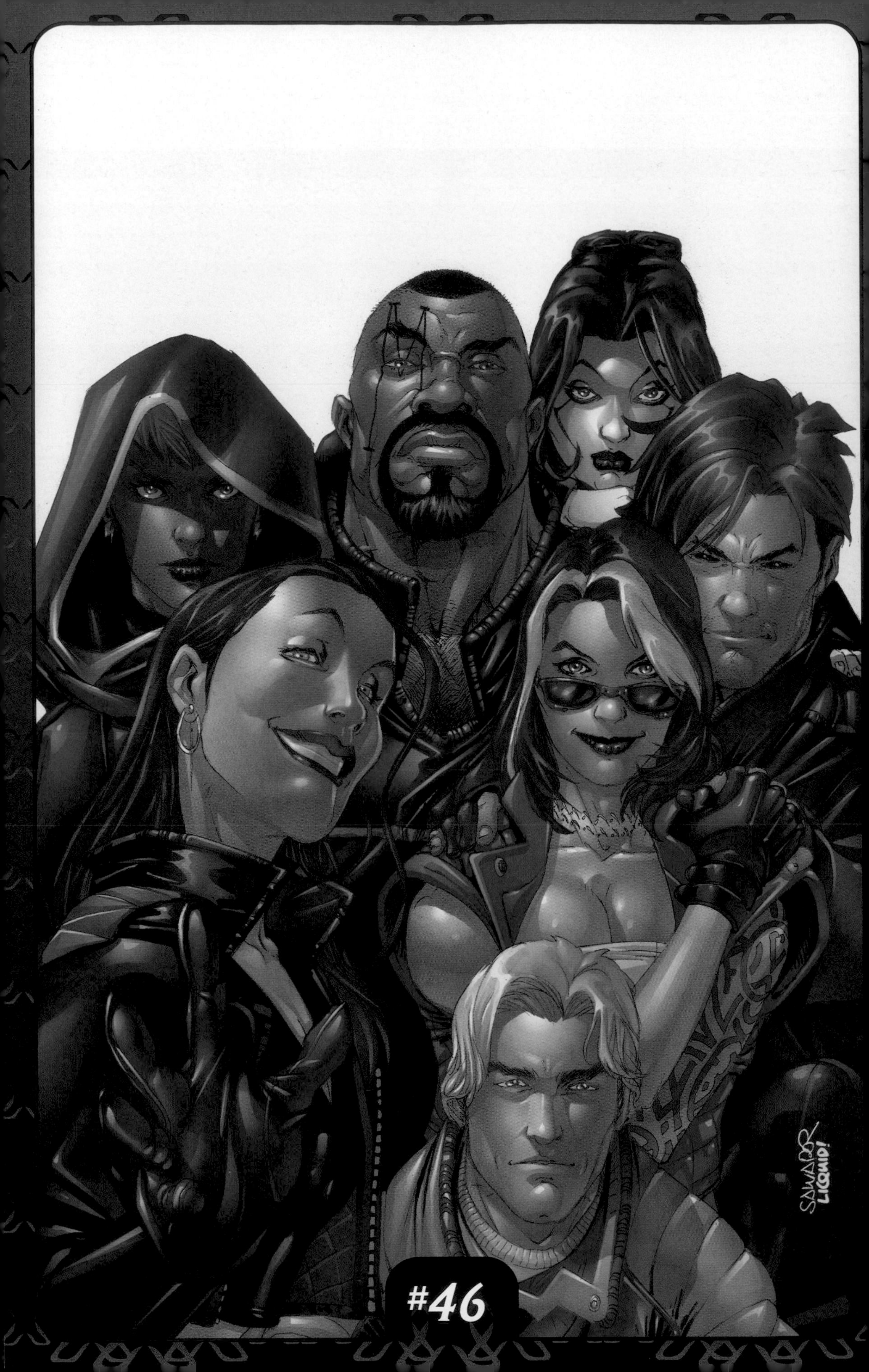
SALVADOR
LIQUID!
#46

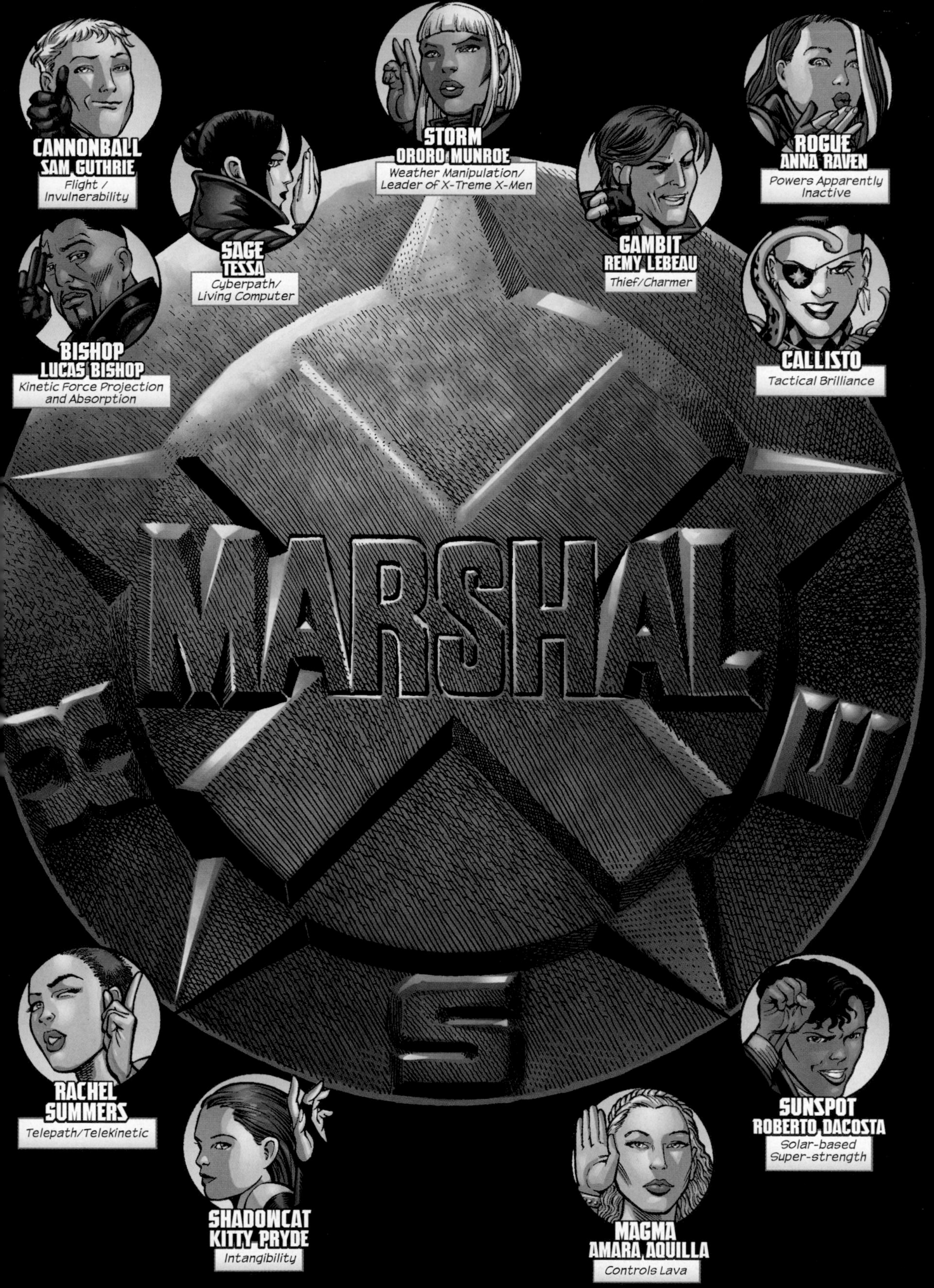
CANNONBALL
SAM GUTHRIE
Flight / Invulnerability
STORM
ORORO MUNROE
Weather Manipulation/ Leader of X-Treme X-Men
ROGUE
ANNA RAVEN
Powers Apparently Inactive
SAGE
TESSA
Cyberpath/ Living Computer
GAMBIT
REMY LEBEAU
Thief/Charmer
BISHOP
LUCAS BISHOP
Kinetic Force Projection and Absorption
CALLISTO
Tactical Brilliance
MARSHAL
S
RACHEL SUMMERS
Telepath/Telekinetic
SUNSPOT
ROBERTO DACOSTA
Solar-based Super-strength
SHADOWCAT
KITTY PRYDE
Intangibility
MAGMA
AMARA AQUILLA
Controls Lava

STAN LEE PROUDLY PRESENTS THE FINAL ISSUE OF *X-TREME X-MEN*

One For My Lady...

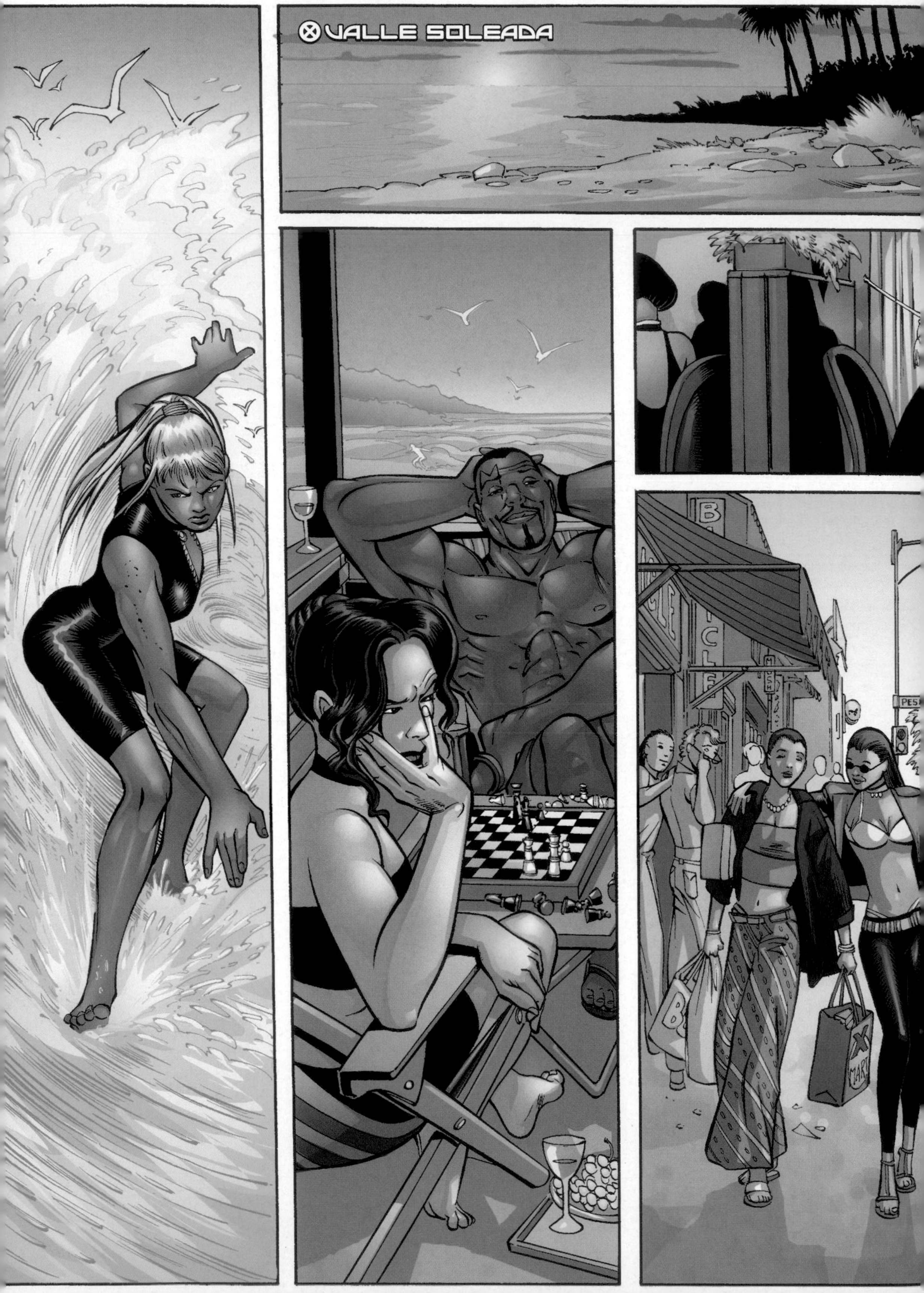

VALLE SOLEADA

...One More For The Road

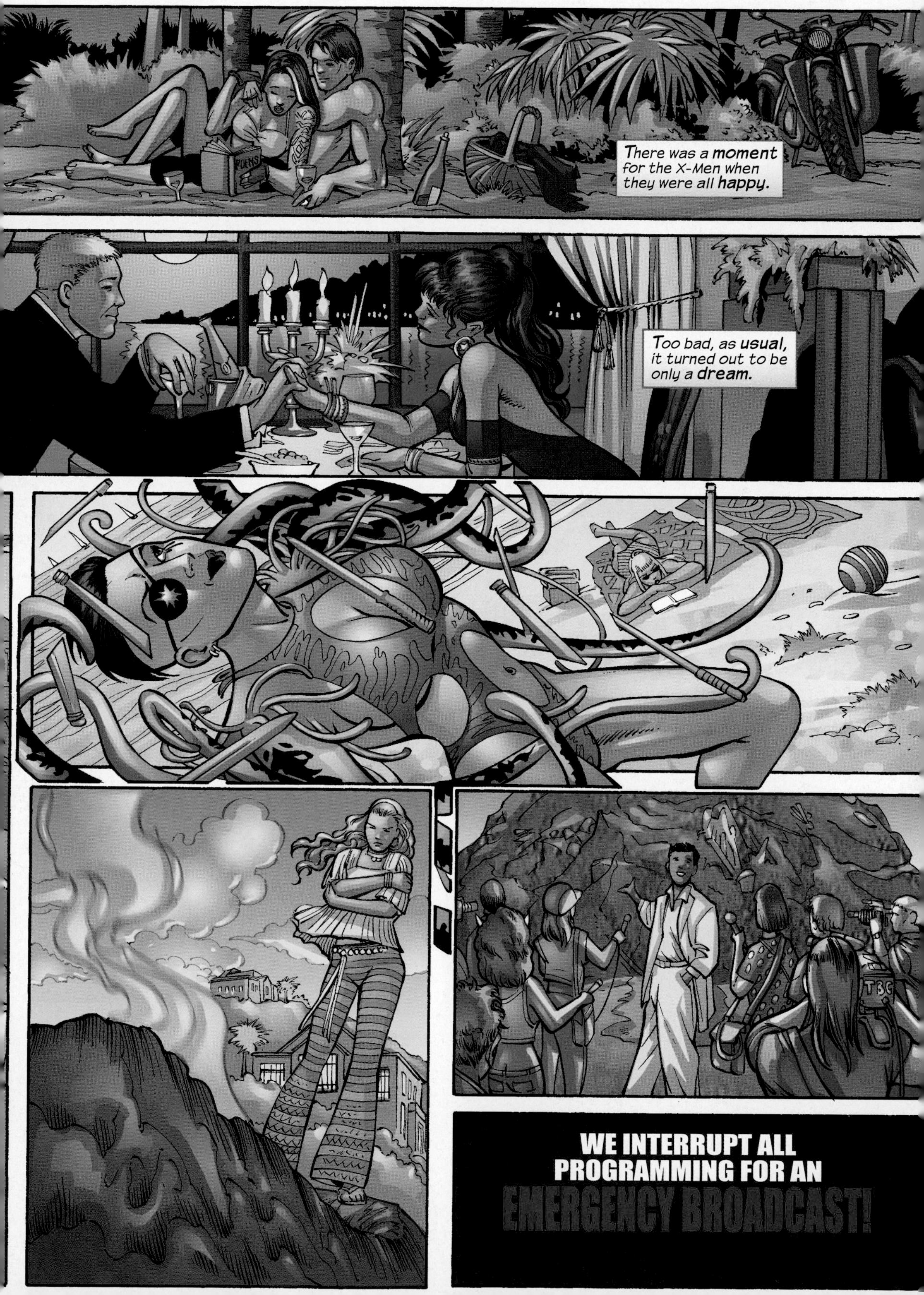
POEMS
There was a moment for the X-Men when they were all happy.
Too bad, as usual, it turned out to be only a dream.
TBG
WE INTERRUPT ALL PROGRAMMING FOR AN
EMERGENCY BROADCAST!

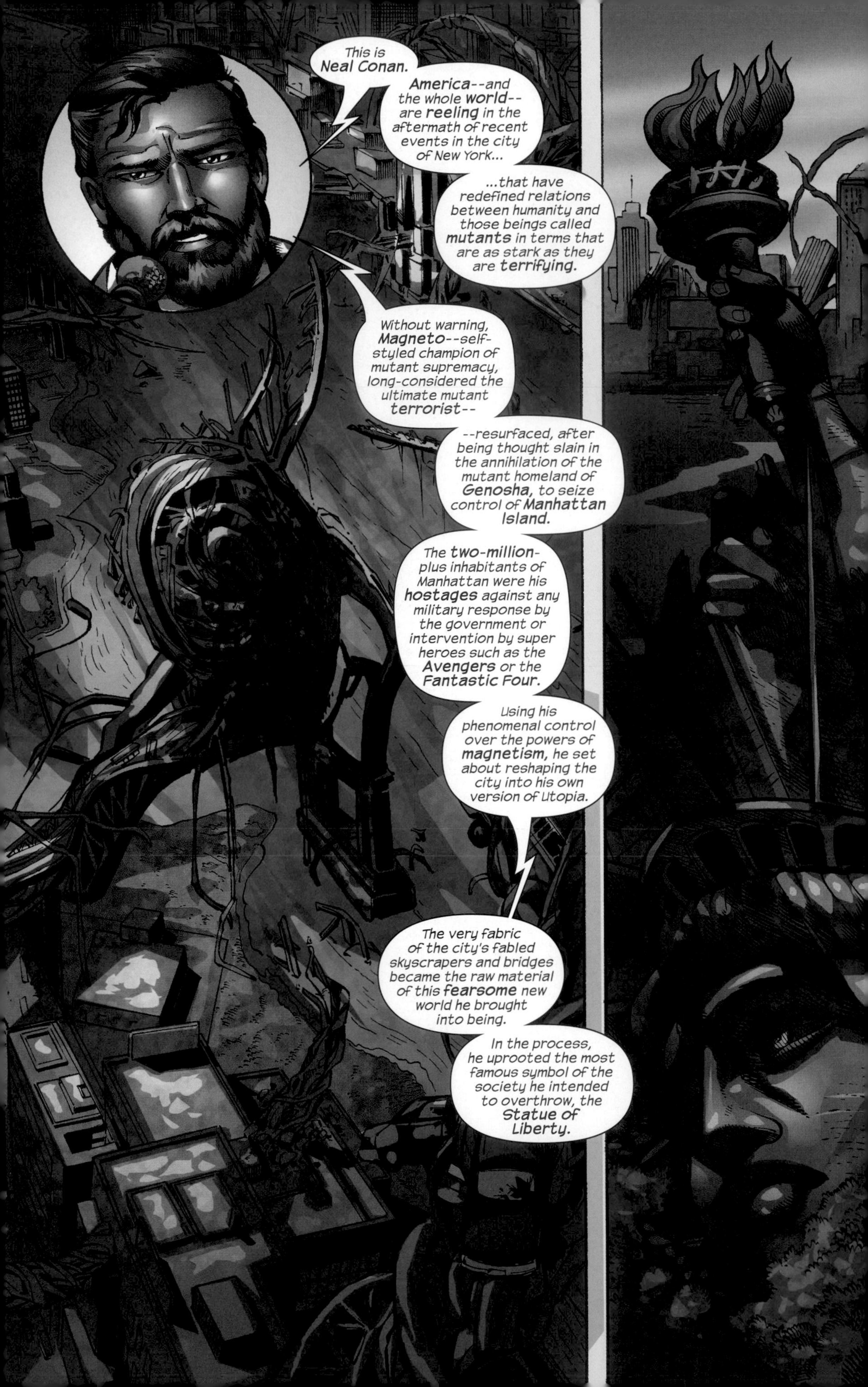
This is Neal Conan.
America--and the whole world--are reeling in the aftermath of recent events in the city of New York...
...that have redefined relations between humanity and those beings called mutants in terms that are as stark as they are terrifying.
Without warning, Magneto--self-styled champion of mutant supremacy, long-considered the ultimate mutant terrorist--
--resurfaced, after being thought slain in the annihilation of the mutant homeland of Genosha, to seize control of Manhattan Island.
The two-million-plus inhabitants of Manhattan were his hostages against any military response by the government or intervention by super heroes such as the Avengers or the Fantastic Four.
Using his phenomenal control over the powers of magnetism, he set about reshaping the city into his own version of Utopia.
The very fabric of the city's fabled skyscrapers and bridges became the raw material of this fearsome new world he brought into being.
In the process, he uprooted the most famous symbol of the society he intended to overthrow, the Statue of Liberty.

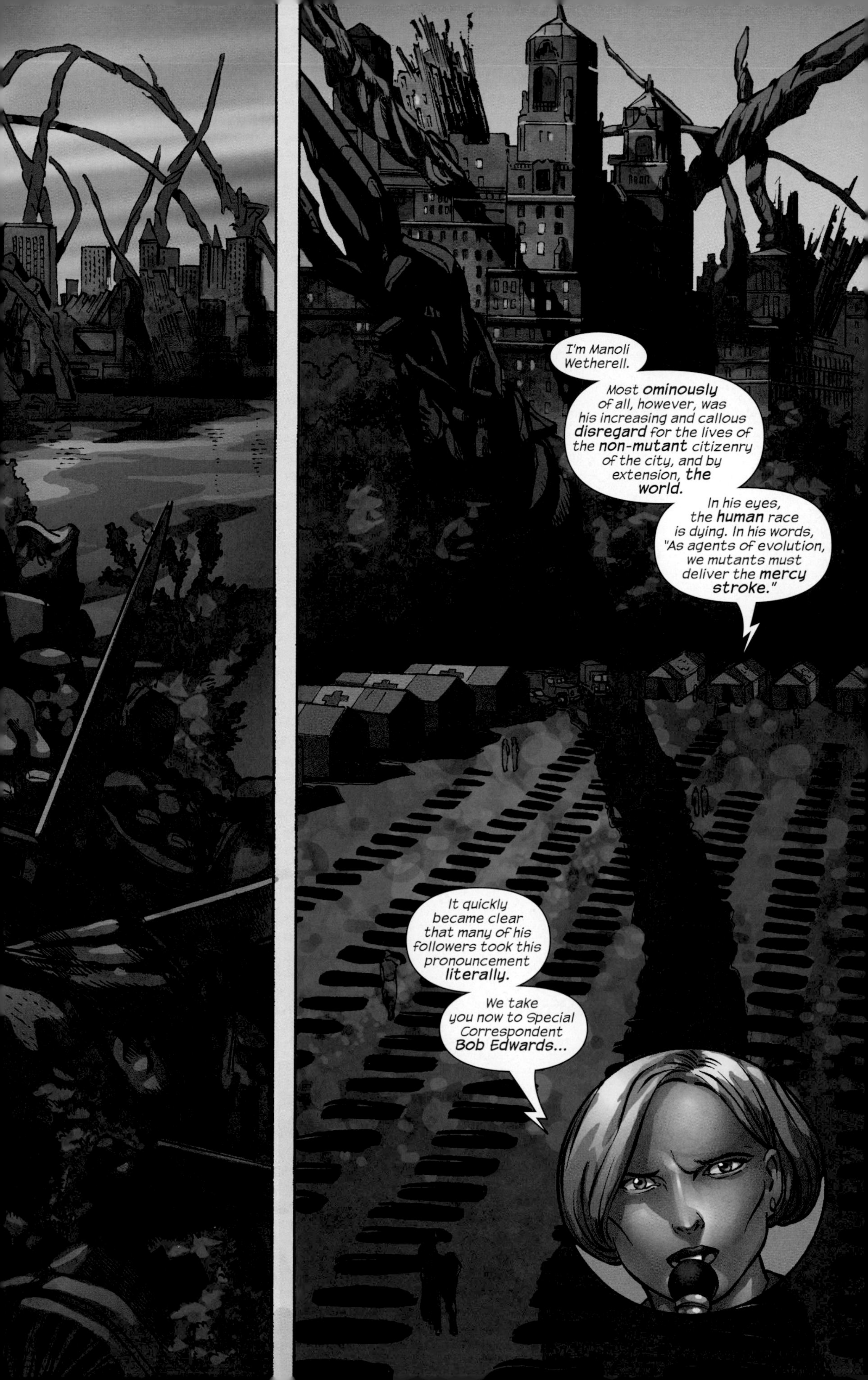
I'm Manoli Wetherell.
Most ominously of all, however, was his increasing and callous disregard for the lives of the non-mutant citizenry of the city, and by extension, the world.
In his eyes, the human race is dying. In his words, "As agents of evolution, we mutants must deliver the mercy stroke."
It quickly became clear that many of his followers took this pronouncement literally.
We take you now to Special Correspondent Bob Edwards...

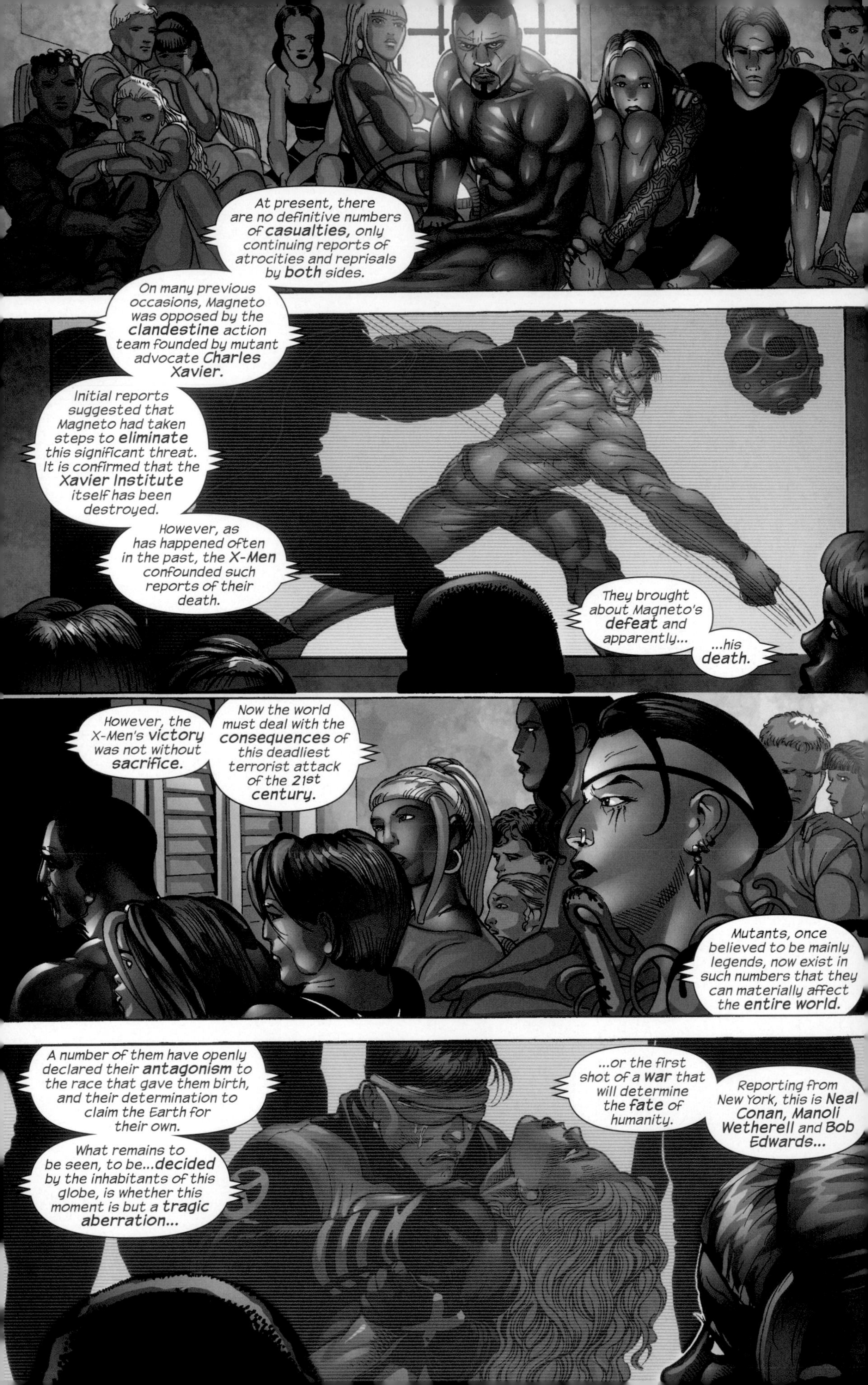
At present, there are no definitive numbers of casualties, only continuing reports of atrocities and reprisals by both sides.
On many previous occasions, Magneto was opposed by the clandestine action team founded by mutant advocate Charles Xavier.
Initial reports suggested that Magneto had taken steps to eliminate this significant threat. It is confirmed that the Xavier Institute itself has been destroyed.
However, as has happened often in the past, the X-Men confounded such reports of their death.
They brought about Magneto's defeat and apparently...
...his death.
However, the X-Men's victory was not without sacrifice.
Now the world must deal with the consequences of this deadliest terrorist attack of the 21st century.
Mutants, once believed to be mainly legends, now exist in such numbers that they can materially affect the entire world.
A number of them have openly declared their antagonism to the race that gave them birth, and their determination to claim the Earth for their own.
What remains to be seen, to be...decided by the inhabitants of this globe, is whether this moment is but a tragic aberration...
...or the first shot of a war that will determine the fate of humanity.
Reporting from New York, this is Neal Conan, Manoli Wetherell and Bob Edwards...

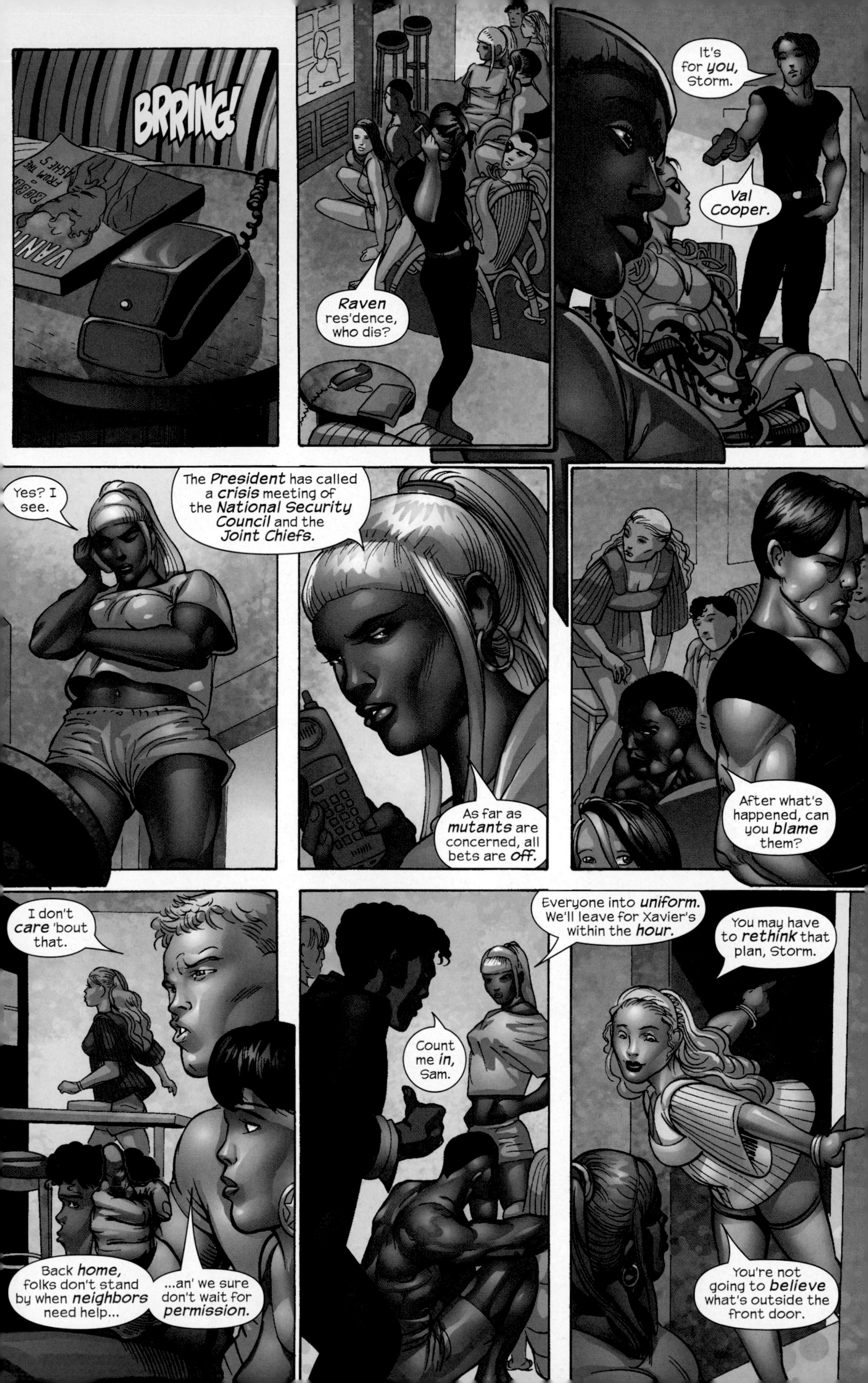
BRRING!
VANITY
Bobby from the Ashes
Raven res'dence, who dis?
It's for you, Storm.
Val Cooper.
Yes? I see.
The President has called a crisis meeting of the National Security Council and the Joint Chiefs.
As far as mutants are concerned, all bets are off.
After what's happened, can you blame them?
I don't care 'bout that.
Back home, folks don't stand by when neighbors need help...
...an' we sure don't wait for permission.
Everyone into uniform. We'll leave for Xavier's within the hour.
Count me in, Sam.
You may have to rethink that plan, Storm.
You're not going to believe what's outside the front door.

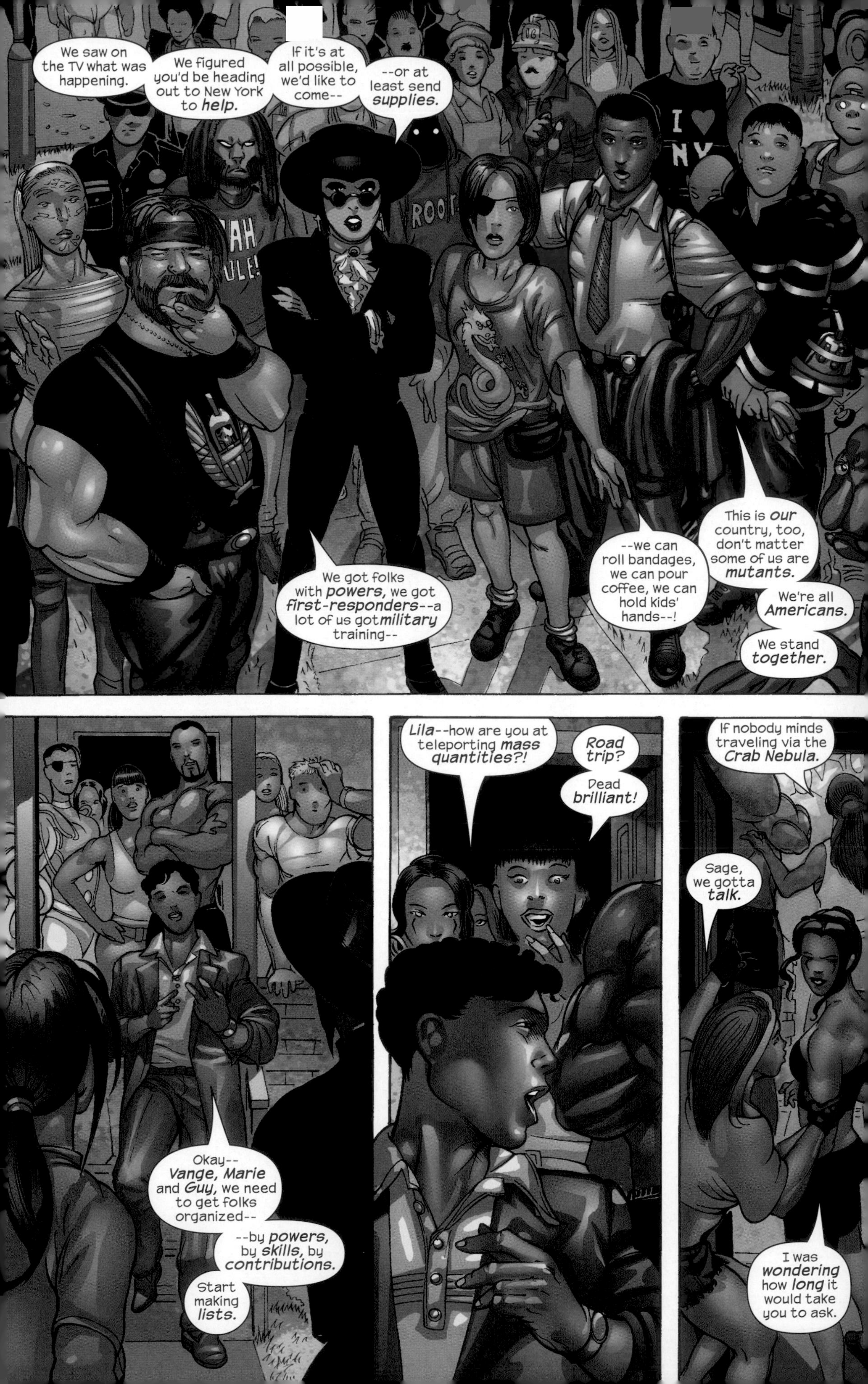
We saw on the TV what was happening.
We figured you'd be heading out to New York to help.
If it's at all possible, we'd like to come--
--or at least send supplies.
We got folks with powers, we got first-responders--a lot of us gotmilitary training--
--we can roll bandages, we can pour coffee, we can hold kids' hands--!
This is our country, too, don't matter some of us are mutants.
We're all Americans.
We stand together.
Okay-- Vange, Marie and Guy, we need to get folks organized--
--by powers, by skills, by contributions.
Start making lists.
Lila--how are you at teleporting mass quantities?!
Road trip?
Dead brilliant!
If nobody minds traveling via the Crab Nebula.
Sage, we gotta talk.
I was wondering how long it would take you to ask.

Dat *Bobby*, he's a *surprise.*

T'anks t' him an' Lila...

...we got a brace o' *semi-trailers* fully loaded an' on dere way.

Oh!

My!

Rogue--chère--did I miss a *cue*, a birthday, our anniversary--*what?*

Rogue, it's *killin'* me t' say dis--

--but dis ain't the time!

In this instance, Ah'd have ta go with *"what."*

Who's the one always sayin'--*carpe diem?*

Moments like this, Remy--and *opportunities*--

--they may never come again.

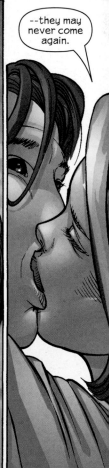

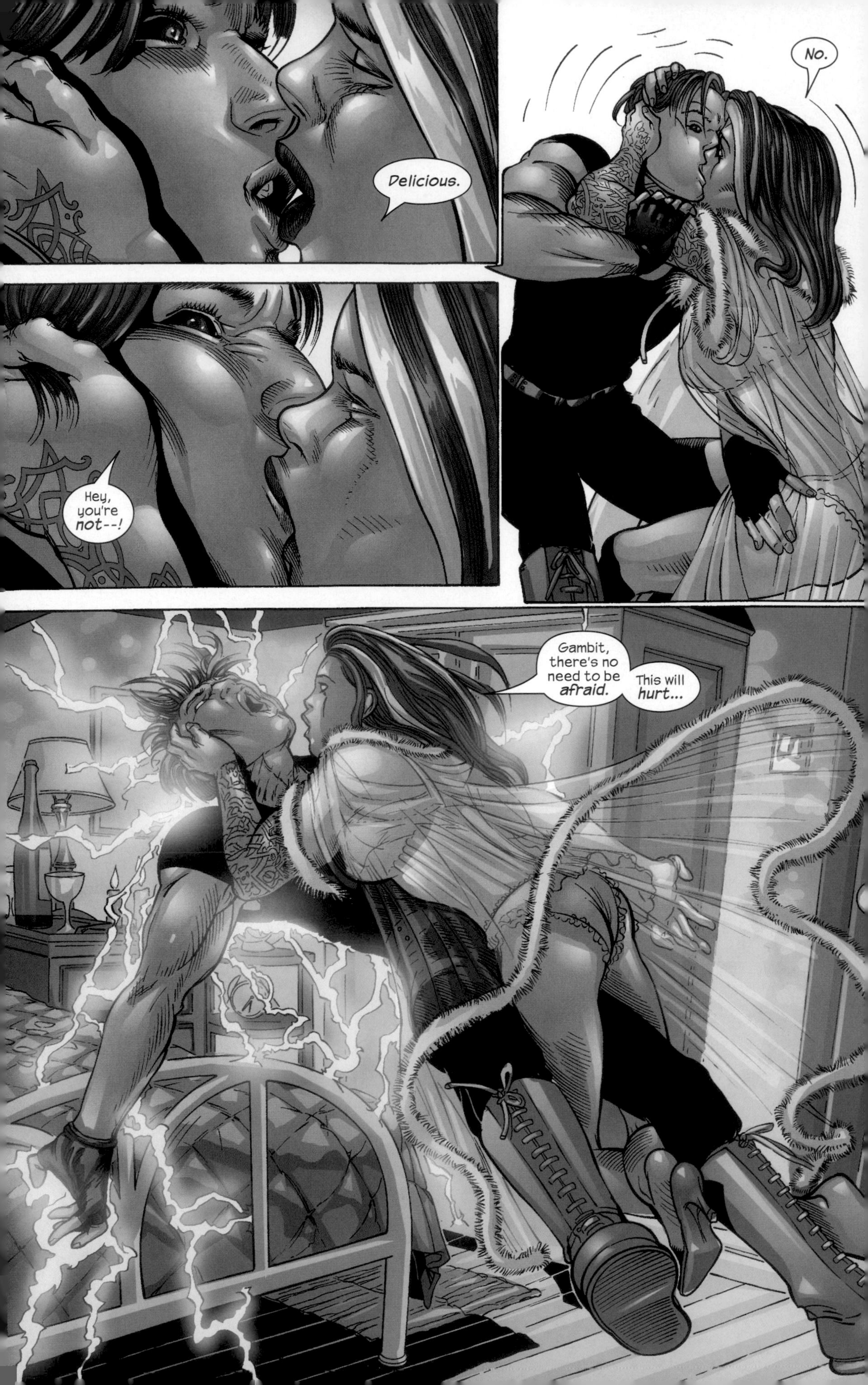
Delicious.
No.
Hey, you're not--!
Gambit, there's no need to be afraid.
This will hurt...

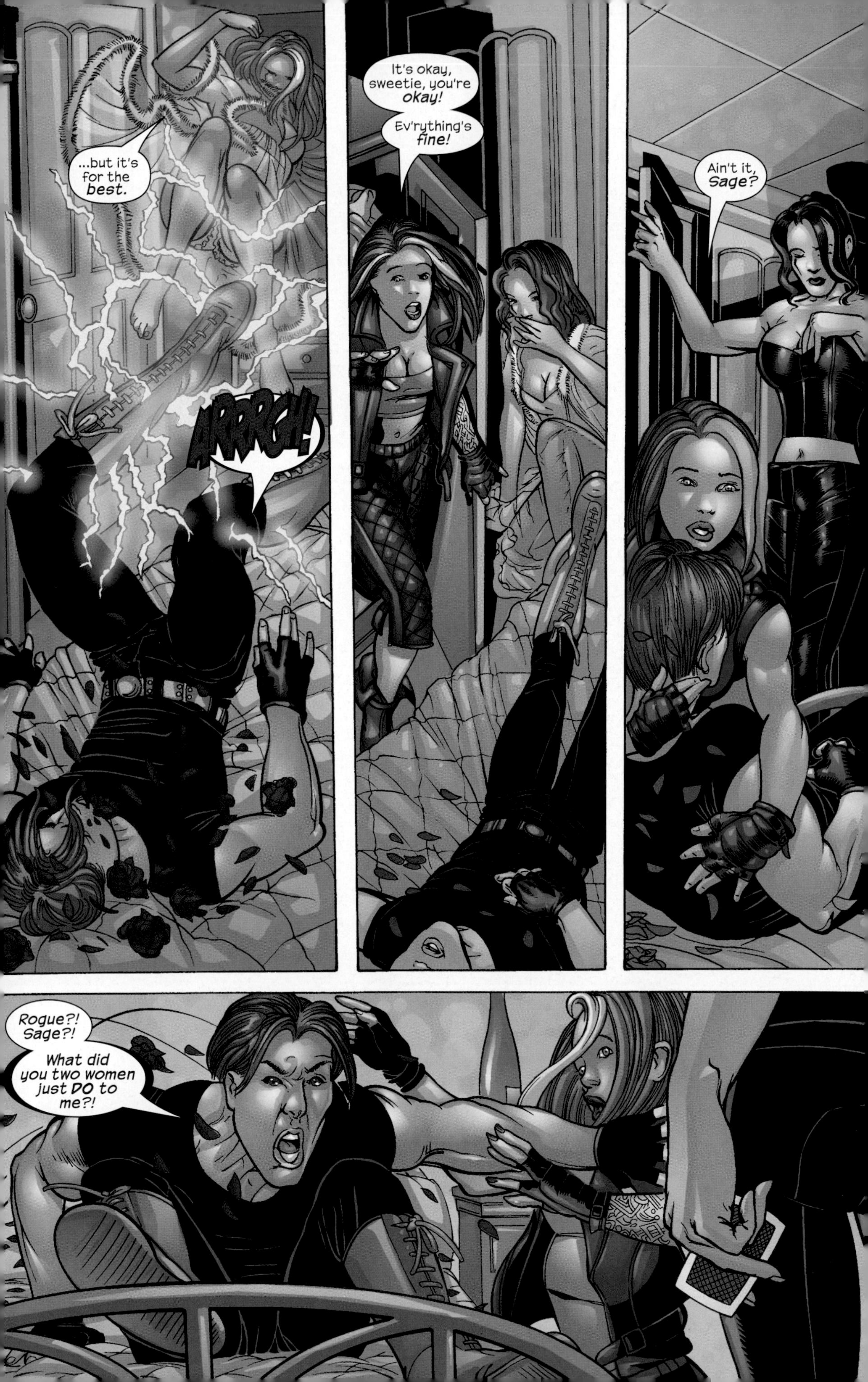

...but it's for the best.
ARRRGH!
It's okay, sweetie, you're okay!
Ev'rything's fine!
Ain't it, Sage?
Rogue?! Sage?!
What did you two women just DO to me?!

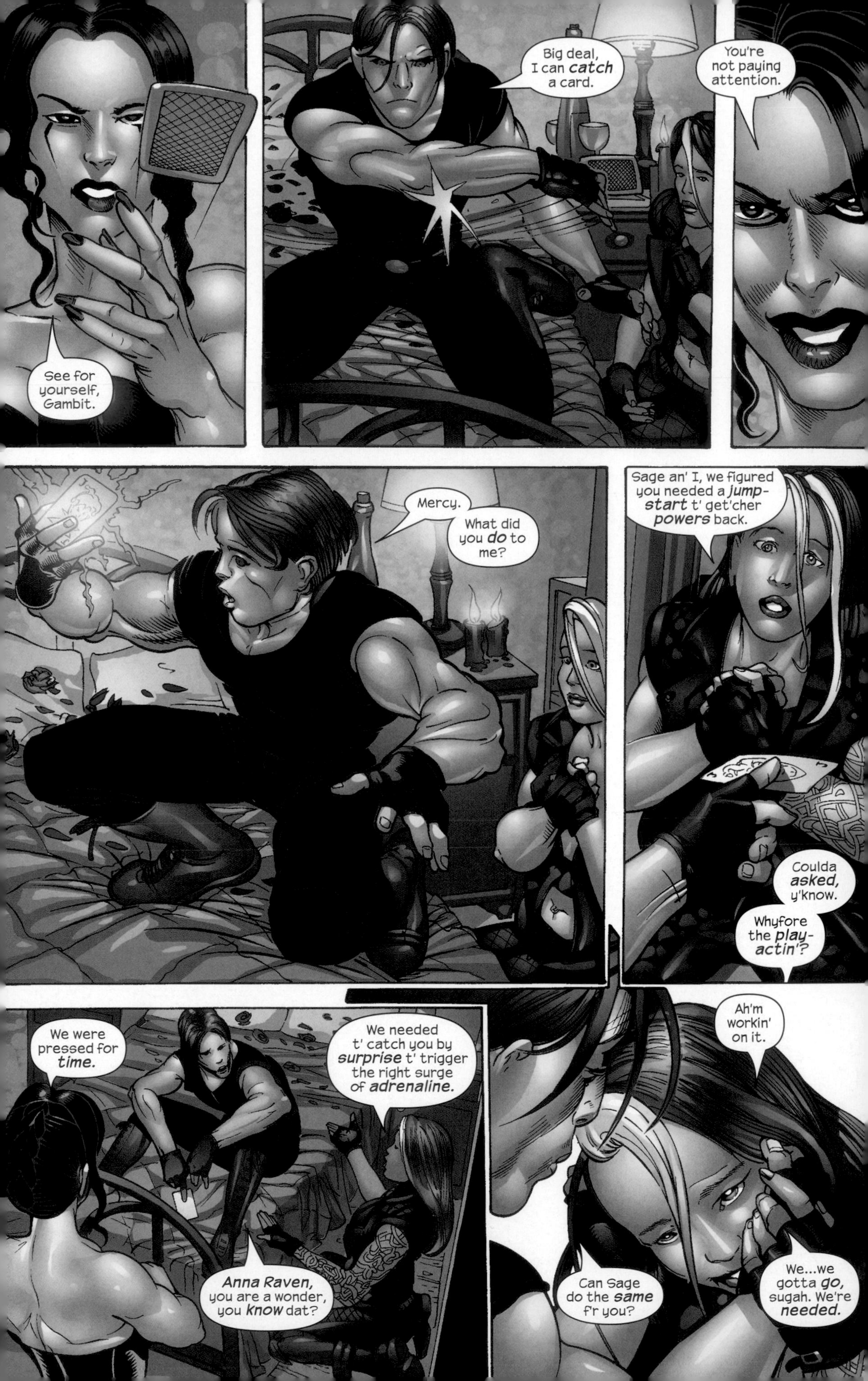
See for yourself, Gambit.
Big deal, I can *catch* a card.
You're not paying attention.
Mercy.
What did you *do* to me?
Sage an' I, we figured you needed a *jump-start* t' get'cher *powers* back.
Coulda *asked,* y'know.
Whyfore the *play-actin'*?
We were pressed for *time.*
We needed t' catch you by *surprise* t' trigger the right surge of *adrenaline.*
Anna Raven, you are a wonder, you *know* dat?
Ah'm workin' on it.
Can Sage do the *same* f'r you?
We...we gotta *go,* sugah. We're *needed.*

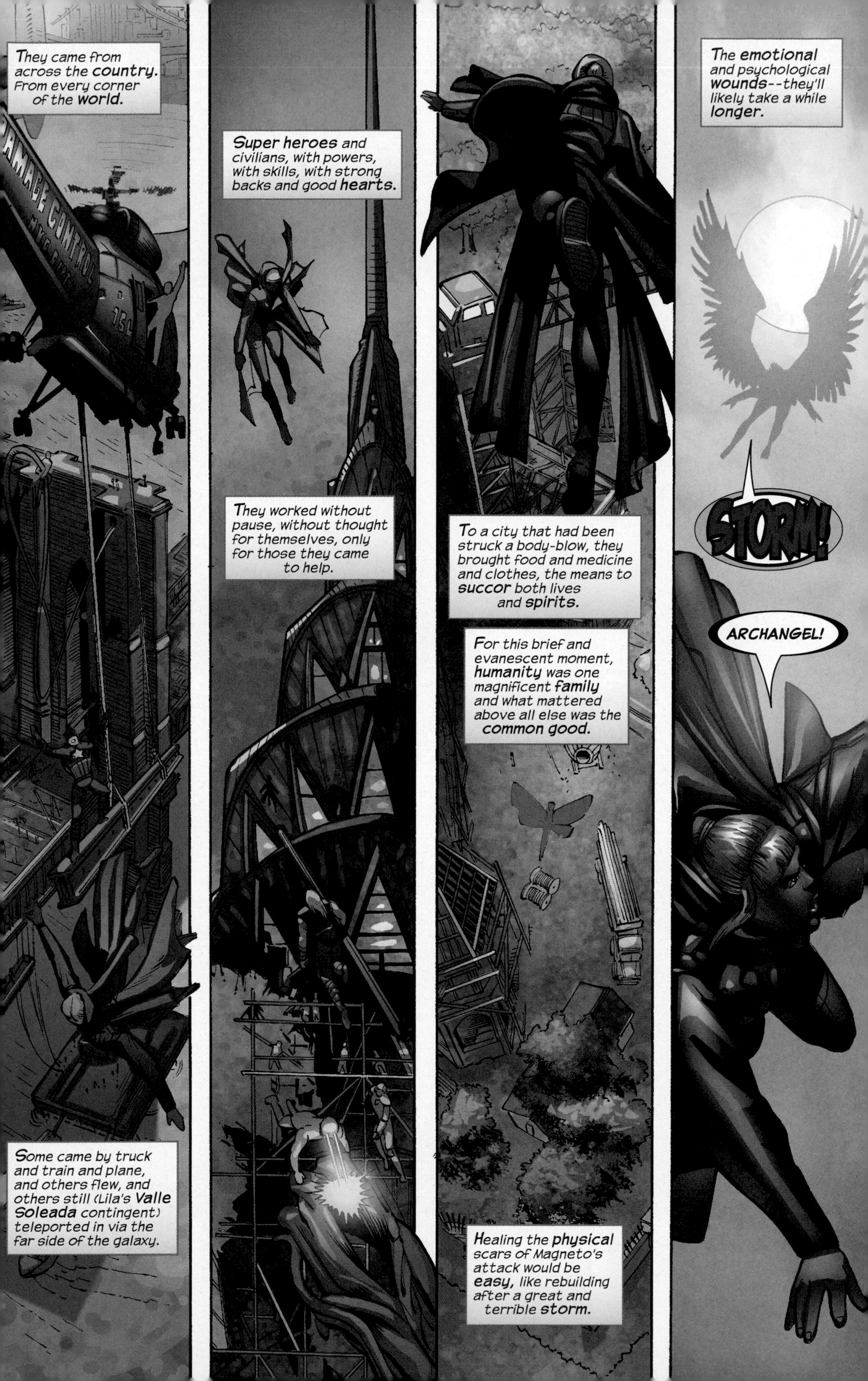

They came from across the country. From every corner of the world.
DAMAGE CONTROL
Some came by truck and train and plane, and others flew, and others still (Lila's Valle Soleada contingent) teleported in via the far side of the galaxy.
Super heroes and civilians, with powers, with skills, with strong backs and good hearts.
They worked without pause, without thought for themselves, only for those they came to help.
To a city that had been struck a body-blow, they brought food and medicine and clothes, the means to succor both lives and spirits.
For this brief and evanescent moment, humanity was one magnificent family and what mattered above all else was the common good.
Healing the physical scars of Magneto's attack would be easy, like rebuilding after a great and terrible storm.
The emotional and psychological wounds--they'll likely take a while longer.
STORM!
ARCHANGEL!

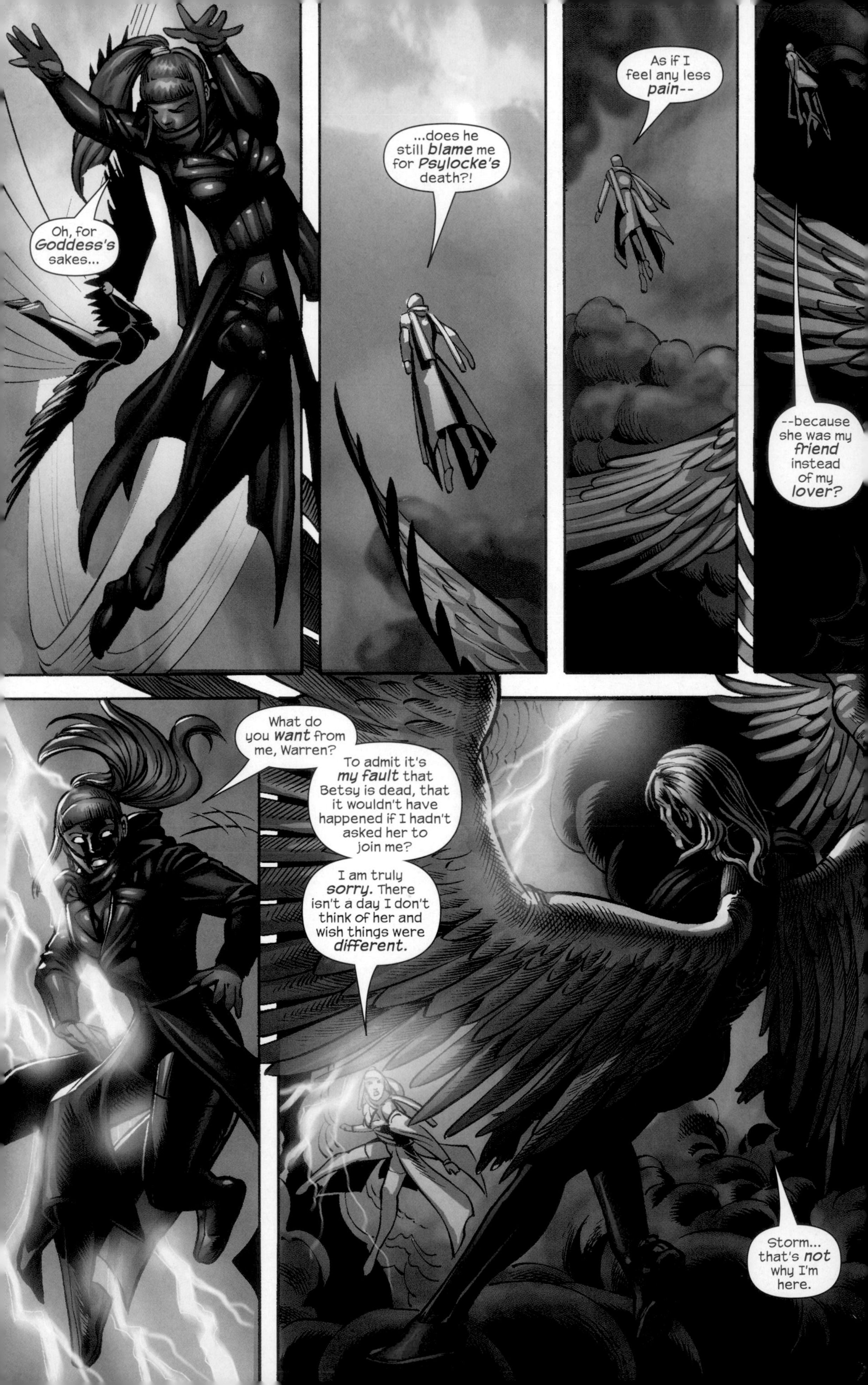
Oh, for Goddess's sakes...
...does he still blame me for Psylocke's death?!
As if I feel any less pain--
--because she was my friend instead of my lover?
What do you want from me, Warren?
To admit it's my fault that Betsy is dead, that it wouldn't have happened if I hadn't asked her to join me?
I am truly sorry. There isn't a day I don't think of her and wish things were different.
Storm... that's not why I'm here.

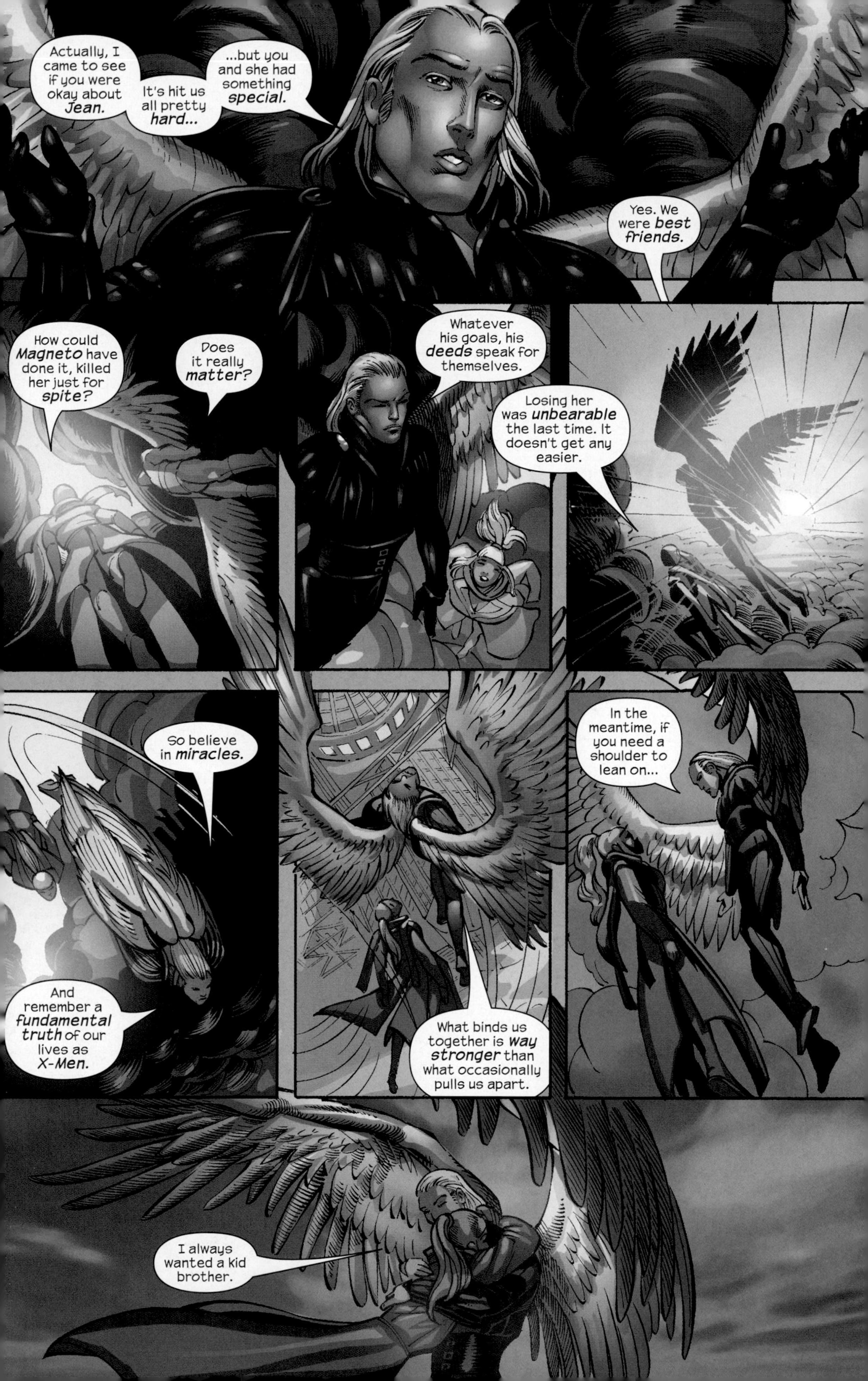

Actually, I came to see if you were okay about Jean.
It's hit us all pretty hard...
...but you and she had something special.
Yes. We were best friends.
How could Magneto have done it, killed her just for spite?
Does it really matter?
Whatever his goals, his deeds speak for themselves.
Losing her was unbearable the last time. It doesn't get any easier.
So believe in miracles.
And remember a fundamental truth of our lives as X-Men.
What binds us together is way stronger than what occasionally pulls us apart.
In the meantime, if you need a shoulder to lean on...
I always wanted a kid brother.

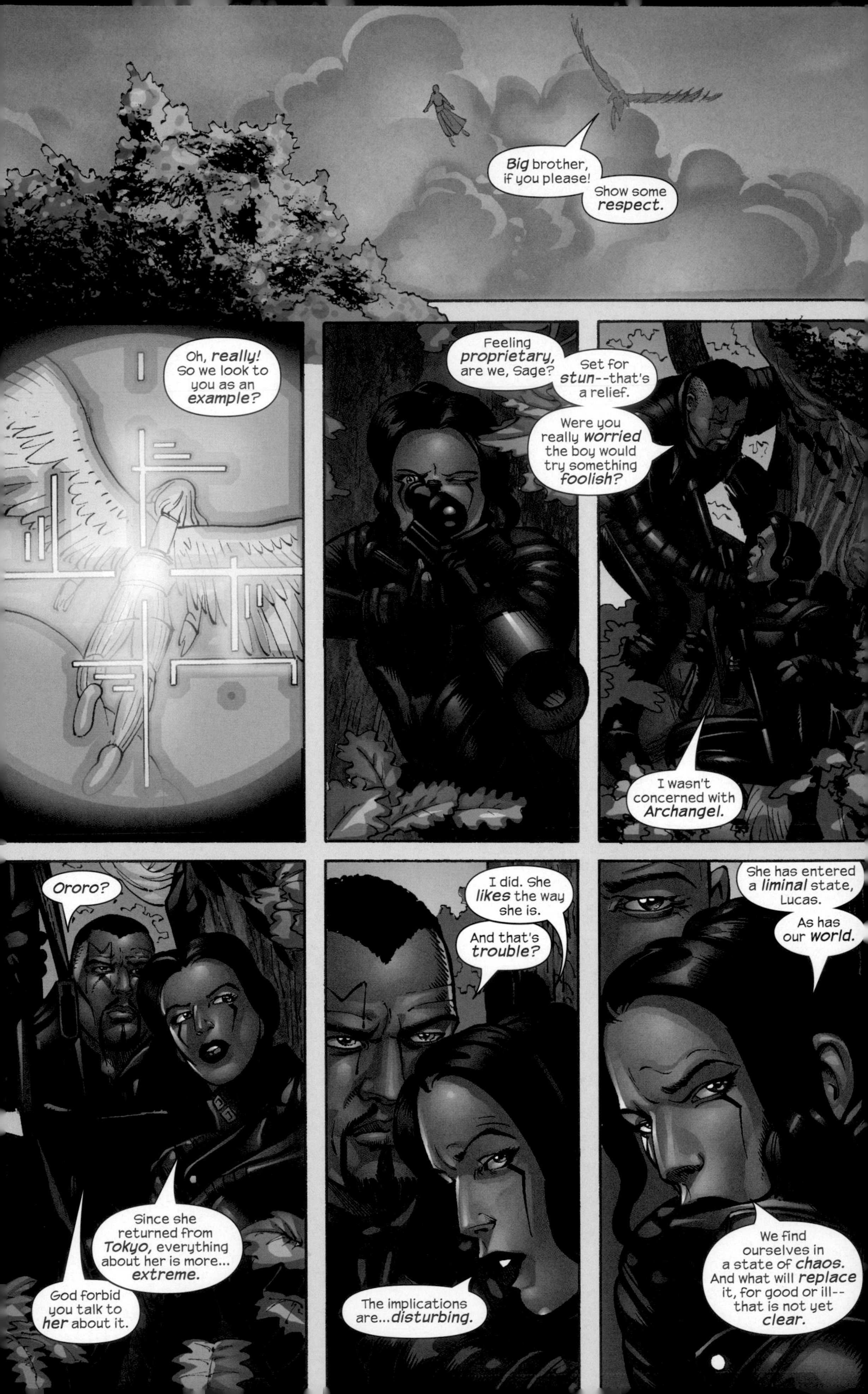
Big brother, if you please!
Show some respect.
Oh, really! So we look to you as an example?
Feeling proprietary, are we, Sage?
Set for stun--that's a relief.
Were you really worried the boy would try something foolish?
I wasn't concerned with Archangel.
Ororo?
Since she returned from Tokyo, everything about her is more... extreme.
God forbid you talk to her about it.
I did. She likes the way she is.
And that's trouble?
The implications are...disturbing.
She has entered a liminal state, Lucas.
As has our world.
We find ourselves in a state of chaos. And what will replace it, for good or ill--that is not yet clear.

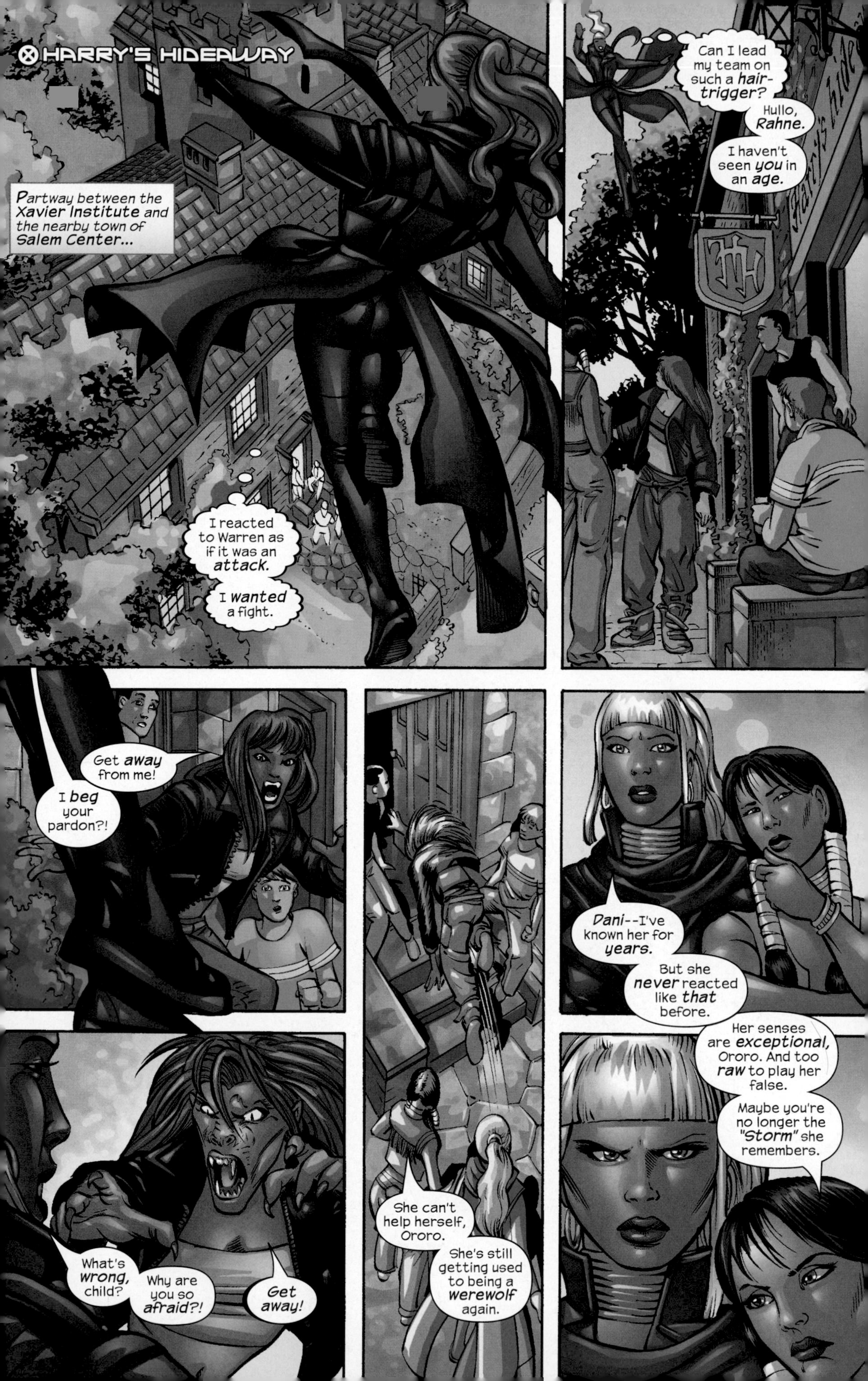
HARRY'S HIDEAWAY
Partway between the Xavier Institute and the nearby town of Salem Center...
I reacted to Warren as if it was an attack.
I wanted a fight.
Can I lead my team on such a hair-trigger?
Hullo, Rahne.
I haven't seen you in an age.
Get away from me!
I beg your pardon?!
What's wrong, child?
Why are you so afraid?!
Get away!
She can't help herself, Ororo.
She's still getting used to being a werewolf again.
Dani--I've known her for years.
But she never reacted like that before.
Her senses are exceptional, Ororo. And too raw to play her false.
Maybe you're no longer the "Storm" she remembers.

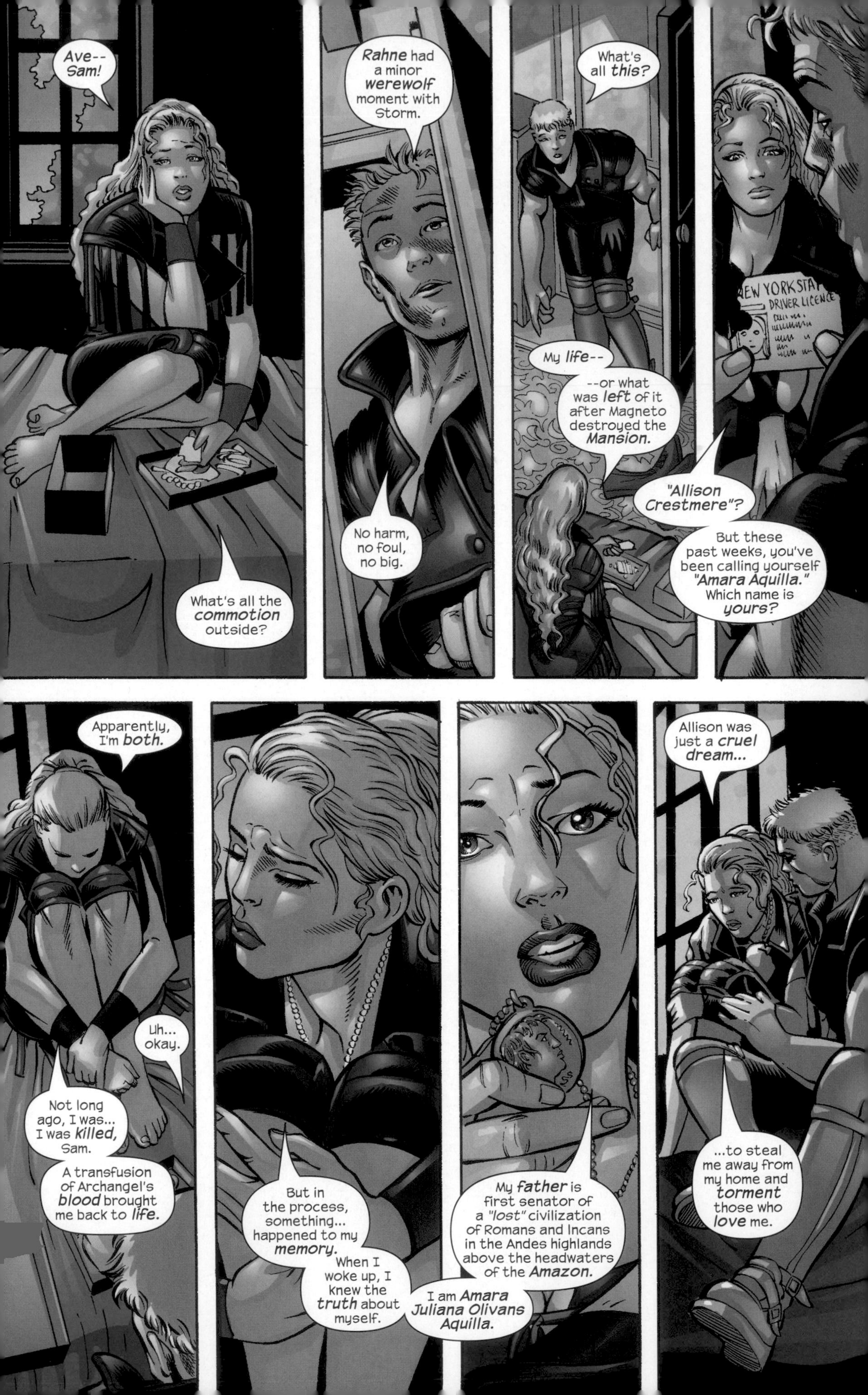
Ave-- Sam!
What's all the commotion outside?
Rahne had a minor werewolf moment with Storm.
No harm, no foul, no big.
What's all this?
My life--
--or what was left of it after Magneto destroyed the Mansion.
"Allison Crestmere"?
But these past weeks, you've been calling yourself "Amara Aquilla." Which name is yours?
NEW YORK STA
DRIVER LICENCE
Apparently, I'm both.
Uh... okay.
Not long ago, I was... I was killed, Sam.
A transfusion of Archangel's blood brought me back to life.
But in the process, something... happened to my memory.
When I woke up, I knew the truth about myself.
My father is first senator of a "lost" civilization of Romans and Incans in the Andes highlands above the headwaters of the Amazon.
I am Amara Juliana Olivans Aquilla.
Allison was just a cruel dream...
...to steal me away from my home and torment those who love me.

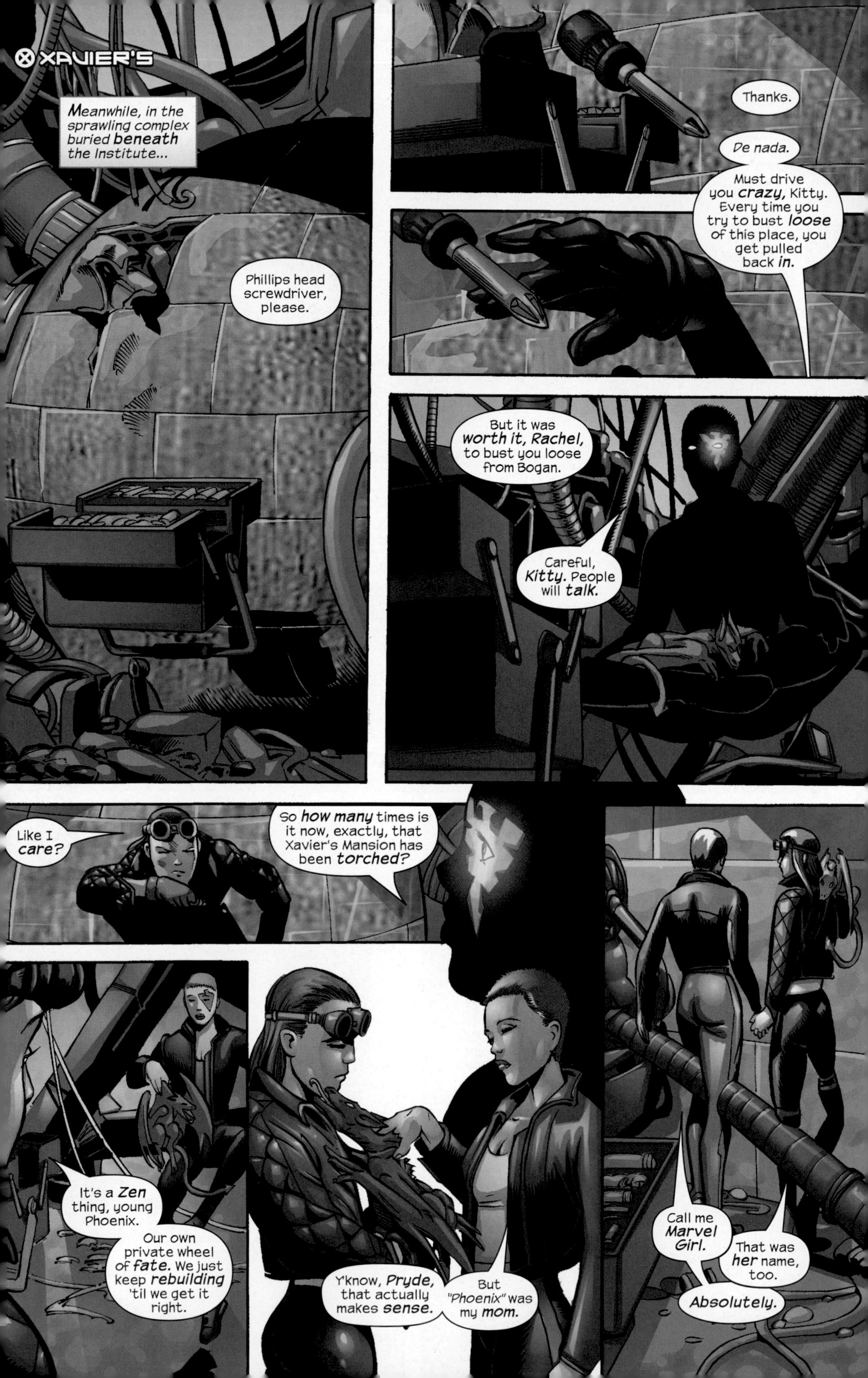
XAVIER'S
Meanwhile, in the sprawling complex buried beneath the Institute...
Phillips head screwdriver, please.
Thanks.
De nada.
Must drive you crazy, Kitty. Every time you try to bust loose of this place, you get pulled back in.
But it was worth it, Rachel, to bust you loose from Bogan.
Careful, Kitty. People will talk.
Like I care?
So how many times is it now, exactly, that Xavier's Mansion has been torched?
It's a Zen thing, young Phoenix.
Our own private wheel of fate. We just keep rebuilding 'til we get it right.
Y'know, Pryde, that actually makes sense.
But "Phoenix" was my mom.
Call me Marvel Girl.
That was her name, too.
Absolutely.

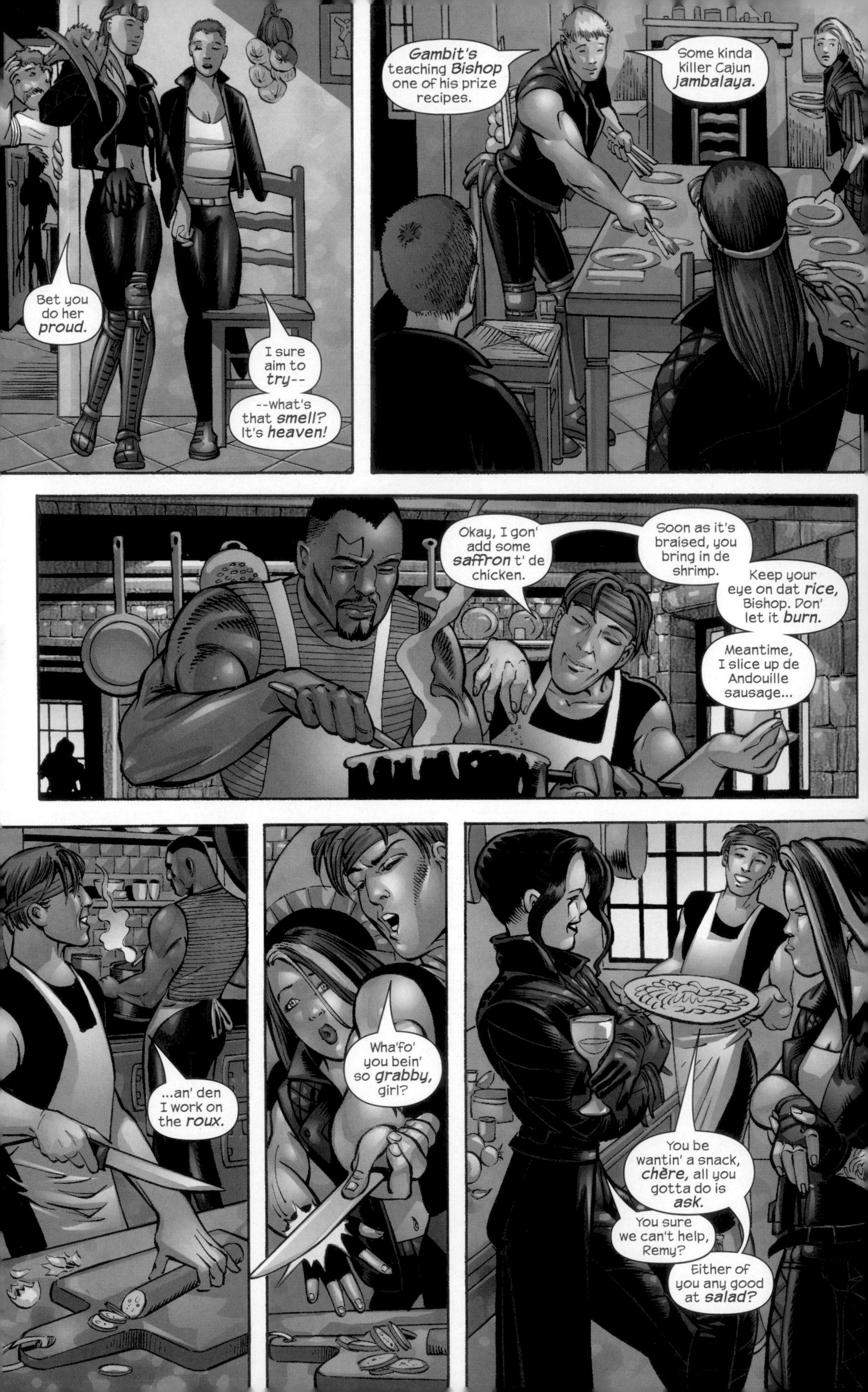
Bet you do her proud.
I sure aim to try--
--what's that smell? It's heaven!
Gambit's teaching Bishop one of his prize recipes.
Some kinda killer Cajun jambalaya.
Okay, I gon' add some saffron t' de chicken.
Soon as it's braised, you bring in de shrimp.
Keep your eye on dat rice, Bishop. Don' let it burn.
Meantime, I slice up de Andouille sausage...
...an' den I work on the roux.
Wha'fo' you bein' so grabby, girl?
You be wantin' a snack, chère, all you gotta do is ask.
You sure we can't help, Remy?
Either of you any good at salad?

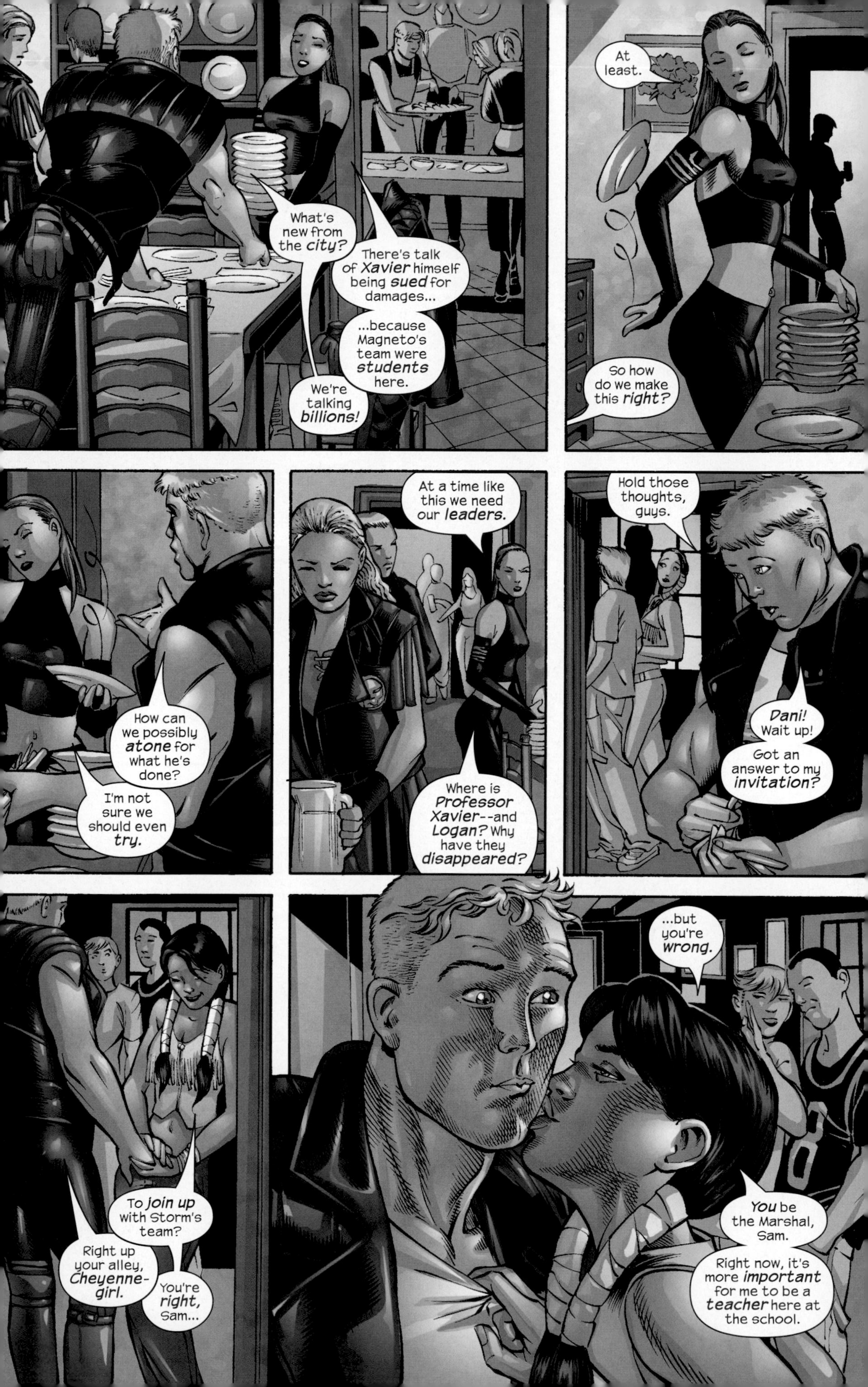
What's new from the city?
There's talk of Xavier himself being sued for damages...
...because Magneto's team were students here.
We're talking billions!
At least.
So how do we make this right?
How can we possibly atone for what he's done?
I'm not sure we should even try.
At a time like this we need our leaders.
Where is Professor Xavier--and Logan? Why have they disappeared?
Hold those thoughts, guys.
Dani! Wait up!
Got an answer to my invitation?
To join up with Storm's team?
Right up your alley, Cheyenne-girl.
You're right, Sam...
...but you're wrong.
You be the Marshal, Sam.
Right now, it's more important for me to be a teacher here at the school.

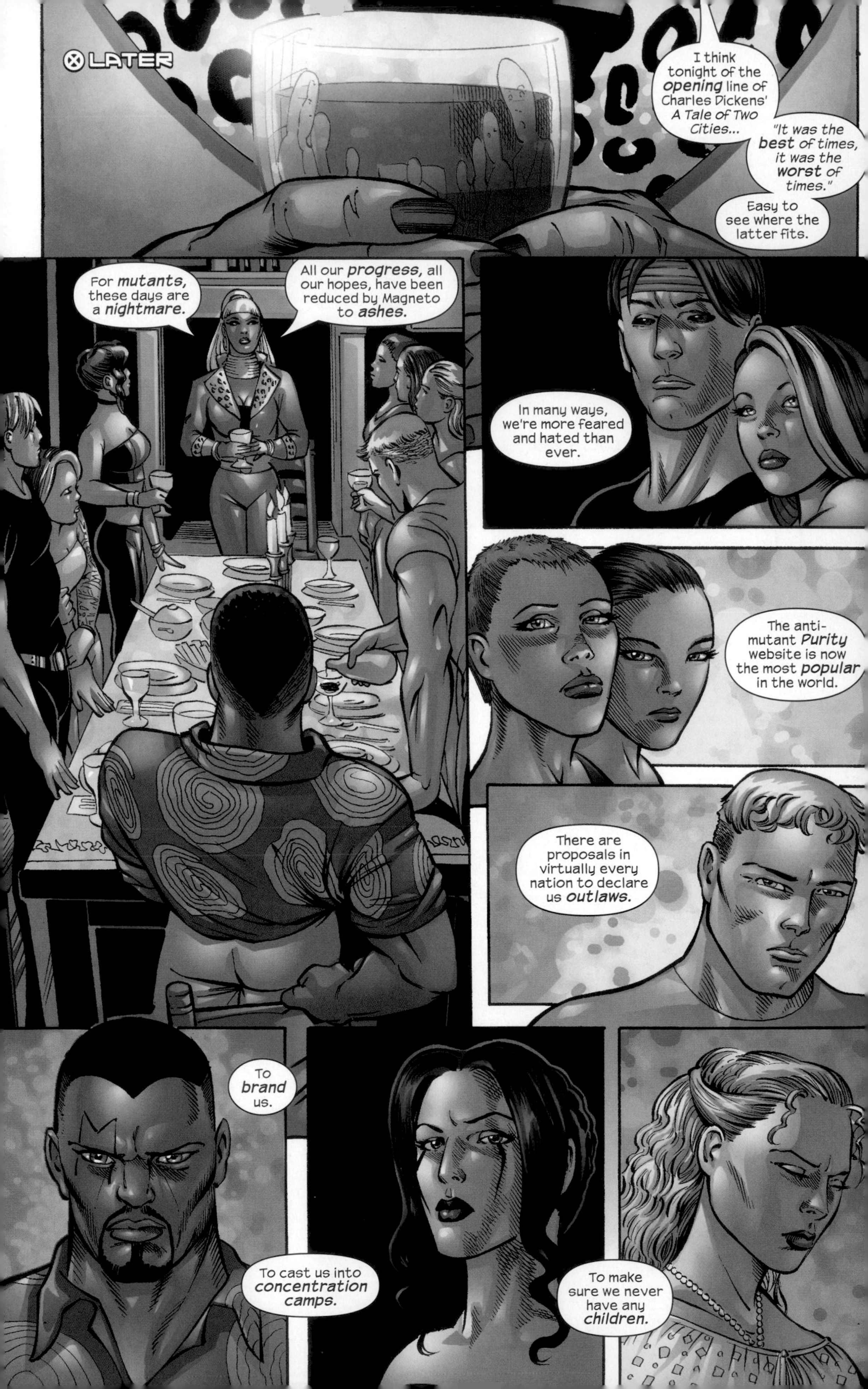
LATER
I think tonight of the opening line of Charles Dickens' A Tale of Two Cities...
"It was the best of times, it was the worst of times."
Easy to see where the latter fits.
For mutants, these days are a nightmare.
All our progress, all our hopes, have been reduced by Magneto to ashes.
In many ways, we're more feared and hated than ever.
The anti-mutant Purity website is now the most popular in the world.
There are proposals in virtually every nation to declare us outlaws.
To brand us.
To cast us into concentration camps.
To make sure we never have any children.

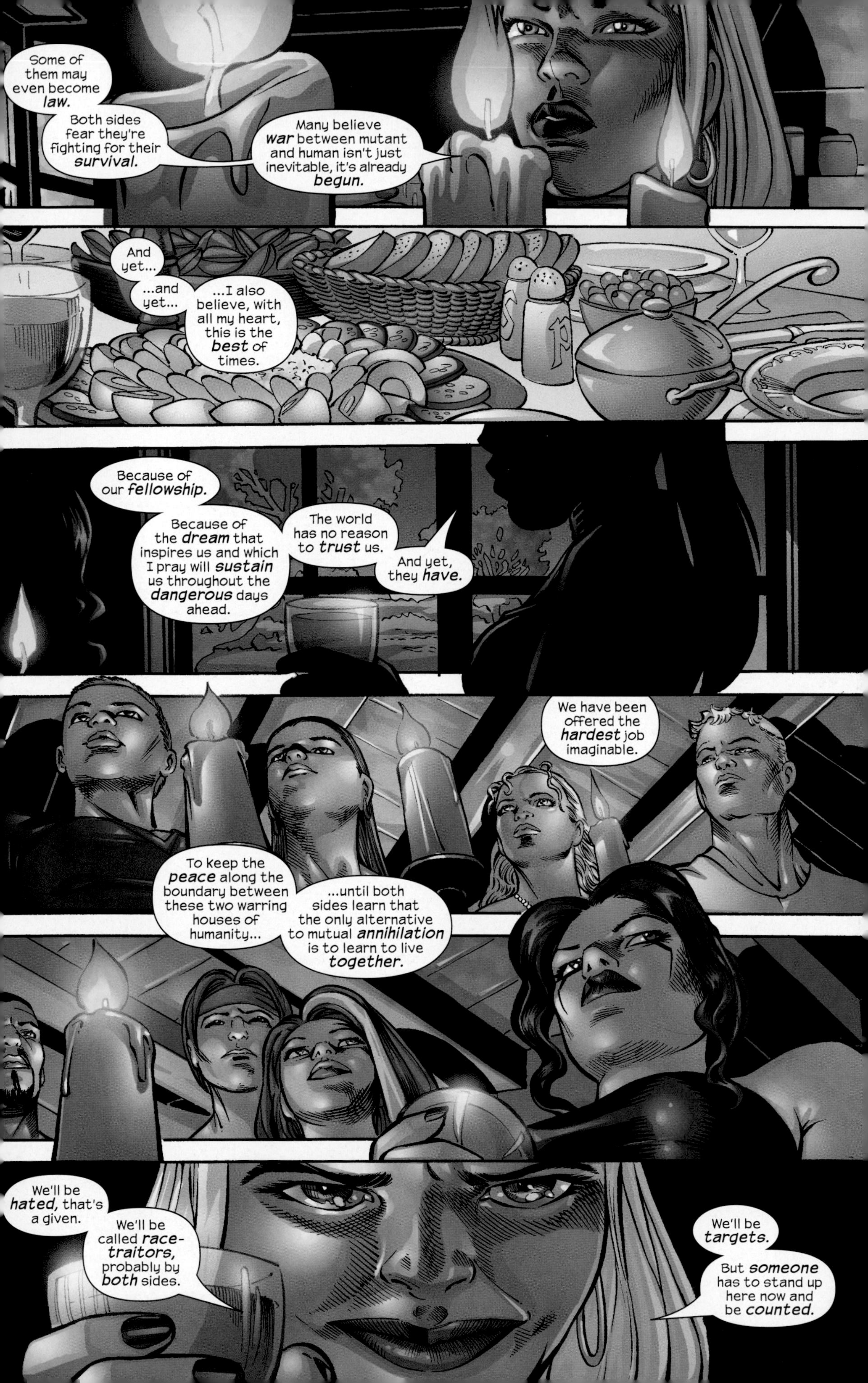

Some of them may even become *law.*
Both sides fear they're fighting for their *survival.*
Many believe *war* between mutant and human isn't just inevitable, it's already *begun.*
And yet...
...and yet...
...I also believe, with all my heart, this is the *best* of times.
Because of our *fellowship.*
Because of the *dream* that inspires us and which I pray will *sustain* us throughout the *dangerous* days ahead.
The world has no reason to *trust* us.
And yet, they *have.*
We have been offered the *hardest* job imaginable.
To keep the *peace* along the boundary between these two warring houses of humanity...
...until both sides learn that the only alternative to mutual *annihilation* is to learn to live *together.*
We'll be *hated,* that's a given.
We'll be called *race-traitors,* probably by *both* sides.
We'll be *targets.*
But *someone* has to stand up here now and be *counted.*

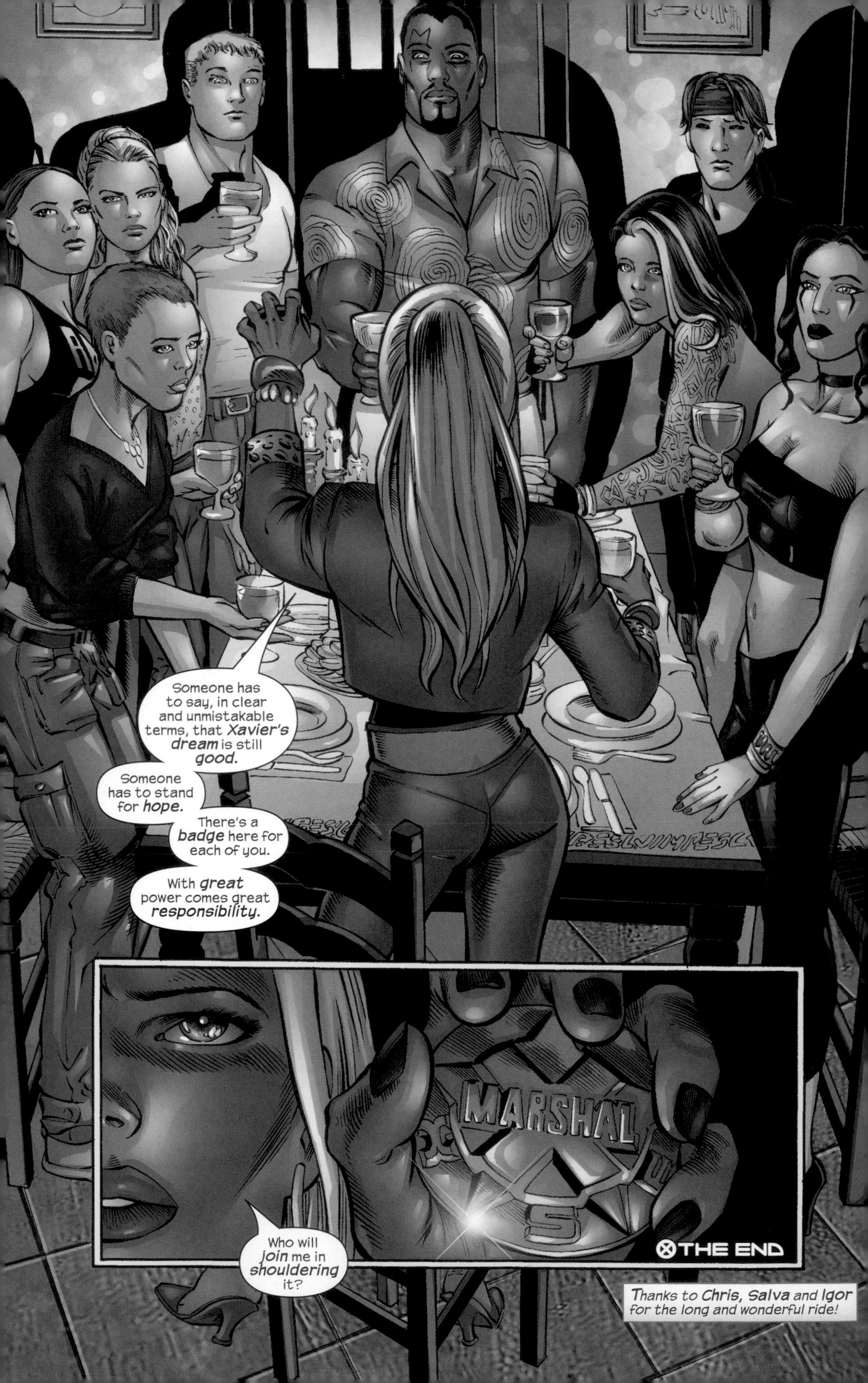
Someone has to say, in clear and unmistakable terms, that Xavier's dream is still good.
Someone has to stand for hope.
There's a badge here for each of you.
With great power comes great responsibility.
MARSHAL
Who will join me in shouldering it?
THE END
Thanks to Chris, Salva and Igor for the long and wonderful ride!

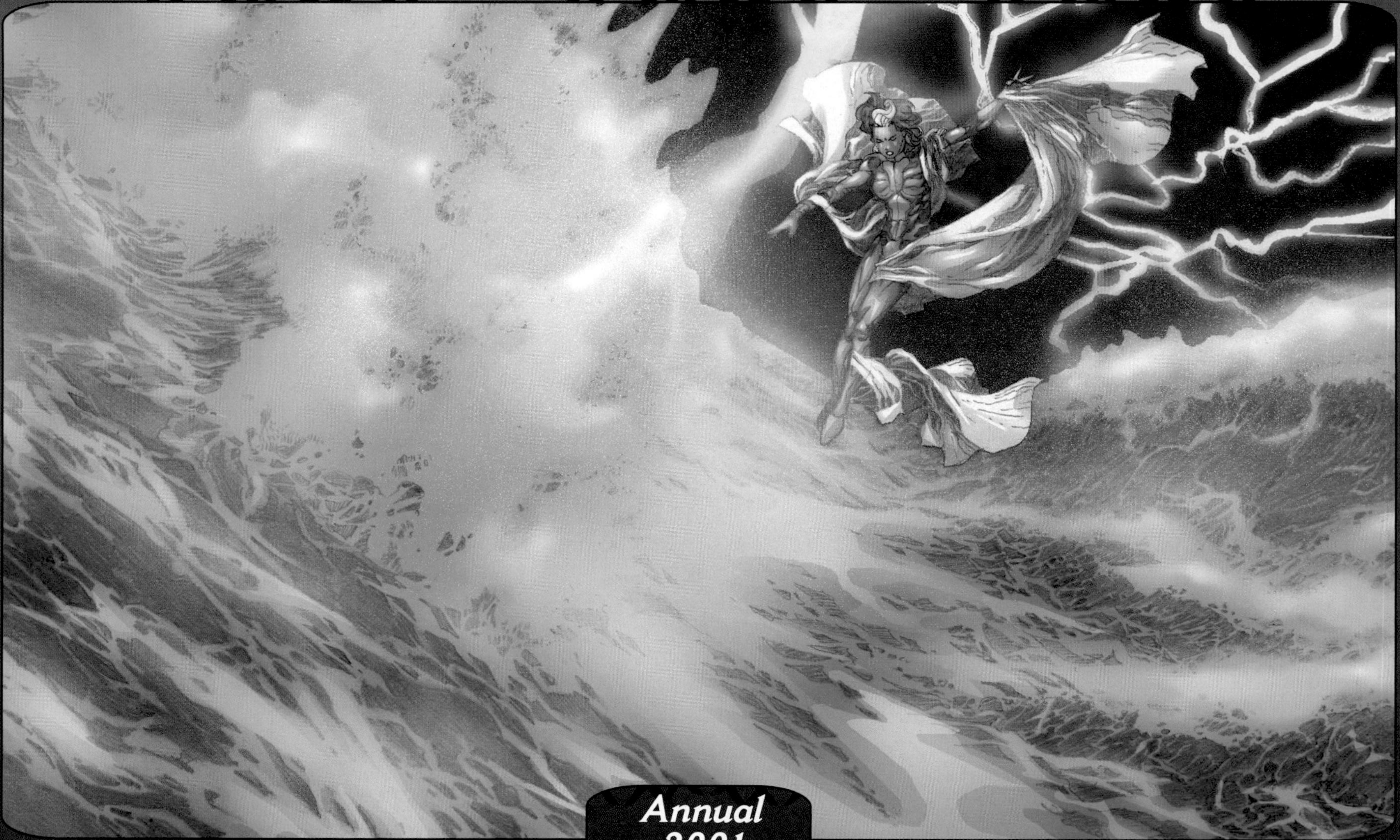

Annual
2001

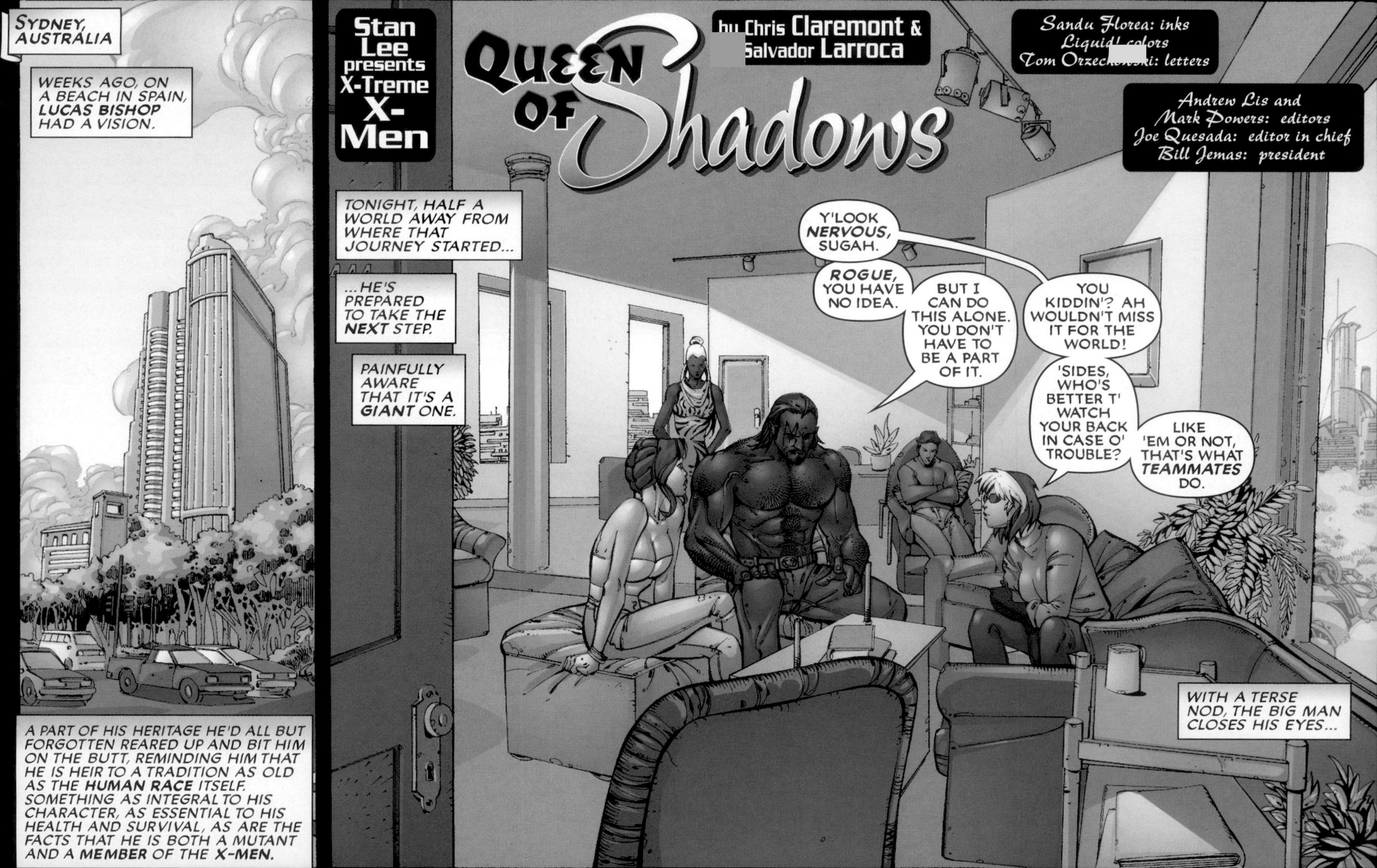
SYDNEY, AUSTRALIA
WEEKS AGO, ON A BEACH IN SPAIN, LUCAS BISHOP HAD A VISION.
A PART OF HIS HERITAGE HE'D ALL BUT FORGOTTEN REARED UP AND BIT HIM ON THE BUTT, REMINDING HIM THAT HE IS HEIR TO A TRADITION AS OLD AS THE HUMAN RACE ITSELF. SOMETHING AS INTEGRAL TO HIS CHARACTER, AS ESSENTIAL TO HIS HEALTH AND SURVIVAL, AS ARE THE FACTS THAT HE IS BOTH A MUTANT AND A MEMBER OF THE X-MEN.
Stan Lee presents X-Treme X-Men
QUEEN OF Shadows
by Chris Claremont & Salvador Larroca
Sandu Florea: inks
Liquid! colors
Tom Orzechowski: letters
Andrew Lis and Mark Powers: editors
Joe Quesada: editor in chief
Bill Jemas: president
TONIGHT, HALF A WORLD AWAY FROM WHERE THAT JOURNEY STARTED...
...HE'S PREPARED TO TAKE THE NEXT STEP.
PAINFULLY AWARE THAT IT'S A GIANT ONE.
Y'LOOK NERVOUS, SUGAH.
ROGUE, YOU HAVE NO IDEA.
BUT I CAN DO THIS ALONE. YOU DON'T HAVE TO BE A PART OF IT.
YOU KIDDIN'? AH WOULDN'T MISS IT FOR THE WORLD!
'SIDES, WHO'S BETTER T' WATCH YOUR BACK IN CASE O' TROUBLE?
LIKE 'EM OR NOT, THAT'S WHAT TEAMMATES DO.
WITH A TERSE NOD, THE BIG MAN CLOSES HIS EYES...

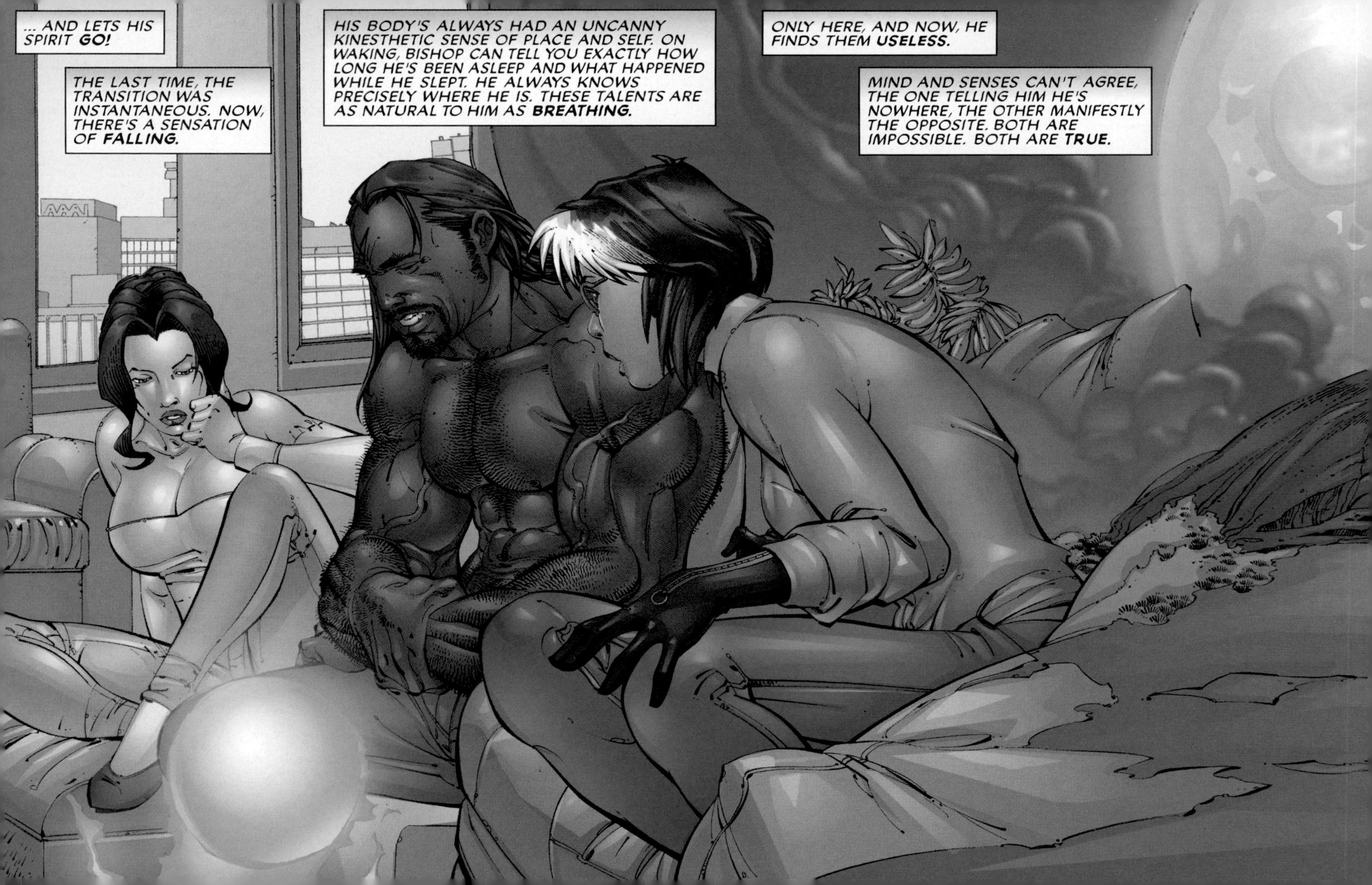
...AND LETS HIS SPIRIT **GO!**
THE LAST TIME, THE TRANSITION WAS INSTANTANEOUS. NOW, THERE'S A SENSATION OF **FALLING.**
HIS BODY'S ALWAYS HAD AN UNCANNY KINESTHETIC SENSE OF PLACE AND SELF. ON WAKING, BISHOP CAN TELL YOU EXACTLY HOW LONG HE'S BEEN ASLEEP AND WHAT HAPPENED WHILE HE SLEPT. HE ALWAYS KNOWS PRECISELY WHERE HE IS. THESE TALENTS ARE AS NATURAL TO HIM AS **BREATHING.**
ONLY HERE, AND NOW, HE FINDS THEM **USELESS.**
MIND AND SENSES CAN'T AGREE, THE ONE TELLING HIM HE'S NOWHERE, THE OTHER MANIFESTLY THE OPPOSITE. BOTH ARE IMPOSSIBLE. BOTH ARE **TRUE.**

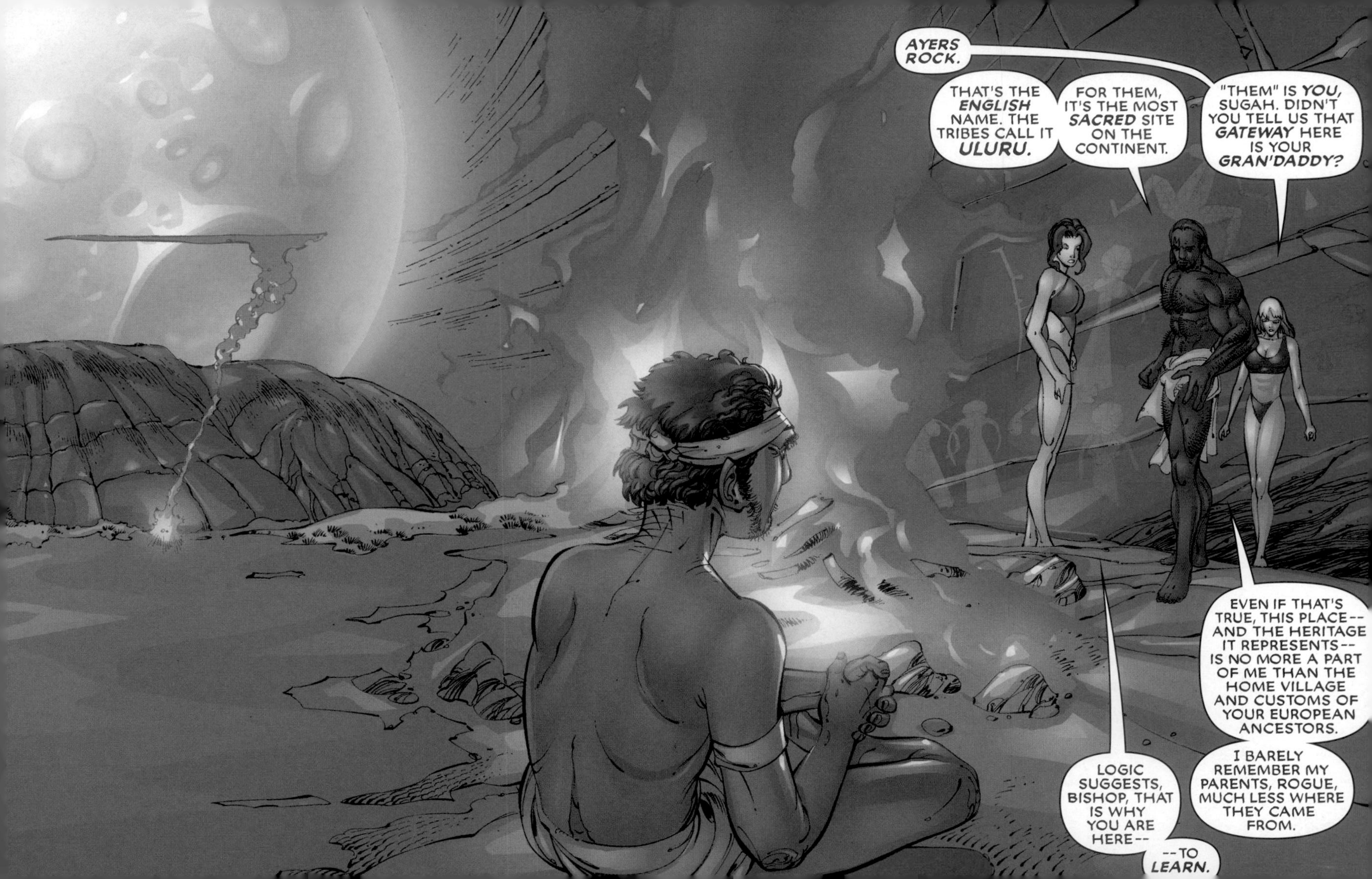

AYERS ROCK.
THAT'S THE ENGLISH NAME. THE TRIBES CALL IT ULURU.
FOR THEM, IT'S THE MOST SACRED SITE ON THE CONTINENT.
"THEM" IS YOU, SUGAH. DIDN'T YOU TELL US THAT GATEWAY HERE IS YOUR GRAN'DADDY?
EVEN IF THAT'S TRUE, THIS PLACE-- AND THE HERITAGE IT REPRESENTS-- IS NO MORE A PART OF ME THAN THE HOME VILLAGE AND CUSTOMS OF YOUR EUROPEAN ANCESTORS.
I BARELY REMEMBER MY PARENTS, ROGUE, MUCH LESS WHERE THEY CAME FROM.
LOGIC SUGGESTS, BISHOP, THAT IS WHY YOU ARE HERE--
--TO LEARN.

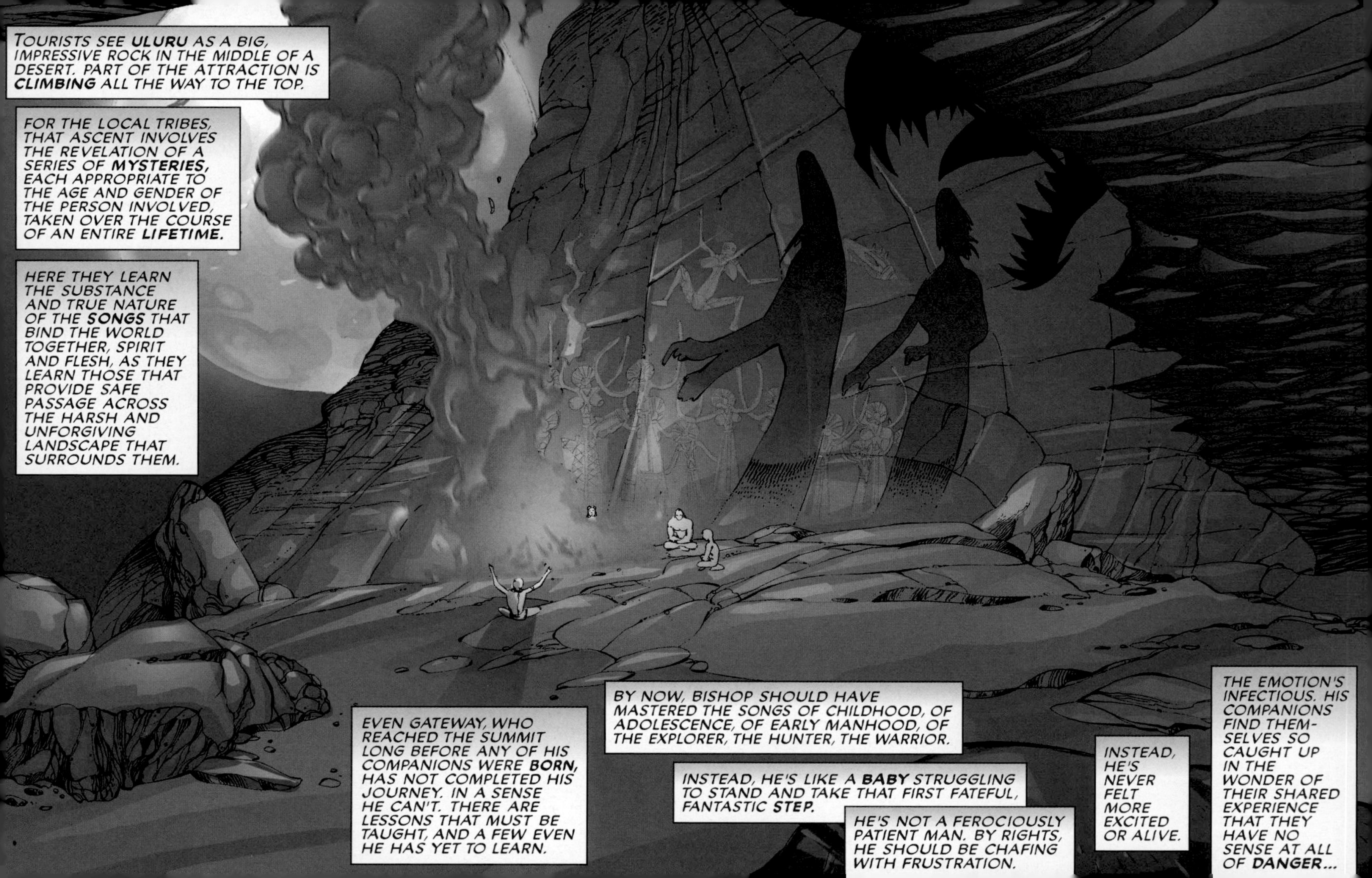
TOURISTS SEE **ULURU** AS A BIG, IMPRESSIVE ROCK IN THE MIDDLE OF A DESERT. PART OF THE ATTRACTION IS **CLIMBING** ALL THE WAY TO THE TOP.
FOR THE LOCAL TRIBES, THAT ASCENT INVOLVES THE REVELATION OF A SERIES OF **MYSTERIES,** EACH APPROPRIATE TO THE AGE AND GENDER OF THE PERSON INVOLVED, TAKEN OVER THE COURSE OF AN ENTIRE **LIFETIME.**
HERE THEY LEARN THE SUBSTANCE AND TRUE NATURE OF THE **SONGS** THAT BIND THE WORLD TOGETHER, SPIRIT AND FLESH, AS THEY LEARN THOSE THAT PROVIDE SAFE PASSAGE ACROSS THE HARSH AND UNFORGIVING LANDSCAPE THAT SURROUNDS THEM.
EVEN GATEWAY, WHO REACHED THE SUMMIT LONG BEFORE ANY OF HIS COMPANIONS WERE **BORN,** HAS NOT COMPLETED HIS JOURNEY. IN A SENSE HE CAN'T. THERE ARE LESSONS THAT MUST BE TAUGHT, AND A FEW EVEN HE HAS YET TO LEARN.
BY NOW, BISHOP SHOULD HAVE MASTERED THE SONGS OF CHILDHOOD, OF ADOLESCENCE, OF EARLY MANHOOD, OF THE EXPLORER, THE HUNTER, THE WARRIOR.
INSTEAD, HE'S LIKE A **BABY** STRUGGLING TO STAND AND TAKE THAT FIRST FATEFUL, FANTASTIC **STEP.**
HE'S NOT A FEROCIOUSLY PATIENT MAN. BY RIGHTS, HE SHOULD BE CHAFING WITH FRUSTRATION.
INSTEAD, HE'S NEVER FELT MORE EXCITED OR ALIVE.
THE EMOTION'S INFECTIOUS. HIS COMPANIONS FIND THEMSELVES SO CAUGHT UP IN THE WONDER OF THEIR SHARED EXPERIENCE THAT THEY HAVE NO SENSE AT ALL OF **DANGER...**

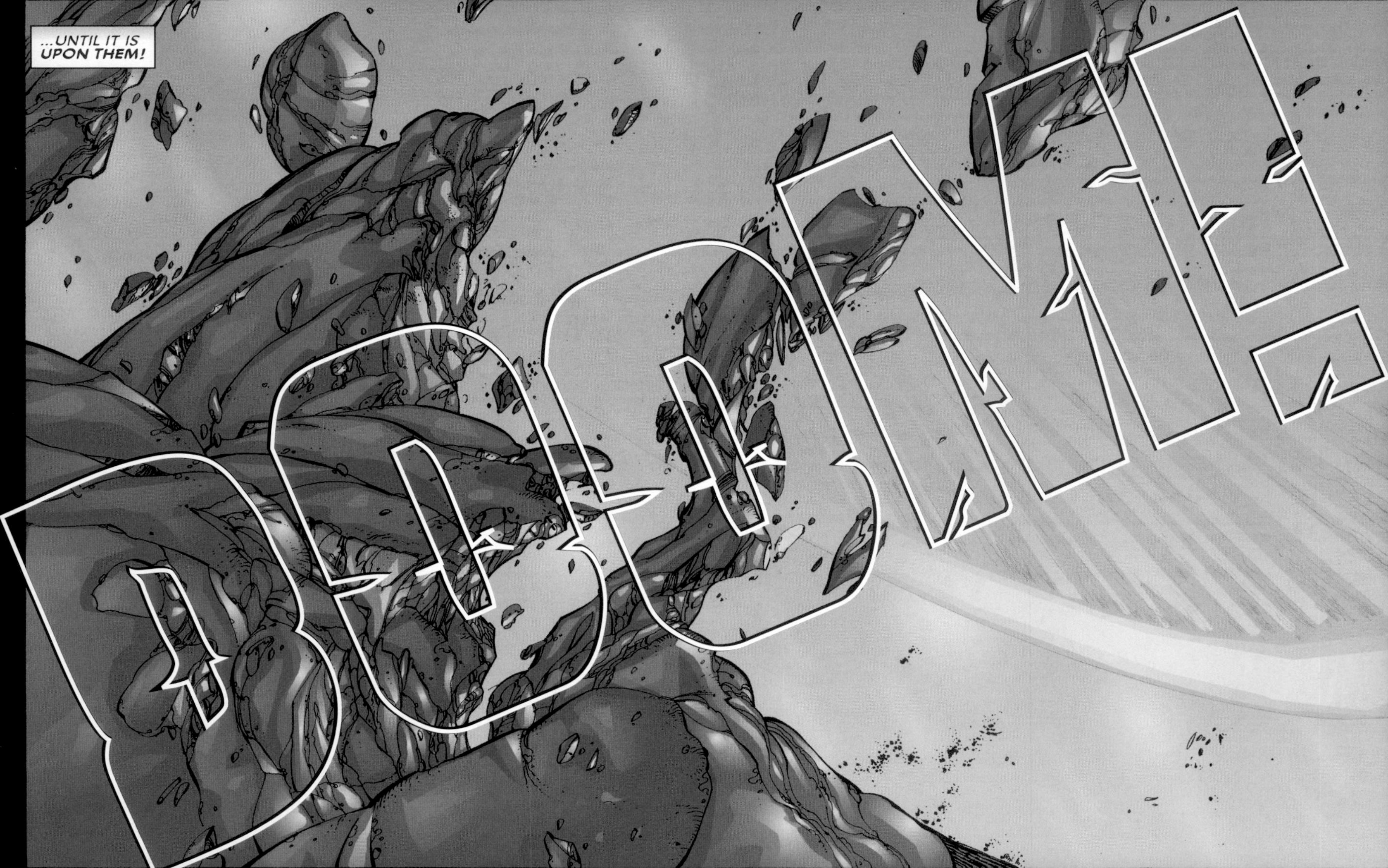
...UNTIL IT IS UPON THEM!
BOOOM!

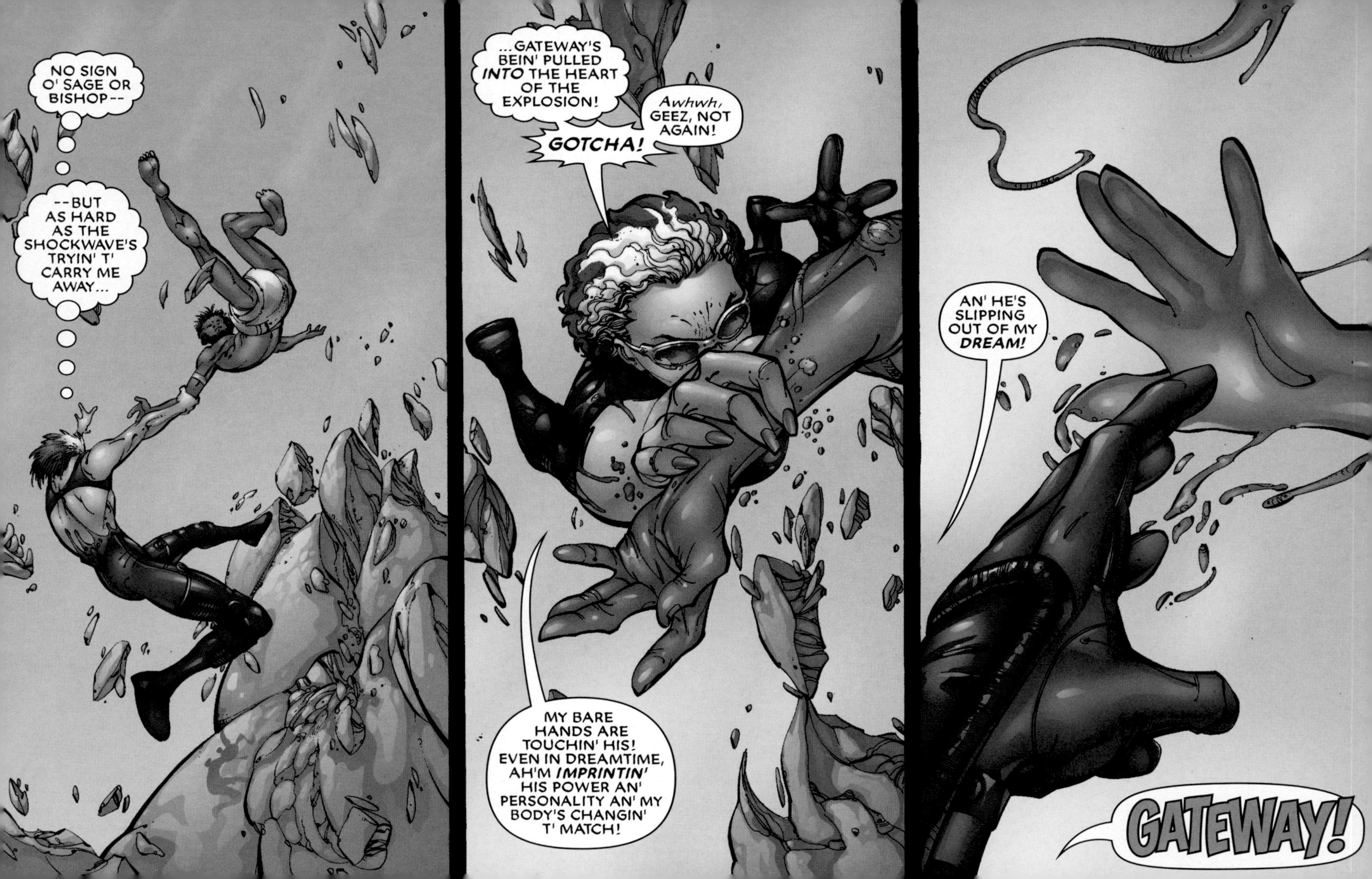
NO SIGN O' SAGE OR BISHOP--
--BUT AS HARD AS THE SHOCKWAVE'S TRYIN' T' CARRY ME AWAY...
...GATEWAY'S BEIN' PULLED *INTO* THE HEART OF THE EXPLOSION!
GOTCHA!
Awhwh, GEEZ, NOT AGAIN!
MY BARE HANDS ARE TOUCHIN' HIS! EVEN IN DREAMTIME, AH'M *IMPRINTIN'* HIS POWER AN' PERSONALITY AN' MY BODY'S CHANGIN' T' MATCH!
AN' HE'S SLIPPING OUT OF MY *DREAM!*
GATEWAY!

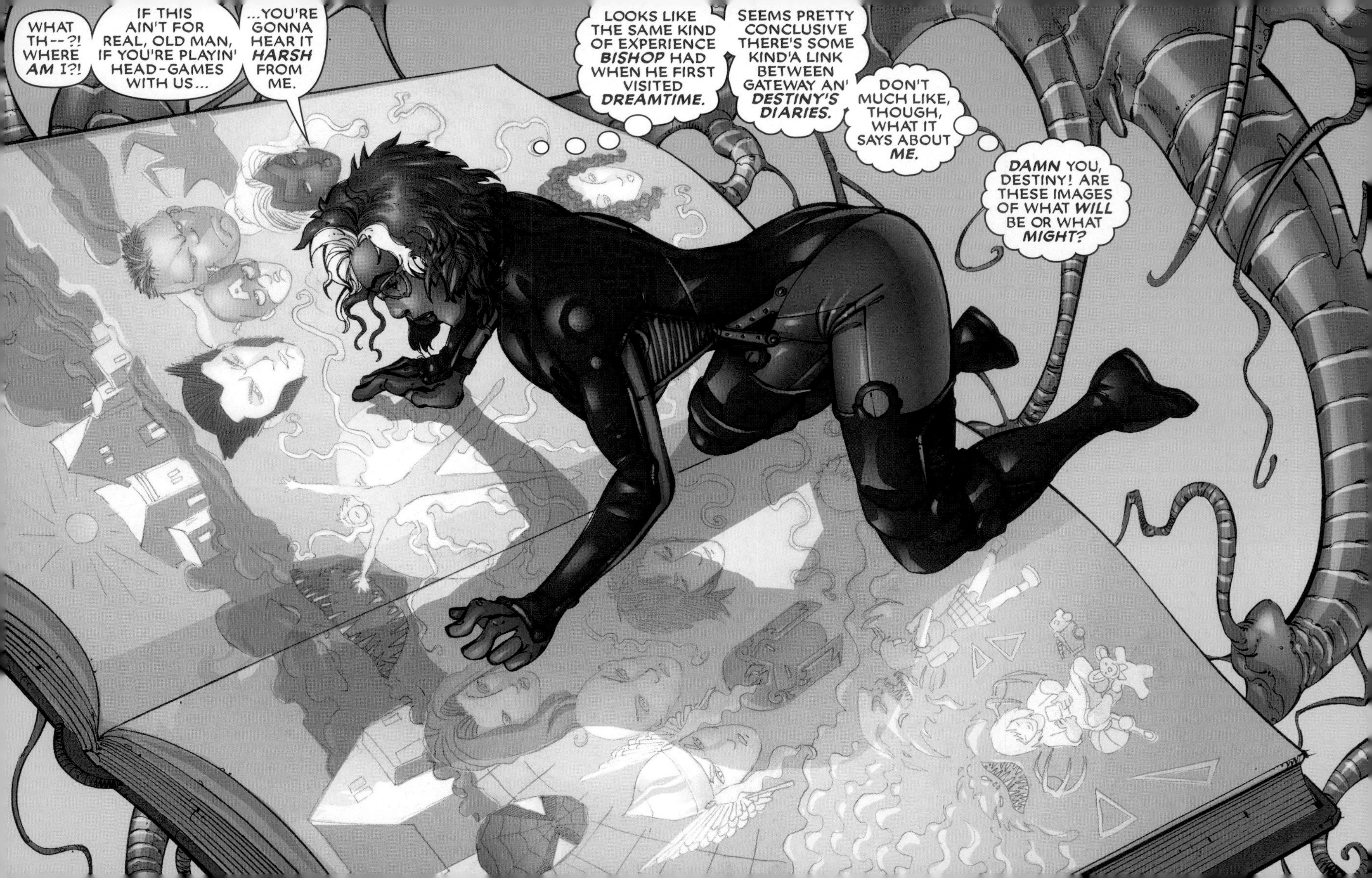
WHAT TH--?! WHERE *AM I*?!
IF THIS AIN'T FOR REAL, OLD MAN, IF YOU'RE PLAYIN' HEAD-GAMES WITH US...
...YOU'RE GONNA HEAR IT *HARSH* FROM ME.
LOOKS LIKE THE SAME KIND OF EXPERIENCE *BISHOP* HAD WHEN HE FIRST VISITED *DREAMTIME.*
SEEMS PRETTY CONCLUSIVE THERE'S SOME KIND'A LINK BETWEEN GATEWAY AN' *DESTINY'S DIARIES.*
DON'T MUCH LIKE, THOUGH, WHAT IT SAYS ABOUT *ME.*
DAMN YOU, DESTINY! ARE THESE IMAGES OF WHAT *WILL* BE OR WHAT *MIGHT?*

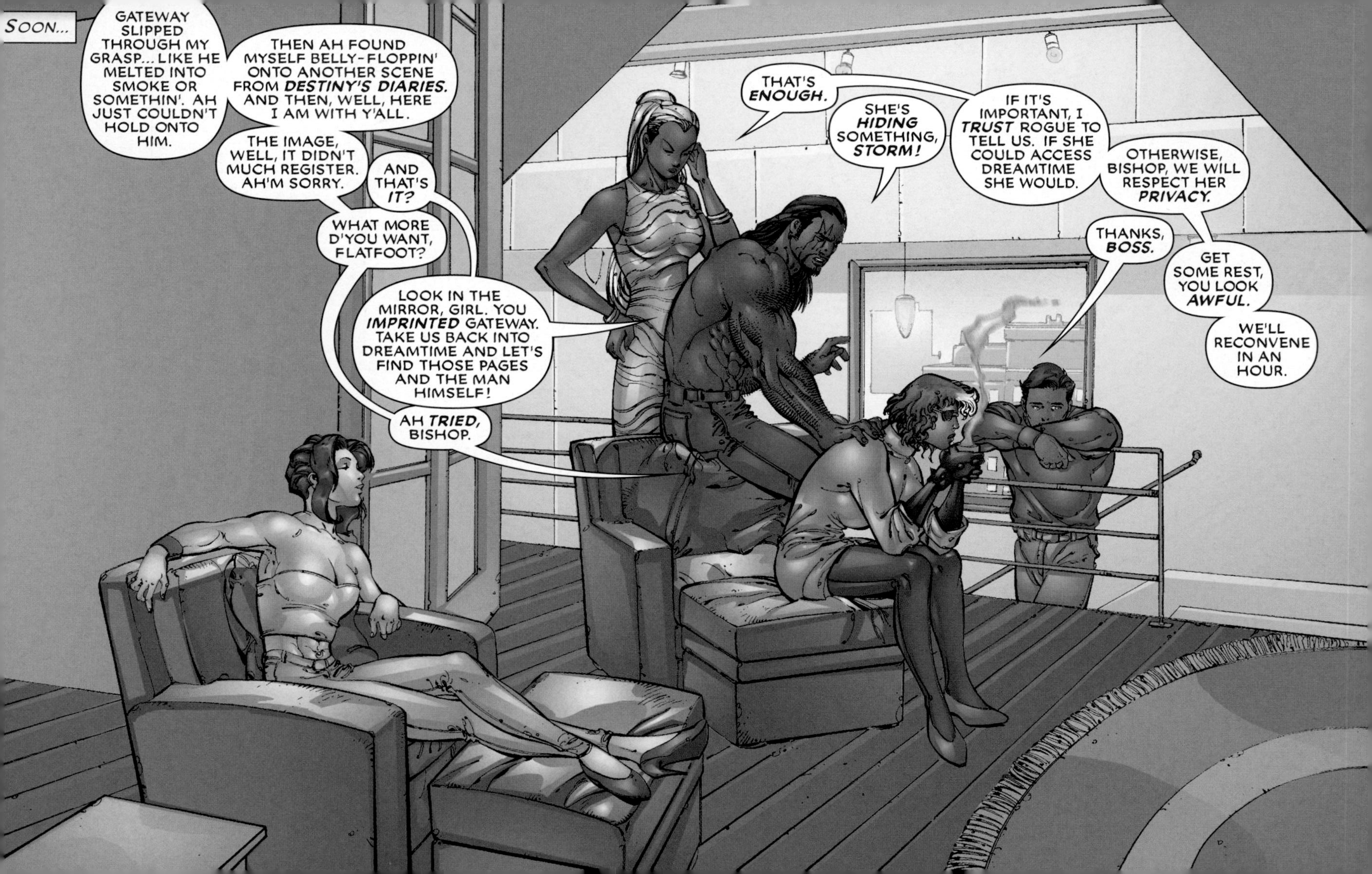
SOON...
GATEWAY SLIPPED THROUGH MY GRASP... LIKE HE MELTED INTO SMOKE OR SOMETHIN'. AH JUST COULDN'T HOLD ONTO HIM.
THEN AH FOUND MYSELF BELLY-FLOPPIN' ONTO ANOTHER SCENE FROM *DESTINY'S DIARIES.* AND THEN, WELL, HERE I AM WITH Y'ALL.
THE IMAGE, WELL, IT DIDN'T MUCH REGISTER. AH'M SORRY.
AND THAT'S *IT?*
WHAT MORE D'YOU WANT, FLATFOOT?
LOOK IN THE MIRROR, GIRL. YOU *IMPRINTED* GATEWAY. TAKE US BACK INTO DREAMTIME AND LET'S FIND THOSE PAGES AND THE MAN HIMSELF!
AH *TRIED,* BISHOP.
THAT'S *ENOUGH.*
SHE'S *HIDING* SOMETHING, *STORM!*
IF IT'S IMPORTANT, I *TRUST* ROGUE TO TELL US. IF SHE COULD ACCESS DREAMTIME SHE WOULD.
OTHERWISE, BISHOP, WE WILL RESPECT HER *PRIVACY.*
THANKS, *BOSS.*
GET SOME REST, YOU LOOK *AWFUL.*
WE'LL RECONVENE IN AN HOUR.

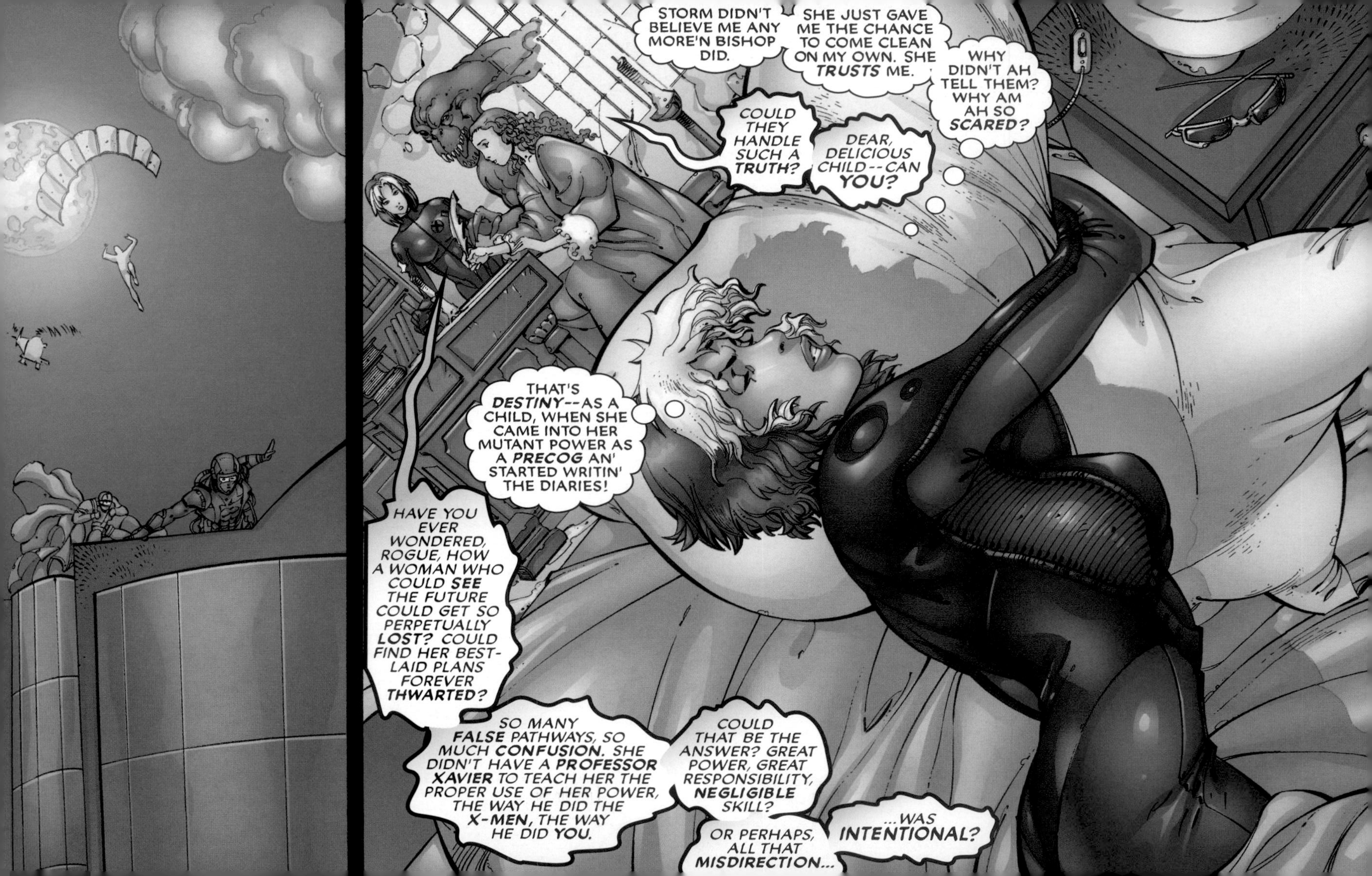
STORM DIDN'T BELIEVE ME ANY MORE'N BISHOP DID.
SHE JUST GAVE ME THE CHANCE TO COME CLEAN ON MY OWN. SHE *TRUSTS* ME.
WHY DIDN'T AH TELL THEM? WHY AM AH SO *SCARED?*
COULD THEY HANDLE SUCH A *TRUTH?*
DEAR, DELICIOUS CHILD--CAN **YOU?**
THAT'S ***DESTINY***--AS A CHILD, WHEN SHE CAME INTO HER MUTANT POWER AS A ***PRECOG*** AN' STARTED WRITIN' THE DIARIES!
HAVE YOU EVER WONDERED, ROGUE, HOW A WOMAN WHO COULD **SEE** THE FUTURE COULD GET SO PERPETUALLY ***LOST?*** COULD FIND HER BEST-LAID PLANS FOREVER **THWARTED?**
SO MANY **FALSE** PATHWAYS, SO MUCH **CONFUSION.** SHE DIDN'T HAVE A **PROFESSOR XAVIER** TO TEACH HER THE PROPER USE OF HER POWER, THE WAY HE DID THE **X-MEN,** THE WAY HE DID **YOU.**
COULD THAT BE THE ANSWER? GREAT POWER, GREAT RESPONSIBILITY, **NEGLIGIBLE** SKILL?
OR PERHAPS, ALL THAT **MISDIRECTION...**
...WAS **INTENTIONAL?**

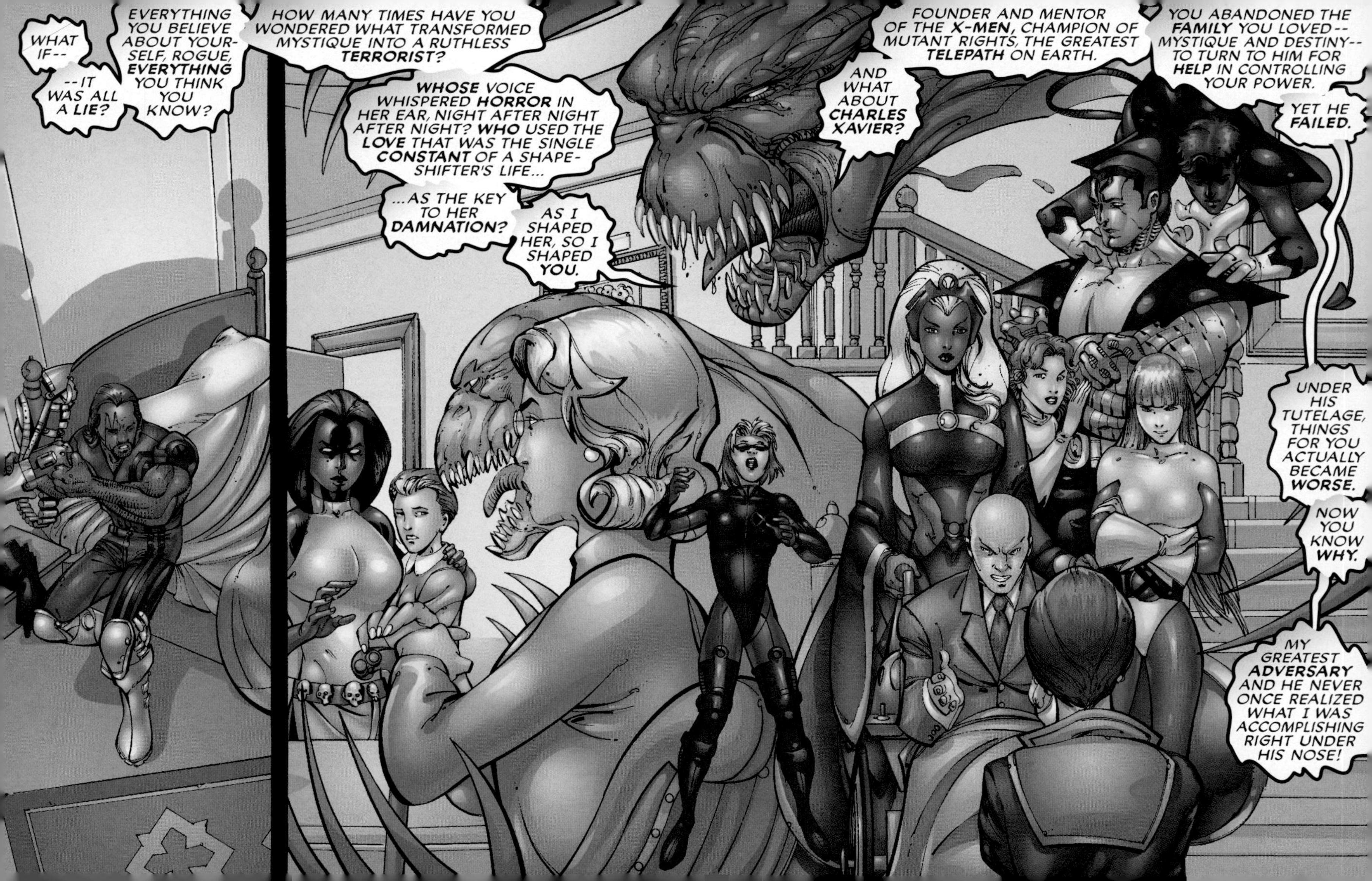
WHAT IF--
--IT WAS ALL A **LIE**?
EVERYTHING YOU BELIEVE ABOUT YOURSELF, ROGUE, **EVERYTHING** YOU THINK YOU KNOW?
HOW MANY TIMES HAVE YOU WONDERED WHAT TRANSFORMED MYSTIQUE INTO A RUTHLESS **TERRORIST**?
WHOSE VOICE WHISPERED **HORROR** IN HER EAR, NIGHT AFTER NIGHT AFTER NIGHT? **WHO** USED THE **LOVE** THAT WAS THE SINGLE **CONSTANT** OF A SHAPE-SHIFTER'S LIFE...
...AS THE KEY TO HER **DAMNATION**?
AS I SHAPED HER, SO I SHAPED **YOU**.
AND WHAT ABOUT **CHARLES XAVIER**?
FOUNDER AND MENTOR OF THE **X-MEN**, CHAMPION OF MUTANT RIGHTS, THE GREATEST **TELEPATH** ON EARTH.
YOU ABANDONED THE **FAMILY** YOU LOVED-- MYSTIQUE AND DESTINY-- TO TURN TO HIM FOR **HELP** IN CONTROLLING YOUR POWER.
YET HE **FAILED**.
UNDER HIS TUTELAGE, THINGS FOR YOU ACTUALLY BECAME **WORSE**.
NOW YOU KNOW **WHY**.
MY GREATEST **ADVERSARY** AND HE NEVER ONCE REALIZED WHAT I WAS ACCOMPLISHING RIGHT UNDER HIS NOSE!

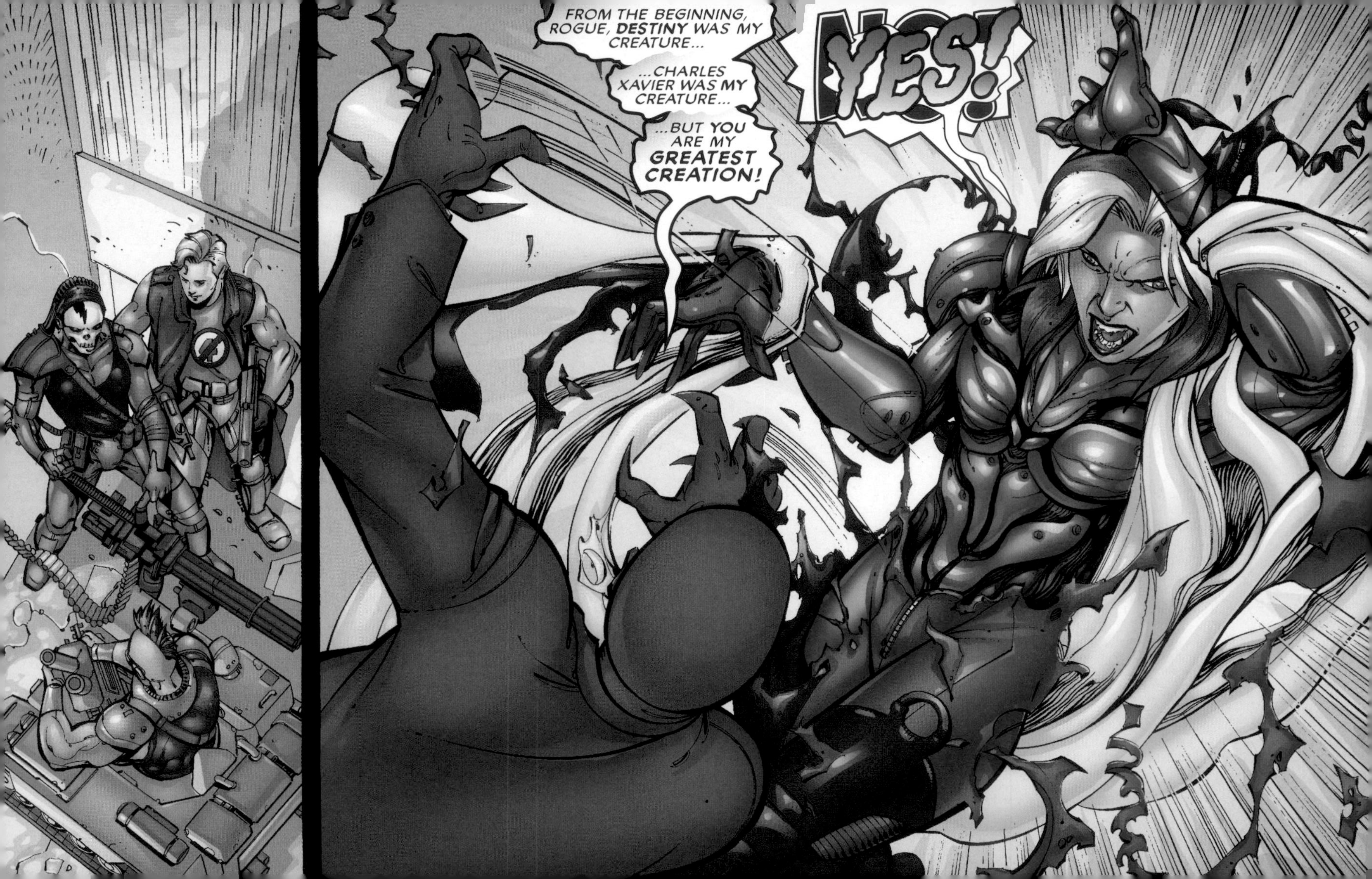
FROM THE BEGINNING, ROGUE, DESTINY WAS MY CREATURE...
...CHARLES XAVIER WAS MY CREATURE...
...BUT YOU ARE MY GREATEST CREATION!
NO! YES!

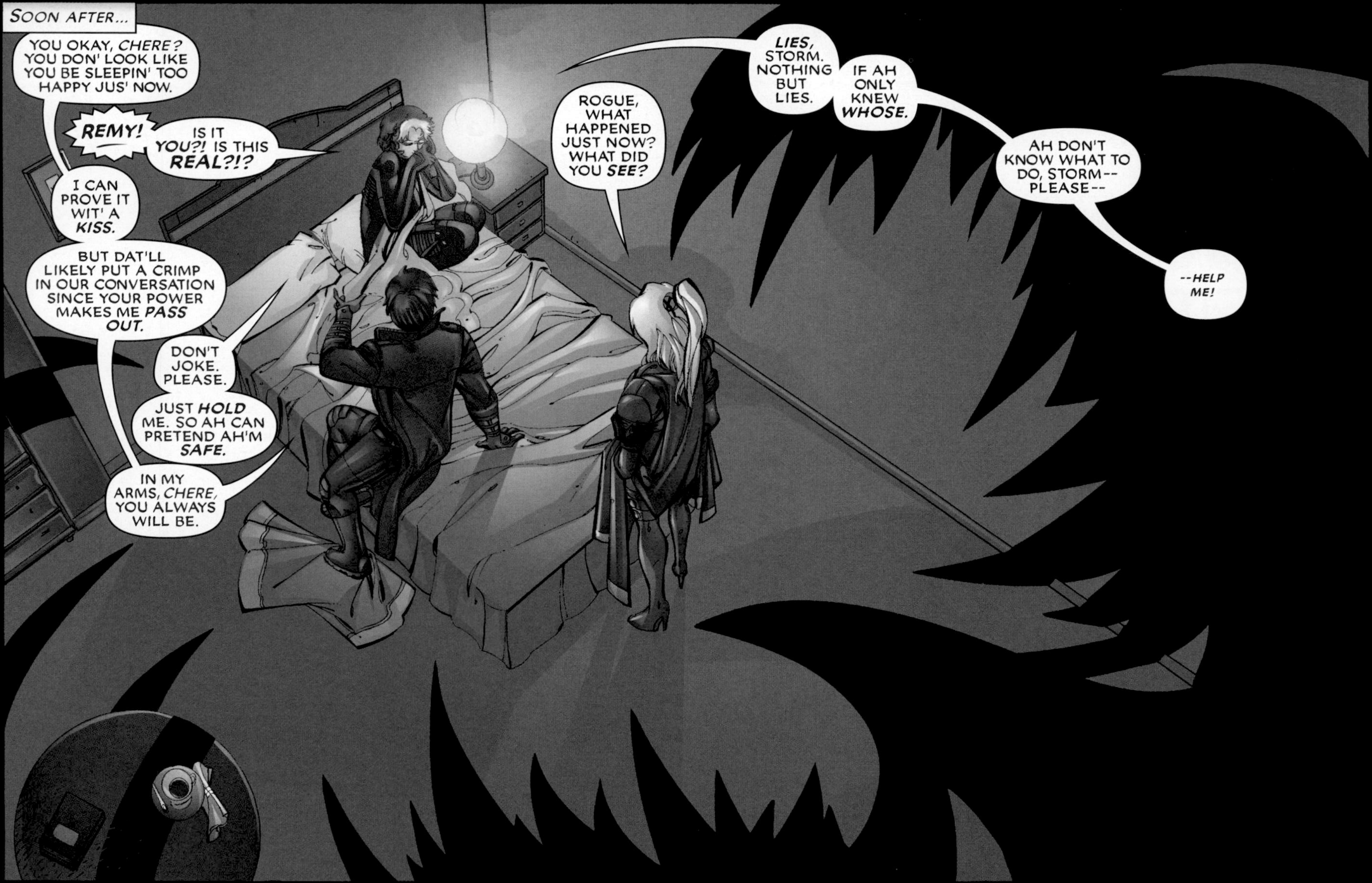
SOON AFTER...
YOU OKAY, *CHERE?* YOU DON' LOOK LIKE YOU BE SLEEPIN' TOO HAPPY JUS' NOW.
REMY!
IS IT *YOU?!* IS THIS ***REAL?!?***
I CAN PROVE IT WIT' A ***KISS.***
BUT DAT'LL LIKELY PUT A CRIMP IN OUR CONVERSATION SINCE YOUR POWER MAKES ME ***PASS OUT.***
DON'T JOKE. PLEASE.
JUST ***HOLD*** ME. SO AH CAN PRETEND AH'M ***SAFE.***
IN MY ARMS, *CHERE,* YOU ALWAYS WILL BE.
ROGUE, WHAT HAPPENED JUST NOW? WHAT DID YOU ***SEE?***
LIES, STORM. NOTHING BUT LIES.
IF AH ONLY KNEW ***WHOSE.***
AH DON'T KNOW WHAT TO DO, STORM-- PLEASE--
--*HELP ME!*

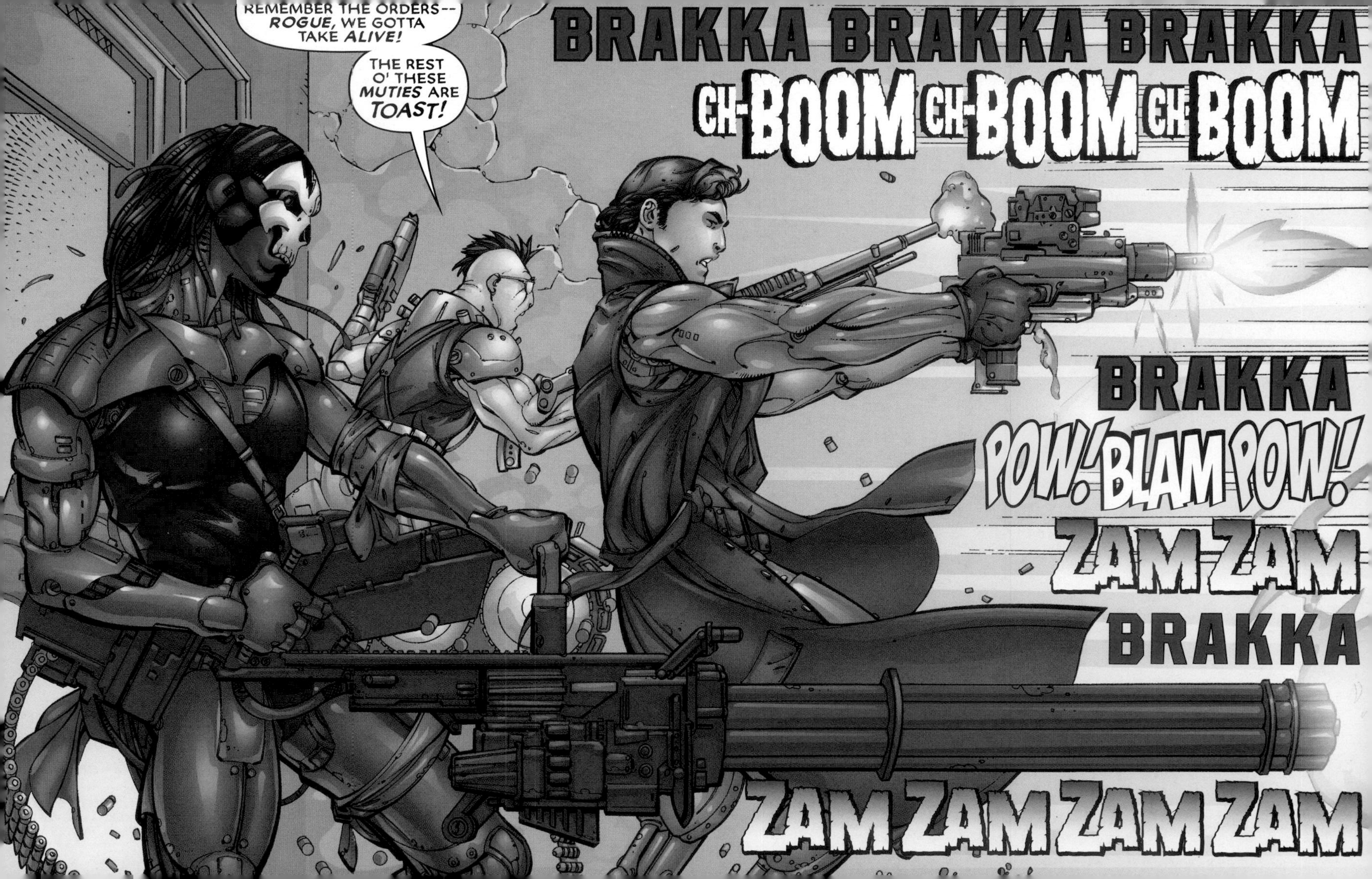
REMEMBER THE ORDERS-- ROGUE, WE GOTTA TAKE ALIVE!
THE REST O' THESE MUTIES ARE TOAST!
BRAKKA BRAKKA BRAKKA
CH-BOOM CH-BOOM CH-BOOM
BRAKKA
POW! BLAM POW!
ZAM ZAM
BRAKKA
ZAM ZAM ZAM ZAM

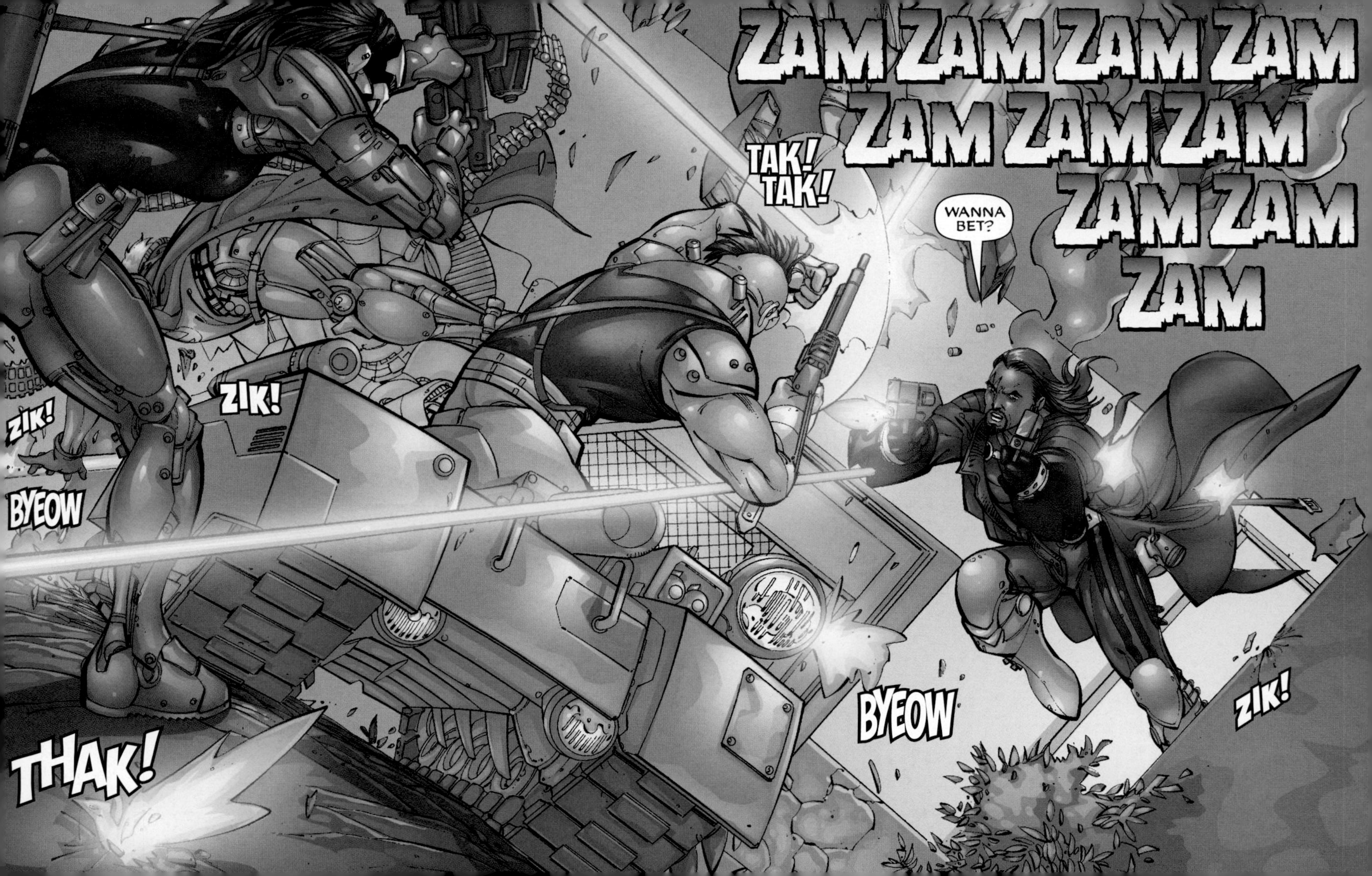
ZAM ZAM ZAM ZAM
ZAM ZAM ZAM
ZAM ZAM
ZAM
TAK! TAK!
WANNA BET?
ZIK!
ZIK!
BYEOW
BYEOW
ZIK!
THAK!

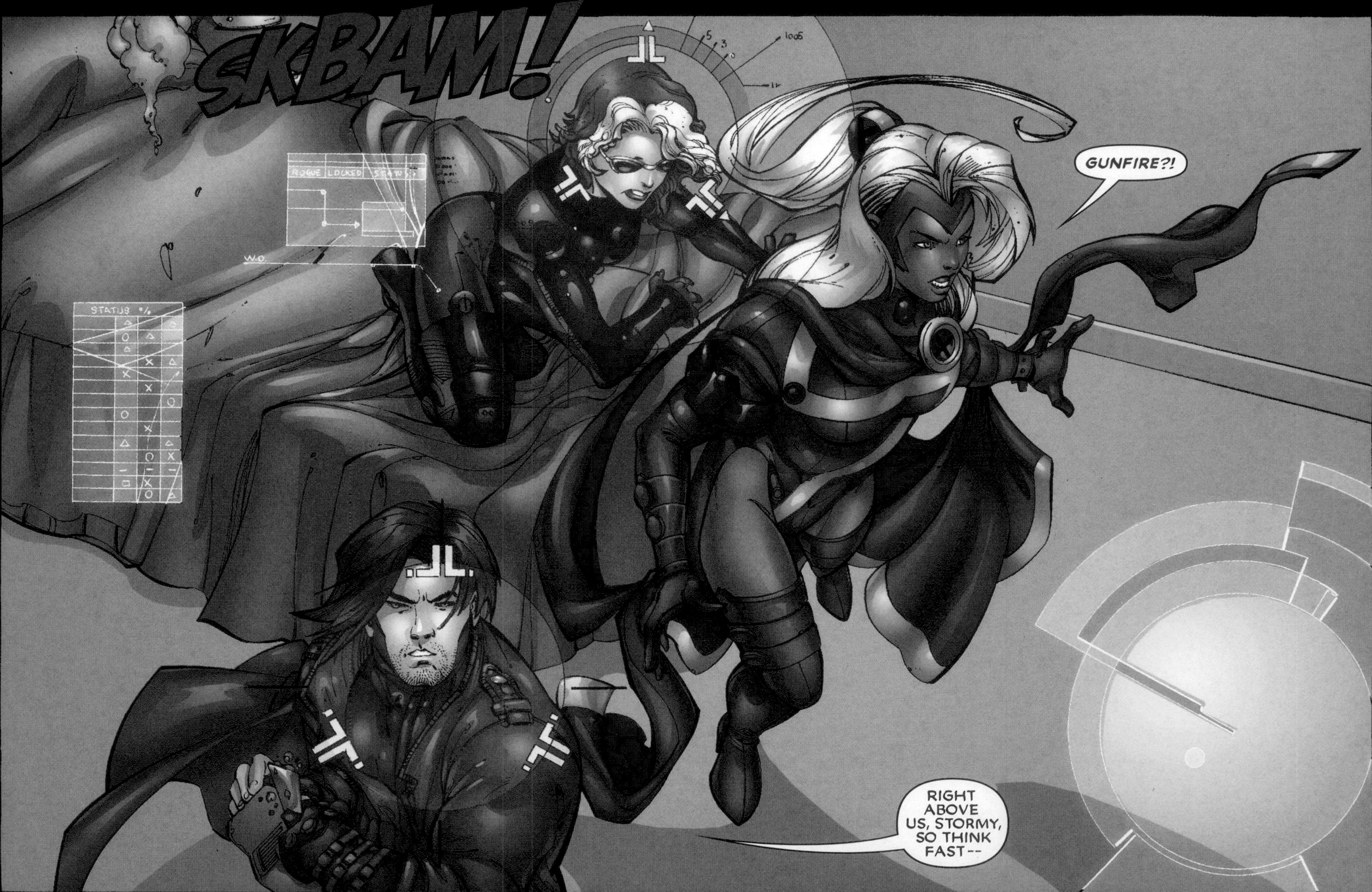
SKBAM!
GUNFIRE?!
RIGHT ABOVE US, STORMY, SO THINK FAST--
ROGUE LOCKED STATUS
STATUS %

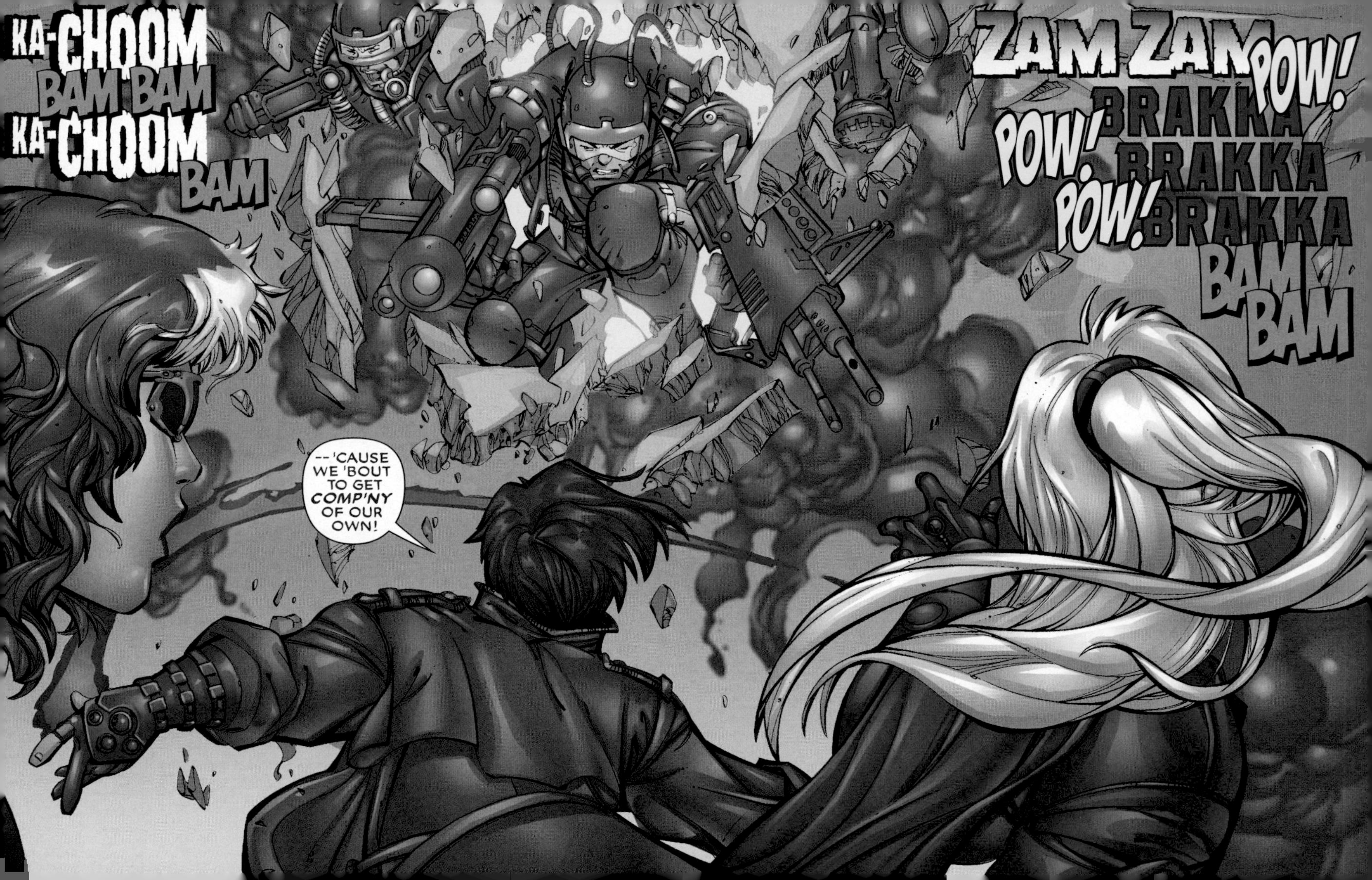
KA-CHOOM
BAM BAM
KA-CHOOM
BAM
ZAM ZAM POW!
POW! BRAKKA
BRAKKA
POW! BRAKKA
BAM
BAM
--'CAUSE WE 'BOUT TO GET COMP'NY OF OUR OWN!

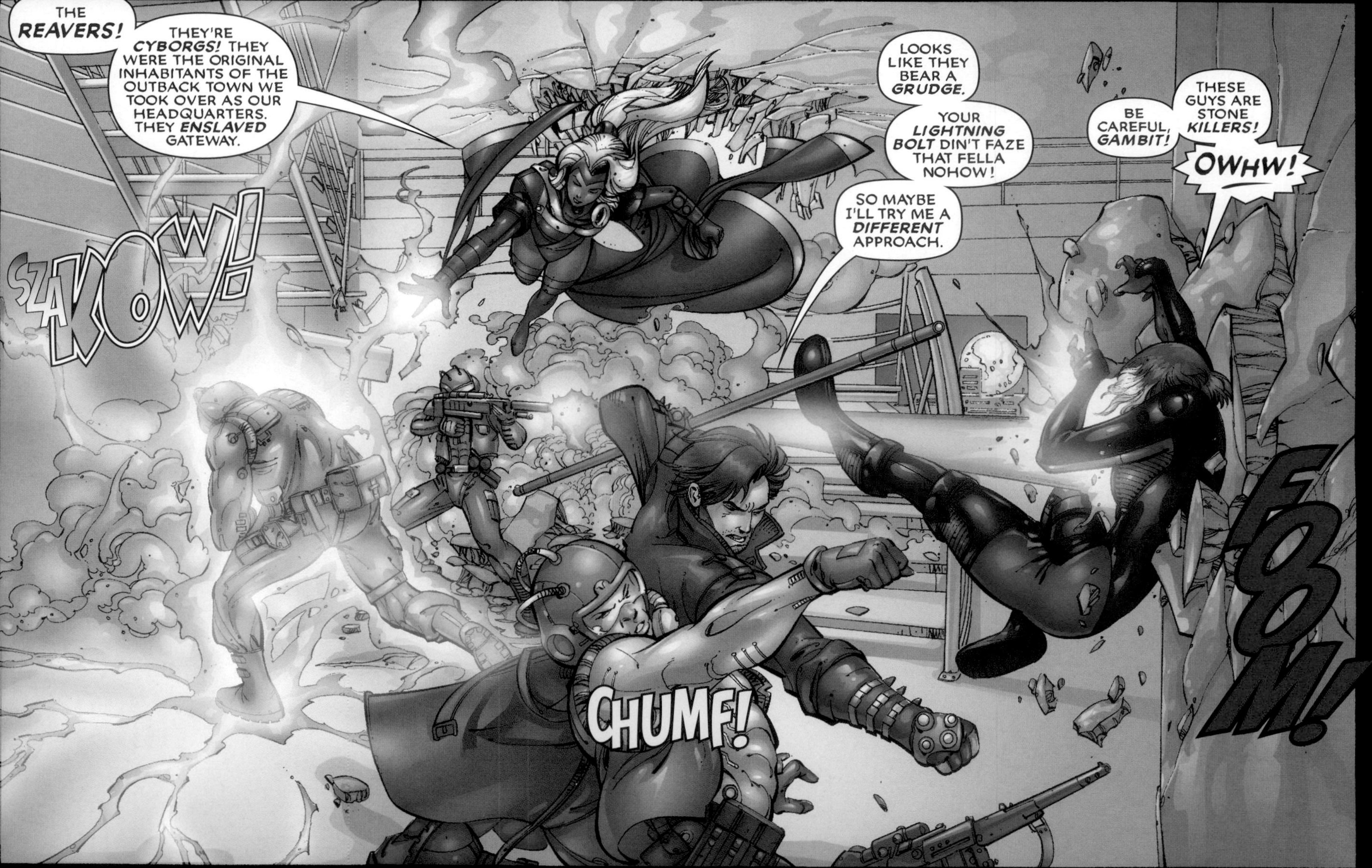
THE REAVERS!
THEY'RE CYBORGS! THEY WERE THE ORIGINAL INHABITANTS OF THE OUTBACK TOWN WE TOOK OVER AS OUR HEADQUARTERS. THEY ENSLAVED GATEWAY.
SZAKOW!
LOOKS LIKE THEY BEAR A GRUDGE.
YOUR LIGHTNING BOLT DIN'T FAZE THAT FELLA NOHOW!
SO MAYBE I'LL TRY ME A DIFFERENT APPROACH.
BE CAREFUL, GAMBIT!
THESE GUYS ARE STONE KILLERS!
OWHW!
FOOM!
CHUMF!

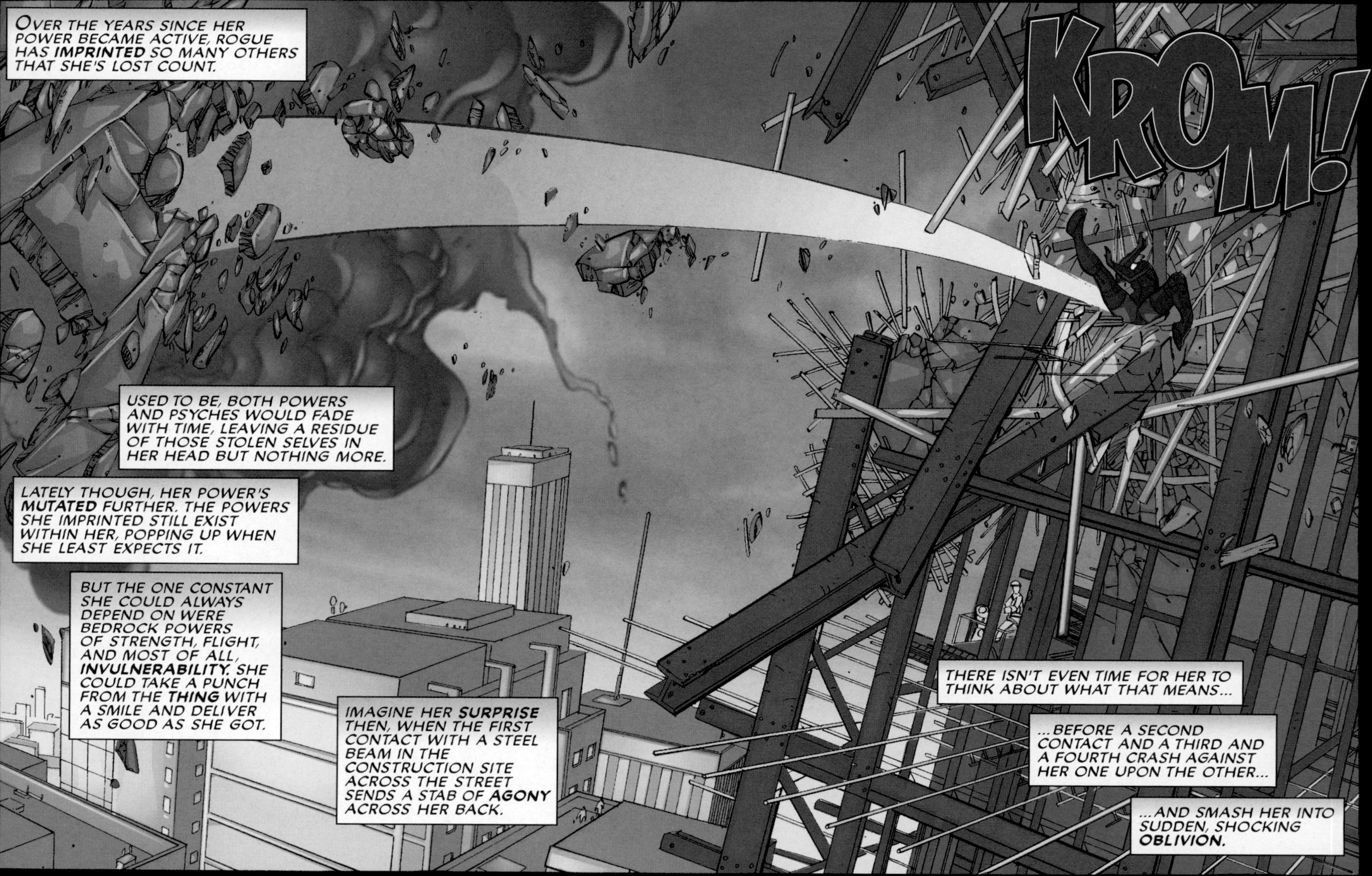
OVER THE YEARS SINCE HER POWER BECAME ACTIVE, ROGUE HAS **IMPRINTED** SO MANY OTHERS THAT SHE'S LOST COUNT.
USED TO BE, BOTH POWERS AND PSYCHES WOULD FADE WITH TIME, LEAVING A RESIDUE OF THOSE STOLEN SELVES IN HER HEAD BUT NOTHING MORE.
LATELY THOUGH, HER POWER'S **MUTATED** FURTHER. THE POWERS SHE IMPRINTED STILL EXIST WITHIN HER, POPPING UP WHEN SHE LEAST EXPECTS IT.
BUT THE ONE CONSTANT SHE COULD ALWAYS DEPEND ON WERE BEDROCK POWERS OF STRENGTH, FLIGHT, AND MOST OF ALL, **INVULNERABILITY.** SHE COULD TAKE A PUNCH FROM THE **THING** WITH A SMILE AND DELIVER AS GOOD AS SHE GOT.
IMAGINE HER **SURPRISE** THEN, WHEN THE FIRST CONTACT WITH A STEEL BEAM IN THE CONSTRUCTION SITE ACROSS THE STREET SENDS A STAB OF **AGONY** ACROSS HER BACK.
KROM!
THERE ISN'T EVEN TIME FOR HER TO THINK ABOUT WHAT THAT MEANS...
...BEFORE A SECOND CONTACT AND A THIRD AND A FOURTH CRASH AGAINST HER ONE UPON THE OTHER...
...AND SMASH HER INTO SUDDEN, SHOCKING **OBLIVION.**

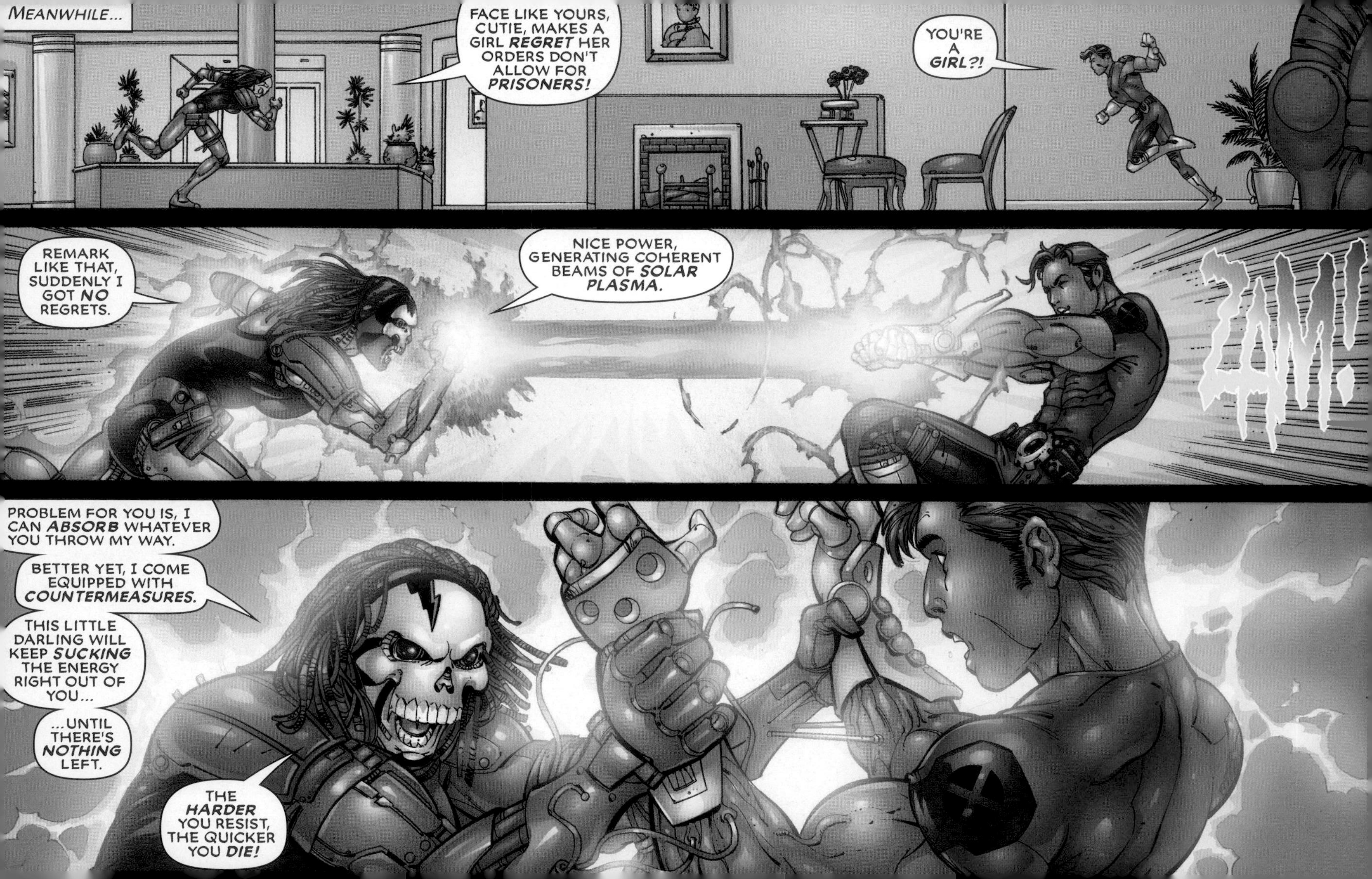
MEANWHILE...
FACE LIKE YOURS, CUTIE, MAKES A GIRL *REGRET* HER ORDERS DON'T ALLOW FOR *PRISONERS!*
YOU'RE A *GIRL?!*
REMARK LIKE THAT, SUDDENLY I GOT *NO* REGRETS.
NICE POWER, GENERATING COHERENT BEAMS OF *SOLAR PLASMA.*
ZAM!
PROBLEM FOR YOU IS, I CAN *ABSORB* WHATEVER YOU THROW MY WAY.
BETTER YET, I COME EQUIPPED WITH *COUNTERMEASURES.*
THIS LITTLE DARLING WILL KEEP *SUCKING* THE ENERGY RIGHT OUT OF YOU...
...UNTIL THERE'S *NOTHING* LEFT.
THE *HARDER* YOU RESIST, THE QUICKER YOU *DIE!*

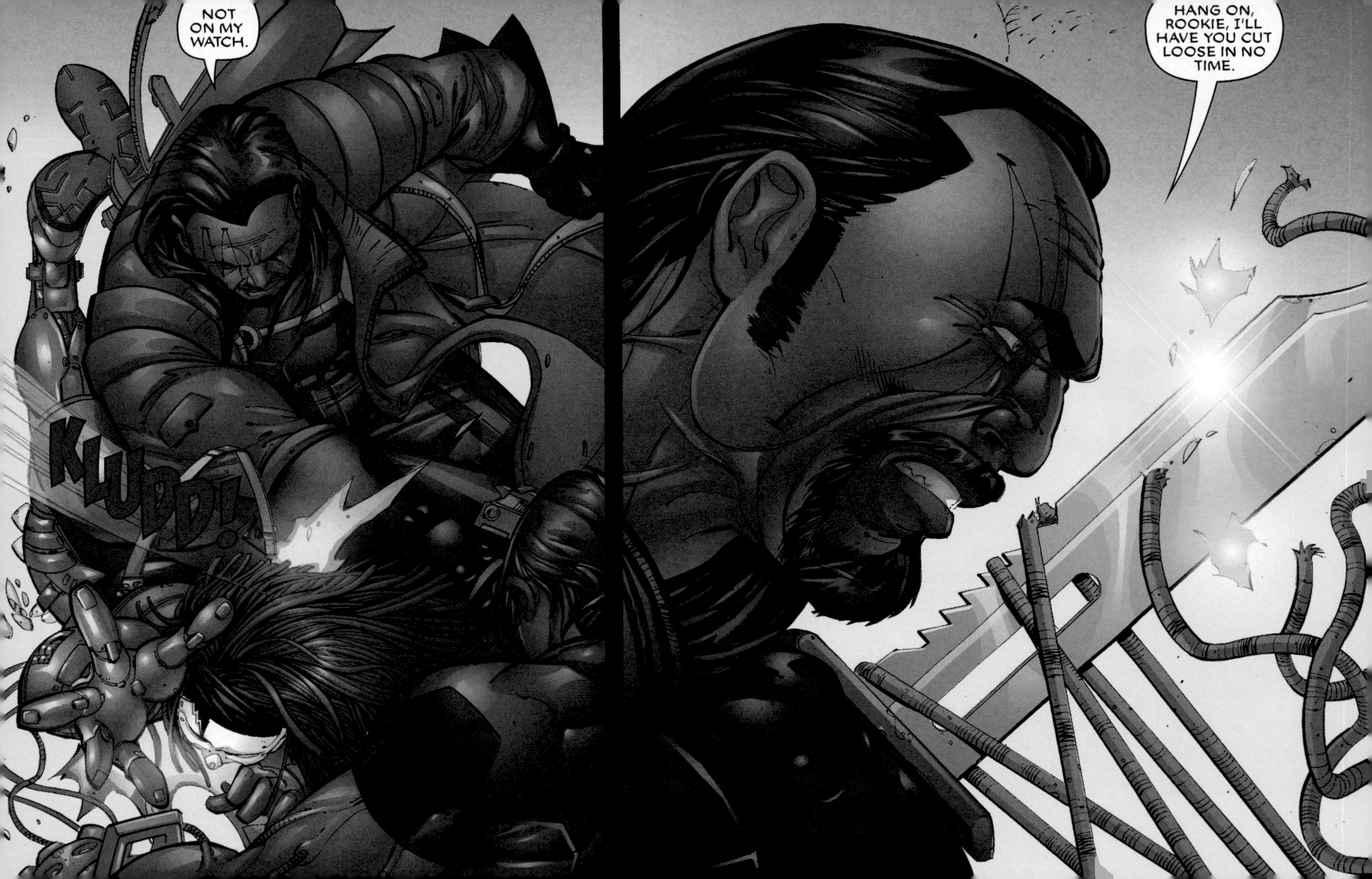
NOT ON MY WATCH.
KLUDD!
HANG ON, ROOKIE, I'LL HAVE YOU CUT LOOSE IN NO TIME.

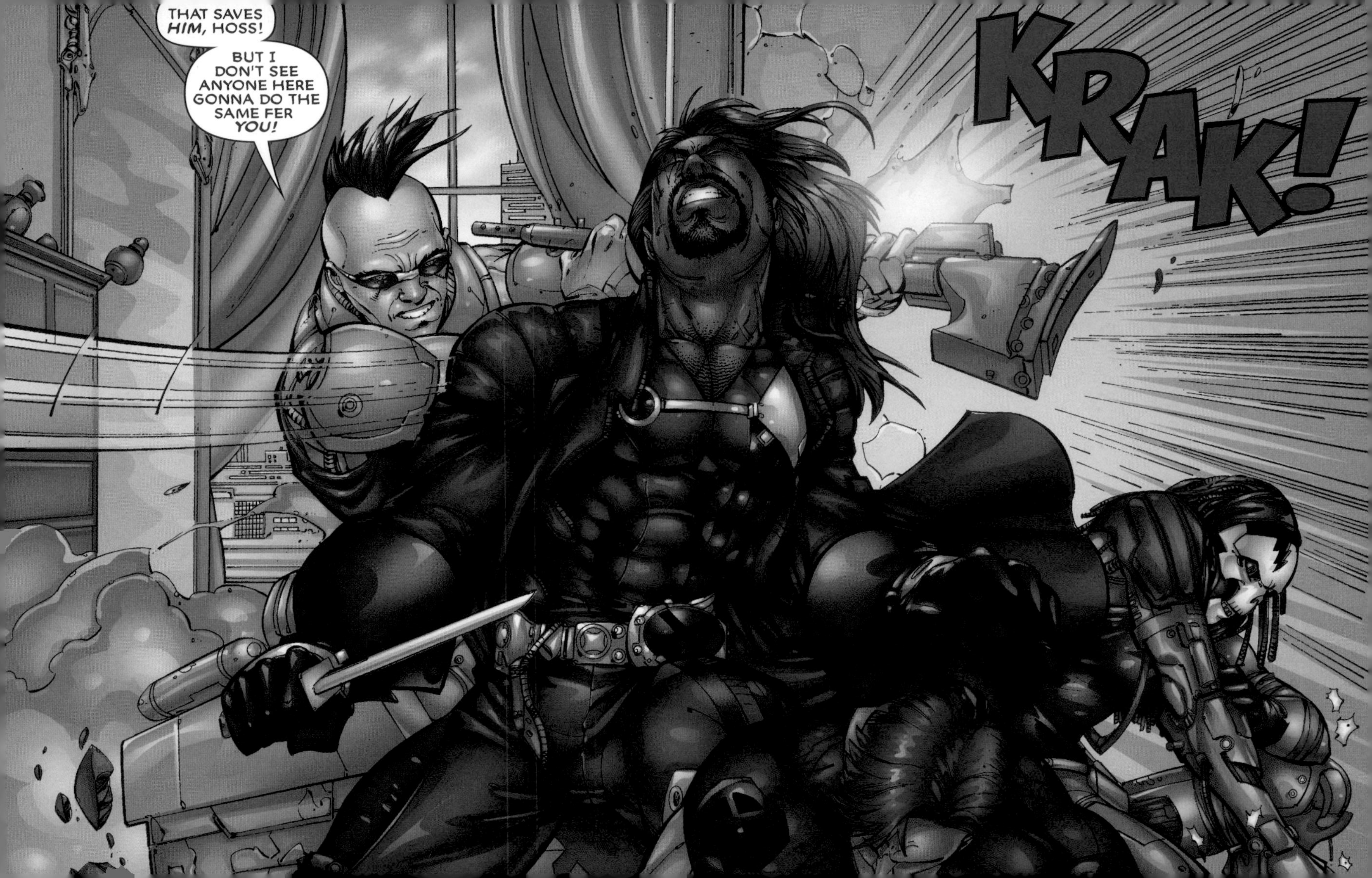
THAT SAVES *HIM*, HOSS!
BUT I DON'T SEE ANYONE HERE GONNA DO THE SAME FER *YOU!*
KRAK!

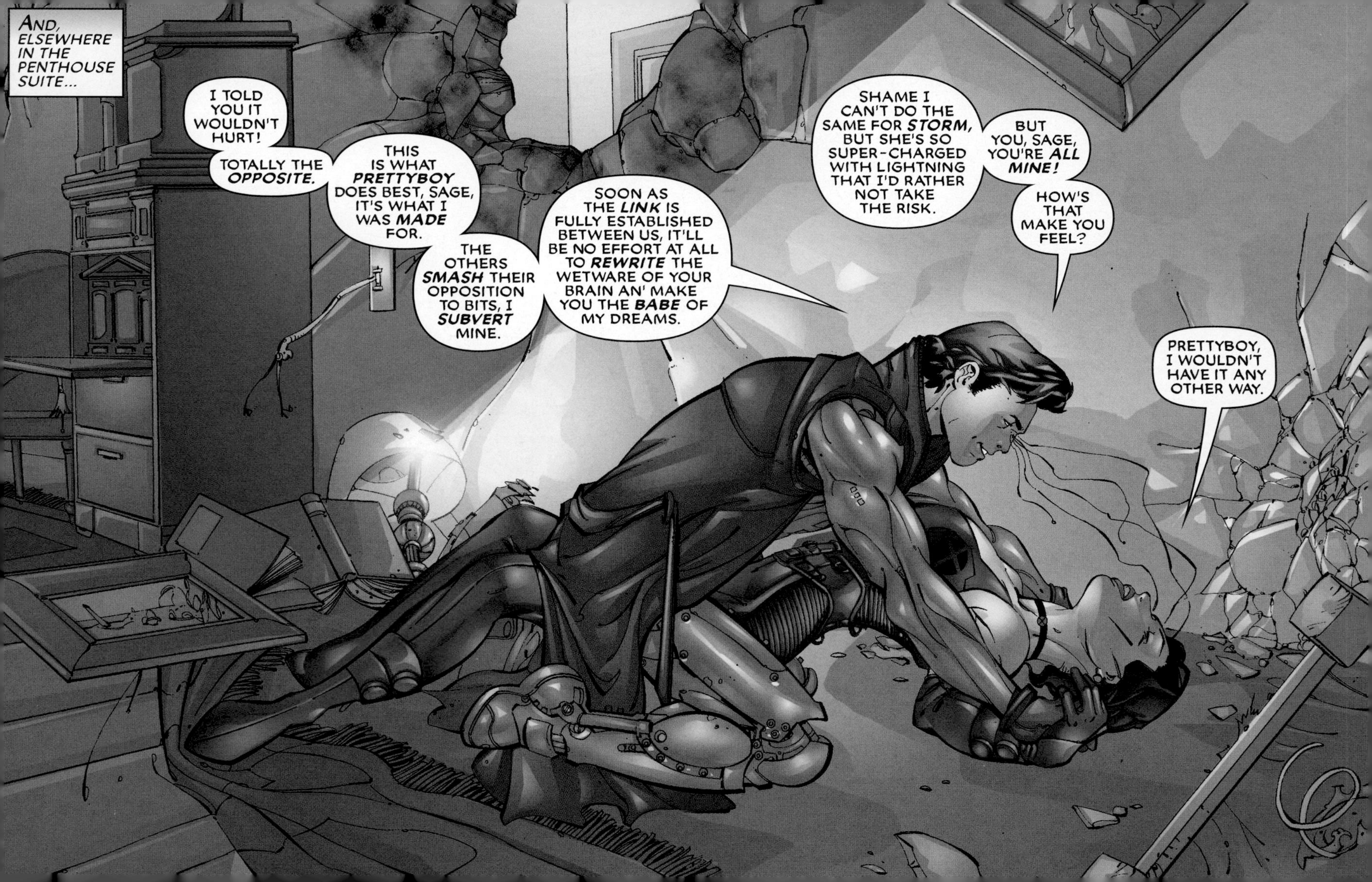
AND, ELSEWHERE IN THE PENTHOUSE SUITE...
I TOLD YOU IT WOULDN'T HURT!
TOTALLY THE OPPOSITE.
THIS IS WHAT PRETTYBOY DOES BEST, SAGE, IT'S WHAT I WAS MADE FOR.
THE OTHERS SMASH THEIR OPPOSITION TO BITS, I SUBVERT MINE.
SOON AS THE LINK IS FULLY ESTABLISHED BETWEEN US, IT'LL BE NO EFFORT AT ALL TO REWRITE THE WETWARE OF YOUR BRAIN AN' MAKE YOU THE BABE OF MY DREAMS.
SHAME I CAN'T DO THE SAME FOR STORM, BUT SHE'S SO SUPER-CHARGED WITH LIGHTNING THAT I'D RATHER NOT TAKE THE RISK.
BUT YOU, SAGE, YOU'RE ALL MINE!
HOW'S THAT MAKE YOU FEEL?
PRETTYBOY, I WOULDN'T HAVE IT ANY OTHER WAY.

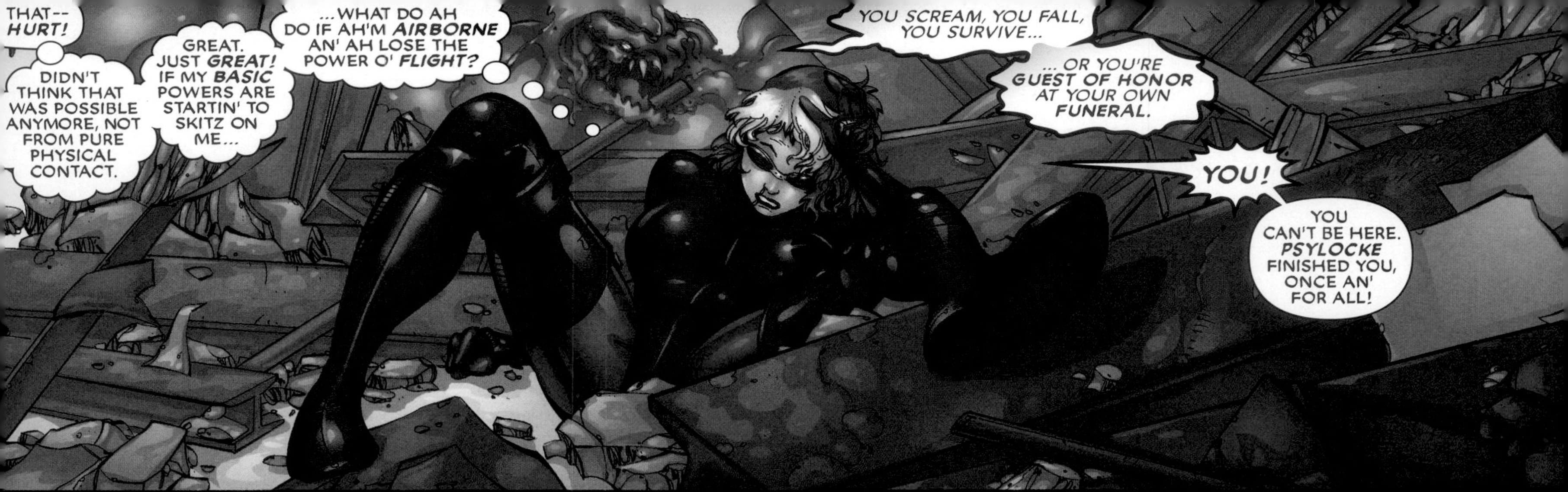
THAT-- HURT!
DIDN'T THINK THAT WAS POSSIBLE ANYMORE, NOT FROM PURE PHYSICAL CONTACT.
GREAT. JUST GREAT! IF MY BASIC POWERS ARE STARTIN' TO SKITZ ON ME...
...WHAT DO AH DO IF AH'M AIRBORNE AN' AH LOSE THE POWER O' FLIGHT?
YOU SCREAM, YOU FALL, YOU SURVIVE...
...OR YOU'RE GUEST OF HONOR AT YOUR OWN FUNERAL.
YOU!
YOU CAN'T BE HERE. PSYLOCKE FINISHED YOU, ONCE AN' FOR ALL!

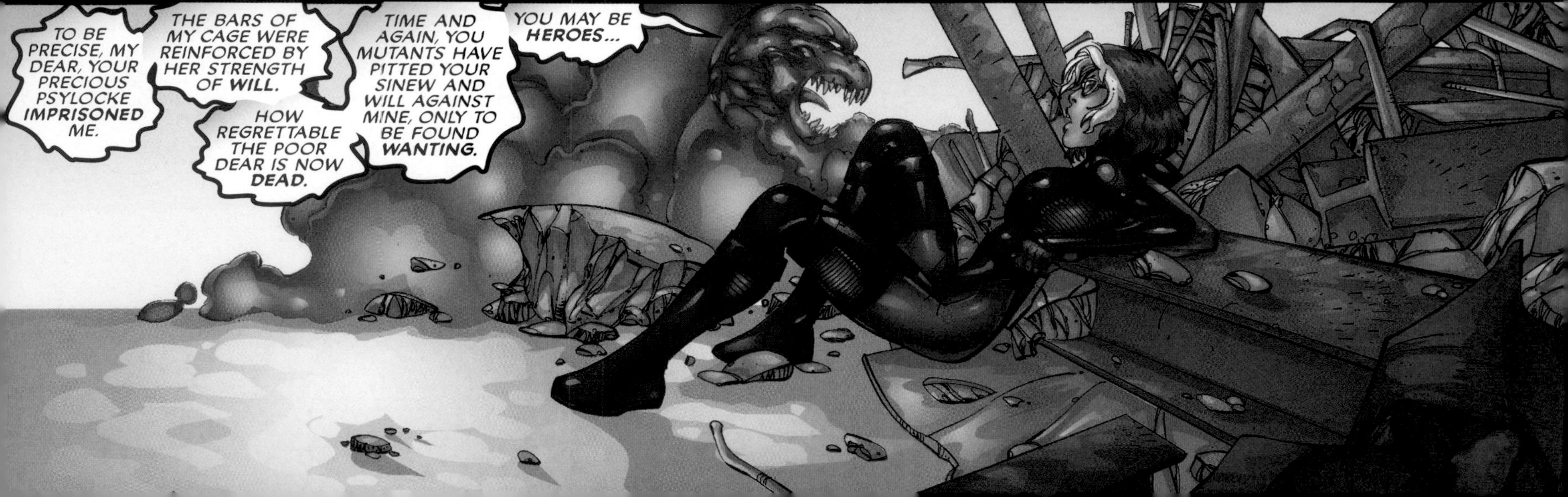
TO BE PRECISE, MY DEAR, YOUR PRECIOUS PSYLOCKE IMPRISONED ME.
THE BARS OF MY CAGE WERE REINFORCED BY HER STRENGTH OF WILL.
HOW REGRETTABLE THE POOR DEAR IS NOW DEAD.
TIME AND AGAIN, YOU MUTANTS HAVE PITTED YOUR SINEW AND WILL AGAINST MINE, ONLY TO BE FOUND WANTING.
YOU MAY BE HEROES...

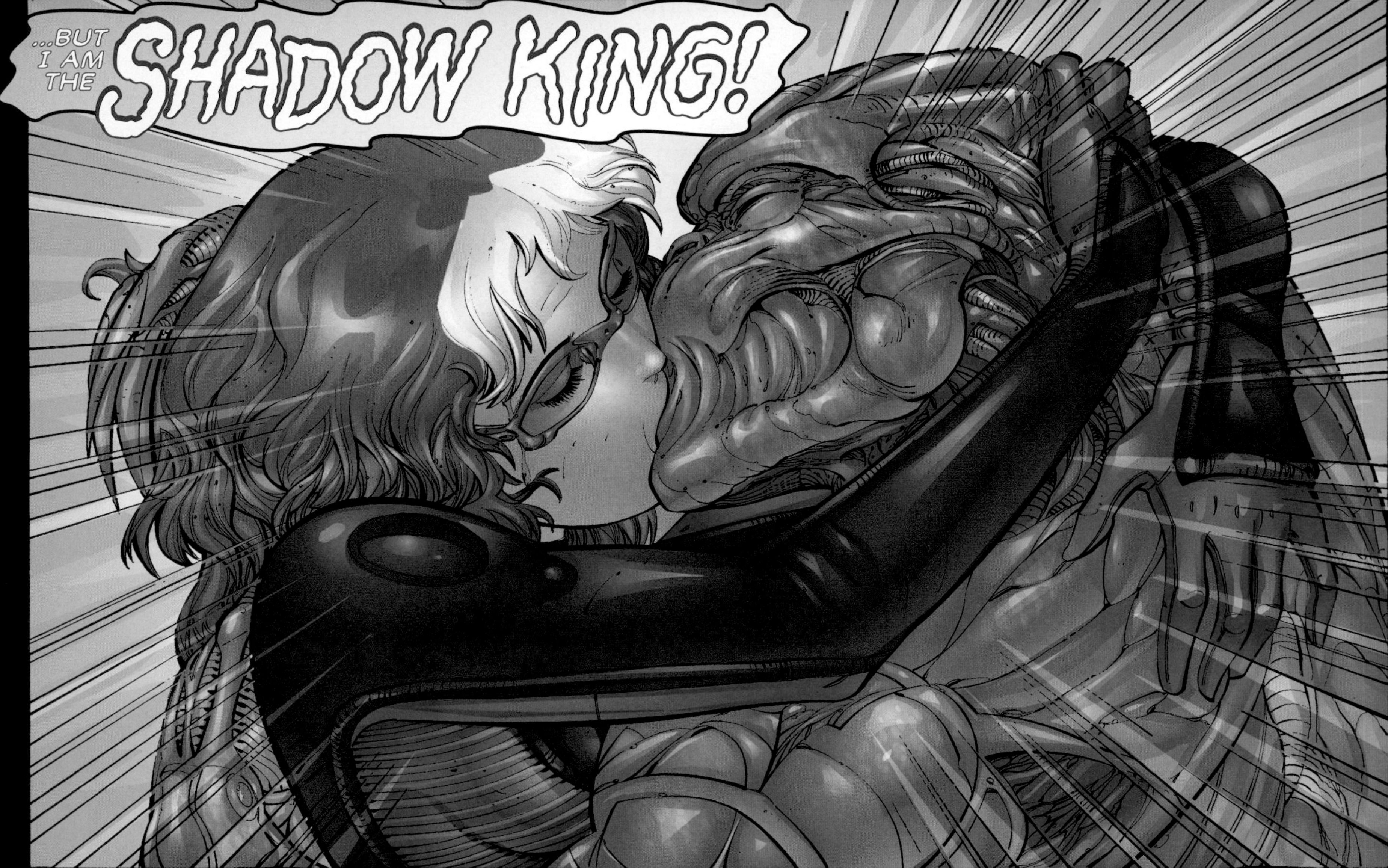
...BUT I AM THE SHADOW KING!

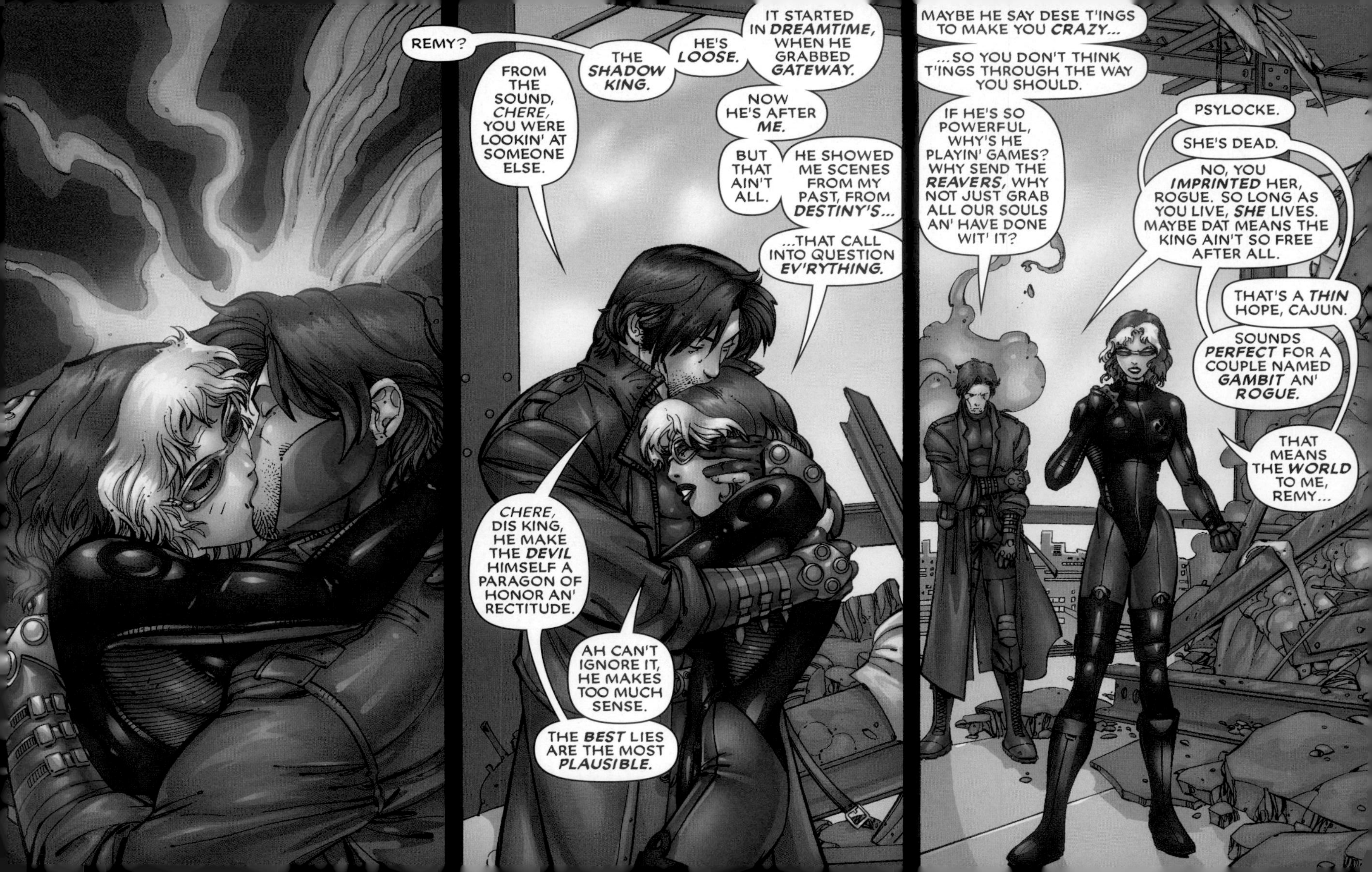
REMY?
FROM THE SOUND, *CHERE,* YOU WERE LOOKIN' AT SOMEONE ELSE.
THE ***SHADOW KING.***
HE'S ***LOOSE.***
IT STARTED IN ***DREAMTIME,*** WHEN HE GRABBED ***GATEWAY.***
NOW HE'S AFTER ***ME.***
BUT THAT AIN'T ALL.
HE SHOWED ME SCENES FROM MY PAST, FROM ***DESTINY'S...***
...THAT CALL INTO QUESTION ***EV'RYTHING.***
CHERE, DIS KING, HE MAKE THE ***DEVIL*** HIMSELF A PARAGON OF HONOR AN' RECTITUDE.
AH CAN'T IGNORE IT, HE MAKES TOO MUCH SENSE.
THE ***BEST*** LIES ARE THE MOST ***PLAUSIBLE.***
MAYBE HE SAY DESE T'INGS TO MAKE YOU ***CRAZY...***
...SO YOU DON'T THINK T'INGS THROUGH THE WAY YOU SHOULD.
IF HE'S SO POWERFUL, WHY'S HE PLAYIN' GAMES? WHY SEND THE ***REAVERS,*** WHY NOT JUST GRAB ALL OUR SOULS AN' HAVE DONE WIT' IT?
PSYLOCKE.
SHE'S DEAD.
NO, YOU ***IMPRINTED*** HER, ROGUE. SO LONG AS YOU LIVE, ***SHE*** LIVES. MAYBE DAT MEANS THE KING AIN'T SO FREE AFTER ALL.
THAT'S A ***THIN*** HOPE, CAJUN.
SOUNDS ***PERFECT*** FOR A COUPLE NAMED ***GAMBIT*** AN' ***ROGUE.***
THAT MEANS THE ***WORLD*** TO ME, REMY...

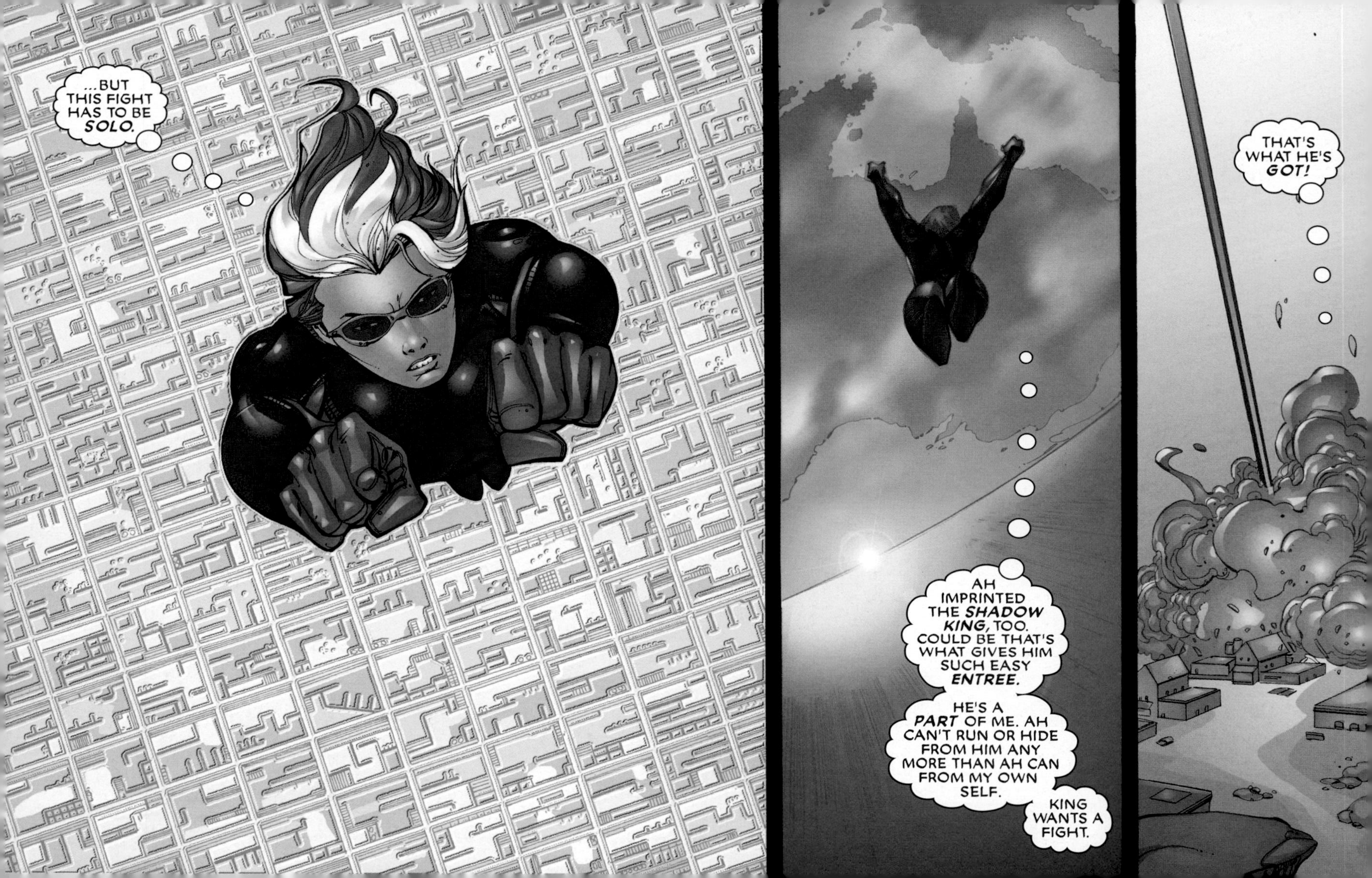
...BUT THIS FIGHT HAS TO BE *SOLO.*
AH IMPRINTED THE *SHADOW KING,* TOO. COULD BE THAT'S WHAT GIVES HIM SUCH EASY *ENTREE.*
HE'S A *PART* OF ME. AH CAN'T RUN OR HIDE FROM HIM ANY MORE THAN AH CAN FROM MY OWN SELF.
KING WANTS A FIGHT.
THAT'S WHAT HE'S *GOT!*

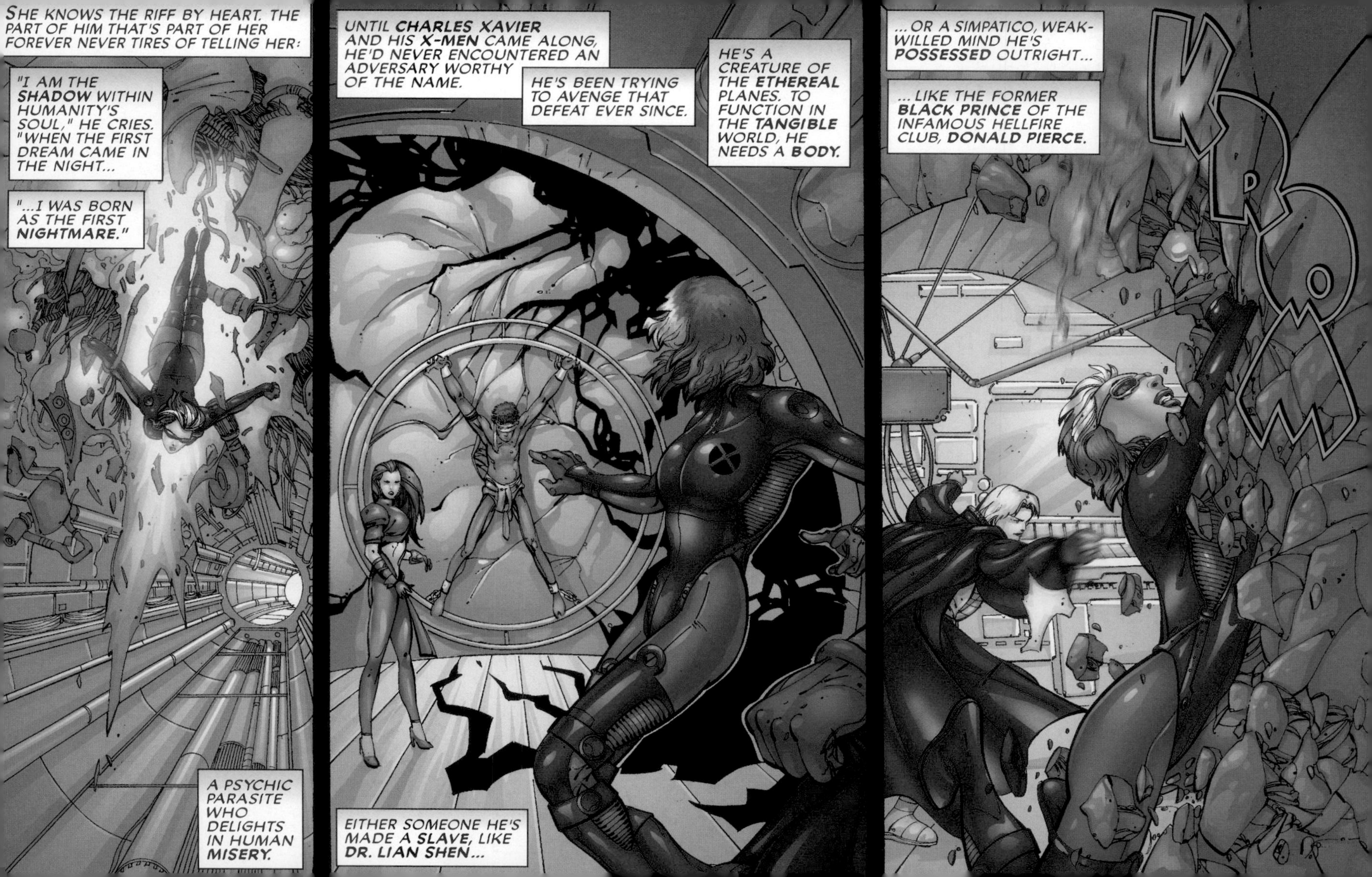
SHE KNOWS THE RIFF BY HEART. THE PART OF HIM THAT'S PART OF HER FOREVER NEVER TIRES OF TELLING HER:
"I AM THE SHADOW WITHIN HUMANITY'S SOUL," HE CRIES. "WHEN THE FIRST DREAM CAME IN THE NIGHT...
"...I WAS BORN AS THE FIRST NIGHTMARE."
A PSYCHIC PARASITE WHO DELIGHTS IN HUMAN MISERY.
UNTIL CHARLES XAVIER AND HIS X-MEN CAME ALONG, HE'D NEVER ENCOUNTERED AN ADVERSARY WORTHY OF THE NAME.
HE'S BEEN TRYING TO AVENGE THAT DEFEAT EVER SINCE.
HE'S A CREATURE OF THE ETHEREAL PLANES. TO FUNCTION IN THE TANGIBLE WORLD, HE NEEDS A BODY.
EITHER SOMEONE HE'S MADE A SLAVE, LIKE DR. LIAN SHEN...
...OR A SIMPATICO, WEAK-WILLED MIND HE'S POSSESSED OUTRIGHT...
...LIKE THE FORMER BLACK PRINCE OF THE INFAMOUS HELLFIRE CLUB, DONALD PIERCE.
KRROOM

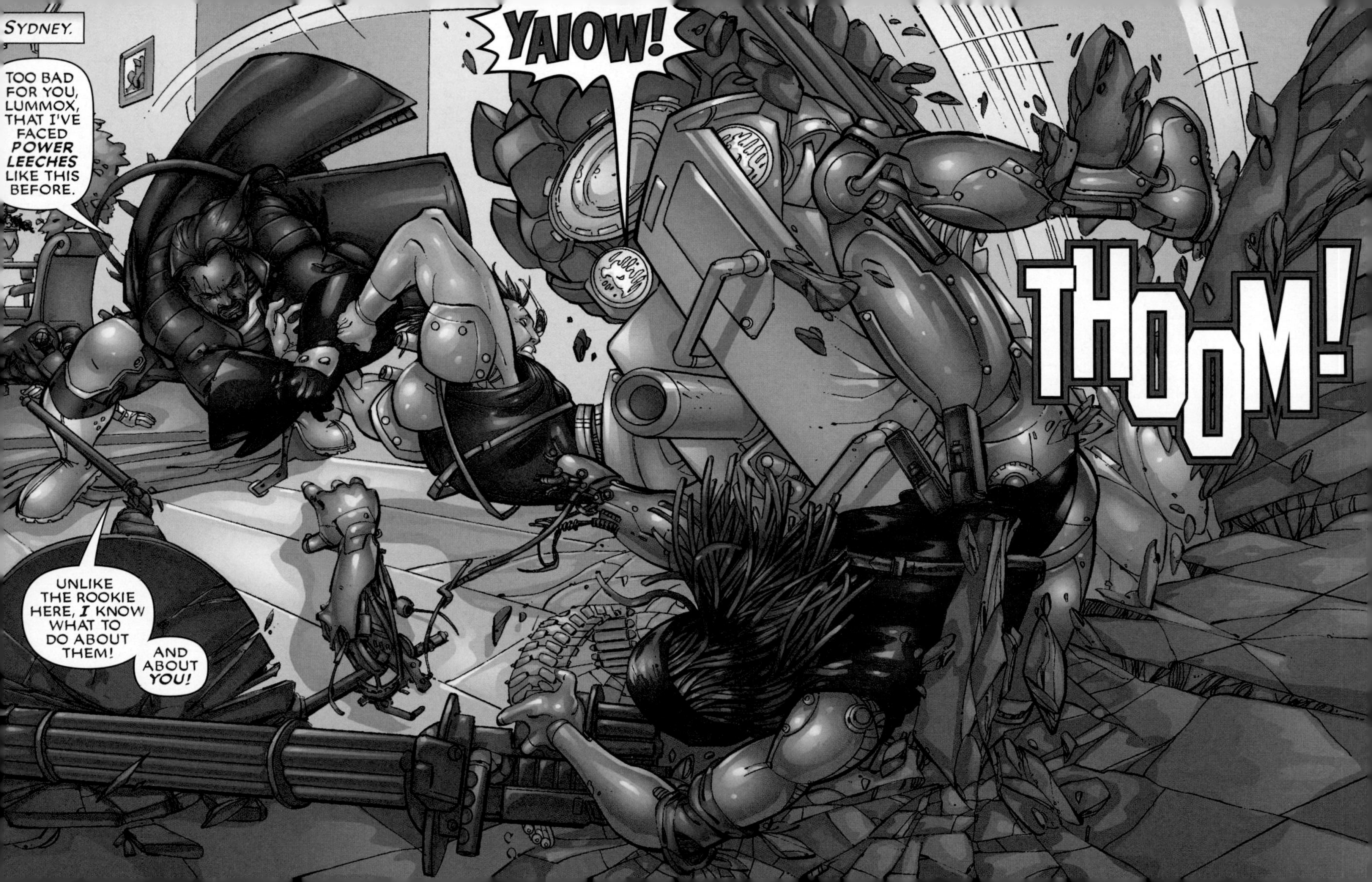
SYDNEY.
TOO BAD FOR YOU, LUMMOX, THAT I'VE FACED *POWER LEECHES* LIKE THIS BEFORE.
YAIOW!
THOOM!
UNLIKE THE ROOKIE HERE, *I* KNOW WHAT TO DO ABOUT THEM!
AND ABOUT *YOU!*

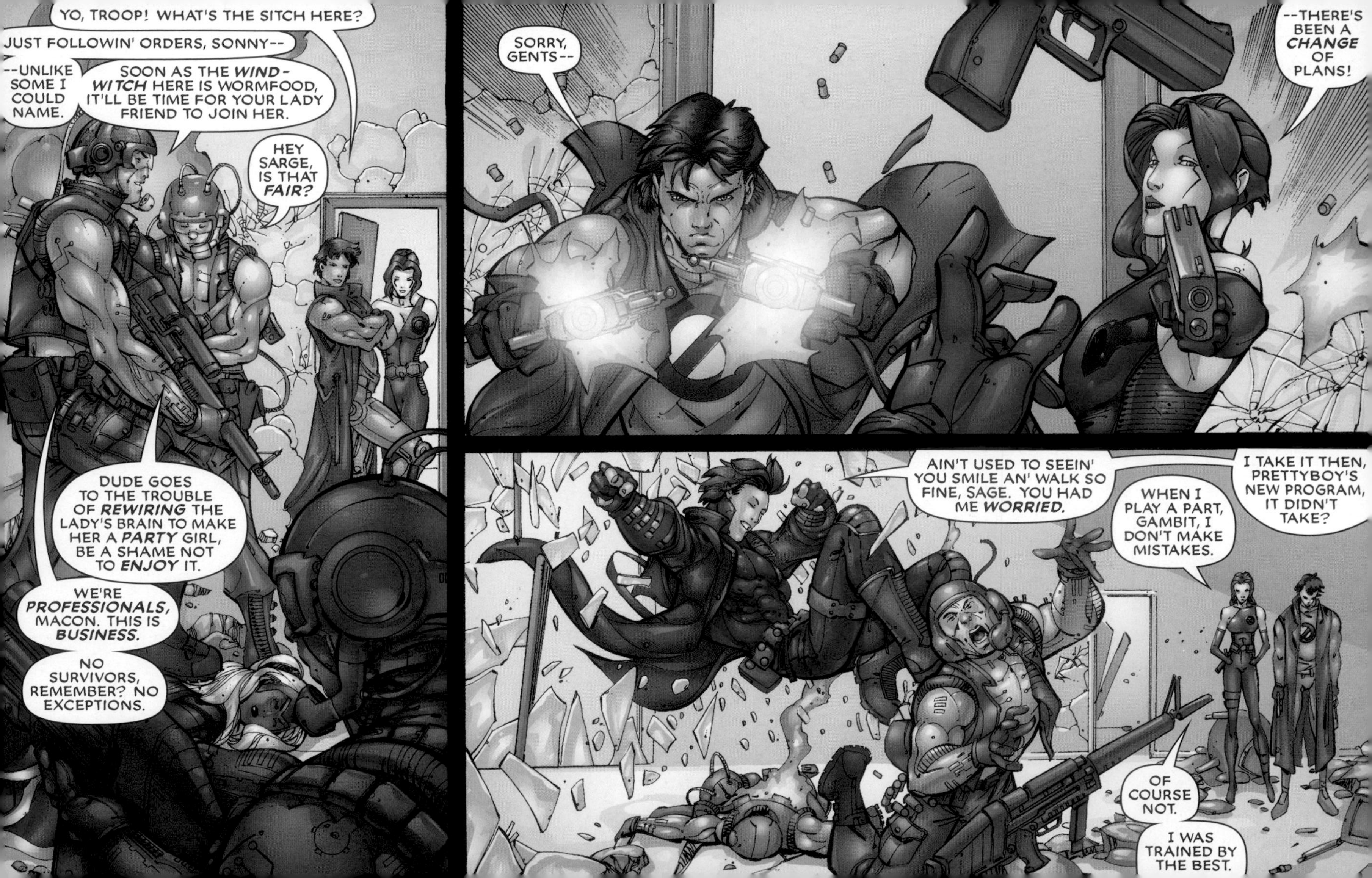
YO, TROOP! WHAT'S THE SITCH HERE?
JUST FOLLOWIN' ORDERS, SONNY--
--UNLIKE SOME I COULD NAME.
SOON AS THE *WIND-WITCH* HERE IS WORMFOOD, IT'LL BE TIME FOR YOUR LADY FRIEND TO JOIN HER.
HEY SARGE, IS THAT *FAIR?*
DUDE GOES TO THE TROUBLE OF *REWIRING* THE LADY'S BRAIN TO MAKE HER A *PARTY* GIRL, BE A SHAME NOT TO *ENJOY* IT.
WE'RE *PROFESSIONALS,* MACON. THIS IS *BUSINESS.*
NO SURVIVORS, REMEMBER? NO EXCEPTIONS.
SORRY, GENTS--
--THERE'S BEEN A *CHANGE* OF PLANS!
I TAKE IT THEN, PRETTYBOY'S NEW PROGRAM, IT DIDN'T TAKE?
WHEN I PLAY A PART, GAMBIT, I DON'T MAKE MISTAKES.
AIN'T USED TO SEEIN' YOU SMILE AN' WALK SO FINE, SAGE. YOU HAD ME *WORRIED.*
OF COURSE NOT.
I WAS TRAINED BY THE BEST.

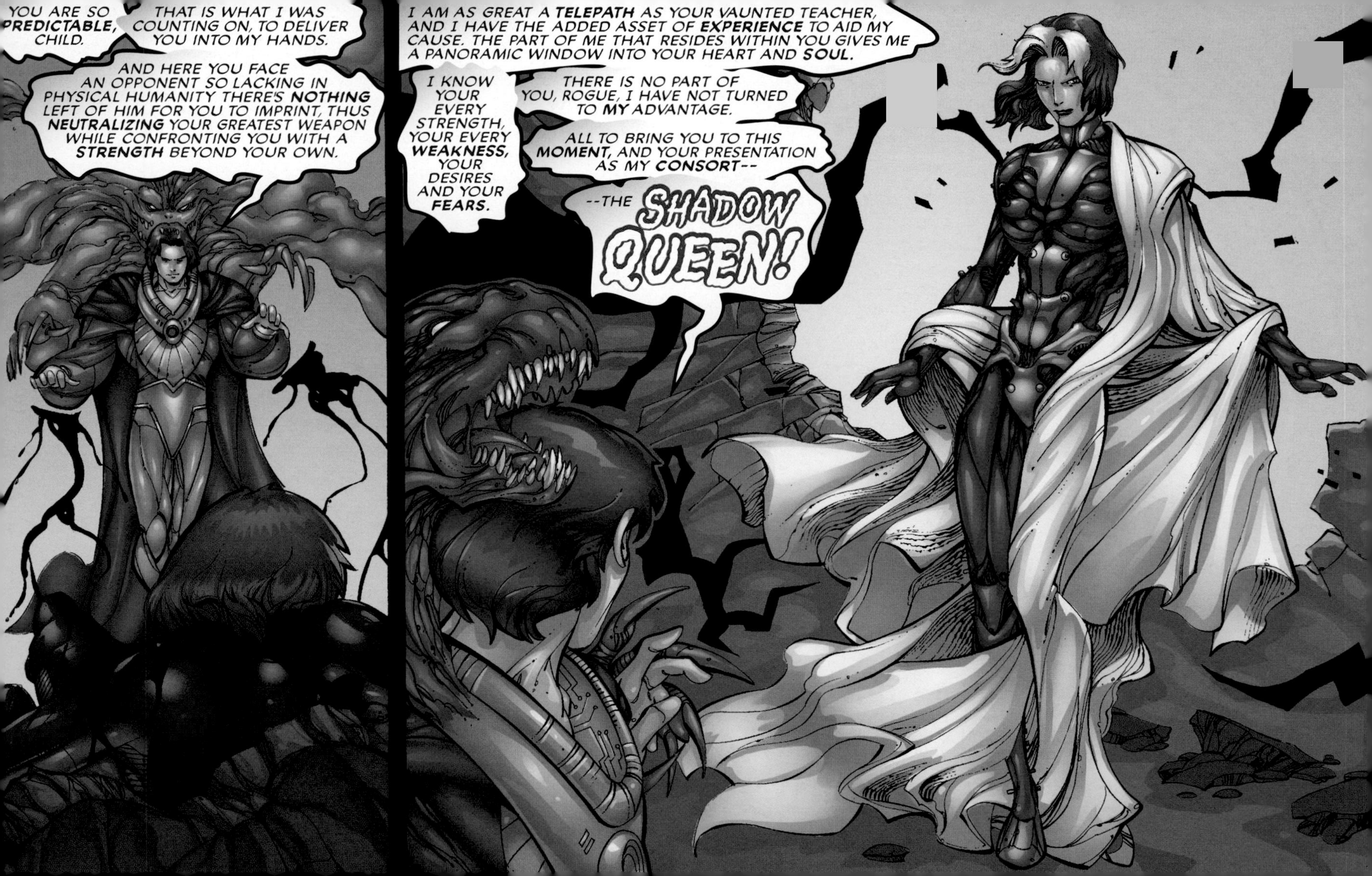
YOU ARE SO **PREDICTABLE,** CHILD.
THAT IS WHAT I WAS COUNTING ON, TO DELIVER YOU INTO MY HANDS.
AND HERE YOU FACE AN OPPONENT SO LACKING IN PHYSICAL HUMANITY THERE'S **NOTHING** LEFT OF HIM FOR YOU TO IMPRINT, THUS **NEUTRALIZING** YOUR GREATEST WEAPON WHILE CONFRONTING YOU WITH A **STRENGTH** BEYOND YOUR OWN.
I AM AS GREAT A **TELEPATH** AS YOUR VAUNTED TEACHER, AND I HAVE THE ADDED ASSET OF **EXPERIENCE** TO AID MY CAUSE. THE PART OF ME THAT RESIDES WITHIN YOU GIVES ME A PANORAMIC WINDOW INTO YOUR HEART AND **SOUL.**
I KNOW YOUR EVERY STRENGTH, YOUR EVERY **WEAKNESS,** YOUR DESIRES AND YOUR **FEARS.**
THERE IS NO PART OF YOU, ROGUE, I HAVE NOT TURNED TO **MY** ADVANTAGE.
ALL TO BRING YOU TO THIS **MOMENT,** AND YOUR PRESENTATION AS MY **CONSORT**--
--THE SHADOW QUEEN!

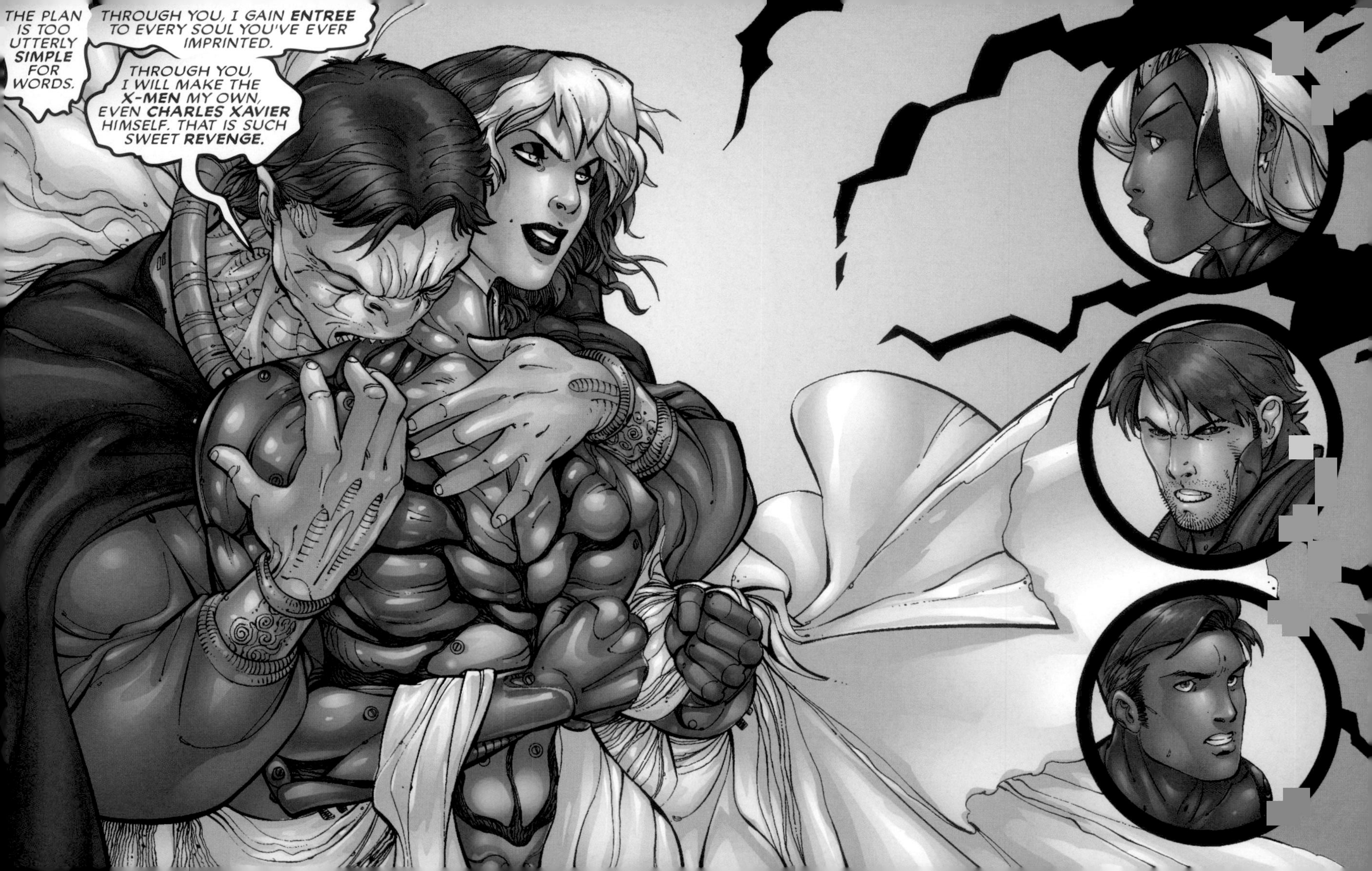
THE PLAN IS TOO UTTERLY SIMPLE FOR WORDS.
THROUGH YOU, I GAIN ENTREE TO EVERY SOUL YOU'VE EVER IMPRINTED.
THROUGH YOU, I WILL MAKE THE X-MEN MY OWN, EVEN CHARLES XAVIER HIMSELF. THAT IS SUCH SWEET REVENGE.

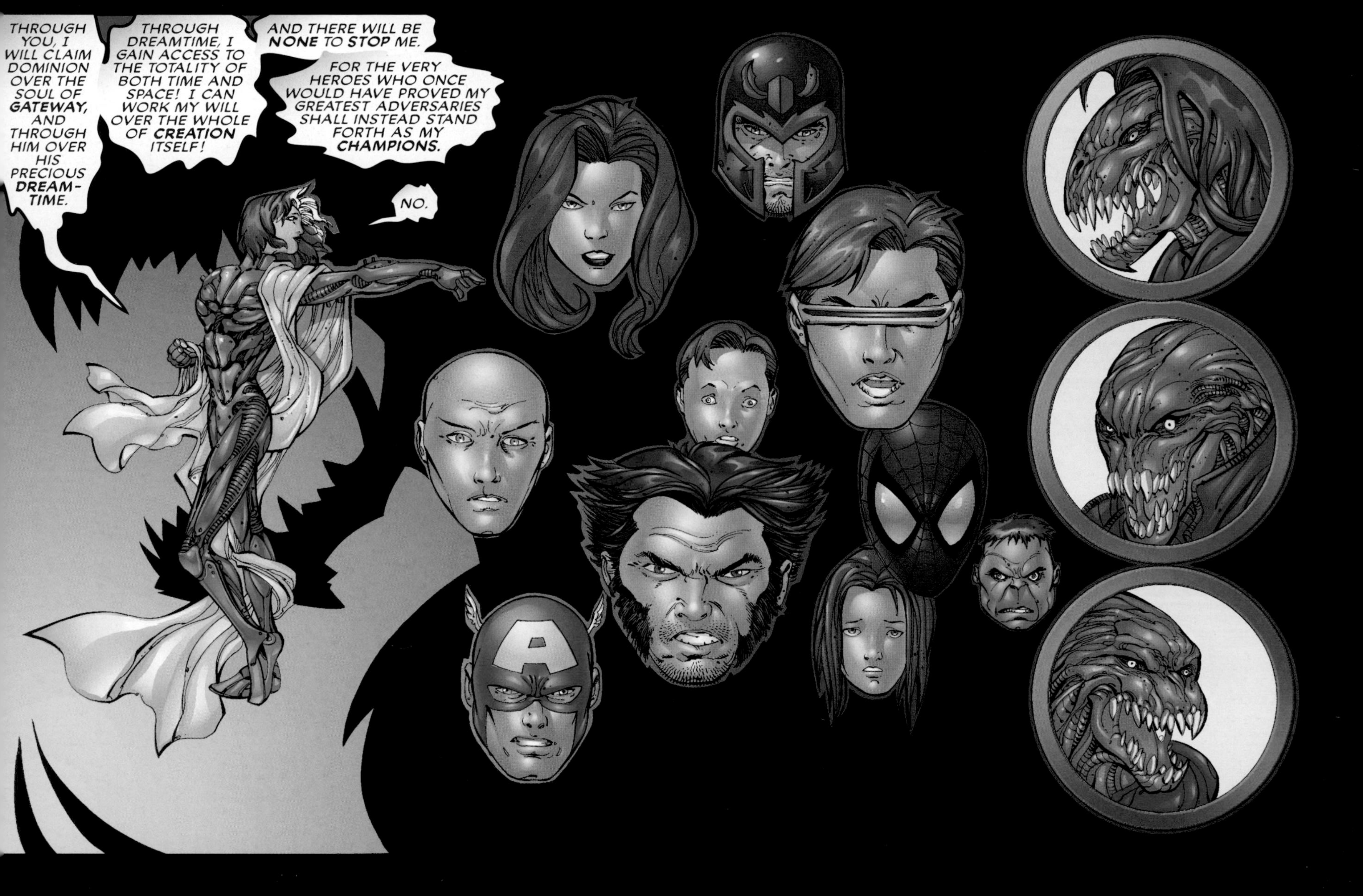
THROUGH YOU, I WILL CLAIM DOMINION OVER THE SOUL OF **GATEWAY**, AND THROUGH HIM OVER HIS PRECIOUS **DREAM-TIME**.
THROUGH DREAMTIME, I GAIN ACCESS TO THE TOTALITY OF BOTH TIME AND SPACE! I CAN WORK MY WILL OVER THE WHOLE OF **CREATION** ITSELF!
AND THERE WILL BE **NONE** TO **STOP** ME.
FOR THE VERY HEROES WHO ONCE WOULD HAVE PROVED MY GREATEST ADVERSARIES SHALL INSTEAD STAND FORTH AS MY **CHAMPIONS**.
NO.

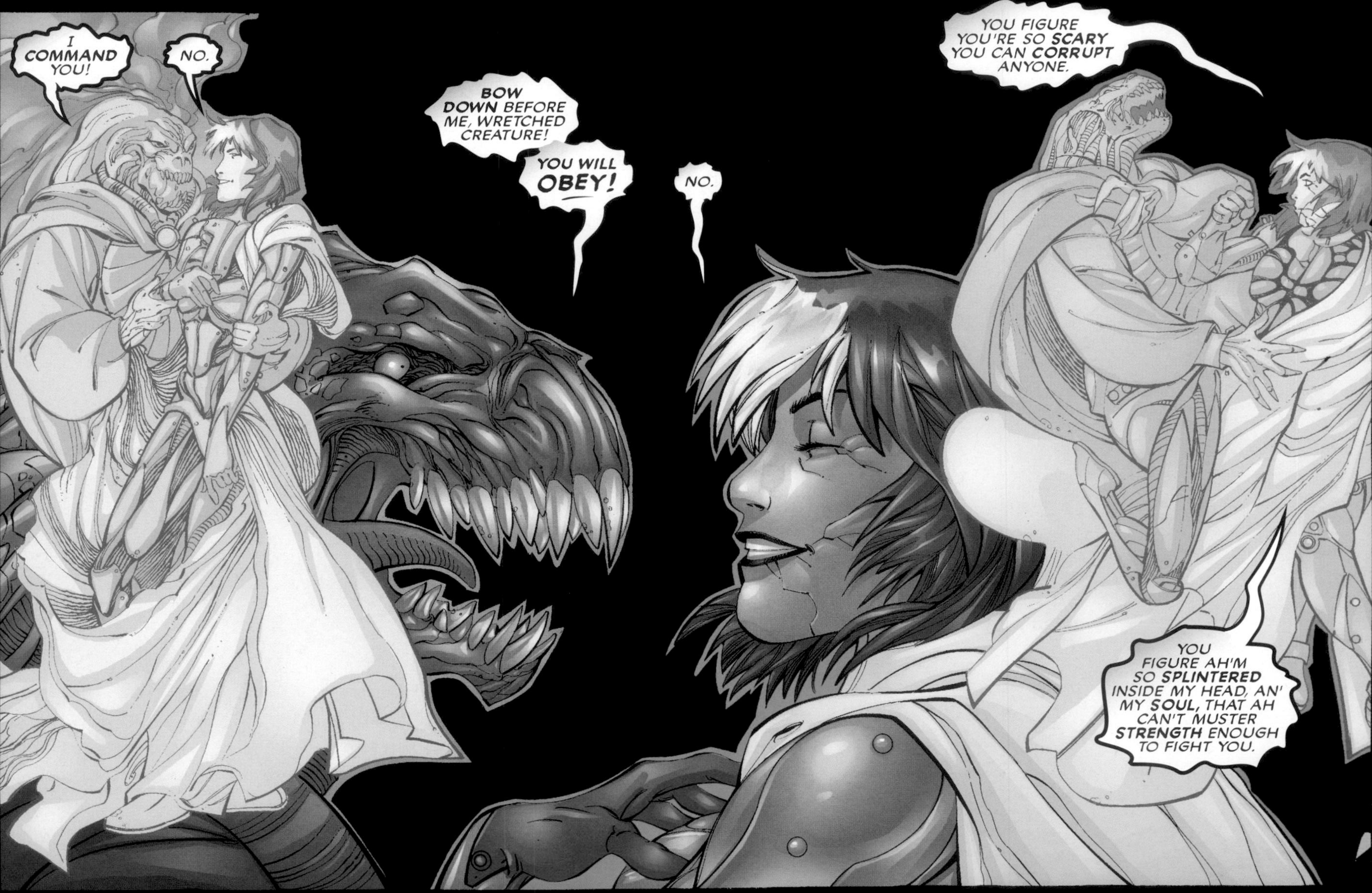
I COMMAND YOU!
NO.
BOW DOWN BEFORE ME, WRETCHED CREATURE!
YOU WILL OBEY!
NO.
YOU FIGURE YOU'RE SO SCARY YOU CAN CORRUPT ANYONE.
YOU FIGURE AH'M SO SPLINTERED INSIDE MY HEAD, AN' MY SOUL, THAT AH CAN'T MUSTER STRENGTH ENOUGH TO FIGHT YOU.

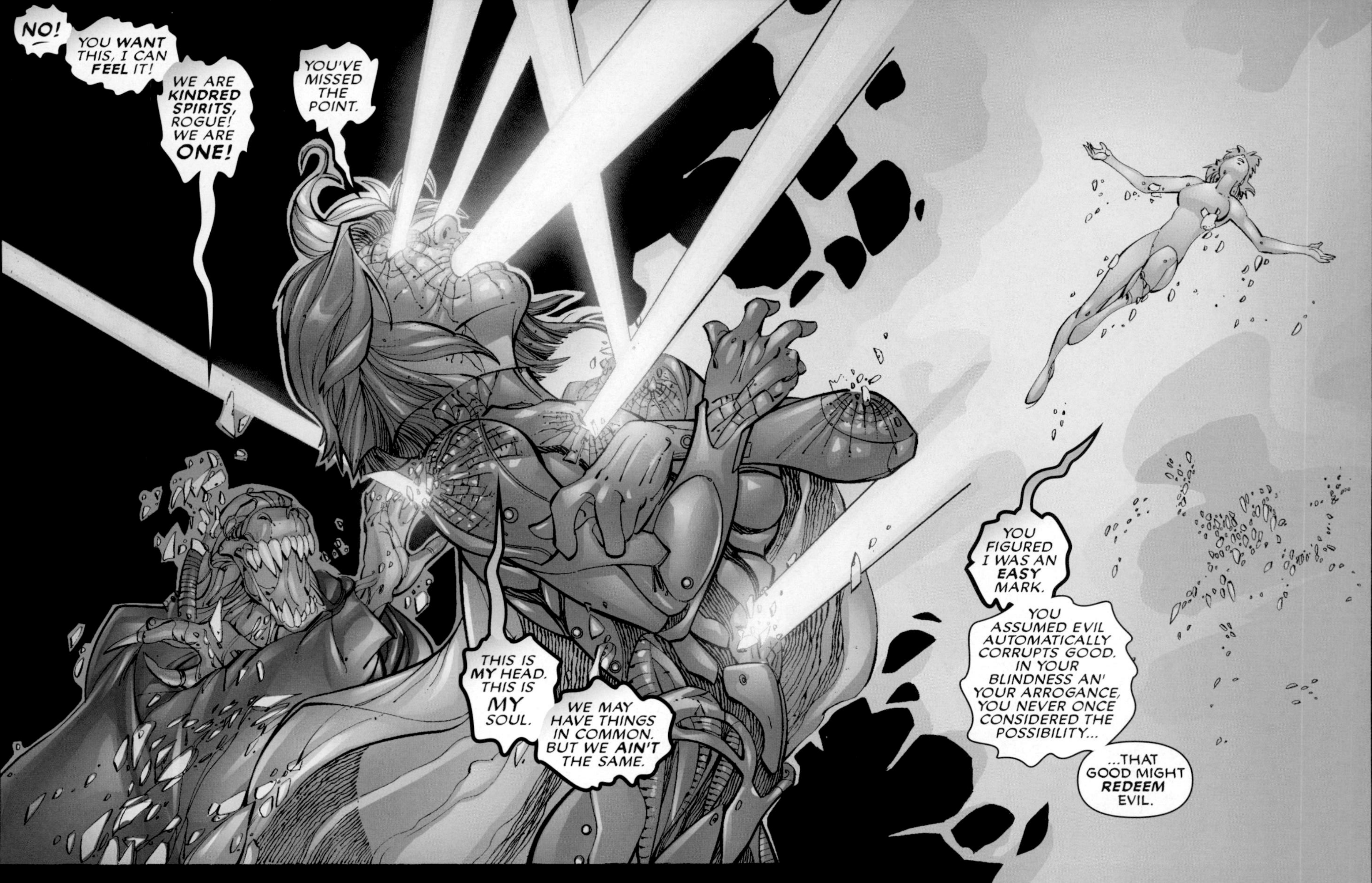
NO!
YOU WANT THIS, I CAN FEEL IT!
WE ARE KINDRED SPIRITS, ROGUE! WE ARE ONE!
YOU'VE MISSED THE POINT.
THIS IS MY HEAD. THIS IS MY SOUL.
WE MAY HAVE THINGS IN COMMON. BUT WE AIN'T THE SAME.
YOU FIGURED I WAS AN EASY MARK.
YOU ASSUMED EVIL AUTOMATICALLY CORRUPTS GOOD. IN YOUR BLINDNESS AN' YOUR ARROGANCE, YOU NEVER ONCE CONSIDERED THE POSSIBILITY...
...THAT GOOD MIGHT REDEEM EVIL.

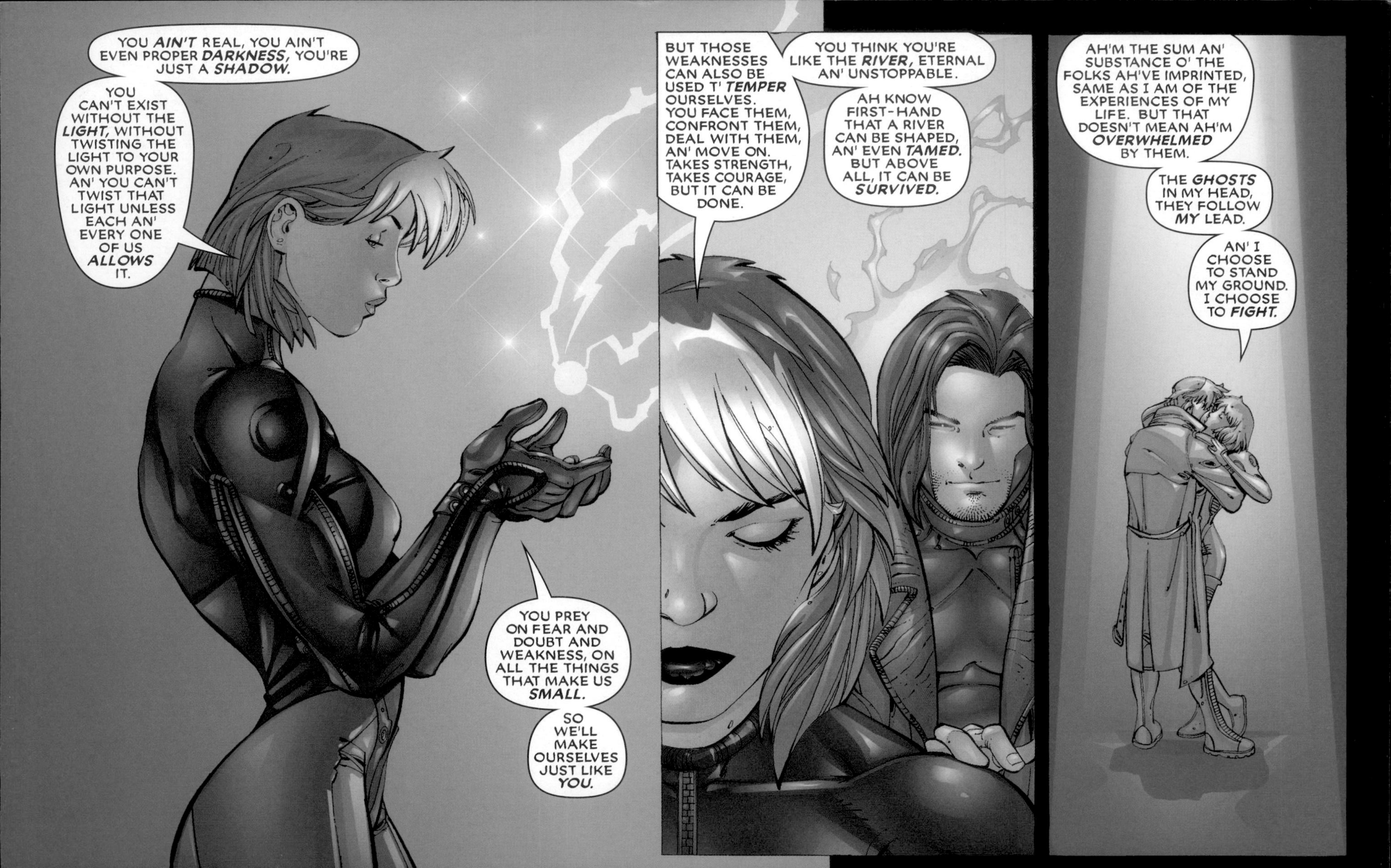
YOU *AIN'T* REAL, YOU AIN'T EVEN PROPER *DARKNESS*, YOU'RE JUST A *SHADOW*.
YOU CAN'T EXIST WITHOUT THE *LIGHT*, WITHOUT TWISTING THE LIGHT TO YOUR OWN PURPOSE. AN' YOU CAN'T TWIST THAT LIGHT UNLESS EACH AN' EVERY ONE OF US *ALLOWS* IT.
YOU PREY ON FEAR AND DOUBT AND WEAKNESS, ON ALL THE THINGS THAT MAKE US *SMALL*.
SO WE'LL MAKE OURSELVES JUST LIKE *YOU*.
YOU THINK YOU'RE LIKE THE *RIVER*, ETERNAL AN' UNSTOPPABLE.
AH KNOW FIRST-HAND THAT A RIVER CAN BE SHAPED, AN' EVEN *TAMED*. BUT ABOVE ALL, IT CAN BE *SURVIVED*.
BUT THOSE WEAKNESSES CAN ALSO BE USED T' *TEMPER* OURSELVES. YOU FACE THEM, CONFRONT THEM, DEAL WITH THEM, AN' MOVE ON. TAKES STRENGTH, TAKES COURAGE, BUT IT CAN BE DONE.
AH'M THE SUM AN' SUBSTANCE O' THE FOLKS AH'VE IMPRINTED, SAME AS I AM OF THE EXPERIENCES OF MY LIFE. BUT THAT DOESN'T MEAN AH'M *OVERWHELMED* BY THEM.
THE *GHOSTS* IN MY HEAD, THEY FOLLOW *MY* LEAD.
AN' I CHOOSE TO STAND MY GROUND. I CHOOSE TO *FIGHT*.

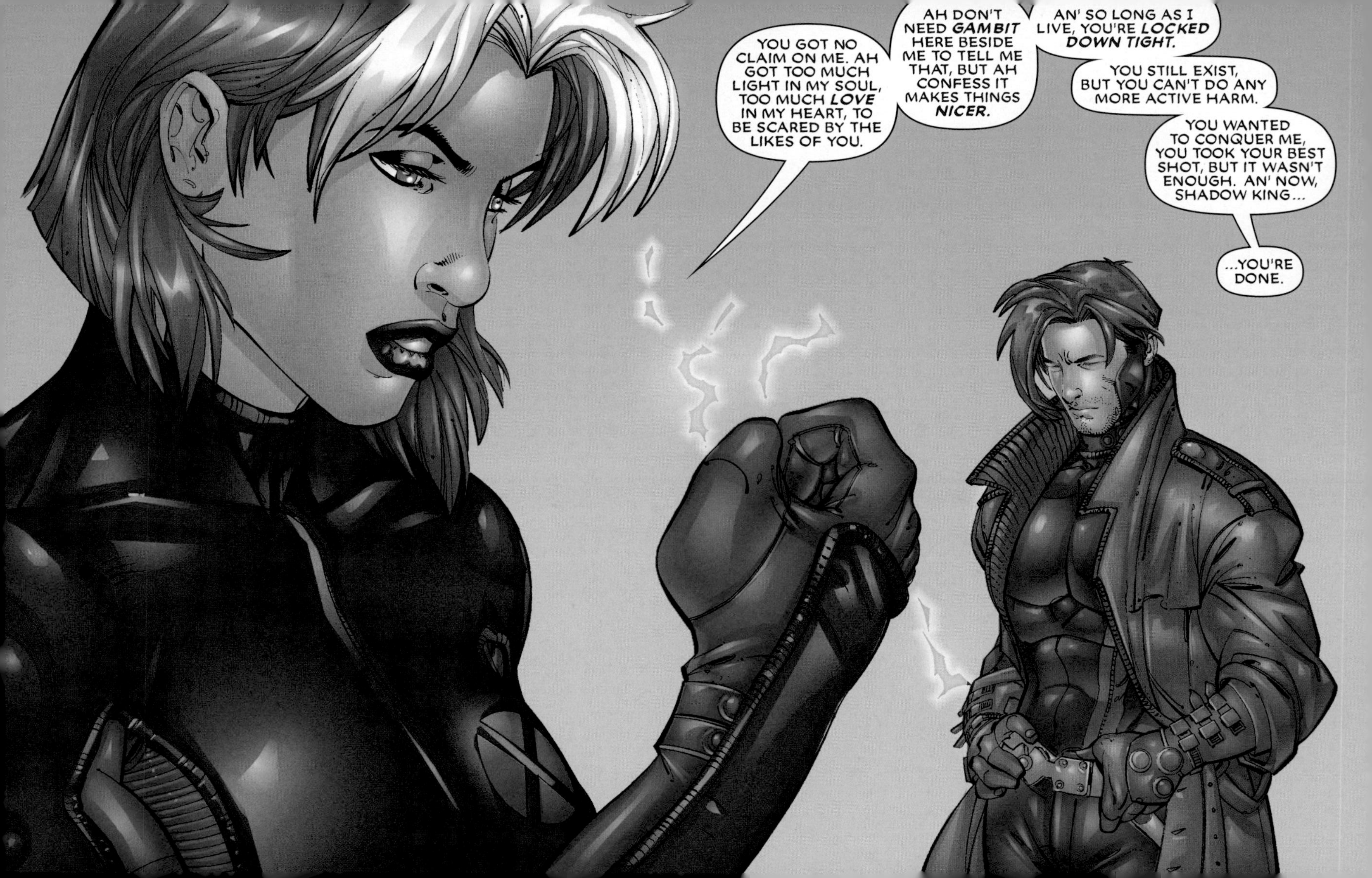
YOU GOT NO CLAIM ON ME. AH GOT TOO MUCH LIGHT IN MY SOUL, TOO MUCH *LOVE* IN MY HEART, TO BE SCARED BY THE LIKES OF YOU.
AH DON'T NEED *GAMBIT* HERE BESIDE ME TO TELL ME THAT, BUT AH CONFESS IT MAKES THINGS *NICER.*
AN' SO LONG AS I LIVE, YOU'RE *LOCKED DOWN TIGHT.*
YOU STILL EXIST, BUT YOU CAN'T DO ANY MORE ACTIVE HARM.
YOU WANTED TO CONQUER ME, YOU TOOK YOUR BEST SHOT, BUT IT WASN'T ENOUGH. AN' NOW, SHADOW KING...
...YOU'RE DONE.

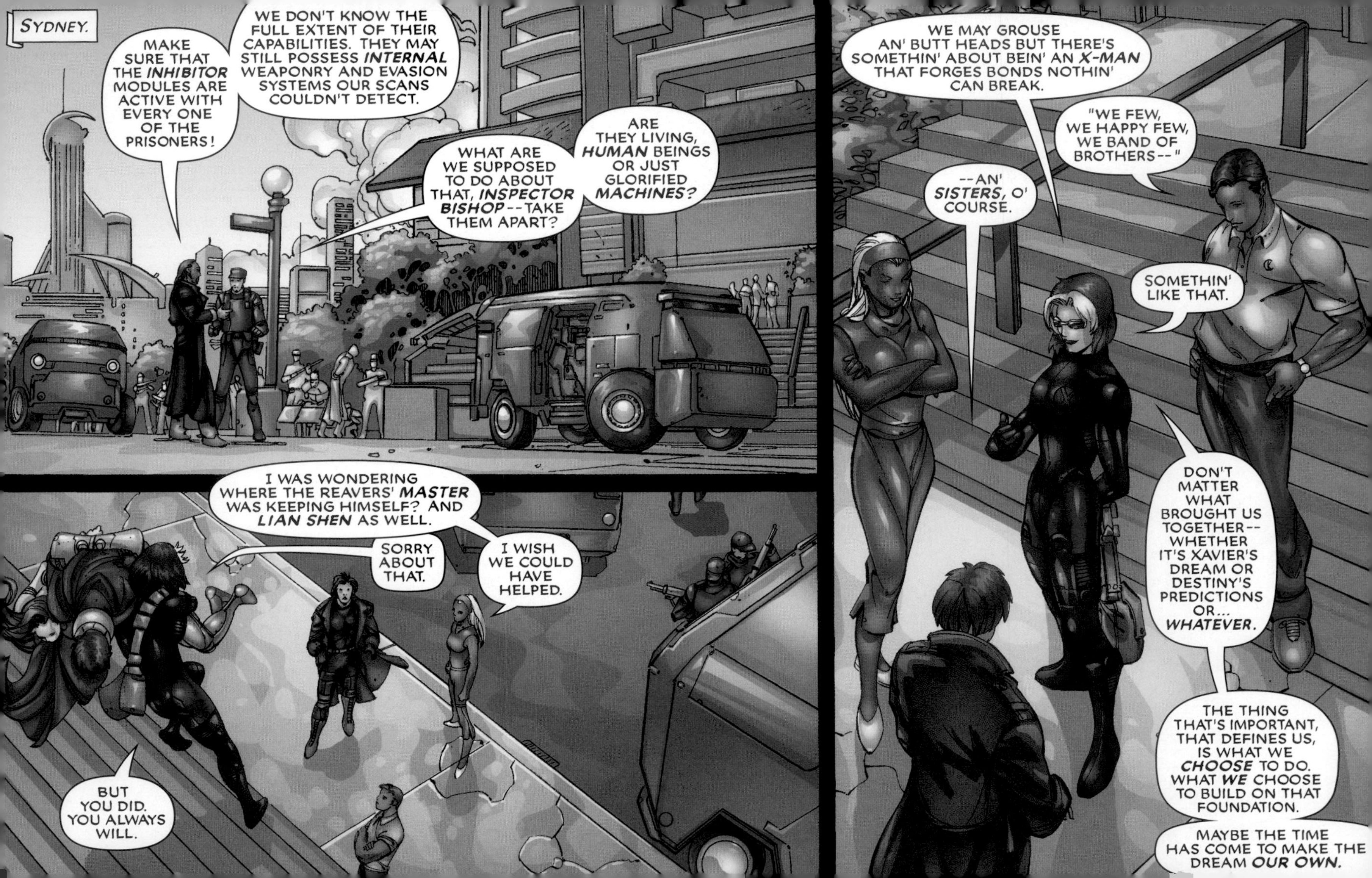
SYDNEY.
MAKE SURE THAT THE *INHIBITOR* MODULES ARE ACTIVE WITH EVERY ONE OF THE PRISONERS!
WE DON'T KNOW THE FULL EXTENT OF THEIR CAPABILITIES. THEY MAY STILL POSSESS *INTERNAL* WEAPONRY AND EVASION SYSTEMS OUR SCANS COULDN'T DETECT.
WHAT ARE WE SUPPOSED TO DO ABOUT THAT, *INSPECTOR BISHOP*--TAKE THEM APART?
ARE THEY LIVING, *HUMAN* BEINGS OR JUST GLORIFIED *MACHINES?*
I WAS WONDERING WHERE THE REAVERS' *MASTER* WAS KEEPING HIMSELF? AND *LIAN SHEN* AS WELL.
I WISH WE COULD HAVE HELPED.
SORRY ABOUT THAT.
BUT YOU DID. YOU ALWAYS WILL.
WE MAY GROUSE AN' BUTT HEADS BUT THERE'S SOMETHIN' ABOUT BEIN' AN *X-MAN* THAT FORGES BONDS NOTHIN' CAN BREAK.
"WE FEW, WE HAPPY FEW, WE BAND OF BROTHERS--"
--AN' *SISTERS,* O' COURSE.
SOMETHIN' LIKE THAT.
DON'T MATTER WHAT BROUGHT US TOGETHER--WHETHER IT'S XAVIER'S DREAM OR DESTINY'S PREDICTIONS OR... *WHATEVER*.
THE THING THAT'S IMPORTANT, THAT DEFINES US, IS WHAT WE *CHOOSE* TO DO. WHAT *WE* CHOOSE TO BUILD ON THAT FOUNDATION.
MAYBE THE TIME HAS COME TO MAKE THE DREAM *OUR OWN*.

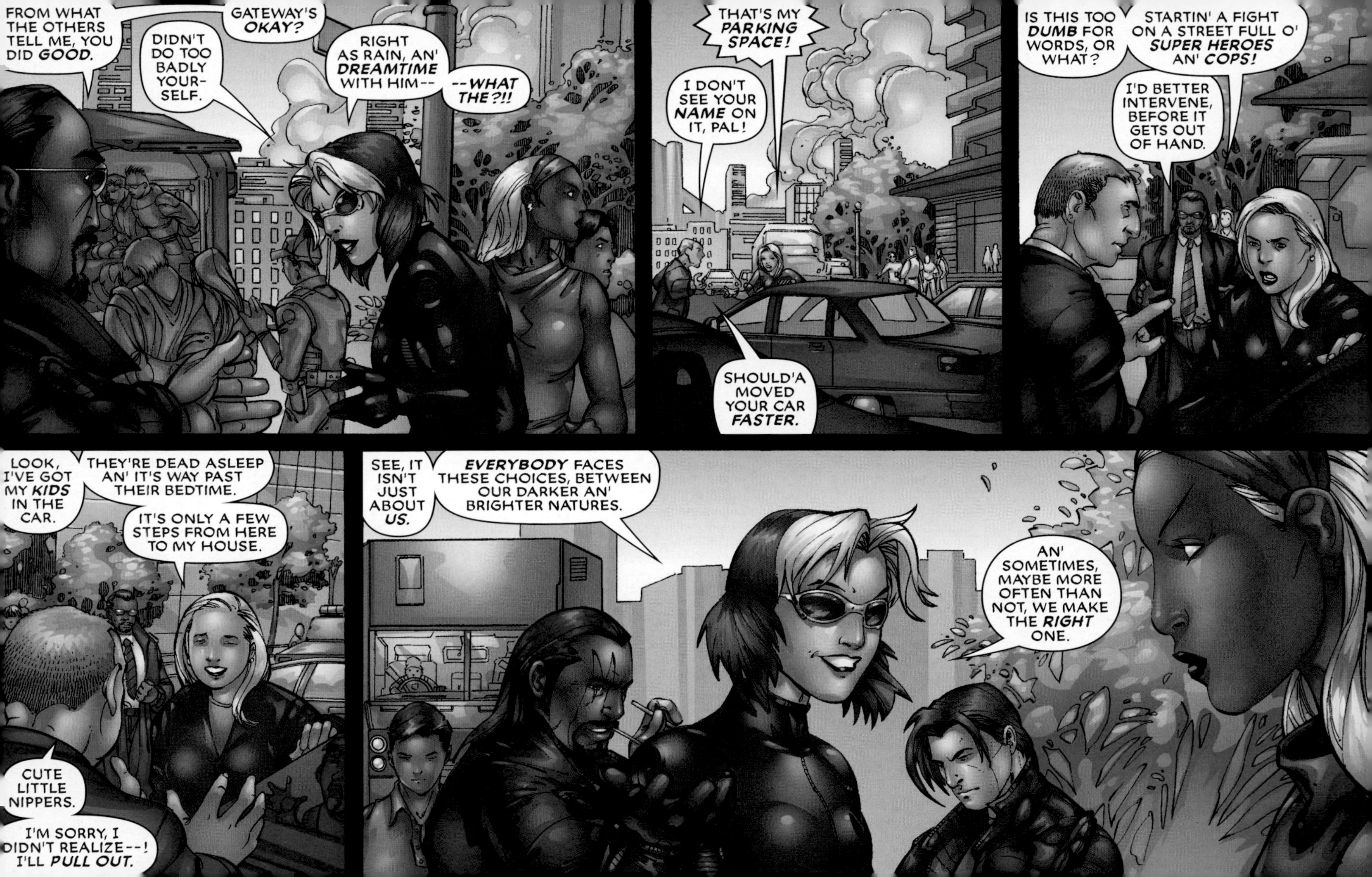

FROM WHAT THE OTHERS TELL ME, YOU DID **GOOD.**
GATEWAY'S **OKAY?**
DIDN'T DO TOO BADLY YOURSELF.
RIGHT AS RAIN, AN' **DREAMTIME** WITH HIM--
--WHAT THE?!!
THAT'S MY **PARKING SPACE!**
I DON'T SEE YOUR **NAME** ON IT, PAL!
SHOULD'A MOVED YOUR CAR **FASTER.**
IS THIS TOO **DUMB** FOR WORDS, OR WHAT?
STARTIN' A FIGHT ON A STREET FULL O' **SUPER HEROES** AN' **COPS!**
I'D BETTER INTERVENE, BEFORE IT GETS OUT OF HAND.
LOOK, I'VE GOT MY **KIDS** IN THE CAR.
THEY'RE DEAD ASLEEP AN' IT'S WAY PAST THEIR BEDTIME.
IT'S ONLY A FEW STEPS FROM HERE TO MY HOUSE.
CUTE LITTLE NIPPERS.
I'M SORRY, I DIDN'T REALIZE--! I'LL **PULL OUT.**
SEE, IT ISN'T JUST ABOUT **US.**
EVERYBODY FACES THESE CHOICES, BETWEEN OUR DARKER AN' BRIGHTER NATURES.
AN' SOMETIMES, MAYBE MORE OFTEN THAN NOT, WE MAKE THE **RIGHT** ONE.

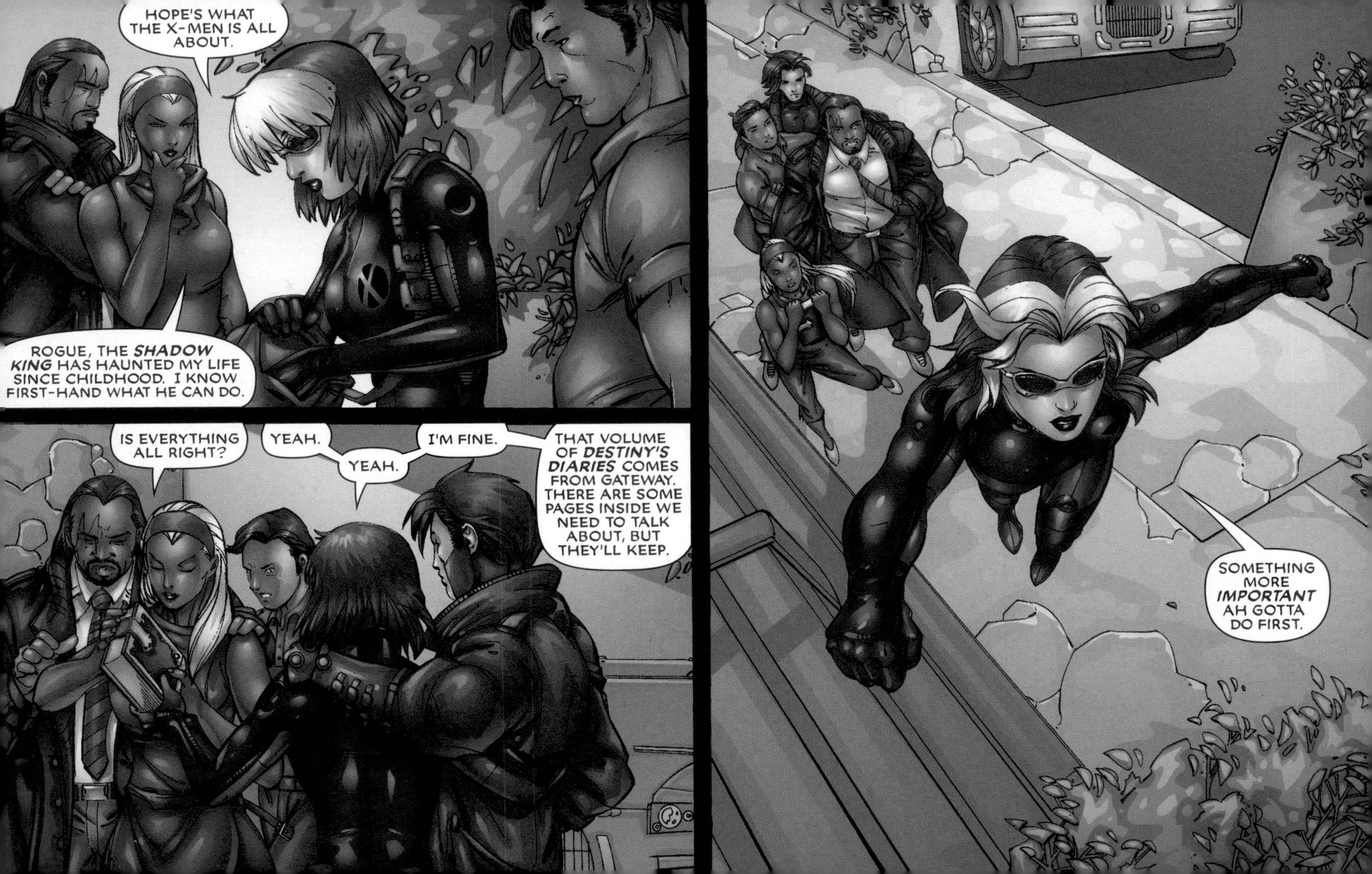

ROGUE, THE *SHADOW KING* HAS HAUNTED MY LIFE SINCE CHILDHOOD. I KNOW FIRST-HAND WHAT HE CAN DO.
HOPE'S WHAT THE X-MEN IS ALL ABOUT.
IS EVERYTHING ALL RIGHT?
YEAH.
YEAH.
I'M FINE.
THAT VOLUME OF *DESTINY'S DIARIES* COMES FROM GATEWAY. THERE ARE SOME PAGES INSIDE WE NEED TO TALK ABOUT, BUT THEY'LL KEEP.
SOMETHING MORE *IMPORTANT* AH GOTTA DO FIRST.

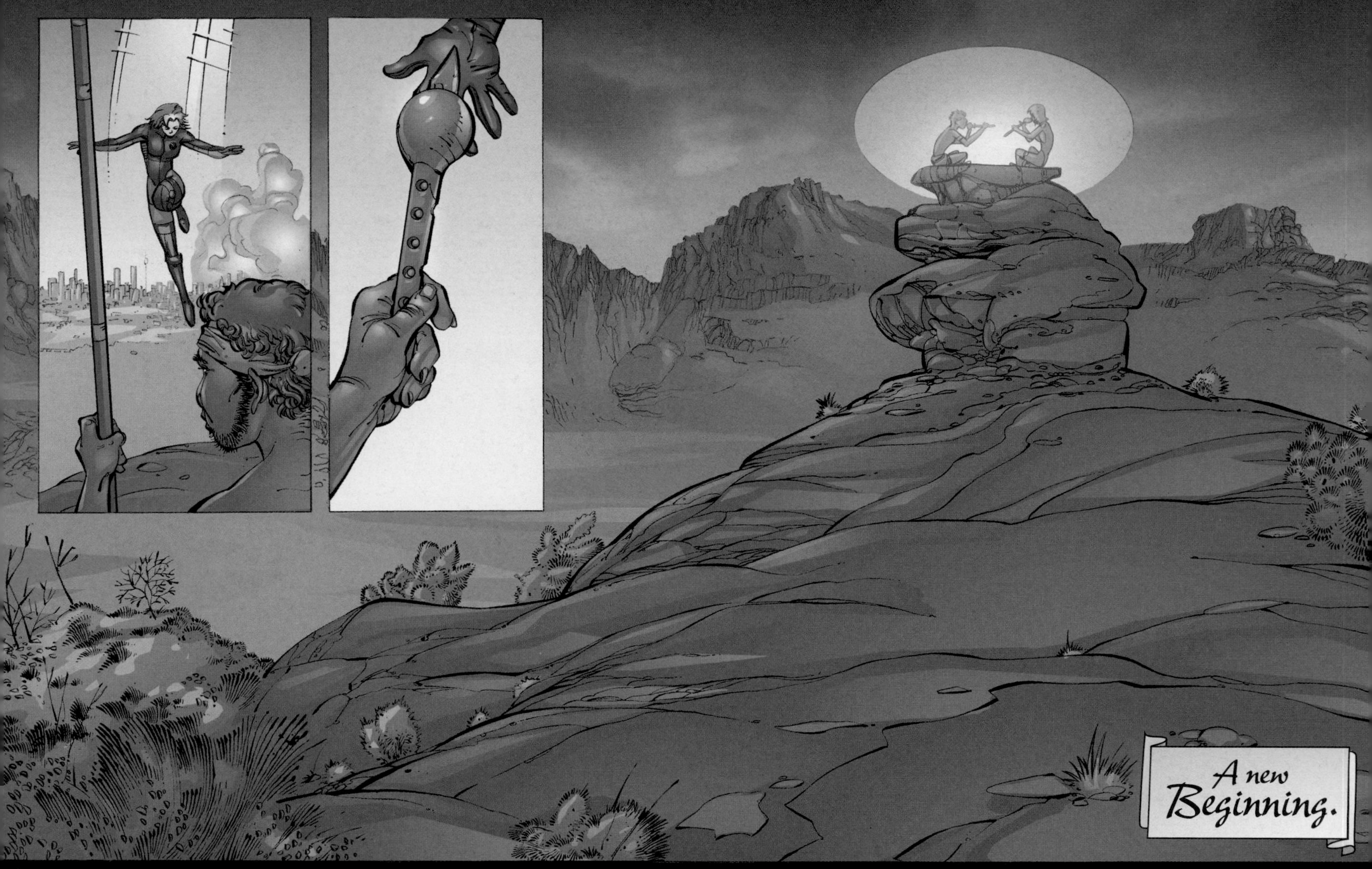
A new Beginning.

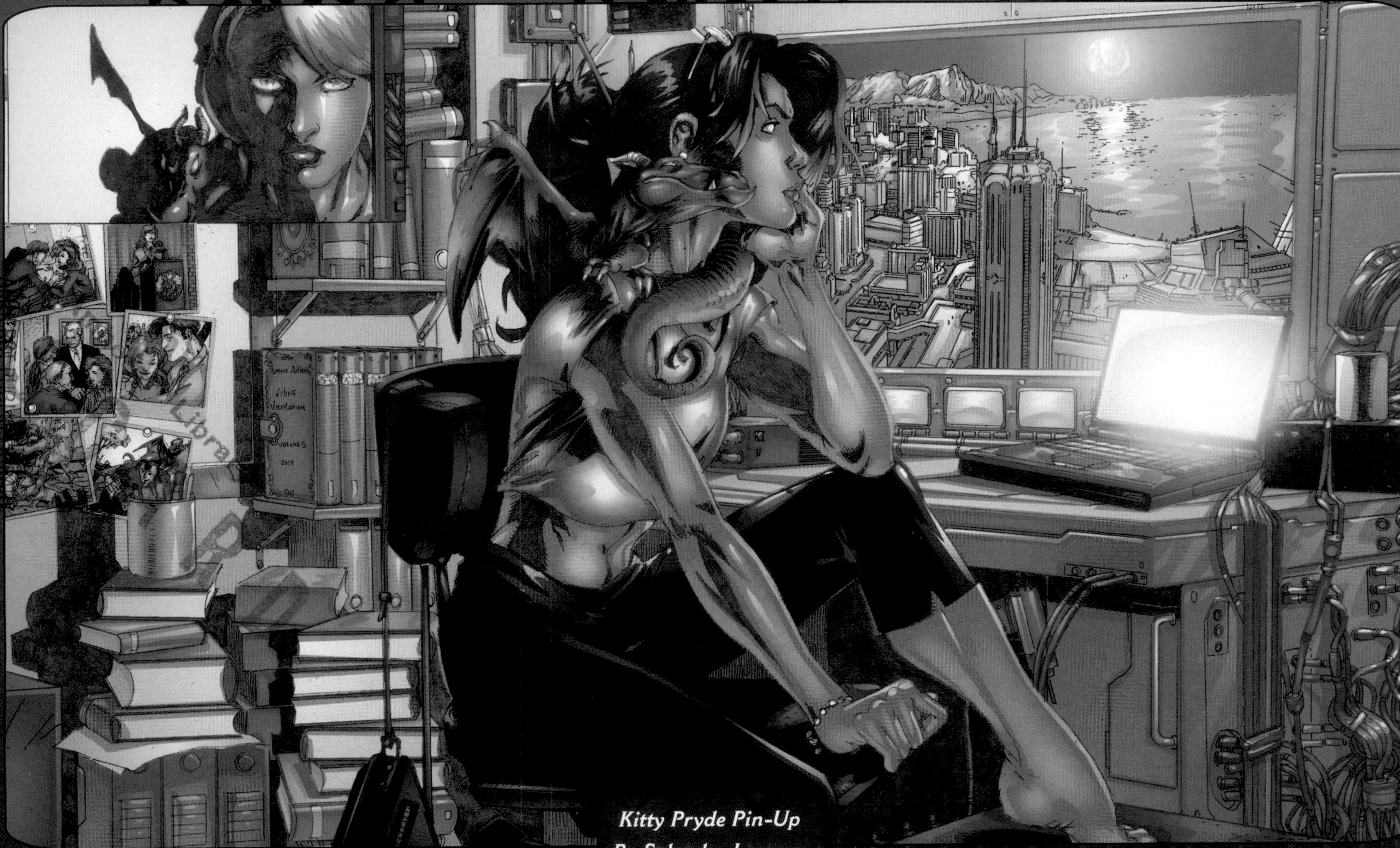

Kitty Pryde Pin-Up
By Salvador Larroca